14th International Conference Mobile Learning 2018

Lisbon, Portugal
14 – 16 April 2018

Editors:

Inmaculada Arnedillo Sanchez
Pedro Isaias
Luis Rodrigues

ISBN: 978-1-5108-6768-0

Printed from e-media with permission by:

Curran Associates, Inc.
57 Morehouse Lane
Red Hook, NY 12571

Some format issues inherent in the e-media version may also appear in this print version.

Printed by Curran Associates, Inc. (2018)

International Association for Development of the Information Society (IADIS)
Rua Sao Sebastiao Da Pedreira
No. 100, 30, 1050-209
Lisbon, Portugal

Phone: 351 21 3151373
Fax: 351 21 3151244

secretariat@iadis.org

Additional copies of this publication are available from:

Curran Associates, Inc.
57 Morehouse Lane
Red Hook, NY 12571 USA
Phone: 845-758-0400
Fax: 845-758-2633
Email: curran@proceedings.com
Web: www.proceedings.com

14th INTERNATIONAL CONFERENCE

MOBILE LEARNING 2018

PROCEEDINGS OF THE 14th INTERNATIONAL CONFERENCE

MOBILE LEARNING 2018

LISBON, PORTUGAL

14 - 16 APRIL, 2018

Organised by

iadis

international association for development of the information society

Edited by Inmaculada Arnedillo Sánchez and Pedro Isaias

Associate Editor: Luís Rodrigues

TABLE OF CONTENTS

FULL PAPERS

SHORT PAPERS

REFLECTION PAPERS

POSTER

DOCTORAL CONSORTIUM

FOREWORD

These proceedings contain the papers of the 14th International Conference on Mobile Learning 2018, which was organised by the International Association for Development of the Information Society, in Lisbon, Portugal, 14 - 16 April 2018.

The Mobile Learning 2018 Conference seeks to provide a forum for the presentation and discussion of mobile learning research which illustrate developments in the field. In particular, but not exclusively, we aim to explore the theme of mobile learning under the following topics:

- Learning analytics and mobile learning
- Cloud computing and mobile learning
- Pedagogical approaches, models and theories for mLearning
- mLearning in and across formal and informal settings
- Strategies and challenges for integrating mLearning in broader educational scenarios
- User Studies in mLearning
- Learner mobility and transitions afforded by mlearning
- Socio-cultural context and implications of mLearning
- Mobile social media and user generated content
- Enabling mLearning technologies, applications and uses
- Evaluation and assessment of mLearning
- Research methods, ethics and implementation of mLearning
- Innovative mLearning approaches
- Tools, technologies and platforms for mLearning
- mlearning: where to next and how?

The Mobile Learning 2018 received 95 submissions from more than 24 countries. Each submission has been anonymously reviewed by an average of 4 independent reviewers, to ensure that accepted submissions were of a high standard. Out of the papers submitted, 16 received blind referee ratings that signified acceptability for publication as full papers (acceptance rate of 17%). A few more papers were accepted as short papers, reflection papers, posters, panel and doctoral consortium. An extended version of the best papers will be published in the International Journal of Mobile and Blended Learning (ISSN: 1941-8647), Interactive Technology and Smart Education (ITSE) journal (ISSN: 1741-5659) and also in the IADIS International Journal on WWW/Internet (ISSN: 1645-7641).

Besides the papers' presentations, the conference also features a keynote presentation from an internationally distinguished researcher. We would therefore like to express our gratitude to Professor Chee Kit Looi (Learning Sciences & Technologies Academic Group Founding Head, Learning Sciences Lab, Nanyang Technological University (NIE/NTU), Singapore), for accepting our invitation as keynote speaker.

The conference also includes one panel presentation entitled "Rain Classroom: Bridging the Gap between Teachers and Learners" by Dr. Michael Zihao Li and Dr. Katrine Wong from University of Macau, Macau S.A.R.

A successful conference requires the effort of many individuals. We would like to thank the members of the Program Committee for their hard work in reviewing and selecting the papers that appear in this book. We are especially grateful to the authors who submitted their papers to this conference and to the presenters who provided the substance of the meeting. We wish to thank all members of our organizing committee.

Last but not least, we hope that everybody has enjoyed Lisbon and their time with colleagues from all over the world, and we invite you all to next edition of the International Mobile Learning in 2019.

Inmaculada Arnedillo Sánchez, Trinity College Dublin, Ireland
Program Chair

Pedro Isaias, The University of Queensland, Australia
Conference Chair

Lisbon, Portugal
April 2018

PROGRAM COMMITTEE

PROGRAM CHAIR

Inmaculada Arnedillo Sánchez, Trinity College Dublin, Ireland

CONFERENCE CHAIR

Pedro Isaias, The University of Queensland, Australia

COMMITTEE MEMBERS

Adamantios Koumpis, Universität Passau, Germany
Agostino Marengo, University of Bari, Italy
Alessandro Caforio, UNINETTUNO University, Italy
Alessandro Pagano, University of Bari, Italy
Alex Voychenko, IRTC, Ukraine
Anastasios Economides, University of Macedonia, Greece
Anastasios Karakostas, ITI CERTH, Greece
Anastopoulou Stamatina, The Open University, UK
Antoanela Naaji, Vasile Goldis Western University, Romania
Antonio Panaggio, Ministry of Education, Universities and Research, Italy
Bahtijar Vogel, Malmö University, Sweden
Boriss F. Misnevs, Transport and Telecommunication Institute, Latvia
Bren Taylor, Service Birmingham, UK
Carmen Holotescu, University "Ioan Slavici" of Timisoara, Romania
Celine Llewellyn-Jones, London Metropolitan University, UK
Charalampos Karagiannidis, University of Thessaly, Greece
Chiu-Pin Lin, National Tsing Hua University, Taiwan
Christos Bouras, University of Patras, Greece
Davide Diamantini, Universita di Milano-bicocca, Italy
Demetrios Sampson, University of Piraeus, Greece
Dumitru Dan Burdescu, University of Craiova, Romania
Elisabetta Parodi, Lattanzio Learning Spa, Italy
Emad Bataineh, Zayed University, United Arab Emirates
Euripides Loukis, University of the Aegean, Greece
Fahriye Altinay, Near East University, Cyprus
Gabor Kiss, J. Selye University, Slovakia
George Magoulas, Birbeck College, UK
Giuliana Dettori, ITD-CNR, Italy
Gülcan Erçetin, Bogaziçi University, Turkey
Gwo-Jen Hwang, National Taiwan University of Science and Technologies, Taiwan
Hannu-Matti Jarvinen, Tampere University of Technology, Finland
Helen Farley, University of Southern Queensland, Australia
Herman Van Der Merwe, North-West University, South Africa
Hsien-sheng Hsiao, National Taiwan Normal University, Taiwan
Inge de Waard, The Open University, UK

KEYNOTE LECTURE

WHITHER SEAMLESS LEARNING: PERSPECTIVES, CHALLENGES AND OPPORTUNITIES

by Professor Chee Kit Looi, Learning Sciences & Technologies Academic Group
Founding Head, Learning Sciences Lab,
Nanyang Technological University (NIE/NTU)
Singapore

Abstract

In this talk, I will attempt a review of the latest state of research and development in seamless learning. Seamless learning is: "… when a person experiences a continuity of learning, and consciously bridges the multifaceted learning efforts, across a combination of locations, times, technologies or social settings." Over the past ten over years, there have been different perspectives, visions, and practices on seamless learning from various diversified (e.g., techno-centric, techno-pedagogical, socio-situated and socio-cultural; informal learning and formal learning; crossover learning, incidental learning and context-based learning) perspectives. While there are researchers in mobile learning, learning sciences, and educational technologies who have been explicitly researching on seamless learning, they are also those who did not think they were studying seamless learning but have indeed accomplished some research work that resembles the spirit and the salient characteristics of the learning approach. It is opportune to review the work in all these fields to inform us of the designs and learning mechanisms for seamless learning. I will discuss their theorization of learning, and the conditions, resources and frameworks for understanding such learning, and probe their relevance and connections to seamless learning.

PANEL

RAIN CLASSROOM: BRIDGING THE GAP BETWEEN TEACHERS AND LEARNERS

by Dr. Michael Zihao Li and Dr. Katrine Wong
University of Macau, Macau S.A.R

Abstract

In the current digital era, gaining new knowledge, skills, or even experience seems to be a click/touch away. Teaching and learning have become increasingly challenging as learners are overly stimulated with information and technology. In classrooms of theater arts and of literature, the component of lecture is usually delivered through conventional sage-on-stage pedagogy. PowerPoint is often used during lectures while many students are, for one reason or another, losing interest: some are trolling on social networking sites or apps, such as WeChat (a close equivalent to Facebook), while others are playing games. As such, a cluster of different modes of technology is simultaneously shaping the dynamic teaching and learning when PPT, mobile device, and social networks are being used, yet their functions and purposes are disconnected from one another. To bridge the gap between teaching and learning, an innovative smartphone-app Rain Classroom, which combines PowerPoint and social network, namely, WeChat, was created by Tsinghua University in April 2016. In less than 2 years, it is used by over 2 million users in 130,000 active classes. This paper discusses key features of Rain Classroom, such as instant feedback through bullet screen, pre/post-lecture push (classroom flipping), pop quiz, survey, and open-ended questions. Researchers also share their insights on using Rain Classroom and how it impacts teaching and learning outcomes in courses on theater arts and on literature.

Keywords: Rain Classroom, Teaching and Learning, Technology, Mobile Learning, Social Media

Full Papers

METHODOLOGY FOR BUILDING VIRTUAL REALITY MOBILE APPLICATIONS FOR BLIND PEOPLE ON ADVANCED VISITS TO UNKNOWN INTERIOR SPACES

Nancy Enriqueta Guerrón Paredes [1,2], Antonio Cobo [1,3], Carlos Martín [1]
and José Javier Serrano [1,3]
[1]Centro de Tecnología Biomédica. Universidad Politécnica de Madrid, 28223, Madrid-España
[2]Universidad de las Fuerzas Armadas ESPE, 170501, Sangolquí-Ecuador
[3]CIBER de Bioingeniería, Biomateriales y Nanomedicina (CIBER-BBN), Spain

ABSTRACT

Virtual reality applications for blind people in smartphones were used to make virtual visits in advance to unknown spaces; these need to include a set of cognitive and sensitive interfaces that allow users to use their other sensory capabilities to understand information about their environment and facilitate the interaction with the application, so that the user can make a mental representation of the unknown space. Some strategies were designed to provide continuous and clear information to the user, so that he can perform exploration activities within a virtual environment generated from a real environment with the help of nineteen blind people and five visually impaired people who participated in the development and tests carried out into six workshops, during twenty-four months. During each workshop took logs about the activities that the user did for the recognized and location of objects and structures indoors. This information was stored in a database to be analyzed and interpreted in order to make subsequent modifications to the application, until achieving a tool that is sufficiently useful, safe and accepted for the user. The last applications were built with voice patterns, beeps, vibrations and gestures called sensitive interfaces, and also with a cognitive interface called "Focus of attention" based on proximity and remote exploration. There was is a thirty-eight percent of improved when the participants choose to remote explore the virtual environment with regard to proximity exploration, also there was preference to be warned with low to medium frequency beeps, a fast reproduction of the voice to receive information on objects and structures and simple gestures for the interaction with Smartphone. In the last experience, we used a structure sensor coupled to the Smartphone for user tracking, and bone conduction headphones to reproduce spatial sounds; they said was pleasing to hear 3D sounds with personalized response in bone earphones, for locating objects inside the test scenario; there was a twenty-one percent of improved when the participants using beeps instead of vocals or musical instruments.

KEYWORDS

Virtual Reality Applications (VRA), Interfaces for Blind People, Cognitive Mapping, Sounds 3D

1. INTRODUCTION

The population with visual impairment on our planet is close to 300 million, of which 45 million are blind, made up mostly of people over 50 years (*WHO | Visual impairment and blindness*, 2014), only a 28% are people of working age; the dependence and the fear to move through new environments limits their social and economic growth. In addition, there are 7.1 billion mobile phone owners and 48% of the population has Internet access, with Europe being the most connected (Silvio P. Mariotti (World Health Organization), 2010). Given the technological evolution, a Smartphone is clearly one of the most useful and necessary things in our daily life, thanks to some services and features that provide user (Anshari and Alas, 2015). It is possible to take advantage of current technology and develop virtual reality applications on phones so that blind people use them to perceive the world around them; mobile learning based on the knowledge of the reality and the experiences of the actors in the training process(Liu *et al.*, 2017), can greatly contribute to the generation of alternatives that will be addressed during the investigation. The operating systems that lead the global mobile market are Android and iOS (Baker *et al.*, no date); Unity3D (Unity, 2017) is a multiplatform game development environment that allows the development of high-contrast virtual reality applications and Vibro-Tactile-Auditory support for people who are blind or very low-vision. The systems which use Braille are getting less used by blind people (Leuthold Stefan, Bargas-Avila Javier, 2008), because of the development of new tools with improved interfaces that seize their other senses and fit better to their needs.

One area of virtual reality applications is assisted navigation that allows people to go from one point to another (Karimi, 2011). Outdoor navigation is done using geo-positioning technologies and assisted navigation in unknown home environments require devices and support tools and Wi-Fi/RFID/Bluetooth technologies to store and deliver data to users. Inland navigation requires the development of information models whose construction depends on the spatial complexity and the amount of static data they generate for processing. When the user is blind, the information is centered on audio description, the use of tactile maps or the combination of both; to be able to make a mental representation of its surroundings.

Cobo (Cobo *et al.*, 2017) proposes the use of virtual reality to simulate real spaces as a means for blind people to obtain spatial knowledge of a place before visiting it.

Picinali (Picinali *et al.*, 2014) investigated the possibilities of helping blind people, through learning in a virtual reality environment, by means the construction of mental maps using spatial audio events and their possible interactions in interior spaces.

Orly Lahav (Lahav *et al.*, 2012)(Lahav, Schloerb and Srinivasan, 2015) uses virtual reality applications to help blind people with an early exploration of an environment, allowing participants to develop cognitive maps of the virtual environment. Subsequently with its results the team creates two rehabilitation programs to improve the orientation and mobility of blind people through training in virtual environments.

Rodríguez (Rodriguez-Sanchez *et al.*, 2014), describes several problems in the use of some tactile interfaces and the possibilities of guiding the user by a route, using a way finding application. This research shows how to combine text, map, auditory and tactile feedback to provide the information, where the user moves his fingers over fixed regions on the touch screen receiving information that allows him to go to different points of interest in a test scenario. Orientation is done by combining DGPS, compass and route information, with an accuracy of about 1 to 3 meters.

Virtual Reality Applications (VRA) used by blind people to know unknown place must allow them built a quality's cognitive-map of that location, through continuous information and relevant content delivered by means physical and cognitive interfaces (Cobo *et al.*, 2017)(Härmä *et al.*, 2004)(Serrão *et al.*, 2012)(Sanabria, 2007), that allows them to explore their environment in advance and build own spatial knowledge over entities and objects of interest to the user.

Kitchin (Kitchin, 2001) mentions that blind people are able to have a spacial thought just like people with vision, if they have enough information, Majerova (Majerova, 2017) emphasizes that spatial mental mapping in an individual with visual impairment should be as an integral and distinctive because the learning is a conjunction between cognitive and perceptual learning skills of an individual. Blind people with no previous visual experience seem to be more dependent on egocentric strategies for coding and representing space during exploration than with allocentric strategies that are more preferred by people with prior visual experience (Pasqualotto *et al.*, 2013).

It is said that sound is very important to develop the sense of orientation and spatial distance (Härmä *et al.*, 2004); and that auditory and haptic feedback allows blind users interacting with different structures and virtual objects (De Felice *et al.*, 2007). For this reason, this work researched the use of different patterns of sounds, gestures and vibrations as physical interface in the construction of virtual reality applications; the use the proximity exploration as a cognitive interface (allocentric & orientation tasks) and the use remote exploration as a cognitive interface to perform egocentric tasks; which together provide the user with an understanding of the virtually visited space. In order to the participants can work with relative ease on their mobile devices, which could significantly increase their willingness to participate in mobile learning programs (Hwang, Chu and Lai, 2017), we proposed and implemented some applications in the iOS system after initially testing Android.

2. VIRTUAL REALITY APPLICATIONS AND THE ACQUISITION OF KNOWLEDGE

We want to help blind users with applications installed on their own phones so they can know in advance the interior of an unknown space, which helps them make their own decisions and feel more comfortable and safe when they go to new places. This is possible thanks to the use of multi-sensitive interfaces that allow explaining and describing the space, so that the user can explore the virtual world in their own way, through egocentric and allocentric activities in this spaces.

2.1 Information Model

Over time two models of information were developed. The Figure **1**.a (first model with only one room) shows the basic relationships between the objects, the avatar and the tools to give information to the user in basic environments. The Figure **1**.b shows the relationships in more complex environments (some rooms on one floor). Where:

The Safety Zones (SZ) are built as physical objects which move and rotate with the user's avatar, their purpose is to alert the user to the presence of objects while your avatar is walking.

The Focus of Attention (FoA) is an object that points in the direction that the user is looking at and move together. We use three methods: flat, spherical and without focus.

Notifications are handled by scripts associated with scene objects. Provide alerts and information to the user during testing.

Avatar represents the blind person inside the application or to the User; the avatar's orientation and movement direction are obtained by the Smartphone's inertial sensors.

Item is each object and structural component in the environment. Common features can group them.

Place represents each space to which the avatar can be directed and if the user chooses one, it adds objects contained in an Entity of the game.

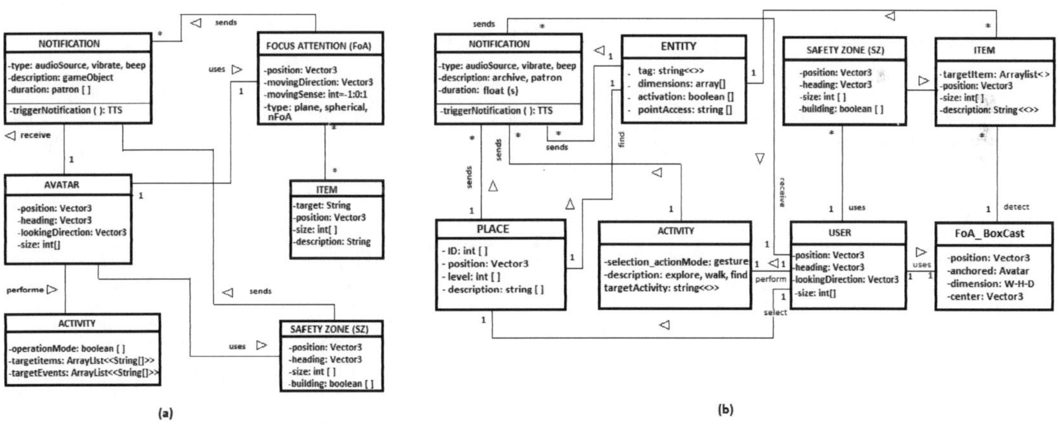

Figure 1. Information Model; a) Basic environment; b) Complex environment

2.1.1 Spatial Coding

The interfaces used in the application depend on the spatial relationship of the avatar with the objects and structures of the environment, for which it is necessary to activate the type of exploration that the user performs (See Table **1**). Where:

Remote Exploration: The locations of objects in space are relative to the axes of the user's body. The user makes gestures on the phone' screen to activate information options (Kozhevnikov, Blazhenkova and Obana, 2017).

Proximity Exploration: The location of an object is defined in relation to the location of other objects. The proximity between the objects and the security zones establishes the information that must be given to the user. The vibration is active as the avatar walks in the virtual environment.

Table 1. Spatial Coding Activation

Mode	Cognitive Interface	Sensitive Interface	Tasks
Remote Exploration	FoA Plane, FoA Spherical	Notification, Gesture	Egocentric
Proximity Exploration.	Safe-Zone, nFoA	Vibration, Notification, Beeps, Gesture	Allocentric

2.2 Methodology

The Smartphone has been used on a number of projects with blind or visually impaired people to provide help to locate, explore and navigate through known and unknown environments (Lahav, Schloerb and Srinivasan, 2015)(Miesenberger *et al.*, 2014)(Hicks *et al.*, 2013)(Callejas Cuervo and Medina Sánchez, 2014); there is talk of the importance of including visually impaired users from an early stage for the design of these systems in order to develop a reality-based learning design (Liu *et al.*, 2017) and also the right develop of interfaces in mobile applications as a basic key for the development of accessibility services (Rodriguez-Sanchez *et al.*, 2014) and . We believe that blind people who use virtual reality applications with sensitive interfaces to make visits in advance to unknown spaces solve with greater confidence and security the tasks of locating objects and structures in the interior of the place visited. Also, we thought that mobile multisensory information along with other various activities help project participants to make a mental representation of their environment.

Six workshops were developed to evaluate the cognitive and physical interfaces used in the development of virtual reality applications, in each workshop were performed, first the welcome, training after, then exploring, at the end of the workshop, participants completed tasks-support. Each experience is recorded with the consent of the participants, observation logs, questionnaires pos-test and application data are stored to the project server. In each new workshop the previous results were considered, as well as the suggestions of the participants listed below.

2.2.1 Workshop I

Fifteen blind and visually impaired people (See Table 2) were recruited through ONCE foundation and through word of mouth, for the initial diagnosis. They signed confidentiality and collaborate agreement with the research group. All the participants had knowledge in the use of the mobile and some applications to convert text into voice. One of the participants has a hearing problem.

Table 2. Participants First Workshop

	Blind people	Visually impaired	Age	Working	Student	Retired	Other
Men	5	3	31-66	13,3%	6,6%	33,3%	
Women	2	5	21-48	33,3%	6,6%		6,6%

With the data collected, it was planned to build a first application based on audio and gestures, taking into account the interests and technical skills of the participants.

2.2.2 Workshop II

Four participants, two blind and two visually impaired (average age 41, SD= 16.5) taken part in the validation of the first VRA where the participant should explore the virtual space sitting on a gyratory armchair. The application was built with three frontals SZ placed to 1, 2 and 3 meters (Figure 2) since centre user's position. There are six objects inside a room placed on different locations. A post-test questionnaire was developed to evaluate the parameters of performance, usability and user satisfaction. For the validation we built scale models of the room and the objects, where the participants were to place this objects in the same position according they remembered. The proximity and remote exploration modes are integrated in a single virtual reality application.

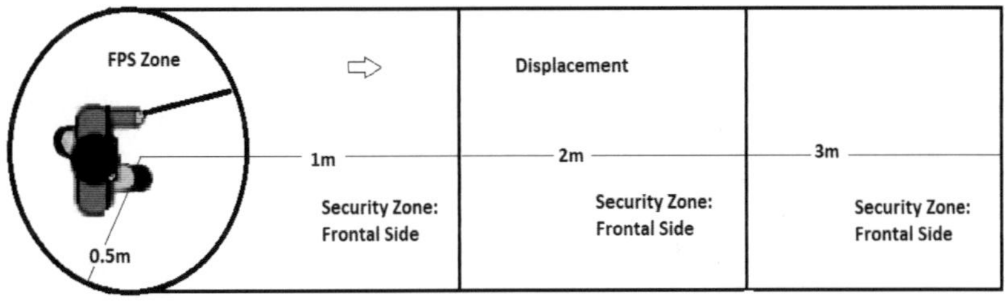

Figure 2. SZ in the first application

The vibration was used to notify the user the avatar is walking, and the variation of the vibration pattern informs the user the closeness to the object. Nevertheless, the users were not sure if the avatar was walking because when the objects entered SZ, the Smartphone kept on vibrating, but the avatar just was stopped. In the construction of this application was used a sphere with a 1 meter diameter as FoA, it was traveling in front the user to know objects ahead. The FoA allowed detecting objects and structures, with some difficulties in the corners. The users suggested numbering the walls and adding beeps to warn on near-avatar objects.

2.2.3 Workshop III

Five participants (average age 40, SD=14.4) took part in the assessment of the second VRA. The same scene with and without objects placed in different places was used for the test. The application had two fronts SZ placed to 1 and 2 meters since centre user's position.

In this application, the user can choose to walk through the virtual scene by touching the screen of the mobile or exploring the virtual environment making a horizontal stroke in the screen. To give information about the type of object, which gets into the safe-zones, high, medium and low frequency beep patterns are created to replace the varying vibration used in the Workshop previous. Since this workshop, the vibration only will have one pattern; it means the avatar is walking in the virtual environment. The participants do the avatar continue colliding with the objects, because there is no chance to stop as an action included in the application. So, for the next application, it was decided to develop an option that allows the avatar to stop, then explore and finally keep on walking by where there are not any objects. The users suggest that the application informs about the objects, which are on their right or on their left, to be able to rotate when there are no objects, so, for the next application, we should be develop Laterals Safety Zones.

The first application built without objects allowed to users recognizes structures as doors, windows and wall indoor, and the second application with objects was used to locate objects. Both applications used two spheres placed one to one into eyes of avatar to reach objects the user is gazing, also we use a voice and vibration patron as output interfaces and gestures on the screen as input interfaces. To assess the application, there was used a small scale model of the room and objects, where the participants were to place this objects in the same position according they remembered, and addition a post-test questionnaire to determine users´ level of satisfaction and efficacy of the tool.

2.2.4 Workshop IV

Three woman, one with visually impaired and two blind (average age 42, SD=8.1) participated in the validation of the next virtual reality application, where laterals SZ was add by to deliver information about objects to the sides (Figure 3).

In Addition the spheres used as FoA was changed by a cube with similar height to the avatar (BoxCastAll) to facilitate programming and reduce changes triggered by any shaking unwanted on the mobile. One application was built to integrate actions as walk, stop and exploring using gestures. Moreover, there were evaluated in four new applications, twenty vibration patterns, thirty-six beep patterns, ten gesture patterns and 25 voice patterns to choose three representative patterns of each option in order to use them in the next application. Owing to the large number of data that we would obtain in the next evaluation, we decided to separate the proximity exploration mode and the remote exploration mode in two applications; these will be used for the next validation with all participants.

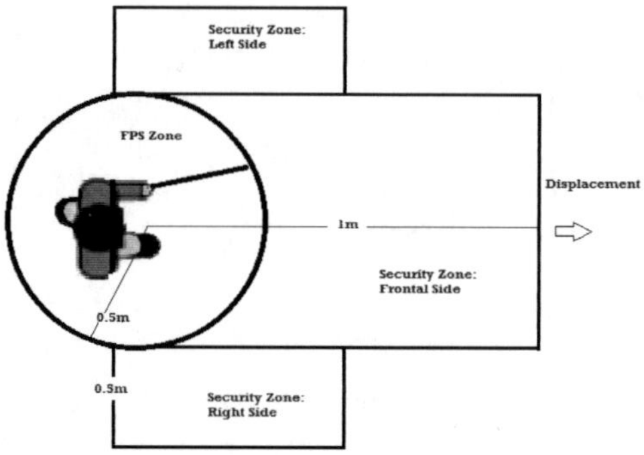

Figure 3. SZ Developed for the Third Application

2.2.5 Workshop V

In this workshop, twelve blind people joined to the work group, totaling twenty blind participants (11 men, 9 women, average age 52.2, SD=14.1) to carry out twelve individual experiences. This workshop is the most representative of the others, since it will allow evaluating the most satisfactory interfaces for the users, their effectiveness and efficiency in the recognition and location of objects and structures with the entire conglomerate of blind people of the project.

Implementation:

A Web server TS140 (Apache, MySQL, PhpMyAdmin) with client-server architecture handles the registration and labeling of users and the database where the registrations of each experience are downloaded. The Smartphone BQ Aquaris E5, SAMSUNG Galaxy S4 and S5, with Android OS 4.4.4 and 5.0, are used to test the developed applications (figure 4). The data about the path are sent to an email address and then they are stored in the SQL Server. The development environment for the Smartphone applications is Unity 3D version 5.3.2 (https://store.unity.com/es), which provides native support for mobile platforms like Android and iOS. Each application has two laterals safety zones and 2 front safety zones placed to 1 and 1.5 meters since centre user's position.

1) Scale models: There were built 24 cardboard scale models (57cm x 32cm) of the structure and 36 scale models of the object for two working teams. Each participant had to identify the scale model of the virtually visited place and put the scale models of the correct objects in this, after having made the virtual visit.

2) Real Environments: There were used three rectangular places in a building that is owned by the Technical University of Madrid. The first space represents an office, the other a bedroom and the third a pub. Each one has the same measure: 10mx6mx3m, where six objects are located in different positions and orientations, totaling 18 actual size objects taken from the building or made with cardboard, wood and plastic.

3) Number of experiences: Twelve experiences per user were defined, making a total of 81 configurations, which make it possible to test three cognitive interfaces and ten sensitive interfaces; taking into account that not every sensitive case can be applied to every cognitive case. Every configuration is labeled with a sensitive interface number (s1-s10), one or two letters for the cognitive interface (sFoA or spherical FoA; fFoA or flat FoA; noFoA or without FoA), three letters for the kind of place (ofi/Office, bed/Bedroom, pub/Pub). Finally, the last letter refers to the position of the objects in the scene (r-Red; b-Black; y-Yellow), as show in the Table 3.

Table 3. Configuration of Application

				Sensitive Interfaces		
Experience	Configuration	Cognitive Interfaces	Scene	Sensitive beeps	Sensitive voice	Sensitive gestures
1 to 12	Sensitive+FoA+Scene+colour	fFoA/sFoA/noFoA	Office/Room/Pub	S1 to S3	S4 to S7	S8 to S10

Sensitive interfaces:

1) Beep patterns: used to alert the user about obstacles. The wave frequency ($f1<f2<f3<f4<f5$) is used to make a difference between the low, middle or high obstacles, and the combination of pulse duration (d) and separation between (δ) waves make the user to know the distance to the obstacle (See Table 4). These patterns (S1, S2, and S3) are shown in the table 4.

Table 4. Sensitive Beep Interface

Pattern	Distance (m)	High object	Middle object	Low object
S1	1.5	f5, δ2, d2	f3, δ2, d2	f1, δ2, d2
S1	1	f6, δ1, d1	f4, δ1, d1	f2, δ1, d1
S2	1.5	f5, δ1, d1	f4, δ2, d1	f2, δ1, d2
S2	1	f4, δ2, d3	f3, δ1, d1	f2, δ2, d1
S3	1.5	f3, δ1, d3	f4, δ1, d2	f1, δ1, d1
S3	1	f3, δ1, d2	f4, δ2, d2	f2, δ1, d3

2) Voice patterns: used to inform the user about the distance and the relative position to the object or structures, and the way to give a feedback when the user activates or deactivates the exploration. The voice patterns (S4, S5, and S6) are specified in the Table 5.

Table 5. Sensitive Voice Interface

Pattern	Voice for distance	Speed	Action modes	Objects in laterals SZ
S4	Steps	Normal	Active/Disable	object out by left/right
S5	Meters	Fast	Start/End	left/right free way
S6	Further, Closer	Very Fast	Enabled/Disable	nothing thing left/right

3) Gesture patterns: determine the better way the user interacts with the system, touching the screen of the Smartphone. They are used to activate/deactivate the exploration as well as identifying structures or objects which are nearer or closer in front of the user. These patterns are detailed in the Table 6.

Table 6. Sensitive Gesture Interface

Pattern	Walk/Stop	Activation/D. Exploration	Object Changing
S7	Single touch	Horizontal swipe	Vertical swipe
S8	Double touch	Vertical swipe	Horizontal swipe
S9	Single touch with sound	Horizontal swipe with sound	Vertical swipe with sounds
S10	Extended touch 1.5 sec.	Vertical swipe with sound	Horizontal swipe with sound

Cognitive Interfaces:

1) Flat Focus of Attention: Consists on a rectangular prism which has the measures of the avatar and moves 30 meters in the horizontal direction (only X and Z coordinates) the person is looking at, and gets the name and the distance to the person of every object it collides with. In this mode, the SZ are not included, and the avatar is always in the same position.

2) Spherical Focus of Attention: Is based on a one-meter-diameter sphere, which moves from the head of the avatar through the vector that represents the direction (X, Y and Z coordinates) the person is looking at. Just as the previous mode, the sphere collides with the objects in that direction and obtains the name and the distance. The SZ do not exist in this cognitive interface. The avatar does not move in the environment, so the user always explores from the same position.

3) No FoA: In this case the user has to explore the virtual environment only with the walking mode and using the information given by the SZ.

2.2.6 Workshop VI

Six blind participants (5 men, 1 woman, average age 48.8 years, SD = 14.9) performed the validation of six VRAs that were installed on an iPhone 6S. The application reproduced 3D sounds in wireless bone headphones to report on the location of objects and structures inside the space. An occipital structure sensor (Occipital, 2017) was also used to track the position of the participant when walking in the real environment and update the position of the avatar in the application (See Figure 4). It was virtualized the Living Lab Smart House (LST-UPM, 2017) of the Polytechnic University of Madrid, which is fully equipped for testing.

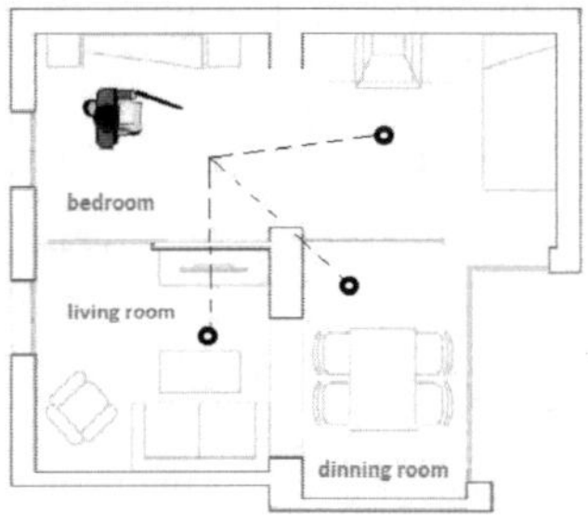

Figure 4. Experience Workshop VI

During the experience each participant should come to three equidistant points, using an auditory output interface. The mobile sends to the bone headphones three types of audio, which are voice, tones and the sound of a musical instrument, using low power Bluetooth. Most users came directly to the proposed points without any difficulty, so we believe that virtual reality applications should include 3D sounds during the exploration.

Most users came directly to the proposed points without any difficulty, so we believe that virtual reality applications should include 3D sounds during the exploration.

2.3 Results

During six workshops, one hundred and twenty-four VRAs were tested, each of which used different sensitive and cognitive interfaces, which were developed to satisfy the majority of participants and to meet the necessary standards of quality. After each workshop, a test based on the Likert scale (5 highest, 1 lowest) and control registers was used to know the level of acceptance of the application in terms of usability and level of satisfaction.

In the Workshop I, the participants gave some information to start the development of the first application. Most the participants had knowledge and experience in using an iPhone, using email, text to speech application and some of them used other electronics devices. One participant appeared to show deafness features.

In workshop II, participants used the first application to explore a room in a virtual way, through a questionnaire the quality and clarity of the information received by voice was evaluated, as well as the intensity of the vibration to recognize the proximity to the inside objects, as well as the gestures used to begin the exploration. The results are showed in Figure 5, where 5 represents fully agree and 1 disagrees. The suggestions of the participants to reinforce the actions with sounds were used to make some modifications in the design of the next application.

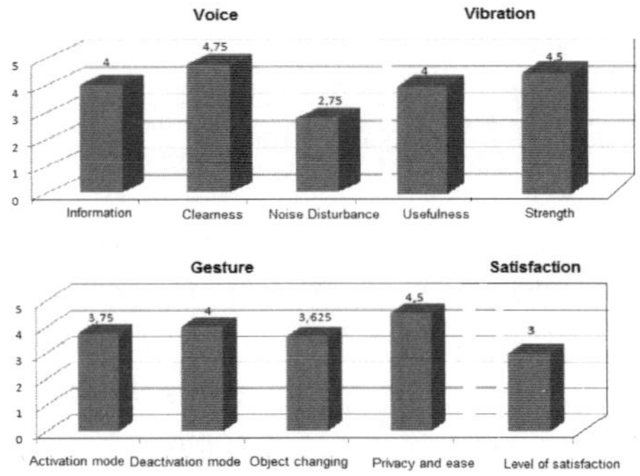

Figure 5. Results Workshop II

In the Workshop III, the activation and deactivation the exploration mode by gestures were reinforced with sounds. The first application allowed environment structure recognizing, with 83.5% success (Figure 6). The second application allowed environment's objects recognizing, with 100% success. Participants performed three tasks that consisted of addressing three points inside virtual environment with a 94.4% success; sometimes the help of researchers was required. In addition, they had to recognize and locate several objects inside a scale model. The participants mention the interest in being informed about objects that appear virtually on their right and left side, because the application only reports about objects in line of sight with the avatar.

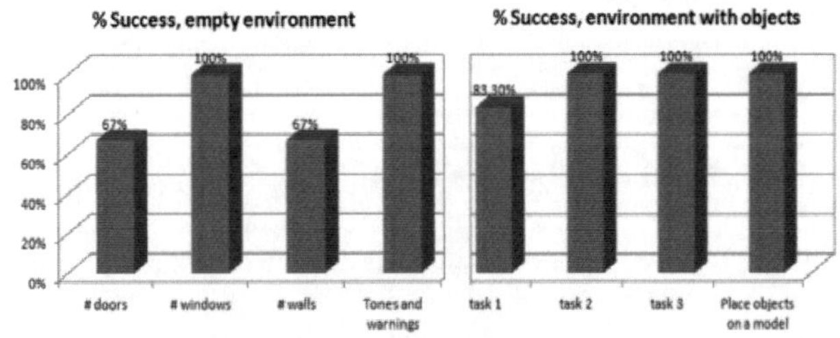

Figure 6. Results Workshop III

In Workshop IV, applications were built with lateral and frontal safety zones, participants assessed proximity and remote exploration with 100% success in the task of localization and recognition, the results are shown in Figure 7, where 5 represents totally agree and 1 disagree.

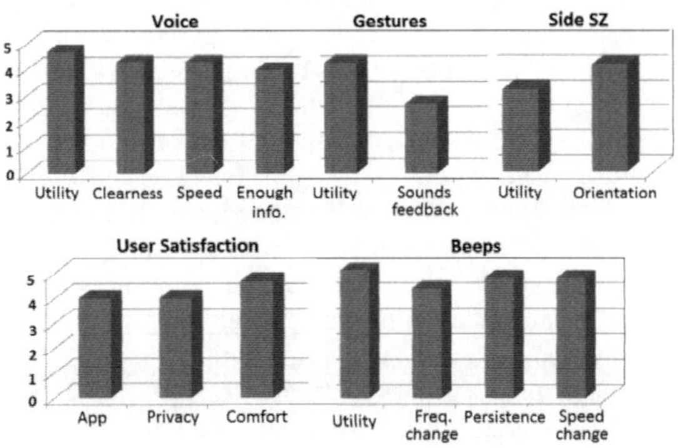

Figure 7. Results Workshop IV

During this workshop they chose patterns of voice, beeps, vibrations and gestures, whose preferences are shown in the Table 7 and Table 8.

Table 7. Vibration, Beep and Voice Patterns Selected

Pattern	P1	P2	P3
Vibration	d=200ms/δ= 400ms	d1=100ms/δ1= 200ms d2=200ms/δ2= 400ms	d=1000ms/δ= 2000ms
Beep High; d>1m	Very sharp and elongated sound	Sharp and fast sound	Sound slow
Beep Medium; d>1m	Cardiac monitor	Sharp and more paused	Cardiac monitor more sharp
Beep Low; d>1m	Slow and paused	Few slow and more paused	Low and fast sound
Beep H-M-L; d<1m	Very sharp, fast and rackety	Cardiac monitor more sharp	Heartbeat
Voice-Mode remote	Exploration mode enabled	Exploration enabled	Exploration
Voice-Mode proximity	Walk mode enable	Walk enable	Walk
Voice- Distance	Meters	Steps	Closer/ Further
Voice- Windows/Doors	Window/Door Open	Size Window/Door + open	Window/Door
Voice- Objects in lateral SZ	Enters from the left/ right	Right blocked/ Left blocked	Enters on the left /right side
Voice-Orientation	Turn right/left	Go to the right/left	Change direction

Table 8. Gesture Patterns Selected

Pattern	Walk /Stop	Exploration Act./Dis.	Object Change
Gesture S7	Single Touch	Horizontal line	Vertical line
Gesture S8	Double touch	Vertical line	Horizontal line
Gesture S9	Single touch with sound	Horizontal line with sound	Vertical line with sounds
Gesture S10	Extended touch of 1.5 sec.	Vertical line with sound	Horizontal line with sound

The logs show that the lateral safety- zones have been well accepted by the participants. They told us that they prefer audio-descriptions of the space and the most representative objects before starting the exploration and that auditory feedback is very important when they made a gesture on the screen to know if they did it correctly. The next step will be build new applications by combining patterns preferred by users to determine their efficiency and effectiveness in the mental representation of space.

In the Workshop V, were assessment separately three cognitive interfaces (flat FoA, spherical FoA, not FoA) and ten sensitive interfaces (S1-S10), totaling eighty one application, where it could be determined that:

1) The remote exploration using a plane FoA reach better users' acceptance and seem to optimize the time in the recognition the structures and objects. There is a 38% of improved when the participants choose the focus of attention to explore the virtual environment remotely. The percentage of correct location of objects in scale models is less than 29%, it is proposed to improve this percentage by using spatial sounds.
2) More than a 70% of the blind users are capable of recognizing high-speed voices, what makes it possible to reduce exploration time.
3) Less than a 33% of the participants are satisfied with the persistence of the beep that takes place when an object enters in his frontal SZ. Nevertheless, their opinion is that it is very useful when avoiding colliding with objects. They prefer since low until medium frequencies as warning, around 500Hz for regular size objects was a beep more comfortable.
4) All participants used a single touch, double touch and vertical and horizontal strokes without difficulty, but the efficiency of the time was greater when using a simple touch. The extended touch and the touch with the sound caused largest time and errors when beginning the exploration.

In Workshop VI, participants used virtual reality applications to locate objects and structures within an unknown environment using 3D sounds with 81.48% success. Users took less time to reach the object when they used the custom audio response, achieving greater efficiency with 440Hz tones (Figure 8).

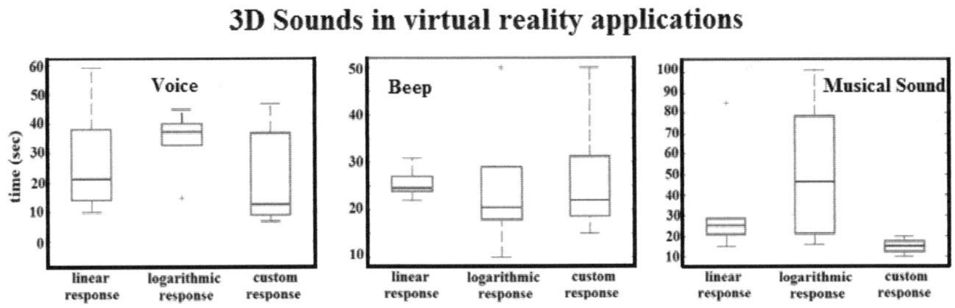

Figure 8. Results Workshop VI

The musical sound seemed to please them as the output interface; however this interface registered the lowest scores in the scale implemented and the highest times to reach the object. According to the participants, the use of 3D sounds produces a substantial improvement in the location of objects and structures in the environment compared to other previously tested applications.

3. CONCLUSIONS

The methodology developed for the construction of virtual reality applications to be used by people who are blind is based on an information model that has allowed us to construct, modify and integrate the physical and cognitive interfaces in each application in a simple way, reusing code and with ease to increase or remove components to the system.

Based on the recommendations provided by users during the evaluation, the logs provided by the system and the observations recorded in each developed experience, an adequate tool has been obtained so that participants with visual impairment can mentally represent the space they visit for the first time, through virtual explorations in advance.

The participants who evaluated the RV applications were able to locate objects and structures within an unknown environment, with confidence and security. The importance of working continuously with a group of people with blindness and low vision is reflected in the level of satisfaction registered in the surveys. Each new application had some modifications and the number of users for evaluation was limited. It will be necessary to carry out a final evaluation with a greater number of users, integrating all the improvements learned during the development of this methodology.

The voice response is very important when: the user touches the screen, because it reinforces the result of the user's intention in each action carried out; also to inform you about objects or structures near your Safety Zone, which allow you to change your orientation and avoid possible collisions. The user's request through a gesture on the screen is also used to remember something that was previously reported. At the same time, it is necessary to limit the amount of information to ensure that it is clear and relevant during the virtual exploration.

The use of 3D sounds to guide the user inside the space and to locate of an object, through a personalized audio response, reduces the amount of information required by the system to produce better results in terms of accuracy and user satisfaction. It is still necessary to integrate all the development achieved with this methodology into new experiences with a greater number of users, which allows establishing the percentages of increase in efficiency and performance with respect to previous applications. It is necessary to increase the number of virtualized scenarios, so that new ones are unknown by the participants.

The percentage of evaluation in the aspects of quality and user satisfaction, allows us to believe that this tool can be used both as training to visit new places in advance and as a tiflo-game (game for blind people); this should be evaluated later.

ACKNOWLEDGEMENT

This research was supported by Cátedra Indra-Fundación Addeco and the colaboration of Fundation ONCE.

REFERENCES

Anshari, M. and Alas, Y. (2015) 'Smartphones habits, necessities, and big data challenges', *Journal of High Technology Management Research*. Elsevier Inc., 26(2), pp. 177–185. doi: 10.1016/j.hitech.2015.09.005.

Baker, S. *et al.* (no date) *IDC Analize the future*.

Callejas Cuervo, M. and Medina Sánchez, E. (2014) 'Aplicación móvil como herramienta de ubicación y demarcación de rutas para invidentes, utilizando realidad aumentada *1', *Ventana Informatica*, (30), pp. 27–42.

Cobo, A. *et al.* (2017) 'Computers in Human Behavior Differences between blind people ' s cognitive maps after proximity and distant exploration of virtual environments Jos e', 77, pp. 294–308. doi: 10.1016/j.chb.2017.09.007.

De Felice, F. *et al.* (2007) 'A haptic/acoustic application to allow blind the access to spatial information', *Proceedings - Second Joint EuroHaptics Conference and Symposium on Haptic Interfaces for Virtual Environment and Teleoperator Systems, World Haptics 2007*, pp. 310–315. doi: 10.1109/WHC.2007.6.

Härmä, A. *et al.* (2004) 'Augmented reality audio for mobile and wearable appliances', *AES: Journal of the Audio Engineering Society*, 52(6), pp. 618–639.

Hicks, S. L. *et al.* (2013) 'A Depth-Based Head-Mounted Visual Display to Aid Navigation in Partially Sighted Individuals', *PLoS ONE*, 8(7), pp. 1–8. doi: 10.1371/journal.pone.0067695.

Hwang, G.-J., Chu, H.-C. and Lai, C.-L. (2017) 'Prepare your own device and determination (PYOD): a successfully promoted mobile learning mode in Taiwan', *International Journal of Mobile Learning and Organization*, 11(2), pp. 87–107. doi: https://doi.org/10.1504/IJMLO.2017.084277.

Karimi, H. (2011) *Universal Navigation on Smartphones:* doi: 10.1007/978-1-4419-7741-0.

Kitchin, R. (2001) 'Cognitive Maps', *International Encyclopedia of the Social & Behavioral Sciences*. Neil J. Sm. doi: https://doi.org/10.1016/B0-08-043076-7/02531-6.

Kozhevnikov, M., Blazhenkova, O. ; and Obana, T. (2017) *Mental Imagery and Human-Computer Interaction Lab.*

Lahav, O. *et al.* (2012) 'A Virtual Environment for People Who Are Blind - A Usability Study.', *Journal of assistive technologies*. NIH Public Access, 6(1). doi: 10.1108/17549451211214346.

Lahav, O., Schloerb, D. W. and Srinivasan, M. A. (2015) 'Rehabilitation Program Integrating Virtual Environment to Improve Orientation and Mobility Skills for People Who Are Blind.', *Computers & Education*, 80(1), pp. 1–14. doi: 10.1016/j.compedu.2014.08.003.

Leuthold Stefan, Bargas-Avila Javier, O. K. (2008) 'contenido accesible', *Elsevier*. doi: :10.1016/j.ijhcs.2007.10.006.

Liu, G. Z. *et al.* (2017) 'Identifying learning features and models for contextaware ubiquitous learning with phenomenological research method', *International Journal of Mobile Learning and Organization*, 10(4). doi: 10.1504 / IJMLO.2016.079501.

LST-UPM (2017) *Smart House*.

Majerova, H. (2017) 'The Person in a Situation of Visual Impairment and its Perception and Imagination from the Qualitative Viewpoint', *Procedia - Social and Behavioral Sciences*. Elsevier B.V., 237(June 2016), pp. 751–757. doi: 10.1016/j.sbspro.2017.02.117.

Miesenberger, K. *et al.* (2014) 'Computers Helping People with Special Needs', in Springer (ed.) *14th International Conference, ICCHP 2014*. Paris, p. 640. doi: 10.1007/978-3-319-08599-9.

Occipital (2017) *Structure*.

Pasqualotto, A. *et al.* (2013) 'Visual experience facilitates allocentric spatial representation', *Behavioural Brain Research*. Elsevier B.V., 236, pp. 175–179. doi: 10.1016/j.bbr.2012.08.042.

Picinali, L. *et al.* (2014) 'Exploration of architectural spaces by blind people using auditory virtual reality for the construction of spatial knowledge', *International Journal of Human Computer Studies*. Elsevier, 72(4), pp. 393–407. doi: 10.1016/j.ijhcs.2013.12.008.

Rodriguez-Sanchez, M. C. *et al.* (2014) 'Accessible smartphones for blind users: A case study for a wayfinding system', *Expert Systems with Applications*. Elsevier Ltd, 41(16), pp. 7210–7222. doi: 10.1016/j.eswa.2014.05.031.

Sanabria, L. B. (2007) 'Mapeo cognitivo y exploración háptica para comprender la disposición del', pp. 45–65.

Serrão, M. *et al.* (2012) 'Indoor localization and navigation for blind persons using visual landmarks and a GIS', *Procedia Computer Science*, 14(Dsai), pp. 65–73. doi: 10.1016/j.procs.2012.10.008.

Silvio P. Mariotti (World Health Organization) (2010) 'GLOBAL DATA ON VISUAL IMPAIRMENTS 2010', pp. 1–17.

Unity (2017) *Unity 3D*. Available at: https://unity3d.com/.

WHO | Visual impairment and blindness (2014) *Visual impairment and blindness*. World Health Organization. Available at: http://www.who.int/mediacentre/factsheets/fs282/en/ (Accessed: 13 September 2016).

A MOBILE CLOUD COMPUTING BASED INDEPENDENT LANGUAGE LEARNING SYSTEM WITH AUTOMATIC INTELLIGIBILITY ASSESSMENT AND INSTANT FEEDBACK

Imen M. Kasrani, Miteshkumar M. Vasoya, Ashutosh Shivakumar and Yong Pei
SMART Lab, Wright State University, Dayton, Ohio, USA

ABSTRACT

In this research paper, we present a novel language learning/training and assessment system that helps people to learn and practice a new language independently at low cost. To achieve an independent-learning workflow, we explore the use of real-time speech recognition, language translation, speech synthesis, and language intelligibility assessment technologies to provide automatic assessment and instant feedback of language-speaking performance. We also propose and adopt an objective assessment methodology that determines the intelligibility based on outcome of speech recognition. Our experimental results demonstrate that the proposed system can sufficiently analyze the intelligibility of one's speaking, accurately identify mispronounced words, and define a feedback that localizes and highlights errors for helping continuous practice toward perfection.

KEYWORDS

Mobile Learning, Language Learning, Speech Recognition, Language Intelligibility Assessment, Instant Feedback, Mobile Cloud Computing

1. INTRODUCTION

Recent advances in computer-assisted language-speaking learning/training technology have demonstrated its promising potential to improve the outcome of language learning in early education, special education, English as a Second Language (ESL), and foreign language (Krasnova and Bulgakova, 2014). The growing number of readily available mobile app-based solutions help encourage interest in learning to speak a foreign language, but their effectiveness is limited due to their lack of objective assessment and performance feedback resembling expert judgment. For example, in early education, it is a challenging task for students to extend the language learning at school to home without such feedback and intervention available at home.

In this research, our objective is to develop an effective and practical solution that will help people to learn and practice a new language independently at low cost. We have explored the use of real-time speech recognition, language translation, speech synthesis, and language intelligibility assessment technologies to develop a learning/training system that provides automatic assessment and instant feedback of language-speaking performance to achieve an independent-learning workflow.

1.1 Survey of Existing Language Learning Applications

High quality apps continuously arrive for both iOS and Android that help users to learn a new language effectively and efficiently. These apps cover almost all languages at little to no cost, and provide the private, virtual, and all-inclusive environment necessary for learning and perfecting a new language through reading, writing and speaking. They can be classified into 5 categories:

1. **Language courses**: Babbel, Duolingo and Busuu are among the most popular applications of language courses. These applications use translation and dictation to emulate traditional language classes. Learners read text and listen to videos, then interpret and answer questions. These apps are also used to help

memorize vocabulary. For speaking training, they use the pronunciation of a native speaker for every word and phrase. Unfortunately, this is an unorganized way of learning information because these apps start with complex words and tricky phrases, providing only a way for improving vocabulary rather than effective methods for enhancing conversational skills.

2. **FlashCards and SRS**: Memrise, Tinycards, and AnkiApp are popular examples of this category. They provide a way of practicing vocabulary using memorization of words and phrases, structured as a competitive game in which users are rewarded with points for every correct answer. It is worth noting that Memrise also has a unique feature that associates a new word with similar words from the user's native language to help make a link between words for better memorization.

3. **Educational games**: MindSnacks is such an educational game that helps users learn grammar and vocabulary and practice listening. In addition, this application teaches words and phrases by limiting the time in which to guess the correct answer. It is more applicable to children than to adults because it uses cartoon image.

4. **Q&A, chat and social**: The most popular chat and social applications used in learning new languages are HelloTalk, HiNative, and TripLingo. They use real-time conversation with unknown native speakers and a text-to-voice option to help pronounce received messages. TripLingo is different from HelloTalk and HiNative in that it provides the learner with information related to the place that he/she wants to travel. HiNative is a chat application that uses question and answer features so that the learner can ask the native about their language and culture. Hence, it is a place for one to introduce themselves more than it is a place to correctly practice a new language.

5. **Contextual reference**: Leaf is one of the contextual reference applications that explains the necessary words that the learner needs to know when encountering new situations. It is an application used only for learning English.

Clearly, current language training applications are limited in the following aspects:

1. Improve writing more than speaking: Most of the language training applications do not provide an efficient listening or speaking experience. Users can learn some new vocabulary and constructions, but unfortunately cannot carry on a deep conversation with a native speaker of the foreign language. Learning a new language is not only about learning new words and formulating new phrases with appropriate syntax; it is also about being understandable when pronouncing words (Heil, et al, 2016).

2. Lack of performance assessment and feedback: Current applications rarely evaluate speaking skills and language pronunciation quality. To make the learning of foreign language more efficient, applications need to deliver meaningful feedback that evaluates the quality of the user's speech. A successful application for learning new language needs to be able to make a real evaluation of mispronounced speech, and recognize an incorrect accent.

3. It is mostly about gaming: Applications that depend more on gaming than the actual fundaments of a language can be problematic in the long-term, as passing levels and scoring becomes more important than learning and practicing the language.

1.2 Why Automatic Intelligibility Assessment for Language Training?

People can learn vocabulary and grammar, and then read words and even sentences after practicing a new language, but oftentimes the challenge they are facing is speaking fluently in the language. For learners, either beginners or someone who needs a refresher, feedback on their level of speaking is necessary to correct and perfect their speaking. Learners need accurate feedback on their pronunciation practice because they are often unable to recognize the precise problem in their pronunciation by themselves. In traditional language classes, this is often achieved through practice sessions, such as roleplays, with assessment and feedback done by the instructor.

Clearly, instant assessment and feedback for improvement is key to effective independent language-speaking learning/training because they provide accurate evidence of the merits, progresses, and limitations of a learner's skills. The lack of timely, accurate, and consistent assessment capabilities that have acceptable operating complexity and affordable cost significantly limit the effectiveness of using mobile apps as a viable option to learn foreign language.

Thus, in this research, we will address this issue by focusing on the design and development of a performance assessment system that can offer the opportunity for language learners to have a more complete picture of what they learn in pronunciation skills and what they need to enhance. The feedback needs to be modeled after human judgment and should be able to be easily interpreted by the learner. An automatic scoring system is appropriate, as it gives the learner instant information on overall result quality (Neri, et al, 2003). Moreover, providing instant feedback gives the learner an idea about their level of progress and gives them a motive to improve their skills over successive attempts.

2. SYSTEM DESIGNS

In this research, we intend to augment and enhance the existing computer-assisted language training idea, as evident by many existing language training applications, to enable independent learning workflow by building a critical new capability that provides automatic intelligibility assessment and feedback.

2.1 System Architecture

To enable a mobile device-centered solution, we decided to adopt a mobile-cloud computing solution that takes advantage of the processing and storage capabilities and capacities of cloud computing service, and the portability, availability and diversity of personal computing devices, particularly mobile devices, as illustrated in Figure 1.

Cloud computing allows fast processing of data from any place over the Internet in real-time without having to concern about the storage or computing power. It is a virtual on-demand delivery of service that does not require an investment in expensive local hardware and software. Moreover, it avoids the hassles to install, configure, and manage the hardware and the software. It provides low-cost and low-latency access to required resources at any time and from anywhere for the consumers. The most popular providers of cloud computing services are: Google Cloud, Amazon Web Services, Microsoft Azure, IBM Bluemix, and Aliyun.

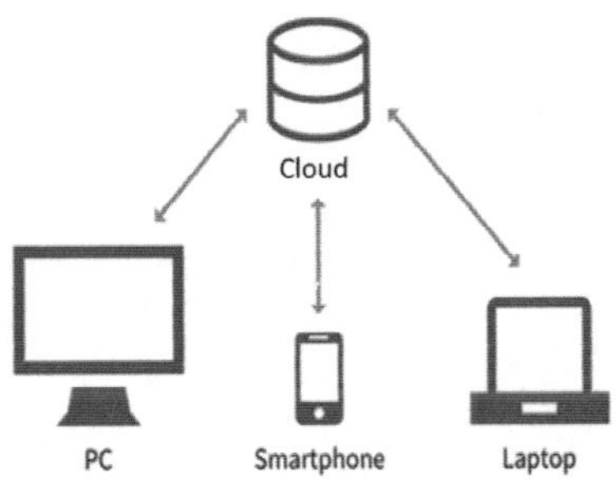

Figure 1. Cloud Computing

2.2 Overview of Our System

The main objectives of this research are: i.) augment the language learning system with accurate and automatic assessment of speaking of a language; and, ii.) enable independent learning workflow. To achieve these objectives, we identify the following key capabilities and features:

- **Recognize the speech**: The most important condition necessary for producing excellent results is accurate speech recognition.
- **Translate the speech**: The application must be able to translate the recognized text in source language (e.g., native language) to the target second language.
- **Synthesize the speech**: The application must be able to convert the translated text into the speech of the desired target language.
- **Assess the intelligibility**: The application must be able to evaluate the user's speech performance in a way that is comparable to human instructors. It should also give instant feedback to the user, e.g., present the overall score as a graded bar, and together with more specific/detailed feedback, such as highlighting the incorrectly pronounced words.

Figure 2 illustrates the workflow of our language learning and assessment system. We have explored the use of real-time speech recognition, language translation, speech synthesis, and language intelligibility assessment technologies to develop a learning/training system that provides automatic assessment and instant feedback of language-speaking performance to achieve an independent-learning workflow. Our prototype system demonstrates the feasibility and effectiveness of such a mobile cloud computing enabled independent learning/training solution. It can be easily used on a smartphone, tablet, computer, or other portable devices, and provides a new learning experience that is augmented and enhanced by objective assessment and significant feedback to improve the language-speaking proficiency of the user.

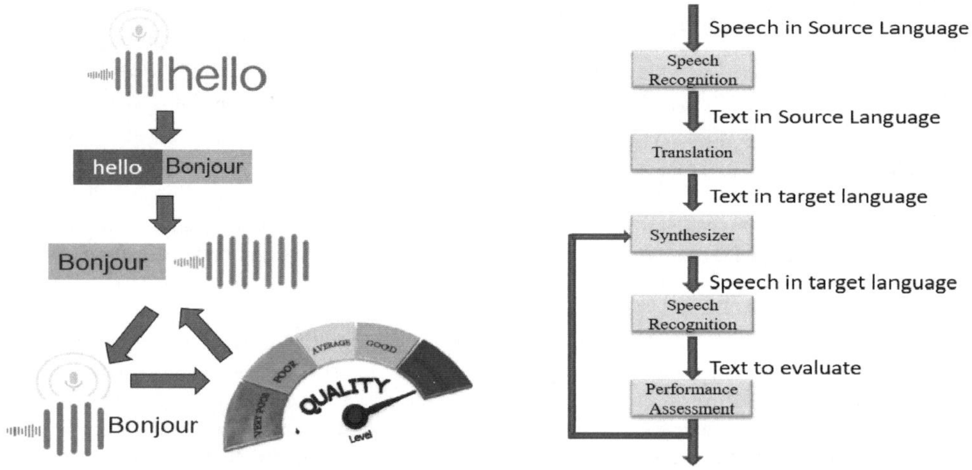

Figure 2. Overview of System Workflow

2.3 Enabling Technologies

In this section, we will discuss the related technologies that help enable the language learning system with accurate and automatic assessment of speaking of a language.

2.3.1 Speech Recognition

Speech recognition software can identify the words of a spoken language, captured from a microphone, and convert them to text. Today, it is used more and more in our daily lives, particularly with the mobile devices. For example, we can give a verbal command for phone calls on smartphones. There are several mature speech recognition services being offered through cloud services, e.g., *iOS* Siri, Amazon Alexa, Android speech to text, IBM Watson, and Google Cloud Speech.

In this research, we take advantage of the handily available cloud speech recognition capabilities offered by the Google Cloud Speech service. First, it produces accurate speech recognition results, even in a noisy environment, by using effective neural network modeling and machine-learning algorithm. Secondly, it recognizes over 110 languages, which fits perfectly with our language learning app. Furthermore, it can give word hints depending on the context provided as well as filter incorrect text results for certain languages. Finally, it is a low-cost service to the user.

2.3.2 Language Translation

Language translation services translate text input from one language to another language. Some of the most popular cloud-based translation services include IBM Watson language translator, Microsoft Translator, and Google Cloud Translation.

In this research, we make use of Google Cloud Translation API to translate the text from the source language to the desired target language in real-time. The Google Cloud Translation API translates text between 2 languages with high accuracy by using the state-of-the-art Neural Machine Translation. It supports over 100 languages, and makes translations between groupings of thousands of languages pairs.

2.3.3 Speech Synthesis

Speech synthesis, also called text-to-speech (TTS), converts natural language text into speech, so a computer, smartphone, tablet, or another device can read the produced audio stream aloud. Speech synthesis is the opposite of speech recognition, as it is a text to speech converter rather than a speech to text converter. The quality of a speech synthesizer is measured in two perspectives: naturalness and intelligibility. Naturalness is the ability to resemble the human voice, and intelligibility is the clearness of the output voice.

There are several available technologies that make conversion from text to speech, such as IBM Watson Text to Speech, FreeTTS, and MaryTTS (Modular Architecture for Research on Speech Synthesis). We use Mary TTS because it is an open source application written in Java and can synthesize many natural languages. MaryTTS was a shared project between DFKI's Language Technology Lab and the Institute of Phonetics at Saarland University. It supports many languages, including, e.g., German, British and American English, French, Italian, Russian, Swedish, Telugu, etc. It can also run in multiple platforms.

2.3.4 Speech Intelligibility Assessment

Speech intelligibility assessment is a complex and subjective process that may vary significantly from one human evaluator to another. In this research, we propose and adopt a more objective assessment methodology by determining the intelligibility based on outcome of speech recognition (Liu, et al, 2006). Following speech recognition, the assessment process is completed by an accurate comparison between speech-recognized spoken text and the original text. For instance, we need to compare the two texts to find the incorrect words that the learner spoke. Then, based on the result from the comparison, the learner will be given feedback of his/her intelligibility in speaking the language. Specifically, we take the following steps:

- Compare the recognized spoken text to the original given or translated text to identify the words that is missing or need to be replaced or removed.
- Assess the percentage of similarity between the two texts to determine the score of intelligibility.
- Highlight the words in green that need to be replaced in the recognized spoken text.
- Highlight the words in red that need to be removed in the recognized spoken text.
- Highlight the words in yellow that is missing in the original text.

To compare and identify the similarity/dissimilarity between two texts, we need to measure the distance between them. There exist different algorithms that count the number of operations needed to transform one string to another string, such as Levenshtein Distance, Hamming Distance, Longest Common Substring Distance and Jaro-Winkler Distance (Cohen, Ravikumar and Fienberg, 2003). In this research, we compare the recognized spoken text and the original text (as the control) word-by-word using the Levenshtein algorithm as illustrated in Table 1. It calculates the minimum numbers of change, including deletion (Missed), insertion (Removed), and substitutions (Replaced), required to transform one string to the other. One potential concern of adopting this algorithm for real-time mobile application is its complexity. The time complexity of the algorithm is $O(n*m)$, where n and m are the lengths of the two sentences being compared. The memory space complexity is $O(n*m)$ because it memorizes in matrix. However, it becomes less a concern nowadays as most of today's mobile devices can provide sufficient computing power and memory space for its operation, even for long sentences.

In Table 1, we illustrate the comparison between 2 sentences using the Levenshtein algorithm. For instance, the comparison between "the weather is nice today" and "the weather is it nice day" give 2 errors: 1 replacement between "today" and "day" and 1 deletion of the word "it".

The accurate analysis of learner speech makes it possible to provide instant feedback on what he/she did not observe otherwise. This feedback includes two parts: 1. The percentage score of intelligibility of the spoken language. 2. Highlight words that the learner needs to work on.

Instant feedback plays a crucial role in learning. It helps the learner clearly know the adjustment needed. Furthermore, it helps the learner to know whether he/she achieved the goal or not. Evaluation system of language learning may also help the trainer to develop training courses that concentrate better on identified weakness and provide highly personalized learning experience. After the Missed, Removed and Replaced words were identified by back tracing, we highlight them with different colors. The feedback of our language learning application provides the advantages of both Constructivist and Behavioristic theories of language learning. The application acts as a virtual facilitator by providing instant feedback that emulates constructivism. Further, it implements behaviorism by identifying errors pertaining to intelligibility and guiding the learner to practice on specific pronunciations (Heil, et al, 2016).

Table 1. Compare 2 Sentences Word-by-Word Using the Levenshtein Algorithm

		the	weather	is	nice	today
	0	1	2	3	4	5
the	1	0	1	2	3	4
weather	2	1	0	1	2	3
is	3	2	1	0	1	2
it	4	3	2	1	1	2
nice	5	4	3	2	1	2
day	6	5	4	3	2	2

We then calculate and report the percentage score of intelligibility use this formula:

Score of Intelligibility = 1- Number of Incorrect Words / Max (lengthSentence1, lengthSentence2);

Where:

Number of Incorrect Words = Missed Words + Removed Words + Replaced Words.

3. EXPERIMENTAL RESULTS

We have designed and implemented a successful prototype system that demonstrates the feasibility and effectiveness of such a mobile cloud computing enabled independent language learning/training solution, as shown in Figure 3. The following results present samples and offer validations for our system.

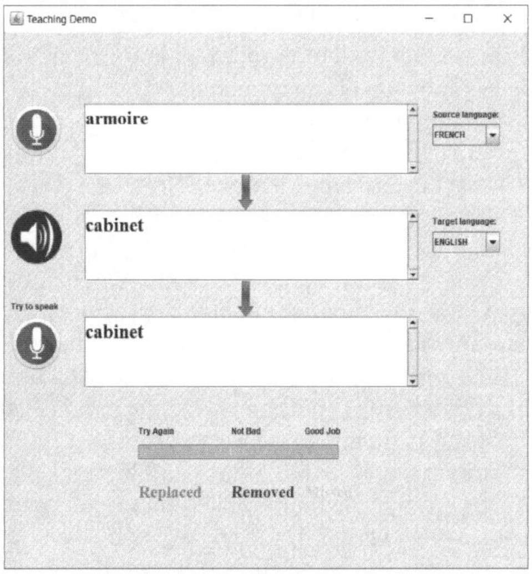

Figure 2. User Interface of the System

When starting the application, the user needs to select the source language and the target language. The user will then click the microphone button to start talking in the source language (e.g., the user's native language). As evident in Figure 3, the speech is successfully converted to text and displayed in the designated text area on the screen. Next, the text displayed in the first text area will be automatically translated to the target language, and then converted to audio for the user. The user can choose to listen again by clicking on the speaker button. When the user is ready to try, he/she needs to click the second microphone button and read the words inside the translated text area. The speech in target language will then be converted to text, but this time in the target language, and displayed in the specified text area. Finally, the system will compare the last recognized text to the translated text. The score of similarity will be displayed, and the missed words, wrong words, and the words that need to be substituted will be highlighted.

3.1 Testing with a Single Word

A user who wants to learn a foreign language will start by pronouncing a single word. So, we will first test with a single word as shown in Figure 4. At the left, the source language is French, and the target language is English. The word "armoire" is translated correctly to the word "cabinet". The user pronounced the word "cabinet" correctly. Thus, the score of intelligibility is 100%. In the middle, the source language is French, and the target language is Italian. The user pronounced the word "scarpe" correctly, but added another word that was not supposed to be there. Consequently, the score of intelligibility is 50%. The word "le" should be removed, thus highlighted in red. At the right, the source language is English, and the target language is French. The user read the word "couverture" wrongly, resulting in a different word "converse". Thus, they are both highlighted in green. The pronunciation is incorrect, so the score of intelligibility is 0%.

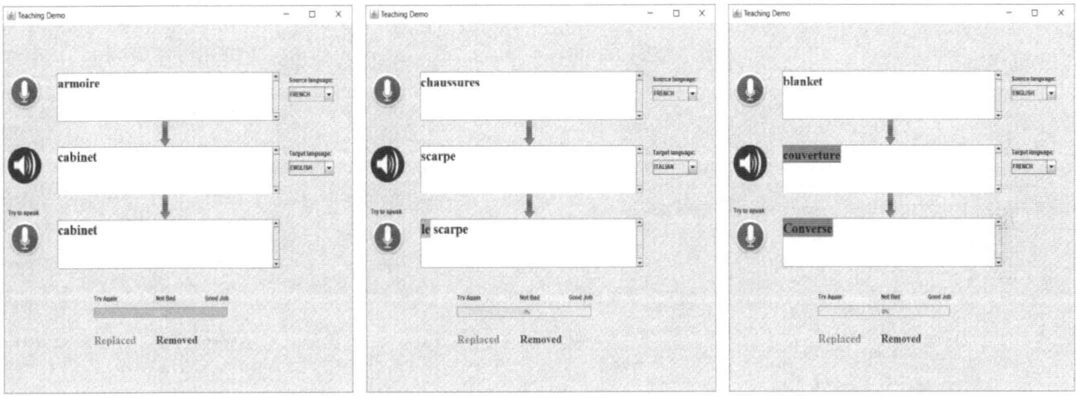

Figure 3. Tests with a Single Word

3.2 Testing with a Single Phrase

Next, we will test with a single phrase as shown in Figure 5. At the left, the source language is English, and the target language is French. The entire phrase is read correctly. Thus, the score of intelligibility is 100%. In the middle, English is the source language, and French is the target language. The feedback gives a score of intelligibility of 33% because only the word "bloc" is correct. The user mispronounced the word "autour" to "retour" and "du" to "de" which are both highlighted accordingly in green. At the right, English is the source language, and Italian is the target language. The user read the entire phrase "correre attraverso i boshi" incorrectly. Thus, the words that need to be replaced are highlighted in green, and the words that need to be removed are highlighted in red. The pronunciation is not correct, so the score of intelligibility is 0%.

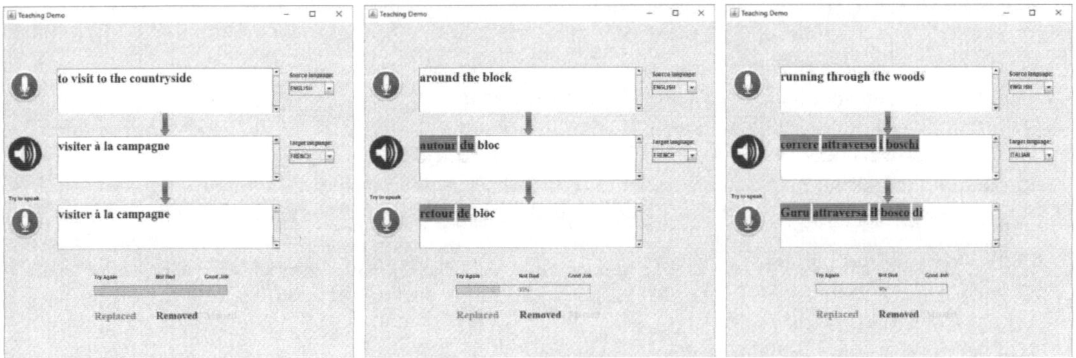

Figure 4. Tests with a Single Phrase

3.3 Testing with a Sentence

Finally, we will test with a sentence as shown in Figure 6. For all three tests, the source language is English, and the target language is French. At the left, the entire sentence is read correctly. Thus, the score of intelligibility is 100%. In the middle, the feedback gives a score of intelligibility of 66% because the user mispronounced the word “il” to “elle”, which is highlighted accordingly with green, and missed the word “si”, which is correctly highlighted in yellow. At the right, the user read the entire sentence incorrectly as highlighted in green, so the score of intelligibility is 0%.

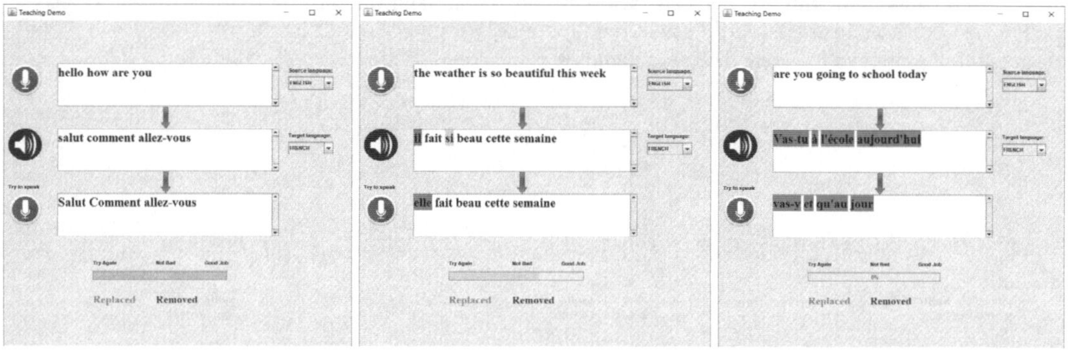

Figure 5. Tests with a Sentence

4. CONCLUSION

An effective and practical solution that helps users to learn and practice a new language independently at a low cost will significantly improve learning efficiency and outcome, as well as encourage more people to learn new languages. In this research, we have successfully developed a mobile cloud computing based language-speaking learning tool that harnesses the latest advances in real-time speech recognition, language translation, speech synthesis and language intelligibility assessment technologies to produce automatic assessment and instant feedback of language-speaking performance to help achieve an independent-learning workflow. Our experimental results demonstrate that the proposed system can sufficiently and accurately analyze the intelligibility of one’s speaking, correctly identify the mispronounced words, and define a feedback mechanism that localizes and highlights errors for helping users to continuously practice towards perfection.

REFERENCES

Google Cloud Speech. Available at: https://cloud.google.com/speech/.

Google Cloud Translate. Available at: https://cloud.google.com/translate/.

Heil, C. R., Wu, J. S., Lee, J. J., & Schmidt, T. (2016). A Review of Mobile Language Learning Applications: Trends, Challenges, and Opportunities. *The EuroCALL Review*, *24*(2), 32–50.

Krasnova E., Bulgakova E. (2014) The Use of Speech Technology in Computer Assisted Language Learning Systems. In: Ronzhin A., Potapova R., Delic V. (eds) Speech and Computer. SPECOM 2014. Lecture Notes in Computer Science, vol 8773. Springer, Cham

Liu, W. M., Jellyman, K. A., Mason, J. S. D., & Evans, N. W. D. (2006). Assessment of Objective Quality Measures for Speech Intelligibility Estimation. In 2006 IEEE ICASSP. https://doi.org/10.1109/ICASSP.2006.1660248

MaryTTS, Available at: http://mary.dfki.de/.

Neri, A., Cucchiarini, C. and Strik, H. (2003) Automatic speech recognition for second language learning: How and why it actually works. Speech Communication.

W. Cohen, W, Ravikumar, P. and E. Fienberg, S. (2003). A Comparison of String Metrics for Matching Names and Records. Proc of the KDD Workshop on Data Cleaning and Object Consolidation.

THE EduPARK MOBILE AUGMENTED REALITY GAME: LEARNING VALUE AND USABILITY

Lúcia Pombo and Margarida Morais Marques
Research Centre Didactics and Technology in Education of Trainers (CIDTFF)
Department of Education and Psychology, University of Aveiro,
Campus Universitário de Santiago, 3810-193 Aveiro, Portugal

ABSTRACT

Augmented Reality (AR) technology and games can enhance motivation for learning. When combined with mobile devices, AR technology can promote authentic learning in outdoor environments, such as urban parks. These spaces can be used for Science Education, particularly, for environmental education and nature conservation. The EduPARK project combines these elements and follows a design-based research approach to develop an interactive mobile AR game to be explored by students, teachers and the general public, as visitors, in a specific urban park, integrating four interdisciplinary educational guides. The app development involved four cycles of user testing and evaluation for progressive refinement, according to the users' feedback in each cycle. The focus of this paper is to analyze the users' perceptions in the two last cycles of the app refinement, regarding its learning value and usability. The users were students of different school levels (24 of Basic Education; and 46 of Higher Education). Data collection involved a focus group interview, a questionnaire and the app's usage data. Content analysis, descriptive statistics, and System Usability Scale (SUS) computing were conducted. Results revealed that the EduPARK app promotes learning, enjoyment and is easy to use. It achieved an excellent usability, according to younger students (85.8 of average SUS) and a good usability according to older students (70.9). From the last refinement cycle, the app's final version has emerged, which is freely available to the public in the Google Store. In the future, more evaluation experiences are needed to better understand the benefits of this mobile AR game for learning in urban parks.

KEYWORDS

Mobile Learning, Gamification, Augmented Reality, Outdoor, Authentic Learning, Science Education

1. INTRODUCTION

In a technology driven society, educators can take advantage of the pervasiveness of technological devices to innovate their educational practices and, therefore, to promote authentic learning. For instance, mobile devices, such as smartphones, can be used as supporting tools of learning activities and can open up new opportunities for digital learning in formal, informal (Parsons 2014) and non-formal settings. The use of mobile games in formal education has been shown to promote student engagement for deeper and authentic learning (Huizenga et al. 2009). When combined with emerging technologies, such as Augmented Reality (AR), mobile devices are claimed to also create conditions to promote students' engagement with learning (Giannakas et al. 2017). Additionally, the recent proliferation of mobile devices and applications (app) makes AR technology accessible to support learning anytime anywhere, even in outdoor environments, such as urban parks.

The EduPARK project, 'Mobile Learning, Augmented Reality and Geocaching in Science Education – an innovator design-based research project' (http://edupark.web.ua.pt), emerged in the above-mentioned context, where original technologies can be used to promote education. The project's aim is to create innovative practices to promote interdisciplinary learning in Science Education, articulated with the school curriculum. For that, Geocaching-based principles are integrated in the game-like activities in a specific urban park, the Infante D. Pedro Park in Aveiro (Portugal), which are supported by mobile AR technologies. The project developed an interactive AR mobile app that integrates four educational guides – two for different levels in Basic Education, one for Secondary and Higher Education, and another for the general public. The latter is also available in English, so that foreign people (external visitors) can explore the app.

Each guide comprises a game with interdisciplinary questions and educational challenges that prompt for the search of interesting places in the Park, so the users can learn while enjoy a healthy walk along the Park. The City Council collaboration allowed the installation of 32 plant identification plaques in the Park with AR information on biological & curiosity aspects of plant species, historical references and a map (Pombo, Marques, Loureiro, et al. 2017). The app can, thus, be used autonomously, using the game mode or exploring it freely, promoting authentic learning.

The project has been organizing and implementing several activities in the Park, frequently integrated in outreach events of its host institution, the University of Aveiro, to test, evaluate and improve the app and its included educational guides, following a design-based research approach (Parker 2011) with four cycles of refinement. The app's description and the first two cycles of development and evaluation were described before (Pombo et al. n.d.; Pombo, Marques, Carlos, et al. 2017; Pombo & Marques 2017). The main purpose of this paper is to evaluate the 3rd and 4th cycles of the app, regarding the users' perspectives on the educational value for authentic learning, as well as the app's usability.

The paper is structured in the following sections: (i) literature review on mobile AR and its relevance in education contexts; (ii) research approach, explaining the 3rd and 4th cycles of the design-based methodology; (iii) presentation and discussion of main results; and (iv) final remarks and recommendations for future work.

2. THEORETICAL FRAMEWORK

According to Crompton (2013), mobile learning denotes a way of learning across contexts, through social and content interactions, with the support of mobile devices. Among their affordances are the mobility (Parsons 2014); the instant access to learning content (Giannakas et al. 2017); and the hardware and applications' panoply that support orientation, measuring, registering, organizing and communicating, among other activities, enhancing contextual and situated learning (Parsons 2014). Regarding its pitfalls, the literature mentions it entrenches digital divides regarding technology access, technological skills and learning competencies (Parsons 2014).

Additionally, AR technology supported by mobile devices creates learning opportunities that go beyond physical environments (Parsons 2014). AR allows overlying virtual objects in a real world environment in real time, producing a new experience. There are already a number of developed AR games for mobile devices that support authentic learning in outdoor settings, such as the ones briefly described below. A trend seems to be the use of AR apps with some sort of geo-location mechanisms.

Alien contact!, developed by Dunleavy et al. (2009), is a curriculum relevant and narrative-driven, inquiry-based AR simulation. In this game, students move around a physical location to get closer to digital artefacts displayed in a map, triggering video, audio, and text files. To successfully discover why the aliens had landed and solve academic challenges (subtasks involving math, language, arts, and scientific literacy skills), students in the same group play different roles and share information. The results included high engagement and motivation supported by the novelty of the use of handheld computers and GPS to learn; collection of data outside the classroom (more authentic learning environment); development of physical space orientation skills; and distributed knowledge, positive interdependence and different roles. The main difficulties pointed out were the GPS errors; screen visualization and audio listening in the outdoors; the high management requirements for teachers (to maintain the activity flowing); student cognitive overload and strong competition between teams.

The AR butterfly ecological learning system (Tarng & Ou 2012), developed using AR and mobile technologies, follows a game-based and mobile learning approach to teach students about butterfly species, ecology and conservation, in a campus environment. The AR was triggered by GPS coordinates (location-based AR), so students could observe virtual butterflies around nectar plants when they approach certain locations. The application also allows the breeding of virtual butterflies to allow observation of the butterfly life cycle and support understanding of their growing process. Students can autonomously use this application.

The EcoMOBILE (Kamarainen et al. 2013) is another project that combines mobile platforms and AR to provide a more interactive way to learn in outdoor contexts and increase student motivation and engagement. In EcoMOBILE the information is accessed by GPS triggers. The information ranges from interactive media, such as images, videos, 3D models and collaborative quizzes (multiple choice and open-ended questions) to

AR visualizations. The authors claim that the use of these technologies keeps the students motivated and allows them to explore the field at their own pace, freeing the teachers to act as a facilitator and move around to check the progress of the different groups. Although these experiences have a lot of positive aspects, an issue found was that some groups just speeded through the activity without reading or fully understanding the accessed contents.

The ZooEduGuide (Srisuphab et al., 2014) is a mobile application to enhance the zoo visits experience in Thailand. This app provides an interactive way to explore a zoo by combining mobile devices and AR. It has three main modes: (i) learning, which presents information about the animals via rich interactive multimedia content, where the information is accessed by scanning QR codes; (ii) educational games, animal sound identification and trivia quiz, where the games' scores are ranked adding a social and competitive component; and (iii) the visit zoo mode, which is a zoo guide where visitors can visualize the map and customize it with their own points of interest and visit path, and check the event schedule. The application makes use of AR to guide the visitor inside the zoo by showing points of interest in the camera view.

The AR competitive game developed by Hwang et al. (2015) is based on the traditional board game concept. The players need to roll a digital dice, but in this game they move around in a butterfly garden. At each location, students need to answer questions or complete a mini-game. Hwang et al. (2015) recommend a three-step design procedure for applying a competitive gaming approach to AR-based outdoor activities: (1) Select the activities that require students to explore or make observations in real-world contexts; (2) Prepare a set of questions related to the real-world contexts for the competitive game; and (3) Determine the location and content for each AR-based events.

Overall, the above-mentioned initiatives provide important insights into the use of AR mobile technology in outdoor educational settings. For example, AR is recognized as a technology that might enhance student interest and motivation, as well as promote self-learning. AR can support the understanding of complex and abstract concepts and, when combined with game-based learning, students may be more willing to overcome challenges and learning difficulties.

3. METHODOLOGICAL OPTIONS

The EduPARK project follows a qualitative interpretative methodology (Amado 2014) with multiple iterations for refinement and evolution of a prototype, justifying a design-based research approach (Parker 2011), as shown in Figure 1. The prototype is a game-like app for mobile devices with AR and the main aim is to collect students' perceptions regarding the app's learning value and usability.

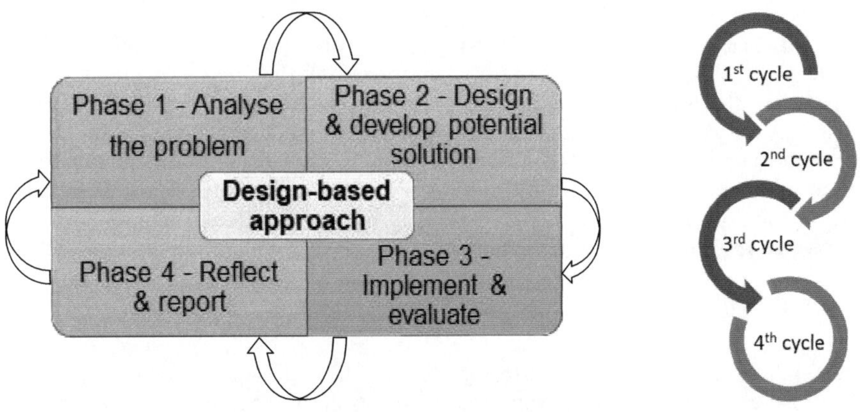

Figure 1. The EduPARK Project Methodology: Design-Based Research (Parker 2011), Comprising four Refinement Cycles

3.1 Context of Development

The first two cycles of prototype development and evaluation were described in other works (Pombo et al. n.d.; Pombo, Marques, Carlos, et al. 2017; Pombo & Marques 2017), so this work presents only a brief description of those cycles below.

In summary, the initially developed version of the app comprised interdisciplinary quizzes with multiple-choice questions and content (text, audio or image) aligned with the curriculum, feedback to the users' answers and scores. The questions included contents from diverse subjects, such as biology (particularly about botanics and zoology), mathematics, local history and physical education. Two educational guides, one for the 1st and another for the 3rd Cycle of Basic Education, were developed to be played by teams of students in a friendly competition approach. These were prompted to search for and locate three physical caches in the Park (Pombo et al. n.d.; Pombo, Marques, Carlos, et al. 2017). During the prototype development, a heuristic evaluation was made, based on the 'usability assessment of interfaces of mobile devices' framework (Neto & Pimentel 2013), which led to improvements prior to tests with users.

In the 1st refinement cycle, under the 2016 UA Open Week of Science and Technology, 74 students (aged 9-10 and 13-14) played with the prototype of the EduPARK app game in the Park and provided feedback. Students reported a positive perception regarding the app's usability and value for authentic learning. For example, a 4th school level student reported: 'I like [this app] because we can learn more about the plants and Nature.' One of the accompanying teachers, while speaking with her students at the end of the activity, mentioned: 'With this game you learn several subjects. You have Mathematics, Sciences, Botany… And you apply, in the outdoors, the knowledge you learnt in the classroom.' However, some inconsistencies were pointed out, such as GPS precision errors, which are widely reported in other studies (Akçayır & Akçayır 2017), and difficulties in the use of some AR markers. Also, the students suggested to include animations, audios and videos (Pombo et al. n.d.; Pombo, Marques, Carlos, et al. 2017), supporting Srisuphab et al. (2014), who claim that information in AR mobile apps should be available in different formats.

The 2nd cycle involved the refinement of the 1st version of the app, namely the development of more reliable markers. The new markers served as a way of triggering AR content, instead of being used as a checkpoint of the game, as in the 1st cycle. Also, physical plaques were developed comprising two main functions: i) botanical species identification; ii) markers to trigger AR contents. This option allows addressing difficulties in the use of the initial markers. Additionally, markerless tracking was also implemented, using 2D imagery, as historical tiles, already located at the Park, increasing the number of opportunities of authentic learning. Under this cycle, two future primary teachers, enrolled in a Master's degree in Basic Education, developed an educational guide for young pupils (aged 9-10). This guide was integrated in the new version of the EduPARK app and was tested in two events: i) the UA Open Campus 2017, when 23 students (aged 15 to 19) tested the app in the University campus to point strengths and weaknesses; and ii) an activity in the Park involving the 1st Cycle class with 21 pupils (aged 9-10) assigned to the two future primary teachers (masters' students) mentioned above.

Once more, the students reported a positive perception of the app usability and value for learning: 'I would like to play the game again because it was really fun to use cell phone in a lesson to review the content we've learnt' (4th school level student). Younger students proposed improvement suggestions exclusively regarding the game features, such as to include riddles to unlock treasure chests, to include time limit for question answering or to add more questions. Older students also pointed some usability-related suggestions, like to increase the app's responsiveness to the touch.

3.2 The 3rd Cycle

Among the new features introduced in this app version was the inclusion of audios, videos and animations, to diversify the formats of information, as suggested by pupils in the 1st refinement cycle. Other improvement was related to the GPS-based search for virtual *caches* (treasure chests) containing virtual objects and prompted by riddles. Users received instructions to search for a virtual *cache* and received GPS-based information about their distance to it. A new educational guide with an interdisciplinary quiz was developed for the 2nd cycle of Basic Education. The students' suggestion of limiting the time for question answering, although it could increase the game's competitiveness, it was not considered in the revised app, as the literature has long shown that time to think is relevant for learning performance (Tobin & Capie 1983).

Students with 10 to 12 years-old tested and evaluated this app version in the Park under the UA Summer Academy 2017, organised after the end of the school year, in a non-formal context of learning. The integration of the app's test in this event was as a way to gather a convenience sample of users, as students were enrolled in this event. The sample was composed by 16 girls and 8 boys (total of 24), who had just finished the 5th year (5 students) and the 6th year of Basic Education (19 students), in eight schools of the region. The students tested the app in the project's mobile devices, in 8 groups of 3 elements, each one accompained by an accompanying researcher. The test lasted 60 to 90 minutes, approximately.

3.3 The 4th Cycle

In the last refinement cycle included the guide for the Secondary and Higher Education according to Science curricular contents related to those levels. The search for *caches* was based in riddles to find a specific marker, instead of using GPS to avoid problems of geolocalization. The change in the AR triggering technology is due to the frequently reported GPS precision errors, both in the literature (Akçayır & Akçayır 2017) and in previous app refinement cycles. Addittionally, 32 permanent plaques of botanic specimens identification, with AR markers, were installed in the Park (with proper authorization of the City Council) to allow autonomous exploration of the app by users, as proposed in Pombo and Marques (2017).

Under the curricular unit 'Nature Integrated Sciences', the app was tested in the Park by 46 Basic Education graduating students, future-teachers, of which 45 were female students. Ages varied from 18 to 42 years-old, with an average age of 21 years. The students' academic backgrounds varied, being 25 from humanities studies, 12 from sciences, and the remaining from other areas, such as Arts or Sports. For the first time, the app was tested with the users' own mobile devices (instead of the project's smartphones), which involved a wide typology of devices and created some technical problems. Students tested the app in 16 groups of 3/4 elements during 74 to 110 minutes, approximately.

In both the 3rd and 4th refinement cycles, data were collected through a focus group interview (FGI), a questionnaire and the app's usage data. Both, FCI and questionnaires, were described before (Pombo et al. n.d.; Pombo, Marques, Carlos, et al. 2017) and were applied immediately after testing. Data analysis involved: i) content analysis of the FGI; and ii) descriptive statistics of the app's usage data and of the questionnaire's answers. Data were triangulated to provide a comprehensive knowledge of the students' perceptions regarding the app and their learning. This analysis will be presented in the next section.

4. RESULTS AND DISCUSSION

In the 3rd refinement cycle, the collected data allowed profiling the users (24 students enrolled in the UA Summer Academy 2017) regarding their demographics and mobile devices proficiency. It is possible to observe that 23 students claimed to own a personal mobile phone, from which 19 were smartphones. Most of them use the device for about 30 and 59 minutes (9 students) or 15 and 29 minutes (7) per day. Besides phone calling and text messaging (both selected by 21), the students use it for: gaming (19 students), video watching (15), internet searching (14), listening to music (12), and using social networks (11). Hence, these results point that the majority of the students was skilled with mobile devices. These results seem to support the literature, regarding the proliferation of mobile devices (Johnson et al. 2014), especially in what concerns young population. Besides that, young students reported feeling enthusiasm and enjoyment by using the app. For example, one student commented 'I really enjoyed playing this game and I would like to do it again' (questionnaire student's cote) and another stated that it 'gave us knowledge, but at the same time we also could have fun.' (FGI student's cote). Additionally, some students also noted they would like the game to last longer, despite the groups' average game time being of about 76 minutes. Such results are in line with the literature that claims that student engagement and motivation to learn can be promoted by the use of games (Freitas, 2008), supported by mobile (Kamarainen et al., 2013) and AR technologies (Akçayır & Akçayır 2017; Dunleavy et al. 2009).

The students' perception of the app's usability was positive; and 22 students agreed or strongly agreed with the statement 'I thought the app was easy to use' and 18 disagreed or strongly disagreed with the statement 'I found the app more difficult to use than it should be.' The SUS score was computed individually and, afterwards, an average value was computed for all the questionnaires. Values ranged from 60 to 100, with an average of 85.8. Therefore, according to the classification of Bangor et al. (2009), this version of EduPARK app achieved an excellent usability.

Concerning the technology-related difficulties, students reported: i) GPS signal malfunctions – 'The distance meters [from the virtual *cache*] sometimes didn't work very well' (FGI student's cote); ii) displeasure in having to keep the mobile device camera pointed at the marker during the exploration of the AR contents – 'I liked it, but (...) when we saw the markers, we had to keep pointing [the mobile phone] at them. It would be nicer to keep the information [in the screen]' (FGI student's cote); and iii) a few difficulties in handling the app – 'When we were searching for *caches*, it would appear the "quit" button, which was similar to the "continue" button, and we would press it by mistake' (FGI student's cote).

In what concerns the game features, students referred they would like: i) to see the collected virtual objects having a goal – 'I think that the objects inside the *caches* could have some kind of use' (FGI student's cote); and ii) to include different paths in the game – 'To have different routes in the app' (FGI student's cote).

Regarding learning obstacles, students reported some difficulties with the vocabulary used in the app – 'we didn't know several words' (FGI student's cote) and that they found some quiz questions challenging – 'in some questions we had to think harder.' (FGI student's cote). On the other hand, one of the advantages acknowledged by the students was that they were more motivated to learn in outdoor settings – 'It is cooler in the outdoors' (FGI student's cote) – and that the game increased motivation due to the authenticity of the learning environment – 'This way we are more motivated to do the calculus [of an object's area]. We know it will have a purpose.' (FGI another student's cote). Another relevant benefit was learning more about the local Park – 'For example, I've never seen that fountain with fish, where the *cache* was hidden' (FGI student's cote). More specifically, regarding the Mathematics' learning, student claimed this activity 'captivated us to Math' (FGI student's cote), despite being in school holidays period. Figure 2 shows the students' perspectives regarding the Mathematics questions in the app, which are strongly positive.

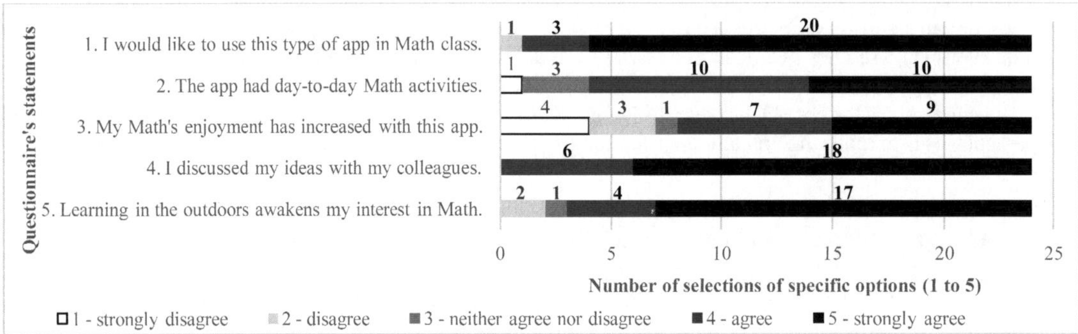

Figure 2. Third Refinement Cycle: Students' Opinion Regarding the Learning Value of the app

In the last refinement cycle, the 46 graduation students/future-teachers reported to frequently (37 students) or occasionally (6) use mobile devices to promote their own learning. They also stated to use mobile devices in the University (22) and their own home (22) for learning purposes, considering that mobile devices allow an easy and quick way of accessing information; although they acknowledged the increase of distracting factors and the risk of becoming addicted to this mobile technology.

Regarding the EduPARK app, students reported positive perceptions. For example, its learning value was acknowledged by 35 students, as illustrated here: 'The EduPARK app is advantageous, essentially, from the pedagogic point of view.' (questionnaire student's cote) and '[with this app] we can see that in each [Park] corner there is something to learn and, thus, enrich our knowledge.' (questionnaire student's cote). Additionally, they also referred the app's value in what respect intrinsic motivation (32 students), engagement (35), authentic learning (33), lifelong learning (28), and conservation habits (31). The average game time was 88 minutes, for a park path with 35 quiz questions, and still there were students suggesting to add more questions to the game.

The students' perception of the app's usability was positive; and 31 students agreed or strongly agreed with the statement 'I thought the app was easy to use' and 35 disagreed or strongly disagreed with the statement 'I found the app more difficult to use than it should be'. The SUS scores ranged from 55 to 95, with an average of 70.9, achieving a good usability, lower than in the previous cycle. This may be explained by two factors: i) the users were older (future educational professionals) and maybe more critical than younger children, which is not a new result, as the literature has had found that SUS scores tend to decrease with increasing age (Bangor, Kortum, & Miller, 2009); and ii) the diversity of cell phones used in this test turn it more challenging, from the technological point of view.

Concerning the technology-related difficulties, students reported: i) the visualization of images and videos, due to the heavy storage space it requires from the device; ii) some lack of responsiveness of the app; iii) the high battery energy requirements; and iv) some app tools did not work (such as the app's compass). Graduating students also suggested to include more AR contents and to have the app available for IOS systems.

5. FINAL REMARKS

The EduPARK project has been developing an interactive mobile AR game to promote authentic learning in a specific Park. The main relevance of the EduPARK project is the articulation between research and development, professional practices, and initial and advanced training, as well as its innovation concerning outdoor learning strategies, in formal, informal, and non-formal contexts. This research also prompts to capitalize urban spaces' educational value, in association with the local City Council.

This work reports the 3rd and 4th refinement cycles of a design-based research for this app development, with the aim of accessing the users' perspectives of the learning value and usability of this app. Hence, it was tested by groups of 10 to 12 aged students, who were enrolled in the UA Summer Academy 2017 and by Higher Education students, future-teachers, from the Basic Education Graduation Course of the UA. The results show that students enjoyed and were enthusiastic about the app. However, some difficulties with the technology were reported in the Summer Academy experience, such as some cases of GPS malfunction, limiting some tasks prompted by the app (the search for the virtual *caches*) and in handling some functions of it. These difficulties were taken in consideration in the following app refinement. Concerning learning, students referred: i) they found the app's quiz challenging in a positive way, e.g., it motivated them to learn; and ii) they could learn in a situated way.

The EduPARK app was released to the public and it is freely available in the Google Store (http://edupark.web.ua.pt/app). In spite of the positive results so far, regarding the users' perspectives about the learning value and usability of this mobile AR game, the samples were convenience ones and the number of users in each target public was scarce. In future the project intends to organize more activities in order to collect systematic data that might be used to better understand the benefits of using AR mobile technology in outdoor settings for learning and for lifelong learning. Additionally, the team expects to triangulate data from different target public besides students, such as teachers, accompanying researchers, external consultants, park visitors, and the general public, as the EduPARK app intends to be a resource with impact in schools, local community and also in the tourism sector.

In summary, the EduPARK app will continue to work to achieve its main purpose: to promote an active participation of students and the wider community in the construction of their knowledge. Thus, the project is fostering authentic learning, both in a formal learning context and in a lifelong learning logic, for the citizens in general. Therefore, the EduPARK project is revealing good educational practices in which digital and social interactions are valued through the use of innovative technologies that combine, in an articulated way, the virtual and real worlds.

ACKNOWLEDGEMENT

This work was financed by FEDER - Fundo Europeu de Desenvolvimento Regional funds through the COMPETE 2020 - Operational Programme for Competitiveness and Internationalisation (POCI), and by Portuguese funds through FCT - Fundação para a Ciência e a Tecnologia in the framework of the project POCI-01-0145-FEDER-016542. The authors would also like to thank the EduPARK researchers, the participant students, teachers, accompanying researchers, and Aveiro's City Council.

REFERENCES

Akçayır, M. & Akçayır, G., 2017. Advantages and challenges associated with augmented reality for education: A systematic review of the literature. *Educational Research Review*, 20, pp.1–11.

Amado, J., 2014. *Manual de investigação qualitativa em educação*, Coimbra: Imprensa da Universidade de Coimbra.

Bangor, A., Kortum, P. & Miller, J., 2009. Determining What Individual SUS Scores Mean: Adding an Adjective Rating Scale. *Journal of Usability Studies*, 4(3), pp.114–123. Available at: http://www.usabilityprofessionals.org. [Accessed February 10, 2017].

Crompton, H., 2013. A historical overview of mobile learning: Toward learner-centered education. In Z. L. Berge & L. Y. Muilenburg, eds. *Handbook of mobile learning*. Florence: Routledge, pp. 3–14. Available at: http://refhub.elsevier.com/S0360-1315(17)30066-0/sref43.

Dunleavy, M., Dede, C. & Mitchell, R., 2009. Affordances and Limitations of Immersive Participatory Augmented Reality Simulations for Teaching and Learning. *Journal of Science Education and Technology*, 18(1), pp.7–22. Available at: http://link.springer.com/10.1007/s10956-008-9119-1 [Accessed March 7, 2017].

Freitas, R., 2008. SMART : a SysteM of Augmented Reality for Teaching 2 nd Grade Students. , (April), p.4.

Giannakas, F. et al., 2017. A critical review of 13 years of mobile game-based learning. *Educational Technology Research and Development*, pp.1–44. Available at: http://link.springer.com/10.1007/s11423-017-9552-z [Accessed January 9, 2018].

Huizenga, J. et al., 2009. Mobile game-based learning in secondary education: engagement, motivation and learning in a mobile city game. *Journal of Computer Assisted Learning*, 25(4), pp.332–344. Available at: http://doi.wiley.com/10.1111/j.1365-2729.2009.00316.x [Accessed February 2, 2017].

Hwang, G.-J. et al., 2015. Effects of an augmented reality-based educational game on students' learning achievements and attitudes in real-world observations. *Interactive Learning Environments*, 4820(April), pp.1–12.

Johnson, L. et al., 2014. *NMC Horizon Report: 2014 K-12 Edition*, Austin, Texas: The New Media Consortium.

Kamarainen, A.M. et al., 2013. EcoMOBILE: Integrating augmented reality and probeware with environmental education field trips. *Computers & Education*, 68, pp.545–556.

Neto, O.M. & Pimentel, M. da G., 2013. Heuristics for the assessment of interfaces of mobile devices. In *Proceedings of the 19th Brazilian symposium on Multimedia and the web - WebMedia '13*. New York, New York, USA: ACM Press, pp. 93–96. Available at: http://dl.acm.org/citation.cfm?doid=2526188.2526237 [Accessed November 9, 2016].

Parker, J., 2011. A design-based research approach for creating effective online higher education courses. In *26th Annual Research Forum: Educational Possibilities*. Fremantle: Western Australian Institute for Educational Research Inc. Available at: http://researchrepository.murdoch.edu.au/5566.

Parsons, D., 2014. The Future of Mobile Learning and Implications for Education and Training. In M. Ally & A. Tsinakos, eds. *Increasing Access through Mobile Learning*. Vancouver: Commonwealth of Learning and Athabasca University, pp. 217–229. Available at: http://oasis.col.org/bitstream/handle/11599/558/pub_Mobile Learning_web.pdf#page=234 [Accessed January 25, 2017].

Pombo, L., Marques, M.M., Carlos, V., et al., 2017. Augmented Reality and mobile learning in a smart urban park: pupils' perceptions of the EduPARK game. In Ó. Mealha, M. Divitini, & M. Rehm, eds. *Citizen, Territory and Technologies: Smart Learning Contexts and Practices*. Aveiro: Springer, pp. 90–100.

Pombo, L. et al., Evaluation of an Augmented Reality Mobile Gamelike Application as an Outdoor Learning Tool. Submitted to *International Journal of Mobile and Blended Learning (IJMBL)*.

Pombo, L., Marques, M.M., Loureiro, M.J., et al., 2017. *Parque Infante D. Pedro, Património Histórico e Botânico - Projeto EduPARK* L. Pombo. (Coord), Aveiro: UA Editora. http://edupark.web.ua.pt/static/docs/Livro_EduPARK.pdf.

Pombo, L. & Marques, M.M., 2017. Marker-based augmented reality application for mobile learning in an urban park - Steps to make it real under the EduPARK project. In C. Ponte, J. M. Dodero, & M. J. Silva, eds. *XIX International Symposium on Computers in Education (SIIE) and VIII CIED Meeting/ III CIED International Meeting*. Lisbon: Polytechnic Institute of Lisbon, School of Education, pp. 174–178. Available at: http://edupark.web.ua.pt/static/docs/EduPARK-SIIE2017.pdf.

Srisuphab, A. et al., 2014. Integrated ZooEduGuide with Multimedia and AR. In *TENCON 2014 - 2014 IEEE Region 10 ConferenceTENCON 2014 - 2014 IEEE Region 10 Conference*. pp. 1–4.

Tarng, W. & Ou, K.-L.L., 2012. A study of campus butterfly ecology learning system based on augmented reality and mobile learning. *Proceedings 2012 17th IEEE International Conference on Wireless, Mobile and Ubiquitous Technology in Education*, pp.62–66. Available at: http://ieeexplore.ieee.org/document/6184998/

Tobin, K. & Capie, W., 1983. The influence of wait-time on classroom learning. *European Journal of Science Education*, 5(1), pp.35–48. Available at: https://doi.org/10.1080/0140528830050104.

MOBILE LEARNING CONSIDERATIONS IN HIGHER EDUCATION: POTENTIAL BENEFITS AND CHALLENGES FOR STUDENTS AND INSTITUTIONS

B-Abee Toperesu and Jean-Paul Van Belle
University of Cape Town, Private Bag, Rondebosch, 7701, South Africa

ABSTRACT

The field of mobile learning has received much attention in both the academic research fields and the practical fields. Yet the implementation rate is low with very few higher education institutions (HEIs) offering full support for this channel. The aim of this research is to evaluate the different mobile learning considerations as identified in available literature with a focus on key benefits and potential challenges which have been identified for students and institutions. A general inductive approach was used to analyze the academic articles as secondary data sources. The final result of the study is a summative framework to be used by HEIs considering fully fledged support for mobile learning.

KEYWORDS

Mobile Phone, mLearning, Optimise, Bandwidth, Information Security

1. INTRODUCTION

Mobile devices have become ubiquitous and in turn have inevitably become a part of our lives. Individuals are using mobile devices to store, process and retrieve information anywhere and anytime. These devices have also become powerful communication tools in the wake of pervasive communication networks such as LTE and WiFi. Not surprisingly, mobile devices are now being used for learning as students integrate these devices with learning processes. Mobile hand held devices have become much cheaper, more powerful and more accessible than computers (Hashemi, Azizinezhad, Najafi, & Nesari, 2011). These and other factors, have made mobile devices to be more popular among university students and the youth in general.

The phenomenon of mobile learning also commonly referred to as m-learning, emerged in recent years through the increased integration and adoption of mobile devices in learning. However, there is lack of consensus on the definition of mobile learning since scholars defined mobile learning in different contexts. This can be attributed to the fact that mobile learning has two distinctive components, notably mobile and learning. The lack of common understanding develops due to the different perspectives from which one views it since mobile learning merges diverse phenomena.

Geddes (2000 as cited in Hashemi et al., 2011) defines m-learning as, “the acquisition of any knowledge or skill through using mobile technology, anywhere, anytime.” (p. 2477). Ozdamli and Cavus (2011) describes mobile learning as a model which allows learners to obtain learning material from anywhere at any time using mobile technologies and the internet. It can be noted that the anywhere and anytime attributes are inherent in both definitions. Kinash, Brand and Mathew (2012 as cited in Marzouki, Idrissi & Bennani, 2013) define mobile learning as simply "the use of mobile devices that can connect to the Internet for educational contexts" (p.567). However, the authors accede to the fact that questions may still abound and that no clear and precise definition can be obtained.

This study will use the following definition as most suitable within the context of the study: *“The exploitation of ubiquitous handheld technologies, together with wireless and mobile phone networks, to facilitate, support, enhance and extend the reach of teaching and learning.”*(Hashemi et al., 2011 p.2478).

Various studies allude to the fact that mobile learning has become popular and suitable among university students as these devices become more affordable resulting in widespread ownership (Abachi & Muhammad, 2014; Gikas & Grant, 2013; Santos, 2015). There has also been a lot of research studies done in the past decade on mobile learning (Marzouki et al., 2013). A meta-analysis literature review examining 163 mobile learning studies done between 2003 and 2010 found that the research purpose of most studies on mobile learning focused on the effectiveness followed by the system design (Wu et al., 2012). The review also found out that the most commonly used device for mobile learning is mobile phones and that mobile learning is being practiced mostly at higher education institutions.

It is in this light that this study seeks to embark on research specifically in higher education institutions. This analysis of academic literature will first look at the key concepts inherent in the title of this research study before identifying the key benefits and challenges of mobile learning as experienced by students on the one hand, and the institutions on the other. The review will then aggregate these into a summative framework to be considered by institutions envisaging the adoption of mobile learning.

2. KEY CONCEPTS

2.1 Smart Phone

A smartphone can be described as a personal digital assistant (PDA) with additional functionality (Park & Chen, 2007). Essential features of a smartphone include the phone function, ability to connect to the internet, camera, and a wide diversity and ecosystem of mobile applications which offer extended functionality.

2.2 Learning

Learning in general can be viewed as a lifelong process. Driscoll (2000 as cited in Siemens, 2014), defines learning as, "a persisting change in human performance or performance potential...[which] must come about as a result of the learner's experience and interaction with the world" (p.2). This definition raises two important attributes of learning, i.e. a change of state and the learner's experience. The former being the result of the latter.

Learning can be classified into two i.e. informal learning and formal learning. Informal learning is when an individual undertakes to develop themselves personally so that they can add value to themselves in their social standing. Informal learning is not linked to a program of study and does not follow a formal path, but is carried out at will. Informal learning is often unanticipated and sometimes un acknowledged even by the leaner (Gikas & Grant, 2013). In this form of learning, mobile learning is perceived as playing a major role. A good example is when integrating a person in a foreign land. They can use their mobile devices at various locations and times to learn at their own pace (Ally, 2013).

Gikas and Grant (2013) defines formal learning as, "where learners are engaging with materials developed by a teacher to be used during a program of instruction in an educational environment, highly structured, institutionally sponsored, and generally recognized in terms of a certificate." This study will look at this type of learning i.e. from a formal perspective as the study looks at how a smartphone impacts the student's formal learning experience at university. The study will uncover how students integrate their smartphones into their learning.

2.3 Mobile Technology and Development

There has been a growing emphasis on using information and communication technologies (ICTs) for development in South Africa and other developing countries. ICTs have been considered as crucial for development in society (Magunje, 2013). Mobile technology plays a contributory role as part of the development. People in developed countries are swiftly moving from desktop computers to mobile devices. However, this is not the case in developing countries. Ally (2013) notes that people in developing countries are going directly to acquiring mobile devices skipping the step altogether of first owning desktop computers. This is because of the attractive and affordable prices of mobile devices (Hashemi et al., 2011).

3. RESEARCH METHODOLOGY

3.1 Data Collection

A qualitative research method informed this research study with secondary data sources being used for evaluation. Data from academic peer reviewed literature i.e. journals and conference proceedings published between 2006 -2016 were used. Given the huge number of articles, instead of employing a systematic literature review, a more pragmatic approach was followed in which articles were selected for their direct relevance using a breath-first approach, then selecting the best articles and using these to snowball into other based on forward and backward citations. Articles were specifically chosen on the basis of their ability to sufficiently cover the area of interest. More specifically articles which covered mobile learning benefits and challenges were analyzed so as to derive the actual mobile learning considerations.

3.2 Data Analysis

This research study followed a general inductive approach to carefully analyze the articles. The purposes of a general inductive approach are to reduce raw text into summaries, establish a connection between the objective of the study and the findings in the data and lastly to develop a framework from the structure of the data (Thomas, 2006).

The general inductive approach allowed for the results to arise from the themes which were identified in literature (Thomas, 2006). The subsequent procedure was used in the inductive analysis of the qualitative data.

1. **Preparation of data** (Thomas, 2006). The author used various scholarly databases to collect the relevant articles and reviewed articles which focused on mobile learning, mobile learning benefits, mobile learning challenges and mobile learning in higher education. Raw data from these articles was then formatted into a standard format in terms of the font, margins and style. Articles not relevant to the study were filtered out at this stage.
2. **Close reading of text** (Thomas, 2006). After populating the text and preparing it, the author read the text in detail and identified key themes which emerged from the text. At this point the researcher gained in-depth understanding of mobile learning phenomenon and identified 12 themes.
3. **Creation of Categories**. The author created the following categories for the benefits and challenges based on the themes that emerged from the data. The benefits to the learner and the benefits to the institution categories were used for the benefits. Similarly, challenges to the learner and challenges to the institution were used to categories the themes that emerged under the challenges for mobile learning adoption.

The researcher analyzed the academic literature and came up with a proposed framework in the form of Table 1 and Table 2. In the following sections, we then discuss the elements in the table in detail.

4. POTENTIAL BENEFITS OF MOBILE LEARNING ADOPTION

This section reviews the potential benefits of adopting a mobile learning approach in an institution. The identified potential benefits are listed under Table 1. There are two categories from this section i.e the benefits to the learner and benefits to the institution. The themes that emerged under benefits to the learner include, affordability, efficient and convenience.

Table 1. Potential Benefits of Mobile Learning Adoption

Benefits To the Learner	**Reference**
Affordability	Moldovan, Weibelzahl, & Muntean, 2014; Stanton, 2014; Vishwakarma, 2015
Efficiency	Alrasheedi & Capretz, 2013, 2015
Convenience	Briz-Ponce, Pereira, Carvalho, Juanes-Méndez, & García-Peñalvo, 2016; Gikas & Grant, 2013; Jackson, Sc, Gardens, & Da, 2016; Santos, 2015b
Benefits to the Institution	
Scalability	Ally, 2013; Ebba, 2015; Elfeky & Yakoub, 2016
Ease of updating learning materials	Farley et al., 2015; Koole, 2009; Olalere Mudasiru, Bolanle Idayat, & Mary Bose, 2015; Ozdamli & Cavus, 2011
Lower Costs	Farley et al., 2015; Conejar, Chung, & Kim, 2015

4.1 Affordability

One of the main benefits to the learner is the affordability that comes with mobile devices (Vishwakarma, 2015). The prices of mobile devices compared to more robust technology such as desktop computers is much less. In developing countries like South Africa, the uptake of mobile phones far outweighs that of desktop PCs.

4.2 Efficiency

The efficiency which comes from accessing information on the go is one of the benefits enjoyed by the learner (Alrasheedi & Capretz, 2015). Mobile technologies qualities such as instant access can enhance face to face teaching bringing a more efficient means of learning (Guri-Rosenblit, 2005).

4.3 Convenience

Convenience can be attributed to the fact that the learner does not need to be confined to a certain location in order to learn. Learning can take place at any place and at any time (Jackson et al., 2016).

The benefits to the educational institution include scalable, easy to update and reduced IT costs.

4.4 Scalability

Affordability of the mobile devices becomes a benefit to the learning institutions as they are able to offer learning materials to more students. To accommodate more students, the institutions will only need to expand their network capabilities and increase educators to facilitate the online content (Olalere Mudasiru et al., 2015). There will not be a need for more classroom facilities as an alternative to face to face interactions is offered through mobile devices. Thus education becomes more scalable (Ally, 2013).

4.5 Ease of Updating

Learning material offered online is easy to update (Olalere Mudasiru et al., 2015). Mobile devices are able to update the material as soon as it is made available ensuring that learners use the latest available material. Mobile device features are advancing making the devices much more capable of performing many more functions quicker and efficient (Alrasheedi & Capretz, 2013).

5. POTENTIAL CHALLENGES OF MOBILE LEARNING ADOPTION

The challenges for adopting mobile learning are listed in Table 2. These challenged have also been placed under two broad categories i.e. challenges to the learner and challenges to the institution.

Table 2. Potential Challenges of Mobile Learning Adoption

Challenges to the Learner	**Reference**
Privacy	Afreen, 2014; Alrasheedi & Capretz, 2015a; Elfeky & Yakoub, 2016; Emery, n.d.; S. Nykvist & Lee, 2013
Teacher perceptions	Ally, 2013; Alrasheedi & Capretz, 2015a; Alrasheedi, 2015; Gikas & Grant, 2013; Park & Chen, 2007; Santos, 2015b
Challenges to the Institution	
Security	Abachi & Muhammad, 2014; Ali & Arshad, 2015; Motiwalla, 2007; S. Nykvist & Lee, 2013; Santos, 2015b; Aloul, 2012
Optimization	Chitanana & Govender, 2015; S. S. Nykvist, 2012
Bandwidth	Abachi & Muhammad, 2014; Chitanana & Govender, 2015

5.1 Security and Privacy

Information security and privacy has remained a top priority among IT leaders globally as cybercriminals are on the increase and higher education institutions are no exception. Cybercrime can be described as any criminal activity where a computer or computer network is either a tool, place of crime, source of crime or is a target (Pozar, 2014). According to a leading security firm Symantec, the education sector is now the third most frequently breached public sector ("Internet Security Threat Report," 2015).

Different forms of threats do exist targeting institutional data, the network or personal data residing on an individual's devices. Some examples of information security threats include, malware & virus infections, cyber fraud and hacking. As mobile devices become prevalent in universities, more and more mobile devices become susceptible to these threats. Smartphone hacking software is also now easily available online and this software is used to steal passwords and any personal information.

Another information security factor is that mobile devices can be lost or stolen. Once these mobile device land in the hands of criminals, if not secured, can lead to more harm done to the institution or the network. Although this can be countered by remote wiping the devices that are stolen or lost, this responsibility lies in the owner in some cases as the device personally belongs to them. In most cases educational institutions have no control over personal devices.

Other alternative ways of insuring information security and privacy are available. The most common method is enforcing detection software. Programs that detect and filter infections using algorithms and signature based matching techniques have been developed. These programs identify malware before it reaches the computer system or network (Zolkipli & Jantan, 2010). Further advancements in enterprise systems security include endpoint security. With endpoint security, each device must meet certain standards before it is granted access to the organisation's network. Examples of endpoint security include personal firewalls and antivirus software which is distributed, monitored and updated from the server (Rouse, 2011).

Awareness campaigns can also be done to raise awareness of criminal activities users need to be aware of. An increase in the number of phishing attempts shows that the target is now the user and cybercriminals seek to exploit their lack of knowledge. While organisation are increasing and advancing their security technologies, very little is being invested in increasing safety awareness among the general users consequently causing them to be the weakest link on the organisation's system (Aloul, 2012). Social awareness campaigns can be run to inform people of prevalent security issues. See attached Appendix for an example of one such campaign run in October each year by the University of Cape Town.

Based on the dominance and persisting nature of information security and privacy as reflected in previous research studies, information security and privacy will continue to be a pressing issue for the next few years. IT leaders in higher education need to prioritise and focus on their security as more cyber-attacks are now coming to the education sector.

5.2 Teacher Perceptions

One of the challenges with mobile learning is people's perceptions and attitudes with using mobile technologies for education. Some educators feel that mobile devices cause too much distraction for learners, and or associate mobile device use during lectures with bad behaviour (Ally, 2013).

5.3 Optimisation

Optimising the technologies supporting learning is one of the identified top issues for IT leaders in education. This is attributed to the fact that more and more devices are now accessing institutional resources. If unattended to, the devices will put strain on the available technologies possibly rendering them unusable. The main issues to be addressed by most universities is the availability and efficiency of the network itself.

As digital natives take on higher education life, bringing along a myriad of mobile devices and using them to access online content, network saturation becomes an issue. Institutions did not envisage an influx of mobile devices. According to Nykvist (2012) most university networks were never built to accommodate a heavy load of devices. Technology managers in education have found themselves in a more reactive position as they reconfigure networks to accommodate as much devices as possible. As a means of addressing this problem, Chitanana and Govender (2015) propose that if proper application of policies are enforced, that will be reduced strain on the network.

5.4 Bandwidth

Bandwidth has also increasingly become a challenge in universities as students are exposed to vast amounts of data consuming online resources. Online learning resources such as YouTube have become popular among students. These resources allow for creation and sharing of video resources. However, these resources have a big impact on the network in terms of bandwidth utilisation. Chitanana and Govender (2015) state that bandwidth is a valuable resource to the university which therefore needs to be managed properly. They further propose that for a university to effectively manage bandwidth, the following three critical elements need to be looked at carefully, i.e. visibility, monitoring and optimisation as shown in the figure below.

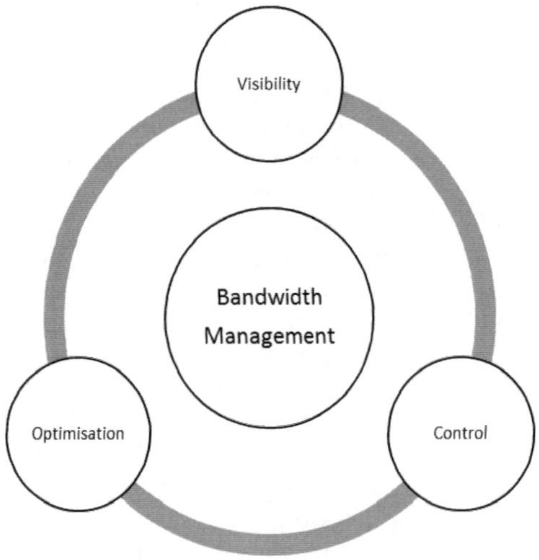

Figure 1. The Critical Interdependent Components of Bandwidth Management (Chitanana & Govender, 2015)

With visibility, the institutions should be able to identify the wireless devices that are connecting to its network. In other words the devices need to be visible in order for policies to be enforced and network access revoked in cases of abuse. Visibility may also include the ability to monitor the applications that run on these devices. The visibility of the apps is relatively important as it allows for the implementation and or enforcement of some policies especially those relating to data usage (Chitanana & Govender, 2015).

Control refers to the network access control whereby the institution is able to control the level of access granted to its users or devices. Andrus (2013) as cited in (Chitanana & Govender, 2015) describes network access control (NAC) as allowing for the defining of the policies which control how users gain access to the network resources on the network. This is of particular importance to university settings with a wide range of users which includes guests and visitors who need to connect to the network.

Optimisation involves the identifying and prioritising of network access to critical applications. In a university setting these can be teaching or research applications. Most universities around the world are making use of learning management systems to deliver learning materials and students can use their mobile devices to access these materials (Abachi & Muhammad, 2014). The resources may include lecture recordings which students through access to the network can download or stream at any time. Such applications can receive priority over others to have a better experience.

6. CONCLUSION

This study has integrated various practical considerations for mobile learning and presented these in a summative framework (Table 1 and Table 2). Previous research studies have not offered a systematic framework for consideration by institutions intending to adopt mobile learning. The practical contribution of this research study is that Higher Educational institutions willing to adopt mobile learning can use the framework as a reference point. The theoretical contribution of this study is that a framework has been proposed which would need to be tested in other studies.

The study only looked at for potential benefits and challenges of adopting mobile learning. Future research could look at other categories to fully address the phenomena, such as necessary capabilities, critical success factors, impacts/outcomes and mediating or contextual variables. Further empirical work to confirm the relative importance of the selected considerations is also essential.

REFERENCES

Abachi, H. R., & Muhammad, G. 2014. The impact of m-learning technology on students and educators. *Computers in Human Behavior*, *30*, 491–496. http://doi.org/10.1016/j.chb.2013.06.018

Ally, M. 2013. Mobile learning: from research to practice to Impact Education. *Learning and Teaching in Higher Education: Gulf Perspectives*, *10*(2), 1–10.

Alrasheedi, M., & Capretz, L. F. 2013. A meta-analysis of critical success factors affecting mobile learning. *Teaching, Assessment and Learning for Engineering (TALE), 2013 IEEE International Conference on*, *8*(1), 262–267. http://doi.org/10.1109/TALE.2013.6654443

Alrasheedi, M., & Capretz, L. F. 2015. Determination of Critical Success Factors Affecting Mobile Learning: A Meta-Analysis Approach. *Turkish Online Journal of Educational Technology - TOJET*, *14*(2), 41–51. Retrieved from http://search.ebscohost.com/login.aspx?direct=true&db=eric&AN=EJ1057286&site=ehost-live&scope=site

Briz-Ponce, L., Pereira, A., Carvalho, L., Juanes-Méndez, J. A., & García-Peñalvo, F. J. 2016. Learning with mobile technologies – Students' behavior. *Computers in Human Behavior*, pp. 1–9. http://doi.org/http://dx.doi.org/10.1016/j.chb.2016.05.027

Conejar, R. J., Chung, H. S., & Kim, H. 2015. A Study of Delivering Education through Mobile Learning. In *Proceedings of the World Congress on Engineering and Computer Science* Vol. 1, pp. 701–702.

Ebba, O. 2015. Quality Enhancement for Mobile Learning in Higher Education. *Promoting Active Learning through the Integration of Mobile and Ubiquitous Technologies*, 167–182. http://doi.org/10.4018/978-1-4666-6343-5.ch010

Elfeky, A. I. M., & Yakoub, M. T. S. 2016. The Effect of Mobile Learning on Students' Achievement and Conversational Skills. *International Journal of Higher Education*, *5*(3), 20–31. http://doi.org/10.5430/ijhe.v5n3p20

Farley, H., Murphy, A., Johnson, C., Carter, B., Lane, M., Midgley, W., ... Koronios, A. 2015. How Do Students Use Their Mobile Devices to Support Learning? A Case Study from an Australian Regional University. *Journal of Interactive Media in Education*, *2015*(1), 1–13. http://doi.org/http://dx.doi.org/10.5334/jime.ap

Gikas, J., & Grant, M. M. 2013. Mobile computing devices in higher education: Student perspectives on learning with cellphones, smartphones & social media. *Internet and Higher Education*, *19*, 18–26. http://doi.org/10.1016/j.iheduc.2013.06.002

Guri-Rosenblit, S. 2005. "Distance education" and "e-learning": Not the same thing. *Higher Education*, *49*(4), 467–493. http://doi.org/10.1007/s10734-004-0040-0

Hashemi, M., Azizinezhad, M., Najafi, V., & Nesari, A. J. 2011. What is mobile learning? Challenges and capabilities. In *Procedia - Social and Behavioral Sciences,* pp. 2477–2481. http://doi.org/10.1016/j.sbspro.2011.10.483

Jackson, E. A., Sc, B., Gardens, A., & Da, K. 2016. M-Learning devices and thier impact on postgraduate researchers scope for improved intergration in the research community. *The Online Journal of New Horizons in Education*, *6*(1), 104–113.

Kinash, S., Brand, J., & Mathew, T. 2012. Challenging mobile learning discourse through research: Student perceptions of Blackboard Mobile Learn and iPads. *Australasian Journal of Educational Technology*, *28*(4), 639–655.

Koole, M. L. 2009. A model for framing mobile learning. *Mobile Learning: Transforming the Delivery of Education and Training*. Edmonton: Athabasca University Press.

Magunje, C. 2013. *Using mobile phones to support learning: A case of UCT first year female science students in the Academic Development Program me.* Retrieved from http://www.thecasecentre.org/files/downloads/research/RP0302M.pdf

Marzouki, O. F., Idrissi, M. K., & Bennani, S. 2013. Mobile Education– Effective Integration of new mobile technologies into existing learning systems using MISA Method. In *Proceedings of International Conference on Advances in Mobile Computing & Multimedia - MoMM '13*, pp. 567–575. New York, New York, USA: ACM Press. http://doi.org/10.1145/2536853.2536862

Moldovan, A., Weibelzahl, S., & Muntean, C. H. 2014. Energy-Aware Mobile Learning : Opportunities and Challenges. *IEEE Communications Surveys & Tutorials*, *16*(1), 234–265. http://doi.org/10.1109/SURV.2013.071913.00194

Olalere Mudasiru, Y., Bolanle Idayat, L., & Mary Bose, O. 2015. Effectiveness of Using Mobile Technologies in Teaching and Learning. In *Promoting Active Learning through the Integration of Mobile and Ubiquitous Technologies,* pp. 155–166. IGI Global. http://doi.org/10.4018/978-1-4666-6343-5.ch009

Ozdamli, F., & Cavus, N. 2011. Basic elements and characteristics of mobile learning. In *Procedia - Social and Behavioral Science,s*(pp. 937–942. Elsevier B.V. http://doi.org/10.1016/j.sbspro.2011.11.173

Park, Y., & Chen, J. V. 2007. Acceptance and adoption of the innovative use of smartphone. *Industrial Management & Data Systems*, *107*(9), 1349–1365. http://doi.org/10.1108/02635570710834009

Santos, I. M. 2015a. Mobile Devices in Higher Education Classrooms : Challenges and Opportunities. In *Promoting Active Learning through the Integration of Mobile and Ubiquitous Technologies,* pp. 37–39. IGI Global. http://doi.org/10.4018/978-1-4666-6343-5.ch003

Santos, I. M. 2015b. Mobile Devices in Higher Education Classrooms : Challenges and Opportunities. *Promoting Active Learning through the Integration of Mobile and Ubiquitous Technologies*, 37–39. http://doi.org/10.4018/978-1-4666-6343-5.ch003

Siemens, G. 2005. Connectivism : A Learning Theory for the Digital Age. *International Journal of Instructional Technology and Distance Learning (ITDL)*, *2*(1), 1–9.

Stanton, G. 2014. *Developing a Method for a Holistic Design of Mobile Learning.*

Thomas, D. R. 2006. Method Notes A General Inductive Approach for Analyzing Qualitative Evaluation Data. *American Journal of Evaluation*, *27*(2), 237–246. http://doi.org/10.1177/1098214005283748

Vishwakarma, A. 2015. Benefits and Challenges of Mobile Learning in Education. In *Promoting Active Learning through the Integration of Mobile and Ubiquitous Technologies,* pp. 24–36. http://doi.org/10.4018/978-1-4666-6343-5.ch001

Wu, W. H., Jim Wu, Y. C., Chen, C. Y., Kao, H. Y., Lin, C. H., & Huang, S. H. 2012. Review of trends from mobile learning studies: A meta-analysis. *Computers and Education*, *59*(2), 817–827. http://doi.org/10.1016/j.compedu.2012.03.016

THE POTENTIAL USE OF SMARTPHONE AND SOCIAL NETWORKS IN PUBLIC SCHOOLS: A CASE STUDY IN NORTH OF BRAZIL

Eva Daltio, José Gama, George França, David Prata and Gentil Veloso
Programa De Pós-Graduação Em Modelagem Computacional De Sistemas - PPGMCS
Universidade Federal Do Tocantins – UFT, Brazil

ABSTRACT

This paper analysis the relationship between smartphones and social networks as compatible technologies with the school´s pedagogical demands in the 21st century. In the classroom there are some challenges imposed by their own dynamics, these analyses aims to highlight the potential of teaching and learning productivity and the contribution of these technologies focus on the production of knowledge. The information contextualized in this analysis has the focus into the base of the research and the objective and it was collected from a public high school in Palmas, the capital of Tocantins state in Brazil. In this study 212 students and 27 teachers participated. The results confirm the need to change from traditional teaching to practice focused on curricular integration of information and communication technologies (ICT), considering the intense relationship and time of students and teachers with the virtual world. This relationship is intensified by the popularization and dissemination of mobile technologies and the importance attached to social networks in the context of social relations.

KEYWORDS

Smartphone, Social Networks, Learning, Digital Technologies, School

1. INTRODUCTION

The advancement of science and technology in the last decades has defined a milestone in contemporary society, the so-called "knowledge society" in Castells´ definitions (1999). This phenomenon consolidated the presence of a new time in communications. In this scenario, ICT (Information and Communication Technologies) assumes an immeasurable importance to the global context, where knowledge generates and improves new technologies, contributing to the production of new knowledge in a continuous process.

In this sense, the United Nations Educational, Scientific and Cultural Organization (UNESCO) gives prominence to mobile technologies, characterized by the use of tablets, iPads, portable book devices, game consoles, and especially the smartphones, defining mobile devices as: "digital, easily portable, owned and controlled by an individual rather than an institution, with access to the internet and multimedia aspects, capable to facilitate a large number of tasks, particularly those related to communication". (Unesco: 8).

This scenario influences and contributes to the transformations in social relations evidenced by the use in different types of media, mainly due to relationship by the internet. These technologies reinvent and are reinvented by every function, thing, or attribute; the innovations, adaptations and discoveries succeed, overlap, interconnect and complement each other in a linear, bidirectional and / or multidirectional sense, characterizing the flow spaces of the (Castells, 1999) society design.

According to this techno-sociocultural panorama, it is possible to visualize and verify the power and influence of social networks in people's lives, as well as the ease of access to different social groups, according to the phenomenon of mobility and portability, characterized by the presence of mobile devices, notably the popularization of smartphones.

Associated with the increasing speed of access to information, competitiveness for the production of smartphone applications intensifies, making it possible to access all types of services and interests of users. This ubiquitous characterization allows the formation of social networks, in which users can carry out any type of business interest, whether consumer or content producer.

In this scenario, it should be noted that young people are connected to the Internet and to the social networks, producing, distributing and consuming a lot of information. This reality has generated increasing demands in the relation between the number of users gradually avid for new electronic devices with capacity for the production and distribution of contents, for the most different purposes. The popularization of the smartphones, associated to the facilities and attributes of ICT, has given a new identity to the youth of the 21st century, regardless of the social class to which it belongs.

Thus, the ICT exerts pressure on the industrial, economic and social processes of production, also does educational policies to their respective didactic-pedagogical processes within Brazilian public schools.

For a better contextualization, this approach will be presented in five sections namely. In the introduction, where will be visualized the theme and its evolution, in agreement with the smartphones, social networks and teaching and learning. In the second section, the relationship between smartphone and social networks is approached in greater depth, based on many authors, such as (Lemos, 2004), (Valente, 2011), (Bonilla, 2005). Statistical data are extracted from the Brazilian Institute of Geography and Statistics (IBGE), the National Telecommunications Agency (ANATEL), the Global System for Mobile Association (GSMA) and the United Nations Educational, Scientific and Cultural Organization (UNESCO). In the third section, the data of a high school of Palmas, capital city of Tocantins federal state, is presented. The database is analyzed in relation to the provision of teachers to integrate the use of ICT in public education. Finally, in the fourth section , the opinions and conclusions built during the survey are carried out.

2. SMARTPHONES AND SOCIAL NETWORKS

From the first telephone call that took place in April 1973 to the present, the cellular device went through a process of evolution that marked the history of telecommunications. Since 2007, with the launch of the iPhone by Apple, smartphones have emerged and have taken a leading position in the world.

The dynamics of this evolution from the cellular apparatus to the smartphones is present, both in its anatomical and functional structure, and in the fact that it becomes a ubiquitous and pervasive phenomenon, according to (Hansmann, 2003). The most part of its popularization is due to the convergence property of applications available to the most different types of users and services, as well as the refinement related to the size, weight and quality of images. These characteristics identify it as a kind of "(...)" handyman ", in the view of (Lemos, 2004).

As new versions are released in the market, smartphones bring more features, in an attempt to overcome previous versions and the version of competitors to meet the requirements of users. In addition, the mobility and portability attributes take advantages and facilities to these mobile devices. Conceptually, the property of mobility can be understood as the possibility of using mobile devices connected during displacements (Lemos, 2008) and (Alves, 2009). In contrast, the portability is the faculty that fixed and mobile telephony users have been given to carry their lines to the operators that best suite them. According to the National Telecommunications Agency, Anatel, numeric portability is "a facility that enables the fixed and mobile telephony services customer to maintain the telephone number (access code) assigned to it." This property now requires a greater investment from telephony companies in order to meet the requirements of an emerging market and a new consumer profile.

According to the estimate made by IBGE, Brazilian Institute of Geography and Statistics, Brazil country has more than 207 million inhabitants. It is the Latin American country best placed in relation to the use of smartphones, with 234.6 million devices connected to the internet (2017). Of this total, 73% use the 4G technology, according to a report from the GSMA agency, responsible for GSM technology.

It is necessary to consider that the evolution of Internet access services in Brazil are boosting the connectivity indexes. According to the Digital Convergence agency, released in November 2017, 3G technology, surpassing the target for 2017, and already reached more than 5 thousand Brazilian municipalities. The 4G network is already present in more than 3,000 municipalities. There are more than 88.5 million accesses by August 2017. This sector is expanding with the advent of 5G technology, scheduled for the market to 2019. This technology promises to be far superior to 4G predecessor. According to a survey released in November / 2017, by the National Telecommunications Agency (ANATEL), Brazil has more than 241 million lines in operation and a density of 116.96 cells per 100 inhabitants.

This context and the evolution in the quality of the provision of services to the user makes it increasingly possible to access information through mobile devices at any time. In this case, besides the numerous applications for mobile devices, it is important to highlight the use of social networks through the smartphone.

According to (Telles, 2010:7), social networks "are environments that focus on bringing people together ... exposing their profile with data such as personal photos, texts, messages and videos, and interacting with other members, creating lists of friends and communities. " Moreover, this activity attracts the majority of young people also contributing to the improvement of abilities to manipulate the smartphone resources.

This relationship can be seen as a potential beneficial to the composition of methodological actions that contributes to the quality of teaching and learning, especially the learning of young students.

It is no longer possible to consider processes of teaching and learning alienated from the technological resources of contemporary society. There is no prospect of regression. On the contrary, there is an increasingly consistent world trend, a panorama, where the real and the virtual world meet, completed and interconnected. A scenario with common places for the internet of things, identity, augmented reality, networks, mobile devices and other technologies classified as emerging technologies of the 21st century.

Immersed in this universe of cutting-edge technologies, the smartphone has become an object of personal use of fundamental importance in people's lives, especially in the lives of young people who feel comfortable as part of this context. "In this new spatial logic there is a social pressure that demands the necessity of belonging, awakens in individuals a greater need for consumption of goods that identifies them with groups they want to contact." (Daltio, Franca and Prata, 2017:8).

In this sense, this study aims to understand the relevance of the use of social networks and smartphones in the teaching and learning process of the students of a public school in Palmas, State of Tocantins, Brazil, allowing the expansion of knowledge production possibilities.

It is necessary to consider that "it is necessary to extrapolate the classroom, to participate in the daily life, to dare." (Bonilla, 2005:70). It is also possible to contribute to the dynamics of the classroom by allowing and initiating the practice of knowledge production by students in public schools. Rather than the traditional practice of informational consumption where "students and teachers close themselves between the four walls of the classroom, as in a vial, without communicating and establishing relations with the external context " (Bonilha, 2005:69/70).

This distancing between contemporary technologies and pedagogical practices contrasts with the affinity and interest of young people for technologies and constitutes the great challenge for teachers of this century, who according to (Valente 2007:56) "the knowledge society requires that all people be able to learn continuously and become lifelong learners", and Medeiros corroborates with:

> An important challenge to face is therefore the appropriation of the multiple ICT and the media languages as effective teaching and learning instruments. To do this, in addition to the resources themselves, are necessary measures to provide training by teachers for their use, when it is desired to bring about significant changes in the way of teaching and learning. (Medeiros, 2007:29).

In this context, this approach has the purpose to provoke a structural change in the institutions and in the way of teaching and learning, based on the positioning evidenced in the answers of students and teachers to the questions addressed to them. The next session analyze the applied research data in a public school in Palmas

3. DATA AND ANALYSIS R

Considering the expressive use of social networks, the school and teachers can apply these resources in pedagogical actions due to the affinity and predisposition of students for the use of virtual communication, allying them to the process of teaching and learning.

The investigation starts by questioning the use of social networks by students and teachers of a public high school in Palmas, capital of Tocantins. It is verified that the social networks of Instagram and Twitter have predominance access of students in relation to the percentage of teachers, Figure 1.

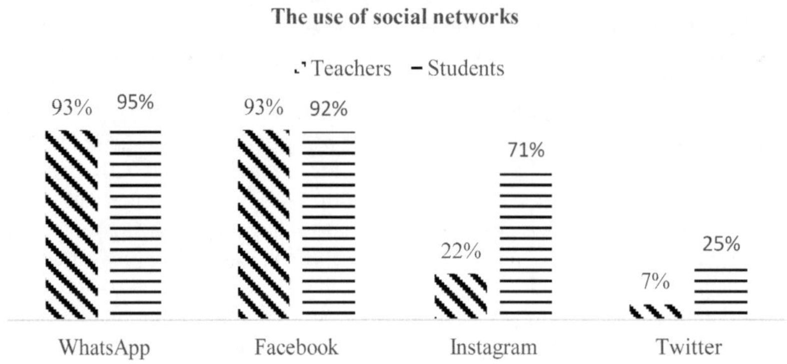

Figure 1. The Use of Social Networks

When teachers and students were asked about "on average, how much time per day do you spend accessing social networks?" the most of them are connected almost every day, Figure 2. Varying from 1h to 5h per day there is 30% of teachers and 35% of students. Up to 8 hours per day, there is 7% of teachers and 20% of students. It is clear with this result that social networks are part of the everyday life´s people, interconnecting them, facilitating communication, entertainment and relationships, and indicating a greater time of use by the students.

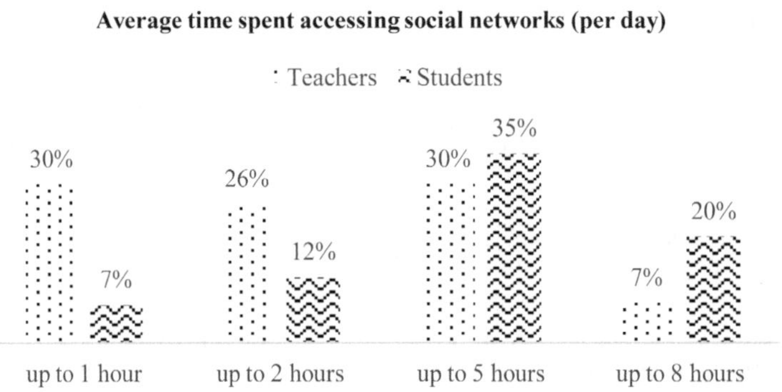

Figure 2. Average Time Spent Accessing Social Networks

Seeking the "purpose of the use of social networks" by students and teachers, 74% of teachers and 85% of students said they use social networks for leisure and entertainment, Figure 3. Of these, 93% of teachers and 49% of students use for communication. Finally, 67% of teachers and 31% of students use networks for work. For 56% of teachers and 86% of students social networks are used for educational purposes.

The indicators point to a potential investment in the training of teachers for the pedagogical use of social networks, since, teachers and students in an inseparable invasion into the school space, making use daily. Students use social networks for longer and educational purposes, that is, teachers have the advantage of benefiting from the inherent use of this resource by the student, with a view to the teaching and learning process.

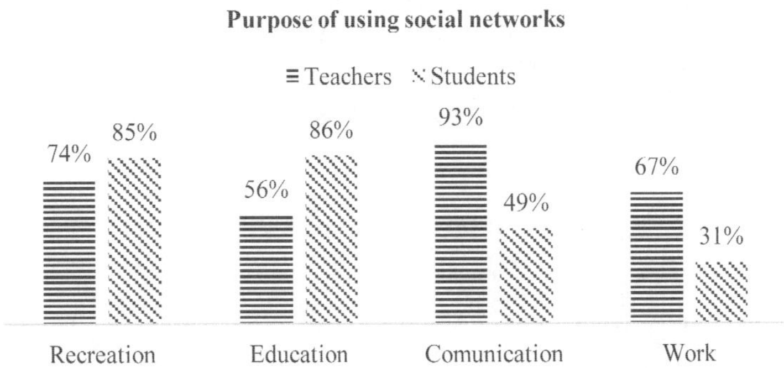

Figure 3. Purpose of Using Social Networks

When questioned about "the belief that social networks definitely influence people's opinions," 74% of teachers and 59% of students think so; the others, 26% and 34% respectively answered that "partial", Figure 4. This paradigm of belief in social networks is based on the fact that today's society is networked, which in turn dictates rules, changes habits, customs, incorporates values and influences the ways of living and interacting.

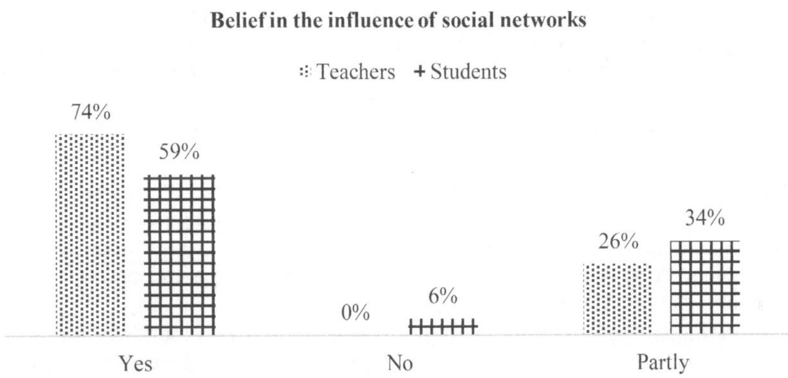

Figure 4. Belief in the Influence of Social Networks on People's Opinions

When questioned if "they did any pedagogical activity at school using social networks", 52% of teachers and 53% of students affirm that they have not done, Figure 5.

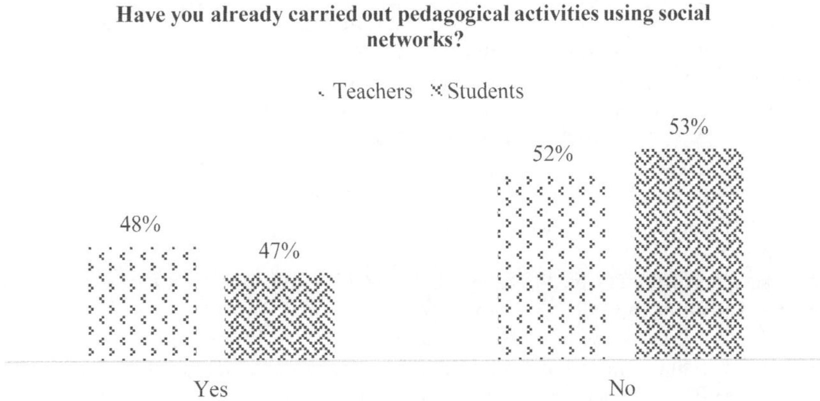

Figure 5. If There are Classroom Learning Activities Using Social Networks

It was also asked, "if it is possible to learn educational content with social networks". The results show, Figure 6, that 85% of teachers and 89% of students said yes. This result shows that so many students and teachers have personal affinities with social networks.

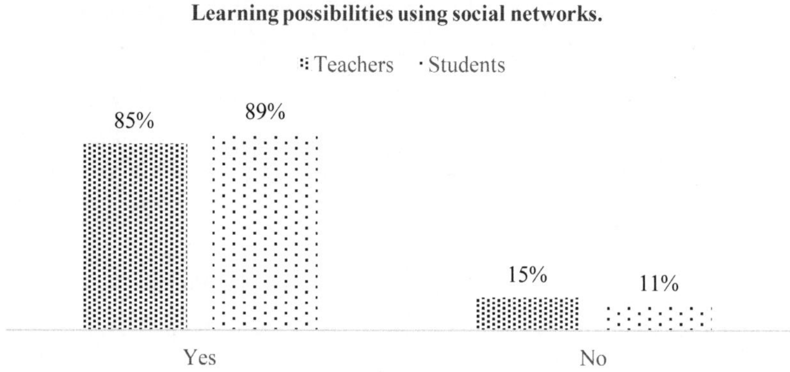

Figure 6. It is Possible to Learn Educational Content Using Social Networks

Given these results, it is evident that social networks are increasingly present in people's daily lives, and it is potential to educational purposes. It is noticed that, often, the use of smartphones is common among teachers and students to access the networks, whose intention is to maintain communication with leisure, education and work. So if 74% of teachers and 59% believe that social networks can influence people's opinions, would not it be an opportunity to be explored for pedagogical purposes and for the application or socialization of experiences between teachers and peers? The students of this generation are articulated in spaces created by social networks, as well as teachers.

During the research, it was verified that many teachers have already noticed and are moving so as not to be unrelated to this virtual universe. Most still do not use social networks as a tool to carry out activities with students, even believing in the potentiality of these tools. However, it can be seen that this is an opportunity to enrich pedagogical work, with not only research and educational games, but also to share ideas, develop projects and disseminate experiences within the school.

The inferences made from the data analyzed show that it is necessary to investigate this topic more widely, since the experiences of teachers regarding the use of smartphones and social networks in their pedagogical practices are slowly evolving.

4. CONCLUSION

This study analyzed to the potential context of didactic-pedagogical use of smartphones and social networks in the context of the Brazilian public School. In this sense, considering:

1. the need for improving the proficiency of Brazilian students in the rankings published by international organizations, such as PISA (2015), where Brazil is among the last 70 countries surveyed;
2. the need to integrate school practices with ICT;
3. technologies are means and ends, according to specific intentionality;
4. access facilities to social networks and other productivity applications;
5. the possibilities and potential of pedagogical activities for the use of smartphones associated with social networks;
6. in Brazil, according to data released by ANATEL, the density of mobile lines per inhabitant is 116.96%, and in Tocantins the density is 115.23%;
7. and, finally, considering that ICT, presented in all fields of human knowledge, has shown no downward trend. On the contrary, researches in emerging technologies, such as the areas of artificial intelligence, connectivity, augmented reality, among others, have intensified and, more and more, researchers are committed to developing new products and contents with new functions and skills for the service and adaptation of different spaces and situations in the life and activities of people.

Therefore, why not the use of smartphone and social networks, so present and accessible, in the service of teaching and learning? This is the challenge for change that is directly related to the need for teacher training, in order to develop pedagogical activities in harmony with this new scenario marked by the mastery of technologies.

In this context, this study is considering the several Brazilian federal states schools where students are legally prohibited to use the cell phone in class, including the schools of Tocantins. In the School Rules of the State Teaching Network of Tocantins, article 41: "It is forbidden to the student, in the school premises: II - to use a cellular device, smartphones, tablets cameras, headphones and any other sound system in the classrooms, except when contemplated in school planning".

In this sense, it is perceived that the integration of ICT resources into classroom pedagogical actions is still more challenging. If, on the one hand, the institutional organization itself imposes restrictions, legalizing the lack of skills to creatively and productively deal with technologies. On the other hand, there is a demand for professionals lacking training in the field of emerging technologies to the contemporary world.

This context can be verified by the analysis of the answers given by teachers and students in the questionnaires, which signaled to the urgency of pedagogical actions using ICT resources in the universe of the school. The reality researched is, only, a cut of daily situations experienced in schools, but representative in the Brazilian educational universe.

It was verified the need for changes in school planning, in the sense of using social networks in the pedagogical proposal of the school, in the projects and actions developed. The use of the Facebook platform and the WhatsApp tool, for example, can bring benefits to teaching and learning. In individual practice, both teachers and students make effective use of social networks in their daily lives, which makes it possible to obtain positive results regarding the integration of technologies in school practices.

As can be seen, the challenge lies in both the appropriateness of the institutional process and the internal changes of each individual, in this case, the teachers, who need to be open and willing to invest in their own formation. This context must be intrinsically related to quality of teaching and learning, capable of raising the scores and ranking of Brazilian students, making them competitive in any labor market. Likewise, these results should reflect the perspectives of social, political and economic development of the country.

The Brazilian Open University (Universidade Aberta do Brasil) is considering to use smartphones, e.g., the Moodle mobile application, as a support learning tool to the graduate and undergraduate courses of the distance learning environment of the Federal University of Tocantins (UFT, Universidade Federal do Tocantins). This is an amount of more than two thousand students.

ACKNOWLEDGMENTS

Authors would like to thank DTE, Ensino a Distância da Universidade Federal do Tocantins (UFT), Universidade Aberta do Brasil – UAB, for the financial support.

REFERENCES

Almeida, M. E. B.; Valente, José Armando. (2011). *Tecnologias e currículo*: trajetórias convergentes ou divergentes? 1. ed. São Paulo: Paulus, v. 1.

Almeida, M. E. B; ALVES, D. R. M. OSB; Lemos, S. D. V. (Orgs). (2014). *Web Currículo*: Aprendizagem, pesquisa e conhecimento com uso das tecnologias digitais. Rio de Janeiro: Letra Capital.

Alves, Mário J. (2009). *Mobilidade e acessibilidade*: conceitos e novas práticas. Revista Indústria e Ambiente.

ANATEL. (2017). Brasil registra 240,9 milhões de linhas móveis em operação em outubro de 2017. *Agência Nacional de Telecomunicações.* Available at: http://www.anatel.gov.br/institucional/noticias-destaque/1848-brasil-registra-240-9-milhoes-de-linhas-moveis-em-operacao-em-outubro-de-2017. (accessed 08 January 2018).

Beecreative. (2017). Telefone celular completa 40 anos de vida. *Beecreative.* Available at: *http://www.beecreative.com.br/telefone-celular-completa-40-anos-de-vida/. (accessed 08 January 2018).*

Bonilla, M. H. (2005). *Escola Aprendente*: para além da sociedade da informação. Cibercultura e Educação. Quartet. Rio de Janeiro-RJ.

Canabarro, M. Margarete. Basso, L. de Oliveira. (2013). Os Professores e as Redes Sociais – É possível utilizar o Facebook para além do "curtir"? *Renote.* V. 11 Nº 1. Available at: <http://seer.ufrgs.br/renote/article/viewFile/41625/26405>. (accessed 26 November 2017).

Castells, Manuel. (1999). *A Sociedade em Rede.* A era da Informação: economia, sociedade e cultura. Vol. 1. 11º Ed. São Paulo. Editora Paz e Terra,

Daltio, E.; França, G.; Prata, David. (2017). Reflexões sobre o uso dos smartphones com fins educacionais nas escolas. *Linkscienceplace.* v. 4, p. 115. Available at: http://revista.srvroot.com/linkscienceplace/index.php/linkscienceplace/article/view/328. (accessed 26 November 2017).

Freire, Paulo. 1996. *Pedagogia da Autonomia*: saberes necessários à prática educativa. São Paulo. 30. ed. Paz e Terra.

Hansmann, Uwe (2003). Pervasive Computing: *The Mobile Word Springer* [S.l.] ISBN 354-000-218-9.

IBGE. (2017). Estimativas da população residente para os municípios e para as unidades da federação brasileiros com data de referência em 1º de Julho de 2017. *Instituto Brasileiro de Geografia e Estatística.* ftp://ftp.ibge.gov.br/Estimativas_de_Populacao/Estimativas_2017/estimativa_TCU_2017.pdf. (accessed 10 January 2018).

Jenkins, H. 2009. *Cultura da Convergência.* São Paulo: Aleph. Available at: http://lelivros.top/book/baixar-livro-cultura-da-convergencia-henry-jenkins-em-pdf-epub-e-mobi-ou-ler-online/ (accessed 12 November 2017).

Lemos, André. (2007). *Cidade e mobilidade.* Telefones celulares, funções pós-massivas e territórios informacionais. Matrizes, vol. 1, núm. 1, 121-137. Universidade de São Paulo. São Paulo.

Lemos, André. (2004). Cibercultura e Mobilidade: a Era da Conexão. *Razón y Palabra.* N. 41. Available at: https://www.razonypalabra.org.mx/anteriores/n41/alemos.html. (accessed 12 January 2018).

Lemos, A.; Josgrilberg, F. (Orgs). (2009). *Comunicação e Mobilidade*: aspectos socioculturais das tecnologias móveis de comunicação no Brasil. Salvador: EDUFBA.

Libâneo, J. C. Santos, A. (2009). *Educação na era do conhecimento em rede e transdisciplinaridade.* Campinas, São Paulo: Alínea.

Medeiros, L. L. (2007). *Educação a Distância e formação de Professores*: relatos e experiências. Coordenação Central de Educação a Distância PUC – Rio (Org.). Rio de Janeiro. Ed. PUC – Rio.

Merije, W. (2012). *Mobimento*: Educação e Comunicação Mobile. São Paulo: Peiropolis. Available at: https://issuu.com/editorapeiropolis/docs/mobimento_wagner_merije_peiropolis?backgroundColor=. (accessed 12 January 2018).

SEDUC. 2017. Regimento Escolar da Rede Estadual do Tocantins. *Secretaria de Educação do Estado do Tocantins.* Available at: https://central3.to.gov.br/arquivo/371242/. (accessed 08 January 2018).

Tapscott, Don. (2010). *A hora da Geração Digital.* Rio de Janeiro: Agir.

Valente, J. A. (2014). *Aprendizagem e mobilidade*: os dispositivos móveis criam novas formas de aprender? In: Almeida, M. E.; Alves, R. M., OSB; Lemos, S. D. V. (Orgs.). Letra Capital, Vol. 1.

Telles, A. (2010). *A revolução das mídias sociais.* Cases, conceitos, dicas e ferramentas. M. Books do Brasil Ed. Ltda. – São Paulo.

UNESCO. (2013). *Policy Guidelines for Mobile Learning.* 7, place de Fontenoy, 75352 Paris 07 SP, France. Trad. Representação da UNESCO no Brasil. Available at: http://unesdoc.unesco.org/images/0021/002196/219641E.pdf . (accessed 09 January 2018).

Weiser, M. (1991). *The Computer for the 21st Century, Scientific American*, vol.265, no.3, September. p. 94 – 104. Available at: http://wiki.daimi.au.dk/pca/_files/weiser-orig.pdf. (accessed 09 January 2018).

1-DAY MOOC ON MOBILE LEARNING: AN EXPERIENCE REPORT ON THE MODULE 'EDUCATIONAL CONTEXTS'

Carla V. Leite, Ivone Almeida and Luiz Fernando Corcini
Universidade de Aveiro, Portugal

ABSTRACT

Smartphones and tablets have become essential tools in users' daily life, as they include a whole range of digital services, enlarging the connection to the virtual world. Nonetheless, the use of these tools in the educational context, known as mobile learning, is still a recent and scarcely embraced practice. A 1-day MOOC (massive open online course) was devised to raise awareness of the potential of mobile devices in the teaching-learning process, aiming at increasing lower secondary education teachers´ adhesion to this approach. This article is intended to present the experience of creating the first out of four course modules/units. This module, entitled "Contexts", is focused on the change of paradigm in educational contexts due to the fact that mobile devices enable ubiquitous learning. The pedagogical strategies adopted in the development of the module, the technologies used to meet the needs and the purposes are described. Participants' comments on the debate activities were analysed and they reinforce the need to invest in infrastructures, to promote teachers' proactivity and to ensure preconditions for a success of the integration of mobile devices. Participants pointed out both teachers and schools as barriers to the introduction of mobile learning, highlighting teachers' lack of motivation and commitment as well as school infrastructure problems. Conclusions drawn from this experience point to an increasing interest in mobile learning and participants' awareness of both its advantages and the obstacles to implementing it.

KEYWORDS

Mobile Learning, MOOC, Educational Contexts

1. INTRODUCTION

The purpose of this paper is to provide a thorough description of the experience of developing a 1-day MOOC designed for teachers at lower secondary education (ISCED level 2). Usually MOOCs run for a few weeks, however a new format was tested, a combination of asynchronous and synchronous training, compressed in a short time period, to meet the requirements of a course of the Multimedia in Education PhD. Despite being considered by many education and training agents as a viable option, Balula (2015) remarks that there is still few research on the potential of MOOCs in terms of digital inclusion. Moreover, mobile learning is still disregarded by many education agents. Therefore, this 1-day MOOC was devised to shed some light on the purposes and benefits of mobile learning, methodologies supporting m-learning, strategies, practical applications, and show some real examples of implementation.

Bearing in mind the current scenario of use of communication technologies in the teaching-learning context and the main trends concerning the use of new devices and digital services, the theme chosen for this 1-day MOOC was "Mobile devices in the teaching-learning process". Notwithstanding the course was divided in 4 modules (Contexts, Tools and technologies, Interaction and Assessment) developed by different teams, this document only reports to the first one. The aim of this paper is to contribute to the promotion of m-learning practices and make schools and teachers aware of the need to overcome obstacles to the successful integration of mobile devices in the teaching-learning process.

2. CONTEXTUALISATION

The emergence of smartphones and tablets allowed a convenient expansion to the virtual world, as they are progressing towards ubiquitous access to a wide range of services (Leite, 2013). They are constantly being reinvented and reused in unexpected ways, regarding their size, forms of interaction, context and use, and many people argue that mobile applications should be thought as tools which enable people to enjoy intense and fulfilling experiences based on their needs (Cartman & Ting, 2008).

Several authors, namely Trindade & Moreira (2017), Moura (2016), Abreu & Cardoso (2016), are enthusiasts of the use of technology in educational context, claiming that traditional school should change in order to meet students' expectations, open the way for significant and contextualised learning, decentralising the teacher from the teaching-learning process, by including other sources of information provided by technological devices. According to Conole et al. (2008), the environment surrounding students can be a rich learning environment in which they can select and adjust the available technologies to their own personal needs.

It is also believed that the way students explore technology promotes the development of multitasking skills, memory, spatial orientation and communication (Redecker, 2008). Introducing technology in the teaching-learning process is still a recent idea, even though it is clear that globalisation and the evolution in the labour market require new skills, which require new contexts and learning strategies (Moura & Carvalho, 2010). It is important to stress that several tools may be used for technologically mediated learning, such as MOOC and mobile learning, which are the focus of this study. According to Baeta (2016), when planning a MOOC, strategies and work organisation should be explicit, as well as the way to interact, communicate and collaborate: individual work, collaborative, tutorial, under supervision and/or autonomous.

Considering that learning can occur in various places and as a result of information contact from different sources, Rogers (2004) supports the distinction between formal, non-formal and informal contexts, summarized by UNESCO in 2014 (as cited in Costa & Xavier, 2014). Alves (2013) stresses the difficulty to delimit these three contexts and their possible integrations. It is important to highlight several authors, such as Barron (2006) who do not agree with defining learning contexts only by the physical environments where they can occur based on the idea that informal learning can happen inside or outside the classroom. Costa & Xavier (2014) suggest defining educational contexts regarding two factors: physical environment and intentionality. Considering that mobile devices are ubiquitous, learning can occur anywhere and anytime, this paths the way for a new and unique educational context proposed by the authors, the "Mobile learning context" focused exclusively on the intentionality.

According to Costa & Xavier (2014), mobile learning allows the convergence of learning in different contexts, enabling new types of learning, derived from the usability aspects of mobile devices that allow a flow of micro-content, enabling continuous learning (Costa & Xavier, 2014, p.2). Corroborating this idea, UNESCO recognises that integrating mobile phones into the teaching-learning process could potentially break traditional pedagogical paradigms, and because of the usage of mobile technologies in education, the line between formal and informal learning is becoming invisible. Nevertheless, to integrate educational technologies in teaching practices, one needs to consider the context, the curriculum, content and collaboration, so that mobile devices contribute to multimodal, individual and collaborative knowledge between students and teachers (Moura, 2015).

Introducing new mobile technologies in education enables several paradigm changes (Berger & Muilenburg, 2013) such as: time flexibility; personalisation of teaching; increase of interaction and collaboration; possibility of a wide variety of pedagogical strategies and assessment methodologies.

Nowadays there are some projects promoting mobile learning in Portugal (Ferreira et al., 2015): *Tablets no Ensino e na Aprendizagem; A sala de aula Gulbenkian; Comunidades Escolares de Aprendizagem Gulbenkian XXI; Edulabs; Creative Classrooms Lab; ManEEle;* Meanwhile internationally some stand out: *eTwinning; Conexões literárias; Projeto Leituras d'Oriente e d'Ocidente; Projeto ERASMUS+: My city in QR codes.*

3. METHODOLOGY

Designing and implementing the 1-day MOOC initiative took place for three weeks, with tasks distributed for 4 teams, each one responsible for one module. The theme of the course was: "Mobile devices in the teaching-learning process" and the modules: 1- Contexts; 2- Tools and Technologies; 3-Interaction; 4- Assessment. Choosing the platform Sapo Campus was consensual, since it meets the requirements and logistic support was provided by its development team.

The event was advertised by Facebook and via email to Portuguese schools. Registrations were made by Google forms and handled through an email account created for this purpose. Then participants were invited to join the 1-day MOOC activity in Sapo Campus and to save the date of the synchronous session. On platform, the participants could find the 1-day MOOC scenario and two social spaces (Available: http://1daymooc.campus.sapo.pt/_)

The "Contexts" module was the first one, and it aimed to present a theoretical approach to educational contexts and strategies to implement mobile learning. The "Tools and technologies" module, the participants came in touch with some applications, as well as recommendations for the success of the activities. Afterwards, in the "Interaction" module the possibilities of communication and interaction between teacher-student, student-student, teacher-teacher were explored. Finally, the "Assessment" module was focused on trying applications that could be used for evaluation purposes and pedagogical activities. It is worth mentioning that module 1 was strategically planned with one asynchronous and another synchronous session, with the last one happening on the day of the course.

3.1 Module 1 - Asynchronous Session

To enable participants to prepare previously and visualise some examples of practical implementation of mobile learning, a set of training material was created. This followed a narrative including positive reinforcement prompts designed to draw participants' attention, and to provide a guided and motivating learning environment. The need to have an appealing and uniform graphic design was also taken into consideration. In order to create the didactic material, a literature review was carried out on educational contexts, the adoption of technologies in education, the increasing use of mobile devices and the potential of mobile learning. The objectives that directed the literature review were: to identify, present and discuss the theoretical approaches about educational contexts, clarify the aims, benefits and how mobile learning may be implemented, present recent data and examples of implementation of mobile learning.

The asynchronous documentation was made available in slides using Microsoft Office software PowerPoint, which is a format that lower secondary education teachers are quite familiar with. The material was divided into 3 parts, entitled: The basics of m-learning; M-learning nowadays; Practical applications.

The basics of m-learning covered were: Formal, non-formal and informal educational contexts; Statistics about the use of the internet and social media platforms in Portugal; Definition of mobile learning; Methodologies supporting the practice of mobile learning. The second part (M-learning nowadays) focused: Intentionality/purpose in the usage of mobile devices: Strategies to make use of mobile technologies in the teaching-learning process; Examples of transversality in learning contexts; Ways of introducing mobile devices in education. Finally, the third part addressed: The purposes and benefits of the use of mobile technologies in education; Dynamics and strategies of pedagogic implementation; Some real examples of m-learning.

Different resources were alternated in the didactic material: text, images, graphics, photos and videos, many of them from well-known researchers (Moura, 2014; Sabbag, 2017; Luna & Cabral, 2016). (Available: https://goo.gl/8TRtAv). Parts of television reports were selected, namely "Linha da frente - RTP, Made in Europa - Sic Notícias" and videos from Youtube (Sabbag, 2017; Moura, 2014), most of them spoken or subtitled in Portuguese. Language was a deliberate concern, since, according to Balula, language is nowadays a barrier to the participation in MOOCs due to the fact that most of them are conducted in English for non-native speakers (Balula, 2015). This researcher stresses out that when designing a MOOC it is important to bear in mind cultural issues in order to meet the trainees' expectations, so in module 1 there are examples of implementation of mobile learning in the European context.

This material was made available in the Sapo Campus platform 36 hours prior to the synchronous session. A task named "Previous reading" was created in the platform to recall participants of the need to read the material of module 1 in advance. It was also announced that a badge named "Contextualized: previous reading task done" would be granted to those who completed that task, embracing a gamification strategy.

3.2 Module 1 - Synchronous Session

The synchronous session took place on October 7th 2017. Participants were welcomed thirty minutes before the beginning of the session in the chat room. They were invited to introduce themselves in the informal areas (the bar and the gym), promoting interaction and leading them to explore the platform. Interaction between the team and the 1-day MOOC participants was conducted through a single profile, registered in the platform as “Contexts Trainer”.

Then they were led to the 1st module, which took place from 10 to 11 am. The synchronous phase consisted of two activities, both introduced by a question and a video. The videos were selected and edited previously, summing up in a few seconds a critical view of the teachers about the use of technologies in education, so as to trigger the debate between participants. Therefore, a student-centred learning strategy was adopted through inquiry-based learning and problem-based learning pedagogies. The debate was planned so as to allow participants to freely express their opinion, as well as discuss with the purpose of answering the problem/question. Thirty minutes were assigned to each activity and meanwhile some more badges were created according to the interactions taking place and were granted to the participants who stood out.

4. RESULTS

The task named "previous reading" in the asynchronous session was completed by 66 participants. However, on the day of the MOOC event, only 52 participants were online (78%), and 47 chose to participate in the synchronous activity (71%). The synchronous session consisted of two debate activities. Two short videos proved to be powerful drivers for ideas exchanging and to share experiences, with about 200 interactions (comments and publications). It is important to emphasize that the foreseen timeframes for each activity (thirty minutes) were precisely followed by the authors, and the participants showed to be highly motivated so the activity continued in parallel through comments, sharing files and publications, simultaneously while the other modules were happening.

During the synchronous session, the authors had to simultaneously work on: starting and concluding the module 1 debate activities; creating and assigning the badges (some of them requested by participants themselves), responding to messages as well as supporting the remaining modules directing participants to follow the course sequence, managing technical issues and motivating the trainees in the chatroom.

4.1 Results of Activity 1

There were 41 participants in the activity, who created around 83 comments, with 81 of them expressing favourable opinions on the integration of mobile devices in schools (97%) and only 2 against (chart 1).

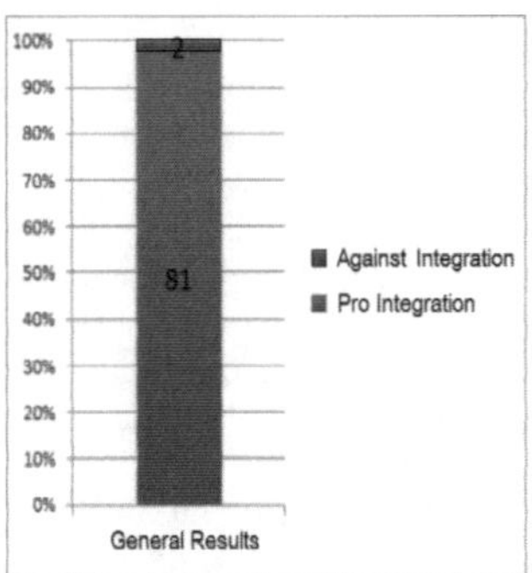

Chart 1. Data referring to activity 1
Source: The authors

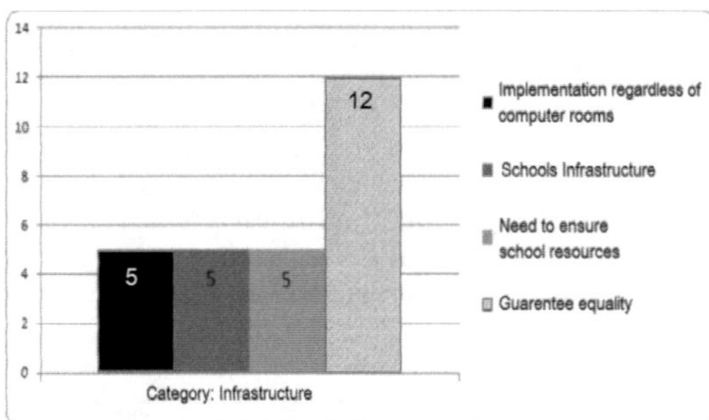

Chart 2. Data referring to 27 comments
Source: The authors

A detailed analysis of the comments enabled the team to address the topics in 3 categories (Infrastructure; Teacher's proactivity; Preconditions for a successful integration). It is important to remark that each comment may address more than one subject, so the sum of the categorized comments adds up to over 83.

Based on the 27 comments that addressed the theme *infrastructure*, it can be said that the main concern of the trainees is guaranteeing equality of resources for the students, that is, in order to be successful in the integration of mobile devices in school activities, students must have the same conditions with regard to the acquisition, capacity and functionality of their devices. The general infrastructure of the school and previous preparation to host activities with mobile devices was also considered relevant, as can be seen in chart 2.

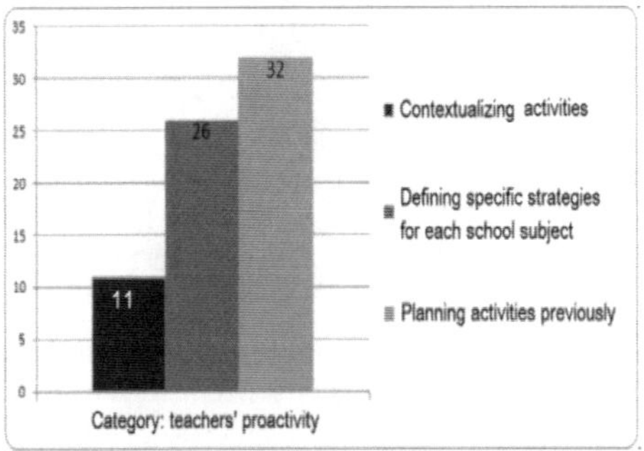

Chart 3. Data referring to 69 comments
Source: The authors

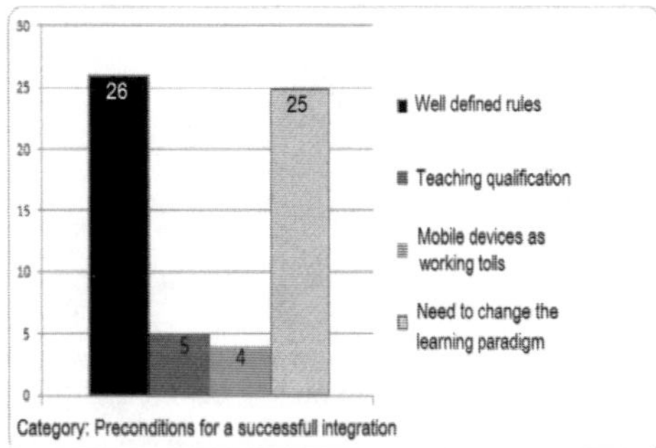

Chart 4. Data referring to comments on preconditions
Source: The authors

Regarding the comments on teachers' proactivity, there are 69 considerations, which are classified in chart 3. It should be noted that these comments demonstrate participants' maturity and sense of responsibility regarding their own limitations and obligations, giving greater emphasis to the subject addressed: "Planning activities". Participants also reveal a clear perception of the need to define different strategies for each school subject, as well as understanding that the same technology can be useful for various contents, but not necessarily in the same way or in the same format. They emphasise the importance of teachers' creativity to choose the most appropriate methodology when adopting mobile technology in school activities. Last but not least, participants understand the need to propose contextualised activities so as to achieve meaningful learnings. It is worth quoting a participant's comment that synthesises this: "There should be a specific objective, a well-defined task, a time, an expected result, and appreciation of students' creativity".

Regarding preconditions for successfully integrating mobile devices in the classroom practices, 60 comments highlight the aspects represented in chart 4. Analysing the 4 items addressed in the comments, the need for well-defined rules and for change in schools' learning paradigm is clear. There is coherence in the comments, given that the preconditions mentioned above have close links with the conditions that would impel teachers' proactivity, such as: "Planning activities" and "Defining specific strategies for each school subject". There are 9 comments reporting positive experiences or attempts to integrate mobile devices in the learning process.

It is worth mentioning two comments describing students' interest in using the mobile phone as being solely for recreational games or applications and not for learning activities, thus stressing that students lack focus in activities related to learning. Therefore, the role of the teacher as a mediator of the learning process using mobile technologies seems to be fundamental. Not all activities of a curricular area need to be bound to technology, but they should be reconsidered so that mobile devices are integrated in a strategic way. Lastly, it is important to stress that setting clear objectives and a limited time for each activity can largely contribute to students' concentration.

4.2 Results of Activity 2

In the second activity there were 43 participants, who produced 83 comments that can also be grouped in similar subjects. From this analysis it can be seen that they highlight the barriers arising from teachers' attitudes, and 72 comments are related to the barriers stemming from school, as shown in chart 5.

Comments regarding the obstacles created by teachers are illustrated in chart 6 and they can be categorized in terms of: Lack of Training, Lack of Motivation; Self-indulgence/lack of commitment.

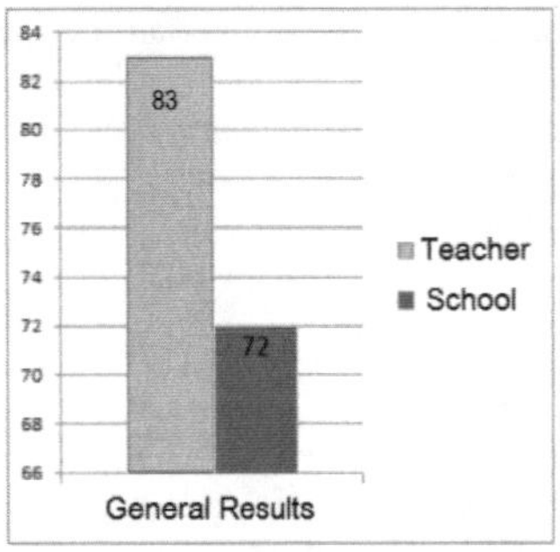

Chart 5 - Data referring to activity 2
Source: The authors

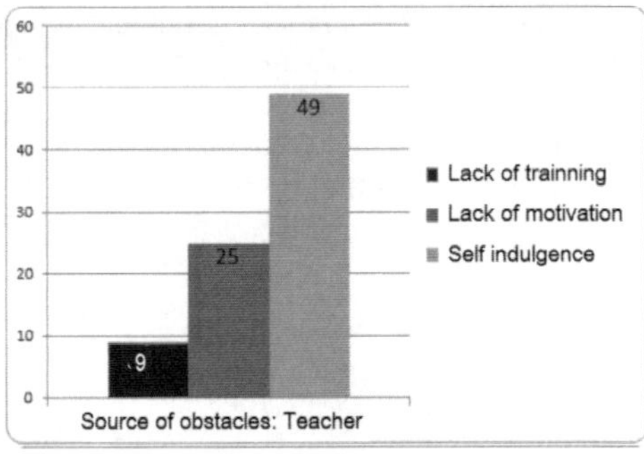

Chart 6 - Obstacles created by teachers
Source: The authors

As shown in figure 6, the barrier defined as "self-indulgence/lack of commitment" was the most frequent and summed up 49 comments, equivalent to approximately 59%. This result is consistent with chart 4, which addresses preconditions for integration, where 41.7% of the comments point to the need for a change in the teaching-learning process paradigm. If we add the indicators that address lack of motivation with those of lack of commitment - considering that they can be cause and effect - they account for approximately 89% of the causes for the barriers pointed out, leaving out only 11% to the lack of teacher training.

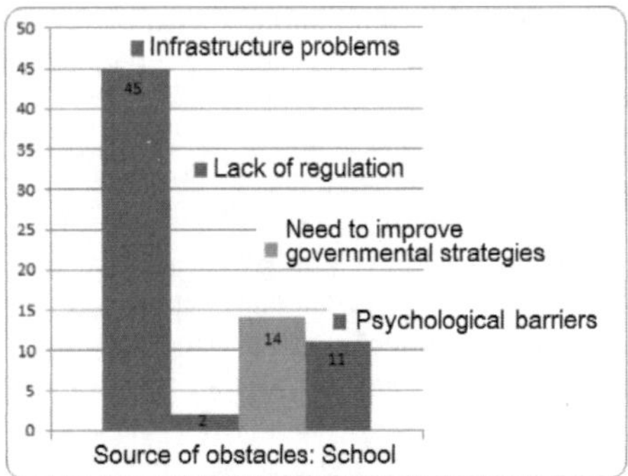

Chart 7. Obstacles created by schools
Source: The authors

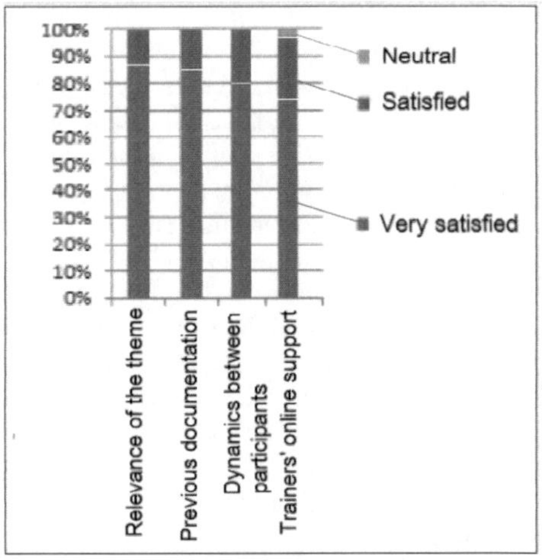

Chart 8. Evaluation of module 1 from the participants' perspective
Source: The authors

Chart 7 shows the distribution of 72 comments regarding obstacles deriving from schools. Analysing chart 7, there is a striking tendency to consider Infrastructure problems as one of the biggest barriers, making up 62.5% in comparison with the other barriers referring to school. It is possible to infer the possibility of an underlying relationship between this barrier and those identified as "lack of motivation" and "convenience" of teachers, shown in chart 6, and these can be directly related to cause and effect. The 15.2% (11 comments) pointing out to psychological barriers could also be summed up to this inference.

The need for a better positioning and strategy of the Ministry of Education about this topic has also been pointed out as significant barrier, with almost 20% of the comments (14 comments). It should be noted that this percentage can contribute to teachers' "self-indulgence" and "lack of motivation" to integrate mobile learning in their classes.

As far as the item "lack of regulation" is considered which only represents 2.7% of the comments, it seems to inconsistent with the large representation in chart 4 regarding the preconditions for the integration of mobile learning, where it was treated as a need for well-defined rules. However, it can be inferred that these apparently similar items deal with the problem from different perspectives. Lack of regulation of the school on the mobile learning issue, in relation to the subject, and teachers' own rules when using mobile devices in the classroom.

4.3 Assessment of the 1-day MOOC

At the end of the 1-day MOOC a questionnaire was applied to the participants in order to evaluate the event as a whole, as well as each module. Thirty-nine answers were registered, that is to say 56% of those who completed the asynchronous tasks made it to the end of the event. The great majority of the participants expressed satisfaction regarding all items: relevance of the theme, previous documentation, trainers' online support and dynamics between participants. There was only 1 neutral opinion and the team did not obtain any negative assessment, as shown in chart 8.

The team tried hard to respond in real time to all questions, to meet participants' needs and to solve technical issues. Regarding the dynamics generated among participants, assigning badges ("Fair play", "Good mood", "Good Speech", "Sharing person", "Pro in m-learning") is likely to have encouraged positive and rich interaction. Participants made hundreds of comments, shared images, scientific articles, ideas, strategies and experiences which also generated interaction among trainees. Their interaction with the "Contexts Trainer" was also a very positive aspect, as trainers encouraged sharing, but did not need to intervene in the debate.

5. CONCLUSION

Participants in the 1-day MOOC showed great interest in improving their understanding of the basics of using digital devices. The theme of this 1 day-MOOC proved to be appealing to a large number of teachers. and the comments in the chat room revealed many affinities between the participants.

It is important to reflect on the timing of the promotion of this initiative. Even though time constraints prevented the team from promoting the event and registrations earlier, adhesion was quite satisfactory. The time for the pre-preparation activities was an aspect that deserved some critical reflection, because it was considered insufficient in some cases. Therefore, two lessons can be taken into consideration in future developments: either to change/reduce the asynchronous material or to increase the time available.

The timetable of the synchronous activities seems to have been favourable for the first module, since it proved to be extremely productive in terms of dynamics between participants. In spite of the fact that the 1-day MOOC took place on Saturday, 78% of the participants interacted actively from the beginning of the session, which is quite representative of the participants' interest in the theme and in the concept of online training condensed into one day.

As the activities progressed, it became clear that participants are aware of the problems, difficulties and limitations of implementing mobile and integrating it into the current educational process, as well as its advantages and benefits. It is consensual that both the learning objectives and the strategies must be clear. Participants didn't stick to the discussion topics proposed and also raised other relevant issues. This demonstrates great interest and adhesion to the theme. Considering the results and also the low dropout rate throughout the day, we can conclude that the team successfully reached its goals. It seems reasonable to suggest new 1-day MOOC experiences designed for teachers of other school levels and about other themes.

ACKNOWLEDGEMENT

This paper is a short and translated version of a course work developed under the supervision of Carlos Santos and Fernando Ramos, to whom the authors are grateful. CVL and IA would like to thank the support of António Moreira, the Coordinator of the Multimedia Education PhD, and acknowledge the fund support through the *Doctoral Programme in Technology Enhanced Learning* and Societal Challenges (PD/00173/2013) by FCT (Fundação para a Ciência e a Tecnologia), research grants PD/BI/135241/2017 and PD/BI/135221/2017.

REFERENCES

Abreu, R., & Cardoso, T. (2016). Mobile Learning e Educação: O que nos diz a Investigação Open Access? *Atas do 3.º Encontro sobre Jogos e Mobile Learning* (Universidade de Coimbra, Faculdade de Psicologia e de Ciências da Educação, LabTE), pp. 28-38.

Alves, M. (2013). *Aprendizagem profissional: Um processo educativo na intersecção de contextos de aprendizagem formais, não-formais e informais* (p. no prelo). Lisboa/Braga: Associação Portuguesa de Sociologia/Universidade do Minho.

Baeta, P. (2016) *Moocs desenvolvidos no ensino superior Português: análise de modelos pedagógicos e estratégias de funcionamento utilizados.* (Dissertação de mestrado). Universidade de Lisboa, Instituto de Educação. Retrieved from: http://repositorio.ul.pt/handle/10451/24293

Balula, A. (2015) The promotion of digital inclusion through MOOC design and use: a literature review. Universidade de Aveiro. *Indagatio Didactica.* Vol 7 (1), 145-164. Retrieved from: http://revistas.ua.pt/index.php/ID/article/viewFile/3451/3196

Barron, B. (2006) Interest and self-sustained learning as catalysts of development: A learning ecologies perspective. *Human Development*, 49, 193-224

Berger, Z. L.; Muilenburg, L. Y. *Handbook of mobile Learning.* New York, NY, USA: Routledge. p. 676, 2013.

Cartman, J., & Ting, R. (2008). *Strategic mobile design: creating engaging experiences.* Berkeley, California, EUA: New Riders Pub.

Conole, G., Laat, Maarten de, Dillon, T. and Darby, J. (2008) "Disruptive technologies", "pedagogical innovation": What's new? Findings from an in-depth study of students' use and perception of technology' *Computers and Education*, vol. 50, pp. 511-524.

Costa, S., G. d., & Xavier, A. C. (2014). Aprendizagem formal, não-formal e informal com a tecnologia móvel: um processo rizomático. *II Congresso Internacional TIC e Educação - ticEDUCA 2014*, p. 8.

Ferreira, A.; Morgado, F; Marques, C.; Manso, A.; Dias, P (2015).Aprender a ler através de dispositivos móveis. Um estudo de caso no Agrupamento de Escolas Artur Gonçalves. *Atas do 3.º Encontro sobre Jogos e Mobile Learning.*

Leite, C. V. (2013) *Otimização da experiência televisiva por reconhecimento de conteúdos.* (Dissertação de mestrado) Aveiro: Universidade de Aveiro. *Retrieved from: http://ria.ua.pt/handle/10773/12308*

Luna, R. & Cabral, E., 2016. Vídeo de animação: "Evolução das Tecnologias na Educação". Projeto de Extensão do Departamento de Comunicação em Mídias Digitais da Universidade Federal da Paraíba.

Moura, A. (2016). Práticas de mobile learning no ensino básico e secundário: metodologias e desafios. *Atas do 3.º Encontro sobre Jogos e Mobile Learning.*

Moura, A. (2015). iPad Program in K-12 Education: The Pilot Year. In Zhang, Y. (ed.) Handbook of Mobile Teaching and Learning. Australia: Springer, pp. 601-616.

Moura, A. (2014) Vídeo "Mobile Learning: Transformar Educação". Retrieved from: https://www.youtube.com/watch?v=JpxsusjQ0FY&t=2s

Moura, A., & Carvalho, A. A. (2010). Enquadramento Teórico para a Integração Móveis em Contexto Educativo. *I Encontro Internacional TIC e Educação.* (pp. 1001 - 1006). Guimarães: Universidade do Minho. Retrieved from: http://repositorium.sdum.uminho.pt/handle/1822/11140, 22 de Abril 2015.

Rogers, A. (2004). Looking again at non-formal and informal education - towards a new paradigm. Retrieved from:

http://infed.org/mobi/looking-again-at-non-formal-and-informal-education-towards-a-new-paradigm/

Redecker, C. (2008) Review of Learning 2.0 Practices: The impact of Web 2.0 innovations on Education and Training in Europe. European Commission. JRS. IPTS - IS unit.

Sabbag, P., 2017. Vídeo "Educação formal, não formal e informal" - Canal Zagaz. Retrieved from: https://www.youtube.com/watch?v=Z4KT_ajZ4fA

Trindade & Moreira (2017). *Tecnologias móveis e a recriação digital na construção do conhecimento histórico.* Retrieved from: http://www.reveduc.ufscar.br/index.php/reveduc/article/view/2230

PROMOTING INTRINSIC MOTIVATION WITH A MOBILE AUGMENTED REALITY LEARNING ENVIRONMENT

Josef Buchner[1] and Jörg Zumbach[2]
[1]*University College of Teacher Education Lower Austria, Mühlgasse 67, A-2500 Baden, Austria*
[2]*University of Salzburg, School of Education, Hellbrunnerstraße 34, A-5020 Salzburg, Austria*

ABSTRACT

In this study the impact of a mobile augmented reality learning environment on motivation, learning effects and cognitive load was tested. Students participated in a two-hour history lesson while using their smartphones to turn static pictures into animations with an Augmented Reality (AR) application. Interest, perceived competence and perceived choice as indicators for intrinsic motivation were assessed. Results of the AR learning group were compared to a non-AR teacher-centered learning environment. The results reveal that augmented reality learning can promote intrinsic motivation and has an impact on history learning. Cognitive load has not been detected as a problem within the AR group.

KEYWORDS

Augmented Reality, Self-Determination Theory, Mobile Learning Environment

1. INTRODUCTION

Augmented Reality (AR) is one of the top educational technology trends since 2010. The Horizon Report (Johnson et al., 2010) assumes a positive impact on learning, creativity and education but the technology was not available on consumer devices at that time. This changed with the rise of smartphones, tablet computers and appropriate platforms (e.g. iOS, Android,...; Yuen, Yaoyuneyong, & Johnson, 2011, p. 120). Nowadays, everything a user needs is a mobile device with camera and an AR application (e.g., Aurasma). Recent surveys from Austria and Germany show that 95% of twelve to nineteen year old students own such a device and 75% of young adults (16-29) in Europe use the Internet on their mobile phone (Education Group, 2015; European Union, 2015; Medienpädagogischer Forschungsverbund Südwest (mpfs), 2016). In summer 2016 Pokémon Go made AR available for the masses and made this technology popular. Since then 750 million downloads of the app have been registered and more than five million active users keep the game still alive (Smith, 2018).

Azuma (1997) defines AR as the coexistence of real and virtual objects in the same space and with real time interaction. For Klopfer and Sheldon (2010) augmented reality (AR) is "(..) a situation in which a real world context is dynamically overlaid with coherent location or context sensitive virtual information" (Klopfer & Sheldon, 2010, p. 205). Milgram et al. (1994) developed a continuum (Figure 1) with two extremes, the real environment and the virtual environment.

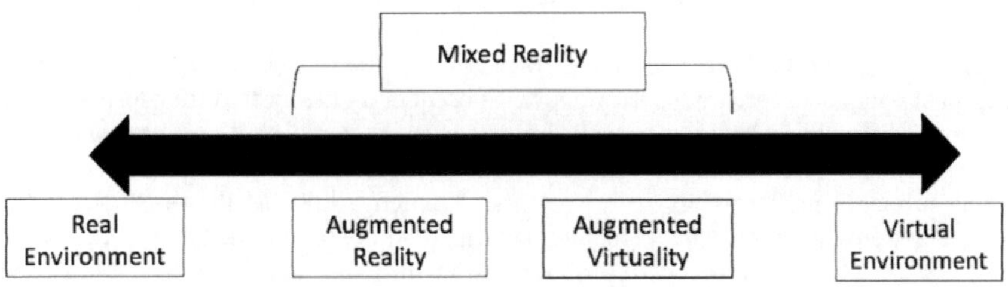

Figure 1. Reality-Virtuality Continuum, Own Representation, Based on Milgram & Kishino, 1994

In this Reality-Virtuality-Continuum, virtual environments are defined as environments that are totally simulated by technology (Yuen, Yaoyuneyong, & Johnson, 2011, p. 121). This side of the continuum is known as Virtual Reality (VR). Between both sides, technology enhanced environments are characterized as "mixed reality". For AR, the real environment is used as background and computer-generated content is displayed. In Augmented Virtuality a computer-generated environment acts as background and real-world objects build an additional layer (Milgram & Kishino, 1994).

Many researchers have already shown that AR can have a positive impact for learning. As for all technology enhanced environments it is important to think about pedagogical aims and learning theories, which can promote the learning process with the help of this technology. For AR Dunleavy and Dede (2014) suggest situated learning theory and constructivism learning as the most important theoretical approaches. Learners can improve their knowledge and skills like problem solving while acting in a real-world and a social-context. Five conditions of constructivist learning theory can enhance learning with AR:

- Learning within relevant environments
- Enable social interaction
- Provide multiple modes of representation
- Provide self-directed and active learning
- Support metacognitive strategies

AR allows also creating problem-based learning environments. Problems can here be solved with collaborative learning approaches like role-play or jigsaw. Another benefit is the possibility to provide multiple learning opportunities, like leaving the physical space, observe new content, manipulate and analyze objects (Dunleavy & Dede, 2014).

Klopfer and Sheldon (2010, p. 86) summarize the potential of AR as „(...)to enable students to see the world around them in new ways and engage with realistic issues in a context with which the students are already connected." Dunleavy and Dede (2014) pointed out that there are typically two versions of AR possible for educators. Location-based AR is linked to GPS-enabled smartphones or devices, which locate the learner in a specific location. Then a multimedia content is displayed which provides relevant information's about this spot. An example for such a location-based is environment is Wikitude (Yuen et al., 2011), which provides specific data about sights in a city or any other place (e.g., about a specific habitat when passing by a specific tree). The other version is vision-based AR. To project the virtual information a trigger image/object is needed. When this image/object is scanned with a camera, virtual objects like text, sounds, videos, animations, 3D models or images appear. An example here is a trigger image near a tree which shows a 3D model of the structure when the camera is focused on it (Dunleavy & Dede, 2014). In this research also a vision-based AR learning environment will be discussed.

2. AR IN EDUCATION

2.1 Impact on Learning Effects

Research showed that AR could support learning in a more effective way than other technology enhanced environments. If content is represented as 3D learners can manipulate objects and handle information's in an interactive way (El Sayed, Zayed, & Sharawy, 2011). Collaborative AR applications can improve spatial abilities (Kaufmann & Schmalstieg, 2003; Kaufmann, Steinbugl, Dunser, & Gluck, 2005) and an authentic AR environment can help understanding dynamic models and complex causality (Rosenbaum, Klopfer, & Perry, 2007). The combination of visual and haptic experience makes AR interesting for the development of psychomotor-cognitive skills (Feng, Duh, & Billinghurst, 2008). For example, in clinical medicine an AR system collected data about learners' performance. Subsequently the system transformed the information's to visual and immediate feedback to support learners' psychomotoric skills (Kotranza, Lind, Pugh, & Lok, 2009). An AR game on science allows students to organize, search and evaluate data and educated their skills in navigating primary and secondary information's (Klopfer, 2008). Mathews (2010) describes a learning environment that helps students to navigate and participate in the digital media landscape by means of an AR simulation. Stanton et al. (2003) reported about AR in museum education and summarized that AR can contribute to student's understanding of history in an authentic way. Ferrer-Torregrosa et al. (2016) compared a video-supported learning scenario to an AR supported one in anatomy learning. The students learned about the muscles of the foot with videos or 3D models. The analysis of the survey indicated a more effective learning with the 3D graphics within the AR setting. Santos et al. (2016) designed a situated vocabulary learning content with ARToolKit (Kato & Billinghurst, 1999). Compared to a non-AR learning content no differences were found in a temporary post-test. A delayed test about vocabulary retention offered a bigger difference in favor of the AR condition.

Additionally to the improvement of content knowledge learning with AR can support collaboration, physical task performance and language learning (Radu, 2014).

2.2 Impact on Motivation

Several studies observed the influence of AR learning environments on students' motivation. Users showed a high enthusiasm while interacting with the AR experiences and reported a higher satisfaction compared to non-AR learning. Also the willing to repeat was higher within an AR setting even though it was more difficult than the offered non-AR environment (Radu, 2014). Santos et al. (2016) tested an AR model for vocabulary learning and found a positive impact on satisfaction and attention. Similar results have been detected by Freitas and Campos (2008), as they developed an AR learning system to teach the meanings of animal and wheeler words for 2nd grade students in Portugal. A visual art course about Italian Renaissance was realized with and without AR. The group learning with AR showed a moderately higher motivation compared to the non-AR learning group. Also an increased interest in and attention for the learning content has been found. Very important for the observed students was the control over the presented learning materials and the learner-centered tasks and activities, which made the whole experience more engaging for them (Di Serio, Ibáñez, & Kloos, 2013). An increase of interest has also been found by Sotiriou and Bogner (2008).

2.3 Limitations

If educators want to implement AR within their classrooms some issues have to be considered. From the technological perspective a device with camera and/or GPS is needed. Most of the applications are also addicted to Internet access. Also the instructional point of view must be considered and needs a change if AR is used in a learning process. A teacher-centered approach can hinder successful knowledge construction, thus a student-centered and explorative character of learning is necessary (Kerawalla, Luckin, Seljeflot, & Woolard, 2006; Wu, Wen-Yu Lee, Chang, & Liang, 2013). Important for teachers and lectures is the flexibility of the AR system. Many systems do not allow changes of the content therefore AR authoring tools are essential to regard the specific needs of the learners. Furthermore the use of AR can cause cognitive overload or the feeling of confusion because of the mixed perception of real and virtual environment (Wu et al., 2013). Attention tunneling, usability difficulties and learner differences are some other challenges to think about (Radu, 2014).

3. CASE STUDY AND RESEARCH QUESTIONS

Based on the findings of former research on learning with AR, this paper studies the impact of a mobile augmented reality learning environment on motivation, learning effects and cognitive load. Three research questions are posed:

First, the impact of the AR learning environment on the learners' motivation is explored. According to self-determination theory (Ryan & Deci, 2000a; 2000b), autonomy, competence and relatedness are the basic needs of humans. If these three needs are satisfied, our motivation to act is more intrinsic than extrinsic. This also applies to learning. Educators can design learning environments that take these needs into account. Free choice opportunities and direct feedback are just two ways for lecturers to support the feeling of autonomy and competence. Other indicators of intrinsic motivation are interest and enjoyment. Beside self-directed learning options Dunleavy and Dede (2014) point out that social experiences are important when learning with AR. Self-determination theory calls this a "social experience relatedness" which can be realized in every classroom when students are allowed to work together in teams. To examine intrinsic motivation the *Intrinsic Motivation Inventory* was designed (Ryan, 1982; Ryan, Mims, & Koestner, 1983). In this questionnaire participants report about interest/enjoyment, perceived competence, perceived choice and pressure/tension as indicators for intrinsic motivation. It is assumed, that the provided learning environment can promote intrinsic motivation by comparison with a more traditional classroom setting (e.g., teacher-centered teaching).

Second, to measure the learning success a pre-and post-test was generated. We assume that the AR learning environment combined with the offered tasks can support the facilitation of historical knowledge.

Third, there are also challenges and burdens when AR is used in classrooms. Dunleavy et al. (2009) covered that learning processes with AR can cause cognitive overload because of the complexity the technology and tasks bring along. According to the Cognitive Load Theory the design of the learning material has an impact on the extraneous cognitive load, which can hinder the learning process (Sweller, 2005). To evaluate the cognitive load within this AR environment an adapted version of the NASA Task Load Index (Hart & Staveland, 1988) is used. With a five-point rating scale the items task requirement, effort in understanding content, mental effort, effort in navigation and stress are self-reported. The students fill the questionnaire after interacting with the learning environment. It is expected that the learners did not experience a high level of cognitive load through the AR elements and the learning tasks.

4. METHOD

4.1 Design and Sample

For this research a two-hour history lesson for students of a secondary school in Vienna was designed as a mobile learning environment with augmented reality elements. Participants used their own smartphones and earphones to experience the contents. The topic of the lesson was "Witch tracing at the beginning of modern times". The design of the study is one-factorial with an experimental and a control group. The control group experienced a traditional classroom setting. A total of 23 learners, eight male and 15 female, participated in the AR group. In the control group 36 students, 21 female and 15 male participated. The average age in the AR group was 12.2 years (SD = 0.42), in the control group 14.74 years (SD = 2.01).

4.2 Procedure

At the beginning of the study, students installed the application *Aurasma* on their smartphones and entered it with a provided username and password. In teams of two they received a list of AR elements they had to completely check. On classroom wall there were trigger images placed by the teacher, every picture contained an AR element. Before the learning phase started a pre was administered. Subsequently, the learners moved around in the classroom and used the smartphones to turn the static pictures into animated ones. The static pictures were taken from diverse websites and all were under a creative commons or public domain license (e.g., a clip art visualization of a witch or the cover of the *malleus maleficarum).* Every trigger image provided a self-made whiteboard video that fitted exactly to the trigger. When the pupils focused their smartphones with the application on it, the images turned into the video. Every AR element (here: video) informed about specific subjects according to the topic of witch hunt. Every video offered a task for the pupils. One task, for example, was to analyze a historical picture about a witch trial. Another task was a rather closed task implemented within the learning application, for example a drag and drop quiz. At the end of the lessons the knowledge post test, the intrinsic motivation questionnaire and the NASA-Task Load Index questionnaire were applied. The intrinsic motivation questionnaire is an adapted German version of the *Intrinsic Motivation Inventory.* Wilde et al. (2009) found strong validity for the short scale of intrinsic motivation and recommended the scale for other learning scenarios. The questionnaire contains twelve items on five-point Likert-scales, three for every subscale (e.g., perceived choice).

The control group had a teacher-centered lesson. Here only the intrinsic motivation questionnaire was administered after the lesson to determine the motivational baseline.

5. RESULTS

The descriptive analysis of the short scale of intrinsic motivation and the NASA-Task Load Index were computed with SPSS Statistics 24. For the knowledge test every correct answer was rewarded with a point and an overall sum score was computed.

5.1 Motivation

Table 1 shows the descriptive results of the subscales assessing intrinsic motivation.

Table 1. Results of the Short Scale of Intrinsic Motivation – AR Group Compared to Control Group

Scale	AR Group		Control Group	
	Mean (SD)	*Cronbach's Alpha*	*Mean (SD)*	*Cronbach's Alpha*
Interest/Enjoyment	7.78 (1.86)	.83	5.09 (3.65)	.94
Perceived Competence	7.09 (1.16)	.52	5.39 (2.58)	.88
Perceived Choice	7.74 (1.57)	.71	2.72 (2.58)	.91
Pressure/Tension	2.04 (1.43)	.27	1.37 (1.31)	.48

The results in Table 1 show a high approval within the scales interest/enjoyment, perceived competence and perceived choice for the AR group, lower means for these scales have been found for the control group. These results tend to confirm the first research question. As a limitation the low value of *Cronbach's Alpha* (0.52) for the scale perceived competence within the AR group has to be mentioned. Thus, this sub-scale will be excluded from further discussion.

5.2 Learning Effects

In the pre knowledge test, students achieved 57 points (out of 184), i.e., 31% of the possible points. The results of the post-test reveal a difference of 64 points compared to the pre test. Students achieved here an average of 121 points (= 66%). Additionally a paired-samples t-test was conducted to compare the historical knowledge before and after the AR experience. There was a significant difference between the pre test scores (M=2.48, SD=1.2) and the post test scores (M=5.26, SD=1.1); $t(22)$=-9.45, $p = 0.000$.

5.3 Cognitive Load

The evaluation of the NASA Task Load Index tends to contradict the findings of Dunleavy et al. (2009). Table 2 shows the means for each item, *Cronbach's Alpha* for the whole questionnaire is 0.63. The answers ranged from 1 (= very) to 5 (= not at all).

Table 2. Results of the NASA Task Load Index

Item	*Mean*	*Standard Deviation*
Mental effort	2.30	1.22
Task requirement	3.26	1.14
Effort in understanding	4.30	1.02
Effort in navigation	4.22	0.99
Stress	4.52	0.99

The learners experienced approximately no stress or navigation problems within the mobile AR learning environment. Also the effort to understand the learning environment could be kept low. The offered tasks have been scored as mentally challenging, but as understandable and solvable.

6. SUMMARY AND DISCUSSION

AR as an educational trend is still not very common within classrooms. The rapid development of mobile devices (e.g., smartphones, tablets) made it possible for teachers and lecturers to integrate this technology in their teaching methods. In this study, AR elements have been offered to a history class while moving around on their own, experiencing a mobile and autonomous learning environment. The learner-centered approach is important when using AR for learning (Dunleavy & Dede, 2014). Benefits are autonomous learning and the feeling of competence. According to self-determination theory these perceptions within a learning environment can promote intrinsic motivation, ascertainable through interest/enjoyment, perceived choice and perceived competence (Ryan & Deci, 2000a; 2000b). Unbeneficial teacher-centered approaches can, however, hinder the learning success (Kerawalla et al., 2006). The results here show that learners rated the learning process as interesting, self-directed and perceived the feeling of competence. Compared to a non-AR and teacher-centered control group, the agreement for these elements of the self-determination theory was higher within the AR group. Therefore it can be stated that the AR learning environment as provided here was able to promote intrinsic motivation.

The influence of the environment on learning effects has been evaluated with a pre and post knowledge test. The scores in the post-test were much better (from 31% to 66%) than in the pre-test. A possible cognitive overload because of the AR learning was not detected.

Limitations of the study are the small sample size and the low internal consistency for the sub-scale of "Perceived Competence" within the AR group and the sub-scale "Pressure/Tension" for both groups.

Future research should also compare the facilitation of skills and knowledge between learning with and without AR. To summarize these findings, we argue that mobile learning environments with AR have a huge potential to motivate learners and to integrate mobile devices as trigger for self-directed learning processes. The latter is important for future generations of learners, because the availability and the use of such offerings will increase. Educators can act as role models here and show that the devices can also be used as learning tools. The benefits of AR are in the area of motivational support, the visualization of complex processes, and can help to foster the pedagogical shift from teaching to learning.

REFERENCES

Di Serio, Á., Ibáñez, M. B., & Kloos, C. D. (2013). Impact of an augmented reality system on students' motivation for a visual art course. *Computers & Education*, *68*, 586–596. https://doi.org/10.1016/j.compedu.2012.03.002

Dunleavy, M., & Dede, C. (2014). Augmented Reality Teaching and Learning. In J. M. Spector, M. D. Merrill, J. Elen, & M. J. Bishop (Hrsg.), *Handbook of Research on Educational Communications and Technology* (S. 735–745). New York, NY: Springer New York. https://doi.org/10.1007/978-1-4614-3185-5_59

Education Group. (2015). 4. Oö. Jugend-Medien-Studie 2015. Abgerufen von https://www.edugroup.at/innovation/forschung/jugend-medien-studie/detail/4-ooe-jugend-medien-studie-2015.html

El Sayed, N. A. M., Zayed, H. H., & Sharawy, M. I. (2011). ARSC: augmented reality student card - an augmented reality solution for the education field. *Computers & Education*, *56*(4), 1045–1061.

European Union (Hrsg.). (2015). *Being young in Europe today*. Luxembourg: Publications Office of the European Union.

Feng, Z., Duh, H. B.-L., & Billinghurst, M. (2008). Trends in augmented reality tracking, interaction and display: A review of ten years of ISMAR. Gehalten auf der 7th IEEE/ACM international symposium on mixed and augmented reality (ISMAR), Cambridge, UK. https://doi.org/http://dx.doi.org/10.1109/ismar.2008.4637362

Ferrer-Torregrosa, J., Jimenez-Rodriguez, M. A., Torralba-Estelles, J., Garzon-Farinos, F., Perez-Bermejo, M., & Fernandez-Ehrling, N. (2016). Distance learning ects and flipped classroom in the anatomy learning: comparative study of the use of augmented reality, video and notes. *BMC Medical Education*. https://doi.org/10.1186/s12909-016-0757-3

Freitas, R., & Campos, P. (2008). SMART: a System of augmented reality for teachning 2nd grade students. In *Proceedings of the 22nd British Computer Society Conference on Human-Computer-Interaction (HCI 2008)* (S. 27–30). Liverpool John Moores University, UK.

Hart, S. G., & Staveland, L. E. (1988). Development of NASA-TLX (Task Load Index): Results of experimental and theoretical research. In P. A. Hancock & N. Meshkati (Hrsg.), *Human mental workload* (S. 139–183). Amsterdam: North Holland.

Johnson, L., Levine, A., Smith, R., & Stone, S. (2010). *The 2010 Horizon Report*. Austin, Texas: The New Media Consortium. Abgerufen von https://www.nmc.org/pdf/2010-Horizon-Report.pdf

Kato, H., & Billinghurst, M. (1999). Marker tracking and hmd calibration for a video-based augmented reality conferencing system. In *Proceedings of IEEE and ACM International Workshop on Augmented Reality* (S. 85–94). San Francisco, CA.

Kaufmann, H., & Schmalstieg, D. (2003). Mathematics and geometry education with collaborative augmented reality. *Computers & Graphics*, *27*(3), 339–345. https://doi.org/http://dx.doi.org/ 10.1016/s0097-8493(03)00028-1

Kaufmann, H., Steinbugl, K., Dunser, A., & Gluck, J. (2005). General training of spatial abilities by geometry education in augmented reality. *Annual Review of CyberTherapy and Telemedicine. A Decade of VR*, *3*, 65–76.

Kerawalla, L., Luckin, R., Seljeflot, S., & Woolard, A. (2006). ''Making it real'': exploring the potential of augmented reality for teaching primary school science. *Virtual Reality*, (10), 163–174.

Klopfer, E. (2008). *Augmented learning: Research and design of mobile educational games*. Cambridge: MIT Press.

Klopfer, E., & Sheldon, J. (2010). Augmenting your own reality: student authoring of science-based augmented reality games. *New Directions for Youth Development*, *128*, 85–94.

Kotranza, A., Lind, D. S., Pugh, C. M., & Lok, B. (2009). Real-time in-situ visual feedback of task performance in mixed environments for learning joint psychomotorcognitive tasks. In *8th IEEE international symposium on mixed and augmented reality (ISMAR)* (S. 125–134). Orlando, FL. https://doi.org/http://dx.doi.org/10. 1109/ISMAR.2009.5336485

Mathews, J. M. (2010). Using a studio-based pedagogy to engage students in the design ot mobile-based media. *English Teaching: Practice and Critique*, *9*(1), 87–102.

Medienpädagogischer Forschungsverbund Südwest (mpfs) (Hrsg.). (2016). JIM 2016. Jugend, Information, (Multi-) Media. Basisstudie zum Medienumgang 12- bis 19-Jähriger in Deutschland. Retrieved from https://www.mpfs.de/fileadmin/files/Studien/JIM/2016/JIM_Studie_2016.pdf

Milgram, P., & Kishino, F. (1994). A Taxonomy of Mixed Reality Visual Displays. *IEICE Transactions on Information System*, *77*(12), 1321–1329.

Radu, I. (2014). Augmented reality in education: a meta-review and cross-media analysis. *Personal and Ubiquitous Computing*, *18*(6), 1533–1543. https://doi.org/10.1007/s00779-013-0747-y

Rosenbaum, E., Klopfer, E., & Perry, J. (2007). On location learning: authentic applied science with networked augmented realities. *Journal of Science Education and Technology*, *16*(1), 31–45. https://doi.org/http://dx.doi.org/10.1007/s10956-006-9036-0.

Ryan, R. M. (1982). Control and information in the intrapersonal sphere: An extension of cognitive evaluation theory. *Journal of Personality and Social Psychology*, *43*, 450–461.

Ryan, R., Mims, V., & Koestner, R. (1983). Relation of reward contingency and interpesonal context to intrinsic motivation: A review and test using cognitive evaluation theory. *Journal of Personality and Social Psychology*, *45*, 736–750.

Ryan, R. M., & Deci, E. L. (2000a). Intrinsic and Extrinsic Motivations: Classic Definitions and New Directions. Contemporary Educational Psychology, 25, 54–67. https://doi.org/doi:10.1006/ceps.1999.1020

Ryan, R. M., & Deci, E. L. (2000b). Self-Determination Theory and the Facilitation of Intrinsic Motivation, Social Development, and Well-Being. American Psychologist, 55(1), 68–78.

Santos, M. E. C., in Wold Lübke, A., Taketomi, T., Yamamoto, G., Rodrigo, M. M. T., Sandor, C., & Kato, H. (2016). Augmented reality as multimedia: the case for situated vocabulary learning. *Research and Practice in Technology Enhanced Learning*. https://doi.org/10.1186/s41039-016-0028-2

Smith, C. (2018). 85 Incredible Pokemon Go Statistics and Facts (January 2018). Retrieved from https://expandedramblings.com/index.php/pokemon-go-statistics/

Sotiriou, S., & Bogner, F. X. (2008). Visualizing the invisible: augmented reality as an innovative science education scheme. *Advanced Science Letters*, *1*, 114–122.

Stanton, D., O'Malley, C., Huing, K., Fraser, M., & Benford, S. (2003). Situating historical events through mixed reality. In B. Wasson, S. Ludvigsen, & U. Hoppe (Hrsg.), *Designing for Change in Networked Learning Environments* (S. 293–302). Dordrecht: Kluwer Academic Publishers.

Sweller, J. (2005). The redundancy principle in multimedia learning. In R. E. Mayer (Hrsg.), *The Cambridge Handbook of Multimedia Learning* (S. 159–167). Cambridge: University Press.

Wilde, M., Bätz, K., Kovaleva, A., & Urhahne, D. (2009). Überprüfung einer Kurzskala intrinsischer Motivation (KIM). *Zeitschrift für Didaktik der Naturwissenschaften*, *15*, 31–45.

Wu, H.-K., Wen-Yu Lee, S., Chang, H.-Y., & Liang, J.-C. (2013). Current status, opportunities and challenges of augmented reality in education. *Computers & Education*, *62*, 41–49.

Yuen, S. C.-Y., Yaoyuneyong, G., & Johnson, E. (2011). Augmented Reality: An Overview and Five Directions for AR in Education. *Journal of Educational Technology Development and Exchange*, *4*(1). https://doi.org/10.18785/jetde.0401.10

PERSONALIZING LEARNING WITH MOBILE TECHNOLOGY IN SECONDARY EDUCATION

Wilfried Admiraal[1], Liesbeth Kester[2], Caressa Janssen[2], Mario de Jonge[2], Monika Louws[2], Lysanne Post[1] and Ditte Lockhorst[3]

[1]*Leiden University Graduate School of Teaching, Kollfpad 1, 2233 BN Leiden, The Netherlands*

[2]*Department of Education, Faculty of Social and Behavioural Sciences, Utrecht University, Heidelberglaan 1, 3584 CS Utrecht, The Netherlands*

[3]*Oberon Research and Consultancy, Slachtstraat 12, 3512 BC Utrecht, The Netherlands*

ABSTRACT

Personalizing learning with technology in secondary schools might be a way to diffuse innovations in both technology and education at the same time. In the current study, personalizing learning with technology is studied from three perspectives: teacher, learner and technology. Data about the implementation and evaluation of the interventions in school were gathered by interviews with teachers and students, teacher logbooks and teacher and student questionnaires. Moreover, test and questionnaire data were collected on achievement, school motivation and self-regulation of more than 4800 students. Effects of 35 personalizing learning interventions with mobile technology in 27 secondary schools in the Netherlands were examined. Generally, three types of personalizing learning interventions seem to increase student achievement: 1) a comprehensive approach across the school organization and programs; 2) personalizing learning with teachers differentiating either convergently or divergently, and 3) learner-control interventions in which students have control of surface aspects such as pacing, sequencing and practicing within limits set by teachers or programs. Too much emphasis on learner control instead of teacher control does not seem to benefit cognitive outcomes. The conclusions with respect to students' motivation and self-regulation are less clear-cut.

KEYWORDS

Personalizing Learning, Mobile Technology, Secondary Education, Learner Control, Teacher Control

1. INTRODUCTION

The increasing use of technology in society in combination with attention for constructivist learning orientations requires secondary schools to change to more suitable learning and teaching practices. Yet innovations in teaching with technology have entered the school sporadically: most classroom teachers use the technology to do what they always have done and choose those activities that will help them accommodate their own perspectives on teaching and learning (Liu, 2011). Many schools have integrated laptops and other digital tools into daily practice, but it is unclear if those devices are being used in ways that best maximize their potential (Greaves, et al. 2010). Despite increased prevalence and use of computers in schools, research on the effectiveness has yielded mixed results (Machin et al., 2007). This problem motivated the Dutch government to setup a tender to stimulate secondary schools to diffuse innovations in both technology and education at the same time. Schools were invited to submit their proposals to receive funds to develop and implement various school-based innovations on personalizing learning with technology. The objective of this study is to provide insights into the effects of the various approaches to personalizing learning with technology in secondary schools.

2. PERSONALIZING LEARNING WITH TECHNOLOGY

In contrast to traditional classroom instruction based on teacher-centered approaches, the use of technology allows educators to empower students to take control of their own learning. Learner control is the degree to which students can direct their own learning experiences (Shyu and Brown, 1992), including path, pace, and instructional approach. Such control could include choices at the curriculum level (sequence of instructional materials), the opportunity to choose how long to focus on a learning objective (pacing), or the ability to select and sequence a variety of review strategies (choice of practice items or amount of review material; Niemiec et al., 1996). As a result of making their own instructional decisions while learning, students would be more likely to explore tactics for different situations. In other words, students would learn how to better learn in the future. This belief is still prevalent today: many educators agree that personalizing learning is a key priority (Marshall et al., 2009). Although giving a student control over their learning has theoretical and intuitive appeal, its effects seem neither powerful nor consistent in the empirical literature base. A meta-analysis of 18 studies by Karich, et al (2014) .found - consistent with previous research (Niemiec et al., 1996)- near zero effects for all components of instruction (pacing, time, sequence, practice, review). Thus, there does not seem to be an advantage to giving the learner control over any particular instructional component. Yet programs that offered a comprehensive approach had larger effects than practice-based applications, suggesting that educators should consider more comprehensive programs that provide the learner with a unique experience beyond what is commonly received in their classroom. Moreover, studies with behavioral variables had larger effects than measures of academic achievement, which suggests that providing learner control within educational technology may enhance engagement, but may not increase student skills.

In personalizing learning with technology, learner-control is not the only dimension to be considered; technology in itself can control students' learning process to some extent (Vandewaetere et al., 2011; Karich et al., 2014). Therefore, we distinguish between three actors influencing student learning: learner, teacher and technology.

Personalizing learning from the perspective of *learner* includes learning across five aspects of program design: pacing, sequencing, time allotment, choice of practice items, and choice of review items (Niemiec et al., 1996). Pacing indicates how quickly teachers present the content to the learner. Sequencing denotes how teachers order information, such as when particular objectives or tasks are presented in relation to other objectives or tasks. Time allotment referred to the amount of time teachers give to the learner to complete the content in its entirety for a particular session. Practice items indicate the type and amount of practice on a particular objective, whereas review items are typically presented at the end of a lesson as a check for understanding. As mentioned above, effects of learner control are ambiguous with small effects mostly found on learners' motivation and learning behavior (Corbalan et al., 2006; Karich et al, 2014). Yet just adding learner control to an existing learning environment does not always lead to learner behavior regulating their learning (Azevedo et al., 2008); students need some guidance or practice in learner control to increase their regulative behavior (Authors, under review).

Personalizing learning from the perspective of *teachers* means that teachers determine what learners need to learn based on learner characteristics and adapt the content and their way of teaching (Tomlinson et al., 2003). Teachers analyze learner characteristics such as achievement, motivation and learning behavior in order to adapt their teaching to what is needed for individuals or groups of students. Although research on personalizing learning from the teacher perspective has a long history (e.g., Snow, 1992), studies show ambiguous findings with respect to effects on cognitive, affective and behavioral measures (Vandewaetere et al., 2011). Personalizing learning from the perspective of *both teacher and learners* is called shared-control (Corbalan et al., 2006). This model combines the two approaches to personalizing learning: Program-controlled instruction, in which an instructional agent (e.g., computer, teacher) makes instructional decisions and learner-controlled instruction, in which learners makes such decisions.

Personalizing learning from the perspective of *technology* refer to the adaptive qualities of the technology that is used to support teaching and learning (Vandewaetere et al., 2011). Empirical findings suggest that the use of adaptive technology in computer-based assessments has a positive impact on students' achievements in various school subjects (e.g. Faber, Luyten and Visscher, 2017), but not all findings are consistent. Findings about the frequency of using these adaptive environments suggest that greater usage of the system by both teacher and students is associated with better student performance.

3. METHOD

The purpose of the current study is to provide insights into the effects of personalizing learning with technology in secondary education, from the teacher, learner and technology perspective. The following research question guided our study:

"What are the effects of personalizing learning with technology on students' achievement, motivation for school and self-regulating behavior?"

3.1 Research Design and Participants

In total, data were collected about 42 interventions in 34 secondary schools (with 6045 students). Seven schools (with one intervention each) were excluded from the final analyses as these school interventions could not be categorized as focused on either teacher, learner or technology. So, data included in this study are from 35 interventions in 27 secondary schools (with 4808 students). The research design mostly included a setup of an experimental condition (the intervention on personalizing learning with technology) and a comparison condition. The latter can be students in another, but similar school (SCHOOL), in the same school, but in another year group (YEAR), in the same school and year group, but in another class (CLASS), in the same class (STUDENT) or the same student for another school subject (WITHIN). In some cases, no reference condition was used (ONE-GROUP). In all cases, a pre-test post-test design has been used. For an overview of the research design of each intervention, see Table 1, 2, 3 and 4. The research was carried out following the guidelines for research ethics and integrity of Utrecht University.

3.2 Interventions on Personalizing Learning with Technology

Interventions in personalizing learning with technology were categorized into three clusters: 1) teacher perspective, 2) learner perspective and 3) technology perspective. Mobile technology (laptops, tablets, smart phones) was used in combination with an electronic learning environment supported by different Learning Management Systems.

Personalizing learning from a *teacher perspective* can be clusters at two levels of differentiating between individual students: 1) at the school level with different streams of schooling like the Dutch system of secondary education, which is called external differentiation, and 2) at the class level which is called internal differentiation (Berben and Van Teesling, 2014). The interventions examined in this study refer to internal differentiation. Internal differentiation by a teacher means that teachers monitor the content, the process and the assessment of student learning based on ability, motivation and learning behavior of their students (Tomlinson et al., 2003). If the learning goal is the same for the whole group of students, internal differentiation is called convergent differentiation; if learning goals within a group of students are different, international differentiation is called divergent differentiation. Finally, convergent differentiation (having the same learning goal for all students) requires thoughts about group constellation during group work with either students with the same ability level (homogeneous groups) or students with different ability levels (heterogeneous groups). In sum, personalizing learning from a teacher perspective have been categorized as 1) divergent (DIV), 2) convergent with homogeneous groups (CON-HO), or 3) convergent with heterogeneous groups (CON-HE).

Personalizing learning from a *learner perspective* refers to the degree students can control program aspects such as pacing, sequencing, time allotment, practicing and reviewing (Karich et al., 2014). A low degree of learner control (LOW) means that learners controlled pacing, whereas other program aspects have been set. High degree of learner control (FULL) means that all or almost all program aspects were controlled by the learner. In-between position (MODERATE) on the degree of control means that students controlled at least pacing, combined with some other program and task aspects, mostly within the limits set by the teacher or program. Low learner control was frequently combined with learner control of surface task characteristics (e.g., various tasks at the same ability level or various forms of testing the same content); full learner control was frequently combined with learner control of structural task characteristics (e.g., various tasks at different ability levels or various sources with variety of information; Corbalan et al., 2011).

Personalizing learning from a *technology perspective* refers to students completing computer-based assessments with either adaptive technology (ADAPTIVE) or non-adaptive technology (NON-ADAPTIVE).

3.3 Measures

Data about the implementation and evaluation of the interventions in school were gathered by interviews with teachers and students, teacher logbooks and teacher and student questionnaires. Although not all these were collected in all cases, in each case evaluation data have been collected from both teachers and students.

Student achievement was measured by student scores on regular exams of the particular school subject related to the interventions.

Student motivation was measured by the Situational Motivation Scale (SiMS; Guay et al., 2000). This questionnaire contains 16 items that are focused on why students are currently engaged in a particular activity concerning a school subject that is object of study. The items are clustered into four scales: 1) intrinsic motivation (example item: "because I think that this activity is interesting"), 2) identified motivation (example item: "because I am doing it for my own good"), 3) external regulation (example item: "because I am supposed to do it", and 4) A-motivation (example item: "I do this activity, but I am not sure if it is worth it"). Students scored each item on a 5-point Likert type scale with 1= does not apply at all and 5= does apply to a great extent. All scales showed satisfying reliability.

Student self-regulation was measured by a questionnaire with 32 items developed by Vandevelde et al. (2013). These 32 items can be clustered into 6 aspects of self-regulation: 1) task orientation (example item: "Before I start my schoolwork, I read the instructions carefully"), 2) planning (example item: "Before I start my schoolwork, I decide what to do first and what later", 3) Persistence (example item: "I carry on until I finish my schoolwork"). 4) self-efficacy regulation (example item: "I am good at connecting new things to what I already know"), 5) product evaluation (example item: "After finishing my school work I go over my answers again", and 6) process evaluation (example item: "I ask myself: 'Have I done it the right way?'). Students scored each item on a 5-point Likert type scale with 1= does not apply at all and 5= does apply to a great extent. All scales showed satisfying reliability.

3.4 Analyses

In the designs with a comparison group, analyses of covariance have been used with the both conditions as factors and one the effect measures (achievement, motivation or self-regulation) as dependent variable. Pre-test scores on the effect measures and background information of the students such as gender, age, and ability level (if available) were used as covariates. In cases of a one-group-only design, t-tests have been performed on the pre-test and post-test scores.

4. FINDINGS

4.1 Personalizing Learning from a Teacher Perspective

The findings for the cluster of interventions that focus on a teacher perspective on personalizing learning are summarized in Table 1.Schools differed in the way they implemented personalizing learning from a teachers perspective with convergent differentiation in seven schools, divergent differentiation in three schools and a combination of both types of differentiation in one school. In all interventions, teachers designed their own educational materials (sometimes together with colleagues), provided instruction and guided the learning process of their students. Students worked individually or in small groups on assignments with guidance of their teacher (all interventions with convergent differentiation and the one of school 18).

In general, the effects of the interventions on student achievement, motivation and self-regulation are mixed. The effects on student achievement are positive in all cases, with divergent as well as convergent interventions. No achievement effects were measured of the interventions with convergent differentiation with homogeneous groups. The findings with respect to students' motivation are difficult to interpret, although interventions with convergent differentiation with homogeneous groups seem to lead to negative effects. In school 17, the degree in which student groups were guided by the teachers varied a lot. Interventions with solely divergent differentiation do not show an effect on student motivation. The findings with respect to student self-regulation only show one positive effect, in school 11. Comparing both schools in which all three effects have been measured (school 10, DIV, and school 11, CON-HE) the intervention in school 11 shows effects on all three measures. The main difference between both interventions is the way of personalizing learning. In school 10, poor-performing students received additional instruction and high-performing students additional tasks; in school 11, students choose their own pacing and sequencing of materials sharing the same learning goal.

Table 1. Personalizing Learning from a Teacher Perspective

School	**Research Design**	$N_{students}$	**Personalizing learning**	**Technology**	**Achievement**	**Motivation**	**Self-regulation**
8	CLASS	362	CON-HE	iPads	n.a.	0	0
9a	CLASS	114	CON-HE	iPads	+	0	n.a.
10	CLASS	106	DIV	iPads	+	0	0
11	CLASS	50	CON-HE	iPads	+	+	+
12	YEAR	104	CON-HE	iPads	n.a.	n.a.	0
13	CLASS	92	DIV	iPads	+	0	n.a.
14	CLASS	563	BOTH-HO	iPads	n.a.	+	n.a.
15	CLASS	234	CON-HO	Laptops	n.a.	+/-	n.a.
16	YEAR	195	CON-HE	Laptops	n.a.	-	n.a.
17	ONE-GROUP	257	CON-HO	No	n.a.	-	n.a.
18a	ONE-GROUP	34	DIV	iPads	n.a.	0	0

Note. 0= no effect; += positive effect, -= negative effect, +/-= mixed and n.a.= not applicable (i.e .not measured). For categories of the research design and personalized learning interventions, see Method section.

4.2 Personalizing Learning from a Learner Perspective

The findings for the cluster of interventions that focus on a learner perspective on personalizing learning are summarized in Table 2.Schools differed in the degree learners controlled aspects of the program and learning tasks. In two interventions (22, 23), students only controlled pacing. In four interventions (26a, 26b, 28, 29b) students controlled pacing and sequencing of the various assignments. In one intervention (20), pacing was combined with a choice of practicing items. All these interventions were categorized as low learner control. All interventions coded as moderate combined learner control of pacing with other aspects, without learner control of structural program aspects. The exception was intervention 11, in which students could choose between tasks with different functionalities (memorizing, analyzing, understanding). Finally, all other interventions were categorized as full control with learner control of most program and tasks aspects.

With respect to the effect on achievement four significant effects were found; two in interventions categorized as moderate and two in other interventions that –although not categorized as such- resembles the moderate ones. More significant effects were found with respect to student motivation, negative, positive and ambiguous, and spread over all kinds of interventions. Finally, with respect to self-regulation, only one positive effect was found (school 22, categorized as low).

Table 2. Personalizing learning from a learner perspective

School	Research design	$N_{students}$	Personalizing learning	Technology	Achievement	Motivation	Self-regulation
19	YEAR	170	FULL	BYOD	n.a.	-	0
20	STUDENT	234	LOW	BYOD	n.a.	n.a.	0
21	CLASS	63	FULL	Laptop	n.a.	-	0
22	WITHIN	111	LOW	No	n.a.	+/-	+
23	WITHIN	37	LOW	iPads	n.a.	0	0
24a	YEAR	315[1]	MODERATE	iPad	0	0	0
24b	YEAR	241[1]	FULL	iPad	+	-	0
25	WITHIN	223	FULL	Laptops	n.a.	+	n.a.
26a	CLASS	240[2]	LOW	Laptops	+	0	n.a.
26b	CLASS	240[2]	LOW	Laptops	0	0	n.a.
26c	CLASS	240[2]	MODERATE	Laptops	0	0	n.a.
27	CLASS	86	MODERATE	BYOD	n.a.	0	0
28	YEAR	426	LOW	BYOD	n.a.	0	0
18b	ONE-GROUP	34[4]	MODERATE	iPad	n.a.	+	0
29a	YEAR	123[3]	MODERATE	iPad	+	+	+/-
29b	YEAR	123[3]	LOW	iPad	0	+	+/-
9b	CLASS	106	FULL	CC	0	+	n.a.
30	CLASS	173	MODERATE	CC	+	+	n.a.
31	YEAR	157	FULL	BYOD	n.a.	0	0

Note. [1] the same control group with 176 students; [2] sharing the same 240 students; [3] sharing the same 123 students; [4] sharing the same 34 students with intervention 18a; BYOD = Bring your own device; CC= Computer Classroom; 0= no effect; += positive effect, -= negative effect, +/-= mixed and n.a.= not applicable (i.e .not measured). For categories of the research design and personalized learning interventions, see Method section.

4.3 Personalizing Learning from a Technology Perspective

The interventions with respect to personalizing learning by technology refer to the use of computer-based assessment as a support of students' learning processes. In the interventions, all aspects of a curriculum (pacing, sequencing, time allotment, practice items and review items) were personalized, either by the technology or the learner, as part of regular classes in a particular topic. Students can choose how much effort they put into completing assignments, and technology determines the other parts - if adaptive technology has been used. Adaptive technology also provided students with feedback about their performance (embedded analytics). In intervention of school 32 and 34a, non-adaptive technology has been used. In intervention 33, 34b and 34c, student receive feedback about their performance (embedded analytics) and teachers are able to get an overview of their students' performance (extracted analytics). In school 33, in-between feedback for students included information about the correct response as well as information on what students still had to learn. In intervention 34 and 36a, only information after completion of the computer-based assessments was available.

No effects on student achievements were measured as none of the school intended to use these computer-based assessment to improve student achievement (see Table 3). With respect to student motivation, no effects or negative effects were found. These negative effects coincide with a low satisfaction of the students with the intervention: for both interventions, students were more satisfied with the regular classes on that topic; they did not see the additional value of practicing with computer-based assessments. With respect to self-regulation, only two significant effects are found: one positive and one negative in school 34. In intervention 34b, teachers use extracted analyses for their classroom instruction with various forms of feedback and instruction (plenary, small-group and individual settings); in intervention 34c. students have the possibility to ask teachers for feedback - which they generally did not do.

Table 3. Personalizing Learning from a Technology Perspective

School	Research design	$N_{students}$	Personalizing learning	Technology	Achievement	Motivation	Self-regulation
32	YEAR	133	NON-ADAPTIVE	iPad	n.a.	0	0
33	STUDENTt	83	ADAPTIVE	Mixed	n.a.	-	0
34a	YEAR	77	NON-ADAPTIVE	Mixed	n.a.	-	0
34b	ONE-GROUP	46	ADAPTIVE	Laptop	n.a.	0	+
34c	ONE-GROUP	52	ADAPTIVE	Laptop	n.a.	0	-

Note. Mixed= students complete assignments on paper and on their laptop or tablet; 0= no effect; += positive effect, -= negative effect, +/-= mixed and n.a.= not applicable (i.e .not measured). For categories of the research design and personalized learning interventions, see Method section.

5. CONCLUSION

The evaluation of personalizing learning interventions in 27 schools from three perspectives (teacher, learner and technology) leads to a number of conclusions and practical implications. Generally, three types of personalizing learning interventions seem to increase student achievement: 1) a comprehensive approach across the school organization and programs; 2) personalizing learning with teachers differentiating either convergently or divergently, and 3) learner-control interventions in which students have control of surface aspects such as pacing, sequencing and practicing within limits set by teachers or program. Too much emphasis on learner control instead of teacher control does not seem to benefit cognitive outcomes. The non-linear relationship between the degree of learner control and cognitive outcomes might also be an explanation for empirical evidence in other studies (Karich et al., 2014).

The conclusions with respect to student motivation are less clear-cut. Similar interventions, either teacher- or learner-controlled, led to different effects. One explanation could be the relationship between learners' autonomy, competence and relatedness influencing student motivation as indicated in the self-determination theory (Ryan and Deci, 2000). Providing students with control of program and task aspects should probably combined with differentiating between students who differ in competence.

With respect to students' self-regulation, only a few effects were found. We provide two explanations for this lack of effects. First, the interventions examined in this study might be too much focused on either teacher control or learner-control; a more balanced approach of personalizing learning might be more effective for students' self-regulative skills. Secondly, the interventions of this study were not focused on increasing students' self-regulation in particular. A more comprehensive approach in which a broach range of metacognitive skills of students are addressed, might lead to more positive effects (Authors., under review).

A final critical reflection refers to the variety of the interventions examined in the current study. Even interventions that are similar in the way learner or teacher control was implemented vary on all kinds of program and task details, the length of an intervention, and the range of implementation. More research on underlying mechanisms of the interventions is necessary to provide a deeper understanding of possible benefits of personalizing learning in secondary education.

ACKNOWLEDGEMENT

Funding: This work was supported by the Dutch Foundation for Scientific Research (NWO), department of Educational Research (NRO), grant number 405-15-823.

REFERENCES

Authors. (under review).

Azevedo, R. et al., 2008. Why is Externally-Facilitated Regulated Learning more Effective than Self-regulated Learning with Hypermedia? *Educational Technology Research and Development*, Vol. 56, No. 1, pp 45-72.

Berben, M. and Van Teeseling, M., 2014. *Differentiëren is te Leren! Omgaan met Verschillen in het Voortgezet Onderwijs.* [Differentiating can be Learned]. CPS, Amersfoort, the Netherlands.

Corbalan, G. et al., 2006. Towards a Personalized Task Selection Model with Shared Instructional Control. *Instructional Science,* Vol. 34, No. 5, pp. 399-422.

Corbalan, G., et al., 2011. Learner-controlledSelection of Tasks with Different Surface and Structural Features: Effects on Transfer and Efficiency. *Computers in Human Behavior*, Vol. 27, No. 1, pp. 76-81.

Faber, J.M. et al., 2017. The Effects of a Digital Formative Assessment Tool on Mathematics Achievement and Student Motivation: Results of a Randomized Experiment. *Computers & Education*, Vol. 106, No. March 2017, pp. 83-96.

Greaves, T. et al, 2010. *The Technology Factor: Nine Keys to Student Achievement and Cost-effectiveness*. Market Data Retrieval, Chicago, IL.

Guay, F., et al., 2000. On the Assessment of Situational Intrinsic and Extrinsic Motivation: the Situational Motivation Scale (SIMS). *Motivation and Emotion*, Vol. 24, No. 3, pp. 175-213.

Karich, A.C. et al., 2014. Updated Meta-analysis of Learner Control within Educational Technology. *Review of Educational Research*, Vol. 84, No. 3, pp. 392-410.

Liu, S-H., 2011. Factors Related to Pedagogical Beliefs of Teachers and Technology Integration. *Computers & Education*, Vol. 56, No. 4, pp. 1012-1022.

Machin, S. et al., 2007. New Technology in Schools: Is There a Payoff? *Economic Journal*, Vol. 117, No. 522, pp. 1145–1167.

Marshall, H. et al., 2009. *Harnessing Technology Schools Survey 2009: Data Report—Part 1, Descriptive Analysis*. Becta, Coventry, UK.

Niemiec et al., 1996. Learner-control Effects: A Review of Reviews and a Meta-analysis. *Journal of Educational Computing Research*, Vol. 15, No. 2, pp. 157–174.

Ryan, R.M. and Deci, E.L., 2000. Intrinsic and Extrinsic Motivations: Classic Definitions and New Directions. *Contemporary Educational Psychology*, Vol. 25, No. 1, pp. 54-67.

Shyu, H.Y. and Brown, S.W., 1992. Learner Control versus Program Control in Interactive Videodisc Instruction: What are the Effects in Procedural Learning? *International Journal of Instructional Media*, Vol. 19, No. 3, pp/ 85–96.

Snow, R.E., 1992. Aptitude Theory: Yesterday, Today, and Tomorrow. *Educational Psychologist*, Vol. 27, No. 1, pp. 5-32.

Tomlinson, C.A. et al.,2003. Differentiating Instruction in Response to Student Readiness, Interest, and Learning Profile in Academically Diverse Classrooms: A Review of Literature. *Journal for the Education of the Gifted*, Vol. 27, No. 2-3, pp. 119-145.

Vandevelde, S. et al., 2013. Measuring the Complexity of Upper Primary School Children's Selfregulated Learning: A Multi-component Approach. *Contemporary Educational Psychology*, Vol. 38, No. 4, pp. 407-425.

Vandewaetere, M. et al, 2011. The Contribution of Learner Characteristics in the Development of Computer-based Adaptive Learning Environments. *Computers in Human Behavior*, Vol. 27, No. 1, pp. 118-130.

IDENTIFICATION OF THE PARAMETERS CONCERNING YOUNG ADULTS' TAKING EPISTEMIC RISKS IN THEIR SOCIAL MEDIA POSTS WITH ACADEMIC CONTENT

Prof. Remzi Y. Kıncal[1], Asst. Prof. Osman Yılmaz Kartal[2] and Asst. Prof. Akan Deniz Yazgan[2]
[1]*Atatürk University, Erzurum, Turkey*
[2]*Çanakkale Onsekiz Mart University, Çanakkale, Turkey*

ABSTRACT

The present study aims to identify and investigate the parameters of taking academic epistemic risks concerning undergraduate young adults who are considered to use social media more frequently than any other users. The study was carried out following a mixed methodology. The study observes the principles of exploratory sequential design of the mixed method. In an exploratory mixed study, initially a theoretical proposition is obtained through a qualitative methodology; then this proposition is tested with a quantitative method. A case study as the qualitative part was conducted over 15 university students who use social media. As a result of the qualitative study, the parameters which were discovered to exert effects on young adults' epistemic risk taking in their social media posts with academic content were identified. A survey research study was carried out with a measurement tool developed by the researchers to assess the obtained parameters. By means of the survey performed over 215 undergraduates, the parameters of epistemic risk were tested. There are individual- and environment-related parameters affecting young adults' taking academic epistemic risk on social media. It was found out from the analyses of these parameters that the parameters knowledgeability, academic knowledgeability, and ethics have direct effects of academic epistemic risk taking. It was also revealed that the parameters self-esteem, responsibility, educational background, and virtual social capital are potentially effective.

KEYWORDS

Epistemic Risk, Epistemic Uncertainty, Young Adults, Social Media, Education, Academic Content

1. INTRODUCTION

When the 21st century's patterns of behavior are taken into account, it can be realized that the pattern of behavior apparently differs from the one in the previous centuries: humans' hunger for knowledge and efforts to suppress this hunger (Gore, 1998; Gupta and Govindarajan, 2000). The interaction and interdependence of the person seeking solutions to this hunger problem have not been so functional and qualified as well as so oppressive and unqualified throughout human history. When the culture of human interaction with information is examined, it is observed that the evolution of technology creates a multidimensional structure in which micro-cultures are formed, opportunities of globalization are spread, and the pluralism and democracy are sustained. Web2.0 technologies, which mediate this interaction, also provide a network of opportunities by offering numerous cultural backgrounds. In view of this cultural background, people in the 21st century display an addiction/preference that spread their social media habits every passing hour assuming the role of consumer, producer, and prosumer (Ritzer, Dean & Jurgenson, 2012; Ritzer and Jurgenson, 2010). This interaction background (Web2.0 platforms) creates an undeniable contribution to the level of information literacy of individuals, creating an educational opportunity that have not been able to be realized up to now in the context of equal opportunity in the history scene. However, these Web 2.0 platforms are becoming a unique tool for epistemic oppression in dualist epistemological belief cultures where dependency cultures dominate (Dotson, 2014; Fricker, 1999; Labbas, 2013). In this framework, the question of how these two extremes (epistemic freedom-epistemic oppression) can emerge on a shared ground is highlighted. The premise and essential tool that provide opportunities for individuals to move from oppression to freedom is epistemic risk. Epistemic risk is the individual's decision about right or wrong when there is uncertainty. Therefore, it is an attempt to end epistemic oppression and enrich the epistemic freedom base (Riggs, 2008; Simon, 2008; Velleman, 1989). In this educational space (social media platforms) where freedom-oppression conflicts are experienced, users have the opportunity to take epistemic risk through social, cultural, entertainment, political, academic and similar contents. However, it is observed that epistemic risk taking behaviors remain weak, especially regarding the academic content, when the stated contents are taken into consideration. This leads to the existence of epistemic violence and epistemic oppression in academic subjects, and causes information elites to consciously or unconsciously conduct social engineering. Individuals must take epistemic risk in academic matters, open themselves to epistemic freedom and avoid the monopolistic acculturation process. In this study, it is aimed to determine the parameters of academic epistemic risk taking in young adults' (university students) social media posts and to test these parameters.

1.1 Conceptual Framework

Risk is a significant determiner between success and failure of learners during the course of their education process. Any educational attempt at micro- and macro-level brings along risks. Risk is a case that can be positioned between the known and the unknown. It is a motivation or anxiety tool between the wanted and unwanted result of any undertaken activity (Bondy & Pritchard, 2016). Risk appearing in an ambiguous setting may lead to beneficial or detrimental results and is likely to affect at least one educational goal. Faced risks and their outcomes become more critical in consideration of the gravity of uncertainty especially over students' academic studies. Uncertainty about educational endeavors is generally referred to as epistemic uncertainty. Epistemic uncertainty occurs when a piece of information is missing or wrong (Curcuru, Galante & La Fata, 2012; Dubois & Guyonnet, 2011; Rohmer & Baudrit, 2011). The educational goals of the 21st century require learners to produce highly functional information by employing their higher-order cognitive skills. In such a case, epistemic uncertainty becomes an inevitable phenomenon for learners in the society of information overload as incurred by the information age. In the face of epistemic risk, learners are required to justify their attempts to retrieve the truth. Therefore, they are to run the risk of making mistakes. This is because knowledge cannot be acquired without taking the risk of failure. In this sense, for a proper epistemic risk management learners should skillfully analyze options and draw rational inferences (Godden, 2017). Constructivism having been located in the center of learning approaches too advocates this statement (Glasersfeld, 1989). Thusly, it can be claimed that epistemic uncertainty faced by learners may serve as an opportunity for intellectual development and this opportunity can be taken advantage of through epistemic risk.

Learners only as passive recipients due to traditional educational mindset and its implications in educational policies cannot develop and hone their skills to produce new knowledge and evaluate the existing one (Lloyd, 1976). Assignment of decision-making capacity in relation to the appreciation of the value of and the subsequent operationalization of knowledge to an authority has turned into a traditional practice. Teachers, books, cultures, media, ideologies, religion, politicians, decision-makers are presented as examples of authority. As a result, learners' epistemological beliefs weaken and they take the authority for a benchmark of what is right or wrong in relation to information retrieval (Haerle and Bendixen, 2007; Jehng, Johnson and Anderson, 1993; Pauler Kuppinger and Jucks, 2017). Hence, social engineering, which some have attempted to end based on the Culture Industry criticism of the Frankfurt School, is still in effect in the information age of the 21st century (Henning, 2017). Learners in the age of informatics have opportunities humans have never availed themselves of throughout the human history. However, in the event that the level of epistemological belief is not high and intellectuality is underdeveloped, people again tend to take authority for a standard. As a consequence, in relation to how learners accept and decide upon information, they should adopt strategies in which they have strong ontological and epistemological assumptions (Haerle and Bendixen, 2007). An analysis of social media habits in 2017 indicates a global consumption of social media (www.statista.com). Excessive interaction with social media poses an opportunity-problem dilemma for individuals. If regarded as an opportunity, one can make a mention of intellectual societies actively generating knowledge and seeking to produce intellectual added value by taking their own epistemic risks in a universe of relative knowledge (Taylor, 2017), for the age of informatics of the 21st century has a culture of information in which the understanding of "a single truth" has come to an end, epistemic uncertainty is in active operation, and there are relatively valid truths. In a culture where dialectical process is regarded as the groundwork for knowledge generation, the views of each and every member of the society should be considered as required by a culture of common sense and reconciliation (Marinopoulou, 2017). Therefore, since members of a society have the potential to generate added value with their individual differences, they are expected to take an epistemic risk avoiding authority as a standard and relying on their intellectual richness.

It is important for individuals to be raised in the aforesaid, culture and have an improved intellectual quality for them to be able to take epistemic risks. Otherwise, epistemic risk turns into a threat rather than an opportunity. Taking epistemic risk with limited knowledge and limited rationalization capability may lead us to mistake wrong (invalid) information and even destructive beliefs for true and beneficial ones (Jain, 2004; Mathiesen, 2006; Phillips, 1995). In this sense, it is imperative that one consider parameters allowing for questioning of epistemic syntheses and epistemic acceptances. For example, in the event that a proposition put forward by taking an epistemic risk turns to be true, the resultant well-being may impede inquiries into the rational and scientific foundation of our acceptances (Freedman, 2015). In each phase of questioning in the presence of epistemic uncertainty, we must never overlook the fact that we tend to make mistakes in our epistemic choices and decisions and may draw wrong (invalid) conclusions (Botterill, 2008; Kukla, 2017; Parascandola, 2010).

Individuals' attitudes and tendencies concerning epistemic risks vary (Fallis, 2007). Moreover, risks taken in the face of epistemic uncertainty are evaluated differently by different individuals (Riggs, 2008). Thus, investigations into epistemic risk taken by individuals and groups constituting a community are likely to produce results that are more valid if they are conducted over groups with similar characteristics. The quality of young adults' (between 18 and 35 years and having completed the basic education) capacity to produce knowledge-oriented added value is a matter of curiosity since they are among the groups most frequently interacting with information in the age of informatics. Consequently, the rate of their social media use is high too. Social media is also used for academic purposes as much as for entertainment, political, cultural and other purposes (Lau, 2017; Manca and Ranieri, 2016; Novakovich, Miah and Shaw, 2017; Sanchez, Cortijo and Javed, 2014). Besides, from this perspective social media looks like an opportunity (Smith, 2016). In this study, parameters pertaining to young adults' epistemic risk taking are investigated. It is both a theory- and practice-based study built on descriptive analyses of young adults' behaviors of epistemic risk taking.

2. METHODOLOGY

The study is performed with Exploratory Sequential Design from Mixed Research Designs (Creswell and Clark, 2011). First, a Case Study was conducted with 15 university students who are social media users in the qualitative method. As a qualitative analysis, parameters affecting the academic epistemic risk taking of young adults in social media sharing have been defined. Subsequently, in the quantitative method, Survey research was carried out with the data collection tool developed by the researchers related to the determined parameters. As a result of the survey conducted with 215 university students, epistemic risk parameters were tested.

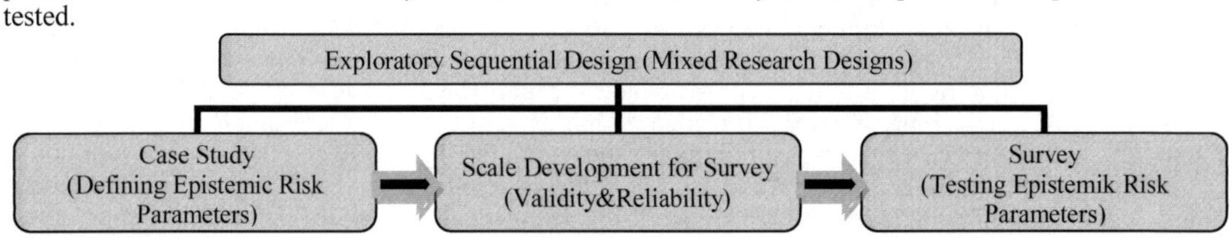

Figure 1. Research Flow Chart

2.1 Participants

The present study was conducted on undergraduate young adults. Young adults between 18 and 35 years were included in the study. All the participants are citizens of the Republic of Turkey. 15 young adult volunteers were included in the case study. The participants were undergraduate students, who received media literacy education, are knowledgeable about epistemic risk and they are known to take and have taken epistemic risks. Besides, the survey was carried out over 215 young adults. The participants were selected assuming that they were undergraduates using social media. In this sense, 151 young adults taking and 64 avoiding epistemic risks in their social media posts with academic contents were included in the study. Whether the participants took epistemic risks was determined by their declaration.

2.2 Data Collection Tools and Data Analysis

A semi-structured interview form was employed for the purpose of the case study. The participants were asked to state "the reasons why they cannot take epistemic risks concerning academic issues in their social media activities". The gathered data were analyzed by content analysis. In content analysis, open coding, axial coding, selective coding, and theoretical coding were employed. With theoretical coding, themes were created and epistemic risk parameters were identified.

For the survey, a scale was produced based on the parameters retrieved in the case study. Each parameter constituted a factor of the scale. It was revised in consideration of the views of faculty members specialized in media literacy and Curriculum and Instruction Programs for improved content validity. The internal consistency coefficient (Cronbach's Alpha) of the measurement instrument consisting of 33 items and 12 factors was calculated to be .906, which means that the measurement instrument is reliable. SPSS 21.0 was used to analyze the data which were also descriptively analyzed.

3. FINDINGS

3.1 Identification of the Parameters of Young Adults' Epistemic Risk Taking in their Social Media Posts with Academic Content

In the table below (Table 1) are the parameters which were discovered to exert effects on young adults' epistemic risk taking in their social media posts with academic content by means of the interviews with 15 participants in the case study, which is the qualitative component of the study.

Table 1. Parameters of Academic Epistemic Risk Taking

Categories - Axial Coding	Concepts - Selective Coding	Themes - Theoretical Coding	Dimensions
Imperfect knowing, knowing wrong, incompetent command of content knowledge, invalid information	Knowledge and knowing	Knowledgeability	Individual-related parameters – Endogenous epistemic risk barriers/opportunities
Academic skill deficit, academic inquiry skill deficit, incompetent academic thinking skills, thinking skills deficit	Academic skills and abilities	Academic knowledgeability	
Destructive criticism, intolerance to criticism, weak criticism, presence of anti-thesis to refute thesis	Criticism culture and individual	Criticism	
Likes, follows, popularity, being center of attention, social status, social reward	Protection and preservation of virtual identity and popularity	Social acceptance	
"I" as the source of failure, incompetent "I", "I" outside of change, anxiety of uselessness	Anxiety over what "I" can do.	Self-esteem	
Failure to self-authorize, failure to associate with the self, the role of recipient, ignorance	Passive recipient-active producer dilemma	Responsibility	
Incompetency, it is not appropriate to affect others despite incompetency, assuming ethical responsibility	Assignment of the area of freedom by ethical principles	Ethics	
Legal responsibility, academic role and responsibilities, authority pressure, authority dominance, authority's reaction	Authority anxiety and freedom restrictions by authority	Authority pressure	Environment-related parameters – exogenous epistemic risk barriers/opportunities
Anxiety over exclusion from group, group reaction, disruption of in-group harmony, social reward/interest loss, acceptance of group norms	Group belonging	Spiral of silence	
Member profile, members' interests, members, member quality	Community profile	Network society profile	
Educational background, education quality, education content, educational achievement	Education support	Educational background	
Trust in social networks, trust in members, trust in groups	Social capital	Virtual social capital	

Table 1 reveals that parameters of academic risk taking in relation to social media posts with academic content consist of two different theoretical propositions. There form two themes, e.g. Individual-related and environment-related parameters concerning epistemic risk. While individual-related parameters are identified as endogenous epistemic risk barriers/opportunities, environment-related parameters refer to exogenous epistemic risk barriers/opportunities. Accordingly, individual's epistemic risk taking in their social media posts about academic matters may be affected by variables such as their own characteristics, knowledgeability, profiles, but also by those such as virtual social environment and roles, groups and cultures created by this environment. Theoretical propositions obtained from the results of the qualitative analyses, which refers to the first part of the research, are as follows:

Epistemic risk taking of undergraduate young adults in their social media posts with academic content is potentially affected by;

- Individual-related parameters such as individual's knowledge repository, quality of academic knowledge, criticism anxiety, social acceptance anxiety, self-esteem level, sense of responsibility and ethical anxiety,

- Environment-related parameters, e.g. authority pressure, spiral of silence, profile of the network society, educational background and level of virtual social capital.

Operational definitions of the parameters are provided below:

Knowledgeability: Individual' holding a basic repository of knowledge on the academic content of the posts.

Academic knowledgeability: Individual's high-order thinking skills (for example, argumentative thinking, creative thinking, critical thinking), tendency to academic inquiry, hold of academic curiosity.

Criticism: Individual's openness to criticism over his/her social media posts with academic content.

Social acceptance: High popularity of individual's profile he/she created in his/her social media account.

Self-esteem: Individual self-esteem to be able to send a functional academic social media post.

Responsibility: Individual's sense of responsibility to the academic social media post.

Ethics: Individual's observation of ethical principles in the academic social media posts.

Authority pressure: Legal status with proven specialization pertaining to academic issues (scientist, researcher author, etc.)

Spiral of silence: Individual's persistence in abiding by the group rules not to be excluded from the group when he/she contradicts the group norms (Noelle-Neumann, 1984).

Network society profile: Characteristics of the virtual society formed by individuals using social media accounts.

Educational background: Individual's educational background as to how to send a social media post with academic content.

Level of virtual social capital: The level of individual's trust in social media networks and users in social media networks.

3.2 Investigation of the Parameters of Young Adults' Epistemic Risk Taking in their Social Media Posts with Academic Content

This part is intended to investigate whether the parameters identified in the previous section are effective in young adults' taking epistemic risks in their social media posts with academic content.

Table 2. Test Results Concerning the Parameters of Academic Epistemic Risk Taking

Dimensions	Parameters	Results of Who take epistemic risks			Results of Who don't take epistemic risks		
		N	Mean*	Standard deviation	N	Mean*	Standard deviation
Individual-related parameters / Endogenous epistemic risk barriers/opportunities	Knowledgeability	151	4.0464	.76016	64	4.3333	.72496
	Academic knowledgeability	151	3.0513	.83333	64	3.5039	.92205
	Criticism	151	2.1104	.81624	64	2.2604	.96950
	Social acceptance	151	1.9007	.74793	64	2.1156	.88142
	Self-esteem	151	2.2958	.86713	64	2.6927	.98723
	Responsibility	151	2.1854	.91399	64	2.7578	1.01962
	Ethics	151	3.1391	1.29120	64	3.5469	1.32053
Environment-related parameters / Exogenous epistemic risk barriers/opportunities	Authority pressure	151	2.3775	.82702	64	2.5885	.93481
	Spiral of silence	151	1.9834	.81938	64	2.1797	.93591
	Network society profile	151	2.3742	.85677	64	2.4688	.94648
	Educational background	151	2.6788	.96669	64	2.9688	1.03078
	Virtual social capital	151	2.4238	.78969	64	2.6250	.94747

*1.00-2.50: Ineffective; 2.51-3.50: Potentially effective; 3.51-5.00: Effective

Parameters' effectiveness was assessed according to the participants taking and not taking epistemic risks.

<u>Assessment of individual-related parameters:</u>

It was inferred from the views of the participants taking epistemic risks that only "knowledgeability" of individual-related parameters was considered to be effective. The parameters deemed potentially effective were "academic knowledge" and "ethical concern". The parameters "criticism anxiety", "social acceptance anxiety", "self-esteem", and "responsibility" were not considered effective.

According to the views of the participants not taking epistemic risks, "knowledgeability", "academic knowledgeability", and "ethical concerns" are effective. The parameters considered potentially effective were "self-esteem" and "responsibility". The parameters "criticism anxiety" and "social acceptance anxiety" were not considered effective.

<u>Assessment of environment-related parameters:</u>

No environment-related parameter was found to be effective in epistemic risk taking.

According to the participants taking epistemic risk, the only parameter potentially effective was "educational background". The parameters "authority pressure", "spiral of silence", "network society profile", and "virtual social capital" were expressed to be ineffective.

According to the participants not taking epistemic risks, the parameters "educational background" and "level of virtual social capital" were potentially effective. The parameters "authority pressure", "spiral of silence", and "network society profile" were not effective.

4. CONCLUSION

Table 3. Parameters Effective in Young Adults' Taking Epistemic Risks in their Social Media Posts with Academic Content

Dimensions	Assessment	Young adults taking epistemic risks	Young adults not taking epistemic risks
Individual-related parameters – Endogenous epistemic risk barriers/opportunities	Effective	"Knowledgeability"	"Knowledgeability", "Ethics", "Academic knowledgeability"
	Potentially effective	"Academic knowledgeability", "Ethics"	"Self-esteem" , "Responsibility"
	Ineffective	"Self-esteem", "Responsibility", "Criticism", "Social acceptance"	"Criticism", "Social acceptance"

Environment-related parameters – Exogenous epistemic risk barriers/opportunities	Effective	--	--
	Potentially effective	"Educational background"	"Educational background", "Virtual social capital"
	Ineffective	"Authority pressure","Spiral of silence","Network society profile","Virtual social capital"	"Authority pressure","Spiral of silence","Network society profile"

The analysis of the parameters of epistemic risk taking by young adults in their social media posts with academic content revealed that the parameters varied according to individuals taking and not taking epistemic risks. Knowledgeability is the most effective epistemic risk parameter of young adults posting (commenting and producing) about academic issue on social media. Therefore, it is imperative to equip individuals with high-quality knowledge reserves for a continued exhibition of epistemic risk taking behavior by young adults. In the cases of epistemic uncertainty, individuals expected to make decisions by justification (rational thinking) instead of relying on beliefs should be intellectually educated. Besides, potentially effective academic knowledge and ethical concerns should be considered for the sustainability of the epistemic risk. Particularly, supporting thinking skills and academic skills of young adults is expected to greatly contribute. Moreover, it is recommended that an individual should sort out ethical dilemmas while taking epistemic risks.

These parameters are directly effective in motivating young adults not taking epistemic risks to take epistemic risks. Thus, it is a considerable finding that the parameters academic knowledgeability and ethics along with knowledgeability are indispensable for individuals not taking epistemic risks. Therefore, it is necessary to equip individuals not taking epistemic risks with these knowledge and skill types. In addition, the parameters self-esteem and responsibility are potentially effective. Individuals should be helped raise consciousness that taking epistemic risks is their responsibility and their self-esteem levels should be increased based on the idea that their individual differences bring in added values.

Young adults' educational backgrounds are potentially effective in taking academic epistemic risks. Thus, individuals should be presented with learning opportunities during formal education intended for academic epistemic risk taking and their educational development should be supported to achieve this goal. Additionally, the level of virtual social capital is potentially effective in young adults' taking epistemic risks. For these individuals to take academic epistemic risks, they should build trust in social networks they are a member of and in their members.

The parameters criticism, social acceptance, authority pressure, spiral of silence, network society profile, level of virtual social capital are not effective in young adults' taking epistemic risks. Young adults' autonomous behavioral characteristics and intention to stand out as autonomous individuals in pursuit of their own goals are considered to underlie this situation.

As a conclusion, individuals are advised to develop cognitive enhancement primarily in epistemic risk taking. This can be done in parallel with the educational opportunities offered to them. In formal and informal education processes, individuals should be equipped and effective in terms of both knowledge and skills. In order for these two factors to function in a functional way, the emotional equipment (as self-esttem, responsibility etc.) of the individual needs to be strengthened. In this framework, the essential requirement for individuals to take epistemic risk is to feel that they are a unique activist with individual differences.

This study has some limitations and suggestions according to these limitations. The study was conducted over young adults who were university students. Therefore, there is a need to examine what result will be reached on different populations. In addition, in the study, participants' epistemic risk-taking situations were described according to their own views. It is suggested to investigate and compare epistemic risk parameters in future studies in which individuals are monitored and tested for epistemic risk performances.

REFERENCES

Curcuru, G., Galante, G. M.,& La Fata, C.M. (2012). Epistemic uncertainty in fault tree analysis approached by the evidence theory. *Journal of Loss Prevention in the Process Industries, 25*, 667-676.

Bondy, P., Pritchard, D. (2016). Propositional epistemic luck, epistemic risk, and epistemic justification. *Synthese*, 1-10.

Botterill, G. (2008) The internal problem of dreaming: detection and epistemic risk. *International Journal of Philosophical Studies, 16*(2), 139-160.

Creswell, J. W. & Clark, V.L.P. (2011). *Designing and conducting mixed method research (2nd edition).* SAGE.

Dotson, K. (2014). Conceptualizing epistemic oppression. *Social Epistemology, 28*(2), 115-138.

Dubois, D., Guyonnet, D. (2011). Risk-informed decision-making in the presence of epistemic uncertainty. *International Journal of General Systems, 40* (2), 145-167.

Fallis, D. (2007). Attitudes toward epistemic risk and the value of experiments. *Studia Logica, 86*(2), 215-246.

Freedman, K.L. (2015) Testimony and Epistemic Risk: The Dependence Account. *Social Epistemology, 29*(3), 251-269.

Fricker, M. (1999). Epistemic oppression and epistemic privilege. *Canadian Journal of Philosophy, 29*(1), 191-210.

Glasersfeld, E. (1988). Cognition, Construction of Knowledge, and Teaching. *Synthese, 80* (1),121-140

Godden, D. (2017). Presumption as a modal qualifier: presumption, inference, and managing epistemic risk. Argumentation: An International Journal on Reasoning, February, 2017, pp-pp. doi: 10.1007/s10503-017-9422-1.

Gore, A. (1998). The digital earth. *Australian Surveyor, 43*(2), 89-91, DOI: 10.1080/00050326.1998.10441850

Gupta, A.K. & Govindarajan, V. (2000). Knowledge management's social dimension: Lessons from Nucor Steel. *MIT Sloan Management Review, 42*(1), 71-80.

Haerle, F.C. & Bendixen, L.D. (2007). Personal epistemology in elementary classrooms: A conceptual comparison of German and the United States and a guide for future cross-cultural research (chapter 7). M.S. Khine (Ed.). Knowing, knowledge and beliefs: epistemological studies across diverse cultures. Springer.

Henning C. (2017) Theories of Culture in the Frankfurt School of Critical Theory. In: Thompson M. (eds) The Palgrave Handbook of Critical Theory. Political Philosophy and Public Purpose. Palgrave Macmillan, New York.

Jain, P. (2004). Validity and its epistemic role. Unpublished Doctorate Thesis, Indiana University: US.

Jehng, J.C.J., Johnson, S.D., and Anderson, R.C. (1993). Schooling and students' epistemological beliefs about learning. *Contemporary Educational Psychology, 18*(1), 23-35.

Kukla, R. (2017). Infertility, epistemic risk, and disease definitions. *Synthese*, pp.1-20, DOI 10.1007/s11229-017-1405-0.

Labbas, R. (2013). Epistemology in Education: Epistemological Development Trajectory. *Journal of International Education and Leadership, 3*(2), 1-10.

Lau, W.W.F. (2017). Effects of social media usage and social media multitasking on the academic performance of university students. *Computers in Human Behavior, 68*, 286-291.

Lloyd,D.I.(1976).Traditional and progressive education(chapter8), D.I.Lloyd(Ed.),Philosophy and the teacher. Routledge.

Manca, S. & Ranieri, M. (2016). "Yes for sharing, no for teaching!": Social Media in academic practices. *Internet and Higher Education, 29*, 63–74

Marinopoulou, A. (2017). *Critical Theory and Epistemology, The Politics of Modern Thought and Science*. Manchester University Press.

Mathiesen, K. (2006). Epistemic risk and community policing. *The Southern Journal of Philosophy, 44*, 139-150.

Noelle-Neumann, E. (1984). *The Spiral of Silence: Public Opinion-Our Social Skin.* Chicago, IL: The University of Chicago Press, ISBN 0-226-58932-3

Novakovich, J. Miah, S. & Shaw, S. (2017). Designing curriculum to shape professional social media skills and identity in virtual communities of practice. *Computers & Education, 104*, 65-90.

Parascandola, M. (2010). Epistemic risk: Empirical science and the fear of being wrong. *Law, Probability and Risk,9,* 201-214

Pauler Kuppinger, L. & Jucks, R. (2017). Perspectives on teaching: Conceptions of teaching and epistemological beliefs of university academics and students in different domains. *Active Learning in Higher Education, 18*(1), 63-76

Phillips, D.C. (1995). The Good, the Bad, and the Ugly: The Many Faces of Constructivism. *Educational Researcher ,24*(7), 5 – 12.

Riggs, W. D. (2008). Epistemic risk and relativism. *Acta Analytica, 23*, 1-8.

Ritzer,G.,Dean,P.,Jurgenson, N.(2012).The coming of age of the prosumer. *American Behavioral Scientist,56*(4), 379-398.

Ritzer, G. & Jurgenson, N. (2010). Production, consumption, prosumption: The nature of capitalism in the age of the digital "prosumer." *Journal of Consumer Culture, 10*, 13-36.

Rohmer, J., & Baudrit, C. (2011). The use of the possibility theory to investigate the epistemic uncertainties within scenerio-based earthquake risk assessments. *Nat Hazards, 56*, 613-632.

Sanchez, R. A., Cortijo, V. & Javed, U. (2014). Students' perceptions of Facebook for academic purposes. *Computers &Education, 70,* 138-149.

Simon, J. (2008). Knowledge and Trust in Epistemology and Social Software/ Knowledge Technologies. In: Arsenault, C., & Tennis, J. T. (Eds.). (2008). Culture and identity in knowledge organization: Proceedings of the Tenth International ISKO Conference (Montréal, Canada, August 5-8, 2008).

Smith, E.E. (2016). "A real double-edged sword:" Undergraduate perceptions of social media in their learning. *Computers & Education, 103,* 44-58.

Taylor, R. M. (2017). Education for autonomy and openmindedness in diverse societies, *Educational Philosophy and Theory, 49*:14, 1326-1337, DOI: 10.1080/00131857.2017.1278673

Velleman, J. D. (1989). Epistemic freedom. *Pacific Philosophical Quarterly, 70*(1), 73-97.

https://www.statista.com/topics/1164/social-networks/, Social Media Statistics & Facts

A SYSTEMATIC REVIEW OF LEARNING AND TEACHING WITH TABLETS

Lechen Zhang and Jalal Nouri
Department of Computer and Systems Sciences, Stockholm University, Sweden

ABSTRACT

Due to the increased popularity of tablets in schools, this systematic review examines the literature on tablet-mediated learning attempting to identify how tablets support the emergence of new teaching and learning practices as well as the transformation of existing ones in primary and secondary schools. 39 studies were selected using predefined selection criteria, most of which concern natural sciences, math and language. The result identified 10 themes of pedagogical teaching and learning practices that are supported by tablets in schools, namely: augmented and virtual learning, collaborative learning, communication, documentation, feedback and assessment, game-based learning, individualized learning, inquiry-based learning, mobile learning, and multimodal learning. The identified themes of practices support and interact with each other to serve learning and teaching purposes.

KEYWORDS

Tablets, iPad, Learning, Teaching, Systematic Review, Mobile Learning

1. INTRODUCTION

Though envisioned by Microsoft already in 2002 (Dray et al, 2002), the tablet computer (tablet PC or tablet) hadn't appealed the public's attention until Apple's release of iPad emerging as the "category-defining blockbuster" of tablets (Pregum et al, 2013). The ownership of tablets has grown greatly since then. By 2013, one third (34%) of American adults had a tablet computer (Zickuhr, 2013).

This popularity of tablets has even extended to schools since 2010 (Henderson and Yeow, 2012). iPads, in particular, being widely adopted in educational settings around the world are the most popular handheld learning device in the schools (Pegrum et al, 2013). Many counties are looking in-depth into the usage of tablets for educational purposes. Apple and ConnectED, an initiative by President Obama, donated an iPad to every student, a Mac and iPad to every teacher for 114 schools across the States (Apple and ConnectED, 2016). Almost 70% of primary and secondary schools in the UK now use tablet-computers to assist learning (Coughlan, 2014). Ontario in Canada announces $150 million investment for iPads in the classrooms (Rieti, 2014). A Chinese company, Shenzhen Scope Scientific Development, has signed a contract for the provision of 400,000 tablets for students (Clarke & Svanaes, 2013). In Sweden, many schools have made tablets available and free of charge for young pupils (Nouri & Cerratto-Pargman, 2016; Bergström & Höglund, 2014).

The research has shown that tablets indeed have promising potentials in facilitating the learning process for pupils of different ages and needs (Cerratto-Pargman, Nouri & Milrad, 2017; Li et al., 2016; Lee, 2015; Gasparini & Culén, 2013; Henderson & Yeow, 2012). For instance, the study of Nouri & Cerratto-Pargman (2016) demonstrated how tablets support teaching and learning practices in Swedish schools through three affordances, i.e. persistence of the digital medium, multimodality of the content and portability and ubiquity. They also discovered that tablets support six themes of learning and teaching practices, namely, organization of teaching and learning, documentation, communication, multimodal learning, assessment and formative feedback, and mobile learning.

Despite of the increased attention and use of tablets in education, previous literature reviews, such as Cobcroft (2012) and Wu et al (2012), have focused mainly on analysis of mobile learning by handling all mobile technologies, that is to say, tablet, portable notebook, smartphone and PDA as one bundle. The reviews focusing on tablets, such as Nguyen et al. (2015), investigated on how iPads have been adopted in the higher education. The literature review by Haßler (2015) is the only review with a focus on the use of tablets by pupils in primary and secondary schools across the curriculum. However, while Haßler's study provides a useful overview on learning outcomes by using tablets, it does not shed light on the teaching and learning practices aided by tablets. Therefore, the significance of this paper is to deepen the understanding on how tablets support the emergence of new teaching and learning practices as well as the transformation of existing ones. This study adopts the systematic review method to close this gap and aims to answer the question "How are pedagogical practices supported by tablets in primary and secondary school?"

2. METHODOLOGY

2.1 Data Collection

2.1.1 Database

The study searched databases that are known for education and information technology: ACM (Association for Computing Machinery), Elsevier Science consisting of Computers & Education, ERIC (Education Resources Information Center), JSTOR consisting Journal of Educational Technology & Society, IEEE (Institute of Electrical and Electronics Engineers), Science Direct consisting of Computers in Human Behavior, SAGE Journal Online, The International Review of Research in Open and Distance Learning, Wiley online library consisting Journal of Computer Assisted Learning, Inderscience Online consisting International journal of mobile and blended learning.

2.1.2 Keywords and Search Terms

The keywords are tablets, iPad, Android tablets, education(-al) app(-lication); education, primary school, elementary school, junior school, middle school, secondary school, high school, pupils, students, teacher, instruction, learning, teaching.

The keywords were combined to form search terms (e.g. "iPad learning high school"). Whenever applicable, Boolean logic was used for constructing search terms (e.g. "tablet" OR "iPad"). When a database didn't allow Boolean logic, individual combinations of the keywords were searched in the databases. The search result generated a large number of studies (>500). Only the articles that were screened by the inclusion and exclusion criteria were selected for this systematic review.

Table 1. Selection Criteria

Inclusion criteria	Exclusion criteria
Formal education from primary school to secondary school	The use of tablets in higher education, informal education (e.g. home learning) or pre-school education
Empirical studies (observation or experimentation) relating to the utilization of tablets in education	Studies not investigating on the physical use of tablets in teaching and learning practices, such as acceptance, attitudes or learning outcomes
Time period from 2010 to 2017	Studies not solely focusing on tablets, such as the use of other mobile devices like smartphone and laptop
Studies with an abstract	

This systematic review intends to investigate the usage of tablets in formal education of primary and secondary school. That excludes pre-schooling and higher education. Besides, this review solely studies tablets, which implies that studies on smartphones and other mobile devices are not considered. The focus of this review is to examine how tablets are engaged in teaching and learning. Other factors like learning outcomes are not the primary concern. The iPad's success in 2010 caught the public attention. Therefore, the search covers the time period from 2010 until now. At last, only articles with an abstract are eligible.

2.1.3 Data Extraction

A data extraction form was designed. The pilot form was refined several times to ensure the quantity and quality of data. Each paper was scrutinized for the following data: general information including source and year of publication, area, context; study characteristics including methodology/study design, sample size; result and research reliability.

2.1.4 Data Analysis

This paper was guided by procedures from content analysis (Braun & Clarke, 2006) in order to code the selected studies. The coding approach was inductively performed to identify the categories of learning and teaching practices supported by tablets. The coding resulted in 10 categories of practices. 20 out of the 39 papers (50%) were coded independently. The inter-rater reliability (r) was 0.92, a good agreement between the two coders.

3. RESULT

3.1 Geographic Distribution of the Selected Studies

The articles examined were published between 2010 and 2016. The research was carried out though out the world, though especially popular in Asia (16 studies) and Europe (12 studies). Interestingly, only 3 studies were found in North America. iPad, an American product, has been given a fair opportunity to be engaged in the American education, such as Apple's effort in donating a large amount of iPads to students and teaching staff (Apple and ConnectED, ibid). The result also shows that the majority (28 studies) of the research was conducted in primary schools while 9 studies in secondary schools. Generally, tablets are used within the classroom (33 studies). The mobility does allow students to carry it outdoors for learning purpose or bring it home. It may imply that a classroom is still the most common learning environment for school education. Another finding is that tablets mostly interest Math (8 studies), Natural Science (10 studies) and Language study (11 studies). Other subjects engage tablets less frequently.

3.2 Tablet-mediated Teaching and Learning Practices

Table 2 below presents the 10 identified categories of tablets-enabled teaching and learning practices. Some studies are listed under different categories as they engage tablets in different pedagogical practices.

3.2.1 Augmented and Virtual Learning

Augmented reality (AR) offers an interface composing of digital information and visualizations blended with physical reality. It allows users to interact with both real and virtual worlds by a tangible interface (Hsu et al, 2015). The app "Video Physics" is introduced to teach motion and velocity (Lohr, 2014). Students film a moving object with the tablet's camera and open it in "Video Physics" so that the position of the moving object can be marked frame by frame through tapping on the object. "Video Physics" then displays the path of the object and drew graphs of the position and velocity of the object. Some physics experiments are conducted through Google Glass's AR (Kuhn et al, 2016). AR provides an alternative to experimental equipment (Grubelnik, 2016). In order to determine the gravity acceleration of a falling body, students record a video of a falling body and use the app "Tracker" to analyze the physical dynamics. None of the tradition physical equipment is needed to measure the acceleration. Furthermore, AR assists leaning in social science as well. Aurasma, an augmented reality software giving students access to the historical videos when reading a textbook, helps student to study history in Hsu's (ibid) experiment. Whenever a student reads the textbook and is interested in a historical figure, s/he can scan the picture with the tablet and the corresponding video of the figure then is played on the screen.

Virtual reality functions in a similar fashion, in form of a substitution of tradition experimental equipment. The app iCircuit is an electronic circuit simulator, which allows students to build electric systems using predefined building blocks just like working with real circuit units (Lohr, ibid). Moreover, it is common that VR enables 3D operation interface on a 2D screen. Chinese calligraphy learners can practice the right stroke order through 3D writing process on a 2D screen on the app "Unity3D", which is a virtual reality-based version of spatial abilities assessment instrument (Wu et al, 2013). Similar apps are utilized in a virtual chemical laboratory (Uchiyama, 2013).

Table 2. Overview of Categories of Pedagogical Practices and Articles (Note: Article Numbers are Referred to the Numbering in Appendix)

Category	Description	Article nr.
Augmented and virtual learning	Learning through augmented reality	11,16,18,29,37
	Learning through virtual reality	27,35,38
Collaborative learning	Knowledge procurement and construction through collaboration: sharing the physical device, planning, discussing, negotiating, solving problems and exchanging opinions.	1,2,8,9,15,25,33
Communication	Communication takes place between teachers and pupils, among pupils online face to face or through virtual environment such as Skype and Google Docs.	9,15,25,27
Documentation	Tools to make markings and important annotations, taking photographs, audio and video recordings, drawing etc.	7,15,17,22,32
Feedback and assessment	Teachers monitor learning process, comment and assess the work using digital feedback systems.	13,14, 19,33,34
Game based learning	Learning through playing digital games.	4,15,24,33,36
Individualized learning	Students learn new content on their on pace and/or by themselves. Tailored difficulty levels in apps.	3,15, 21,27,26
Inquiry based learning	Learning through inquiry. Using the tablet for data collection.	11,15,33,37,39
Mobile learning	The portability enables learning at any given location in the classroom and outdoors.	7,15,17,22,37
Multimodal learning	Learning through different modalities (sound, image, text, video, etc.)	1,2,3,7,8,10,12,22,23, 27,28,39,30,31,32
	eBooks.	3,5,6,15,20,27
	Educational apps (non-game)	1,2,3,7,10,12,19, 22,23,27,32,39

3.2.2 Collaborative Learning

Tablets can facilitate collaborative learning. Tablet-mediated tasks require debates and negotiations, team research and outcome presentations. Students learn to create newsletters in pairs by assigning team roles, searching information online and producing an animated poster (Culén,2012). In order to learn English collaboratively, students need to create and construct digital language productions within their group (Alhinty, 2014). Both studies show that, through tablets, learning can be collaborative and production-based. When combined with external equipment or services, tablets provide more means of collaborative learning. Fallon (2015) examined cloud services such as Google Docs that is characterized by its convenience of synchronicity. Google Docs enables students to share work and allows them to edit, add content or correct each other's mistakes. Several people can work on the same output concurrently. Furuya (2016) tested CSCL (Computer Supported Collaborative Learning) app "edutab". Students write solutions to Math questions in the app, which are later displayed on an LCD screen. In this case, students can see others' solutions, it inspires ideas and encourages exchanging opinions. Mobility and flexibility of tablets are also factors to smooth the collaborative learning (Fallon, ibid). The size of display allows a group to view the same content at the same time. It can be easily repositioned, angled or rotated for different purposes such as viewing YouTube clips. Students can help others or ask for help by being able to carry the device easily to different parts of the classroom or into another environment.

3.2.3 Communication

Supported by hardware infrastructure like Wi-Fi or cellular network, communication can take place at anytime and anywhere through tablets. The communication covers both teacher-learner and learners with their peers. According to Alhinty (2014), online communication is enhanced by the mobility and instant accessibility provided by tablets. The students, through iPad blogging, can meet their classmates virtually, hence, to discuss their learning experience. There are other alternatives to realize virtual communication. For example, Edmodo, Skype, iMessage as well as Google Docs provide audio and video face to face, real time communication (Nikolić, 2013). Edmodo, an application similar to Facebook, makes communication between student and teacher much simpler and faster at all times.

3.2.4 Documentation

Tablets affordances expand the forms of documentation further than pen and paper's reach. Typing text and entering content digitally on tablets are environmentally friendly and don't require physical pen and paper. Photographs, voice recording and videos are convenient and useful tools for documentation, shown in Geer et al. (2017) and Alhinty's (2014) study. The camera and photo can easily document objects that are fragile or hard to move within school or bring to school. Apps like Puppet Pals allow young learners to make the characters image by photographing and to make the characters talk by recording their own voices. However, learners do prefer certain types of documentation methods. Wyeth et al (2011) conducted a study to test typing, recording and drawing for ecological observation and data collection. It was reported that learners found drawing more difficult to use compared to the other two. But this doesn't imply that sketching and drawing stand on disadvantage in all scenarios. Wang et al (2013) considered sketching advantageous for learning. Students, instead of reading information or typing notes on the tablets, were asked to sketch out the image and their impressions on what they have seen and learned from a specific cultural context in a museum. The sketches on tablets were presented and discussed later in a regular classroom. Wyeth et al (ibid) believe that all these new ways of documentation encourage learners to explore different forms of expression. The expressive use of these affordances leads to media-rich work and authentic experiences that accommodate student-centered pedagogies and authentic learning.

3.2.5 Feedback and Assessment

Several studies investigated feedback and assessment through tablets. The common factor in the studies is that tablets are the host for various digital learning platforms. Students' answers or performance are submitted or monitored through tablets. Sun et al (2016) examined iFIT (Interactive, Feedback-based In-class Teaching system). Each member of a learning group in turn uses the tablet to deliver a response, which is sent to a server. The teacher views each student's response on a control screen and analyses the responses of the entire class. Earlier, Harfield et al's study (2013) presented a similar system called Open Monitoring Environment (OME). The OME captures the state of the learning progress of students' though complex visualization on a tablet's screen, which can offer teachers insight on students' progress and difficulties. The teachers can monitor all the students' activities such as ongoing problem solving or finished tasks. Being provided by graphical visualizations of the analyzed data, teachers are able to interpret the visualized information, see indications of students' learning and thereafter adjust their teaching. Another e-learning platform, Moodle, is also used for giving feedback to students by allowing students to upload their work, which is commented and assessed by the teacher (Lohr, 2011).

3.2.6 Game Based Learning

The game based learning materialized through tablets mainly focuses on developing mathematics and literacy skills. Henderson et al (2012) and Culén et al (2012) believe that playing digital games on tablets can reinforce the learning of math while spelling games are widely used for literacy development. Walubita's team (2015) also confirmed the literacy part. They installed GraphoGame on students' tablets, which is an evidence-based computer game that helps early grade learners to master the link between letters and their sounds as a foundation to acquisition of reading skills. The result showed that sufficient practice on GraphoGame led to increase initial literacy skills. As to Math, Deckard et al (2014) observed how digital games helped students to deepen the understanding of fractions. They concluded that the game playing shifted learners' focus from achieving the learning goals to advancing levels of the game. The winning intention became the motivation. The game itself was considered as a non-invasive assessment tool, collecting continuous data throughout play sessions. The progress was automatically tracked.

3.2.7 Individualized Learning

The tablet and its flexibility enable autonomous and individualized learning, meaning students can learn in their paces based on their needs and choose the exercises accordingly. For example, in language classes, pupils who are shy and often tend not to communicate can practice speaking at home on the tablet apps recommended by the teacher and then send their voice recordings to the teacher (Nikolić, ibid and Crnković, 2014). It can be a great opportunity for the less self-confident students to build their confidence gradually. Besides, tablets can help achieve a regular contact between the teacher and the student as the teacher gives each student individually feedback on their strengths and areas for improvement. Tablets are considered helpful especially in a group of students with heterogeneous learning abilities (Ramkalawon et al, 2016). It provides students with greater flexibility to proceed with their own pace and to follow their own interests, potentially increasing their motivation to pursue learning opportunities. For instance, apps like as Dragon Dictation or Spelling Notebook are used for practice spelling or pronunciation. Not only do learners have control on the process or revisit learning material as many times as it requires, but also get immediate feedback about their progress. In this case, students can become more aware of their own learning (Crnković, ibid). In a pilot study, students were able to learn faster on their own by repeating lessons as many times as they wished (Nedungadi et al, 2014).

3.2.8 Inquiry Based Learning

In Lohr's (2014) experiment, students conducted physics experiment with AR. The technology did help the students understand the physics process. Meanwhile, tablets provided them an opportunity for inquiry-based learning. The live data recorded by sensors on the tablet could be analyzed step by step according to a "guided tour" with built-in statistical tools like minimum, maximum, mean or standard deviation on the app "SparkVue". Students could disable the guided tour feature and explore the content and solve problem for themselves implementing the inquiry-based learning model. Grubelnik's (2016) observed inquiry based problem solving as well. Students analyzed a given task in astronomy independently with the assistance of tablet and Internet. They retrieved useful and relevant data such as mass of the planets in solar system from research to complete the task. Learners could even creatively combine different apps in ways that were not immediately apparent for solving open-ended research tasks (Mann et al, 2016). For instance, a student used a web browser for searching news and took a number of screen shots, which were opened in Book Creator app and pasted into a new file. In the end, the student marked certain important text digitally as notes.

3.2.9 Mobile Learning

One of the key findings in the result is the important advantage of tablet's mobility. This allows students to execute different tasks in numerous environments. The tablets could move along a free falling object and record data for physics analysis (Grubelnik, ibid). Because of the portable nature and lightweight, learners could carry the tablets around with them, even if not needed. They could move around in the class or change desks (Mann, 2016), which is a perquisite for ubiquitous learning. It was observed by Henderson (2012) that students could easily work in groups and move from one location to the next when needed. For instance, it allowed students to gather around the teacher and used the tablets to follow what was being read to them while looking up definitions of words. Because of this feature, learning can also take place beyond a physically limited classroom. During a culture observation school trip (Wang, 2013), students could the record the teacher's instructions on their tablet and draw their impressions onto their e-sketch notes anytime anywhere as means of data collection. Wyeth (idib) organized field trip so that learners could experience and capture observations of interesting environmental attributes they encountered, including plants, trees, birds, insects, spiders, reptiles and mammals and recorded them on tablets.

3.2.10 Multimodal Learning

A large number of the included studies are associated to the utilization of multimodal affordances of the tablets (i.e., sound, image, text).

eBooks or digital books are interactive books that have audio, video and interactivity making content alive. Students first and foremost used tablets as textbook when they answered the question "the functions of tablets in lectures" in Švecová et al's survey (2015). eBooks can be used in many contexts of the classroom teaching. Henderson (ibid) observed that Math teachers converted math textbook in PDF format and uploaded onto the iPad for children to use, while other teachers read parts of a novel daily to students through the iPad's iBook. Students also used the iBook to read individually and for peer reading. Geography teachers made "digital books" that provided students with a lot of visualized content and a variety of multimedia materials in order to study waves (Nikolić et al, ibid). Gong et al (2013) also investigated how eBooks were engaged in teaching and learning. The interactive function of eBooks allowed contents to be projected on a bigger screen through Airplay showing students' products from their iPad, highlighting the texts, and providing instant feedback. They stated that students were highly motivated to use eBooks in learning activities. However, technological issues, such as failures of devices and software, delays of systems response, are still the key obstacles for teachers to use eBooks in the classroom. At the same time, Henderson (ibid) pointed out that more attention must be paid to the professional development of teachers' digital competence in order to master the tablets in teaching.

Almost one third of the selected studies (12 out of 39) reported the usage of educational apps. Geer et al's (2016) survey stated that approximately 40% students used educational apps at least six times a week. According to Mann (2016), the App Store offers thousands of free educational applications for every subject and these multimedia applications featuring interactivity make learning easier. For example, digital editors or spelling apps bear advantages for learning the spelling of words. Students can switch between dictionary app, note-taking app and eBook during reading. The book creator app can produce posters or short comics. 'Super Spellers, Crazy Cursive, Sumdog, King of Maths, Brain Training' are designed to train a specific competence such as literacy or numeracy abilities.

4. DISCUSSION

This review aimed to provide an overview on the pedagogical usage of tablets in educational settings. After applying inclusion and exclusion criteria on more than 500 studies, 39 articles were selected for further analysis. The analysis resulted in the identification of 10 themes of learning and teaching practices that are supported by tablets, namely, augmented and virtual learning, collaborative learning, communication, documentation, feedback and assessment, game-based learning, individualized learning, inquiry-based learning, mobile learning, and multimodal learning.

A number of conclusions can be drawn based on the identification of the 10 themes. First, in research studies, tablets supported a large variety of learning and teaching activities. Second, innovative learning and teaching practices emerged such as augmented and virtual learning. Meanwhile practices like documentation and collaborative learning were enhanced and transformed by tablets. Thirdly, the findings in this review confirmed and further complemented Nouri & Cerrato-Pargman (2016) which studied how students and teachers, without any guidance intervention, used tablets. This shows the consistency between the way tablets are used in research settings by scholars and in educational settings by students and teachers. Fourthly, multimodal learning stands out as one third of the selected studies concern some aspects of multimodal learning.

Furthermore, a couple of research gaps were identified. Few of the learning and teaching activities designed by researchers (and teachers in some cases) in the included studies were informed by theories of learning. Additionally, longitudinal studies were rarely employed. As pointed out, tablets are primarily used in subjects such as language, mathematics and natural sciences. The engagement of tablets in other subjects in K-12 education like social sciences, music and PE was not sufficiently presented. Future research may focus on determining the obstacles of integrating tablets in those subjects and conducting longitudinal studies of implementing tablets for teaching and learning.

The main limitation of this systematic review is that it primarily aimed at identifying the types of tablet-mediated learning and teaching practices, and overlooked the effectiveness and the efficiency of these practices in terms of learning and teaching.

REFERENCES

Bergström, A. & Höglund, L., (2014). A national survey of early adopters of e-book reading in Sweden. [online] Available at: http://www.gu.se/english/research/publication?publicationId=200854>

Braun, V. & Clarke, V, 2006. Using thematic analysis in Psychology. *Qualitative Research in Psychology*, 3 (2). pp. 77-101.

Cerratto Pargman, T., Nouri, J. & Milrad, M., (2017), Taking an instrumental genesis lens: New insights into collaborative mobile learning. *British Journal of Educational Technology*. 49: 219–234, doi:10.1111/bjet.12585

Clarke, B., Svanaes, S. &Zimmermann S. (2013). 'One-to-one tablets in secondary schools: an evaluation study', Tablets for Schools, [online] Available at: http://tabletsforschools.org.uk/wp-content/uploads/2012/12/FKY-Tablets-for-Schools-Stage-2-Full-Report-July-2013.pdf

Cobcroft, R. S., Towers, S. J., Smith, J. E., & Bruns, A., (2006). Mobile learning in review: Opportunities and challenges for learners, teachers, and institutions. *Online Learning and Teaching (OLT) Conference*. Brisbane, Australia, pp. 21-30.

Dray, S., Siegel, D., Feldman, E., & Potenza, M., (2002). "Why Do Version 1.0 And Not Release It? Conducting Field Trials Of The Tablet PC". *Interactions,* 9(2). pp.11-16.

Gasparini, A., & Culén, A., (2013). The iPad in a classroom: A cool personal item or simply an educational tool? *International Conference on Advances in Computer-Human Interactions*, Nice, France, pp. 204–209.

Haßler, B., Major, L. & Hennessy, S. (2015) Tablet use in schools: A critical review of the evidence for learning outcomes. *Journal of Computer Assisted Learning*, 32(2). pp. 139–156.

Henderson, S. & Yeow, J., (2012). iPad in Education: A Case Study of iPad Adoption and Use in a Primary School. *International Conference on System Science*, Hawaii, USA. pp. 77-87.

Hirsh-Pasek, K., Zosh, J. M., Golinkoff, R. M., Gray, J. H., Robb, M. B., & Kaufman, J., (2015). Putting education in "educational" apps: lessons from the science of learning. *Psychological Science in the Public Interest*, 16(1). pp. 3–34.

Hung, C. Y., Sun, J. C. Y., & Yu, P. T., (2015). The benefits of a challenge: student motivation and flow experience in tablet-PC-game-based learning. *Interactive Learning Environments*, 23(2). pp. 172-190.

Lee C., (2015). Use of iPad for teaching and learning: a review of the literature. *International Journal of Social Media and Interactive Learning Environments*, 3(3). pp. 184-199.

Li, S. C., Pow, J. W., Wong, E. M., & Fung, A. C., (2010). Empowering student learning through Tablet PCs: A case study. *Education and Information Technologies*, 15(3). pp.171-180.

Nguyen, L., Barton, S. M., & Nguyen, L. T., (2015). iPads in higher education—Hype and hope. *British Journal of Educational Technology*, 46(1). pp.190–203.

Nouri, J., & Pargman, T. C., (2016). When teaching practices meet tablets' affordances. Insights on the materiality of learning. *European Conference on Technology Enhanced Learning.* pp. 179-192. Springer, Cham.

Pegrum, M., Oakley, G., & Faulkner, R. , (2013). Schools going mobile: A study of the adoption of mobile handheld technologies in Western Australian independent schools. *Australasian Journal of Education Technology, 29*(1), *pp.66-81.*

Wu, H. K., Lee, S. W. Y., Chang, H. Y., & Liang, J. C., (2013). Current status, opportunities and challenges of augmented reality in education. *Computers & Education,* 62. pp.41-49.

APPENDIX: SELECTED STUDIES

1. Alhinty, M. 2014. Young language learners' collaborative learning and social interaction as a motivational aspect of the iPad. *International conference on Interactive Mobile Communication Technologies and Learning*, (pp. 64-69). Available from: IEEE.
2. Culén, A., & Gasparini, A., 2012. Tweens with the iPad classroom—Cool but not really helpful?. *International Conference on e-Learning and e-Technologies in Education*, (pp. 1-6). Available from: IEEE.

3. Crnkovic, K., 2014, May. Use of iPads in foreign language classes. *International Convention on Information and Communication Technology, Electronics and Microelectronics*, (pp. 937-939). Available from: IEEE.
4. Deater-Deckard, K., El Mallah, S., Chang, M., Evans, M. A., & Norton, A., 2014. Student behavioural engagement during mathematics educational video game instruction with 11–14 year olds. *International Journal of Child-Computer Interaction,* 2(3). (pp. 101-108).
5. Decano, T., 2013. Willingness of students to use tablets as a learning tool. *International Conference on Educational Media,* (pp. 1-9). Available from: IEEE.
6. Desmon, L. B. J., Soon, L. K., & Peng, Z., 2013. Maths@ RV: A dual-component framework in designing one-to-one computing lessons in mathematics. *International Council for Educational Media (ICEM),* (pp. 1-13). Available from :IEEE.
7. Falloon, G., 2015. What's the difference? Learning collaboratively using iPads in conventional classrooms. *Computers & Education*, 84(C). pp 62-77.
8. Furuya, T., Mizuochi, Y., Yatsushiro, K., & Mizukoshi, K., 2016. A study regarding the effects of synchronous CSCL use involving tablet-type terminals in arithmetic class and through practical experience with fractions using edutab. *International Symposium on System Integration*, (pp. 658-663). Available from: IEEE.
9. Geer, R., White, B., Zeegers, Y., Au, W. & Barnes, A., 2016. Emerging pedagogies for the use of iPads in schools. *British Journal of Educational Technology*, 48(2). pp. 490-498.
10. Gong, C., Chen, G., Cheng, W., Yang, X. & Huang, R., 2013. Potential issues on initiatively utilizing e-textbooks in K-12 classrooms. *International Conference on Advanced Learning Technologies*, (pp. 314-318). Available from: IEEE.
11. Grubelnik, V., & Grubelnik, L.,2016. Teaching physics in primary schools with tablet computers: Key advantages. *International Convention on Information and Communication Technology, Electronics and Microelectronics,* (pp. 847-851). Available from: IEEE.
12. Gu, E., Tzou, M.H. & Hoda, R., 2014. Fill that blank! An iOS-based literacy application. *Software Engineering Conference*, (pp. 80-83). Available from: IEEE.
13. Han, H., Wang, D. & Xu, J., 2013. Classroom Assessment and Analysis System: Using Tablet PCs and Cloud Computing to Improve Effectiveness of Classroom Assessment. *International Conference on Advanced Cloud and Big Data*, (pp. 77-80). Available from: IEEE.
14. Harfield, A., Jormanainen, I., Rungrattanaubol, J. & Pattaranit, R., 2013. An Open Monitoring Environment for primary school children engaged in tablet-based learning. *International Joint Conference on Computer Science and Software Engineering*, (pp. 195-199). Available from: IEEE.
15. Henderson, S., & Yeow, J., 2012. iPad in education: A case study of iPad adoption and use in a primary school. *International Conference on System Science*, (pp. 78-87). Available from: IEEE.
16. Hsu, C. Y., Chen, M.W. & Wu. C.C., 2015. Teaching High School Computer Science with Videos of Historical Figures--An Augmented Reality Approach. *International Conference on Learning and Teaching in Computing and Engineering,* (pp. 22-25). Available from: IEEE.
17. Kim, Y., Lim, C., Choi, H., & Hahn, M., 2012. Effects on training mathematics problem-solving behaviors using a tablet computer. *International Conference on Teaching, Assessment and Learning for Engineering,* (pp. W2C-6). Available from: IEEE.
18. Kuhn, J., Lukowicz, P., Hirth, M., Poxrucker, A., Weppner, J., & Younas. J., 2016. gPhysics—Using Smart Glasses for Head-Centered, Context-Aware Learning in Physics Experiments. *Transactions on Learning Technologies*, 9(4), pp. 304-317.
19. Lohr, M, 2011. e-Learning Using iPads-An e-learning Scenario Using Mobile Devices and Sensors for Measurements. *International Conference on Advanced Learning Technologies*, (pp. 237-238). Available from: IEEE.
20. Lohr, M., 2014. Apps versus demonstration experiments: Improvement of quality of physics teaching in secondary education by the use of tablets. *International Conference on Interactive Mobile Communication Technologies and Learning*, 2014 (pp. 226-231). Available from: IEEE.
21. Lohr, M., 2015. Scientific teaching with tablet PCs: Incorporating Tablet PCs into scientific workflows at schools. *International Conference on Experiment*, (pp. 151-152). Available from: IEEE.
22. LaBelle, D., Alsulami, J., & Leone, J., 2016. Effects of using iPads on First Grade Students' Achievements in Arabic Language Classes In Saudi Arabia. *In Proceedings of Annual Conference on Research in Information Technology,* (pp. 25-28). Available from: ACM.
23. Mann, A. M., Hinrichs, U., Read, J. C., & Quigley, A., 2016. Facilitator, Functionary, Friend or Foe?: Studying the Role of iPads within Learning Activities Across a School Year. *In Proceedings of International Conference on Human Factors in Computing Systems,* (pp. 1833-1845). Available from: ACM.

24. Montrieux, H., Vanderlinde, R., Courtois, C., Schellens, T., & De Marez, L., 2014. A qualitative study about the implementation of tablet computers in secondary education: The teachers' role in this process. *Procedia-Social and Behavioral Sciences*, 112. pp. 481-488.
25. Mouza, C., & Barrett-Greenly, T., 2015. Bridging the app gap: An examination of a professional development initiative on mobile learning in urban schools. *Computers & Education*, 88. pp.1-14.
26. Nedungadi, P., Jayakumar, A., & Raman, R., 2014. Low cost tablet enhanced pedagogy for early grade reading: Indian context. *Humanitarian Technology Conference*, (pp. 35-39). Available from: IEEE.
27. Nikolić, V., Krnelić, L. Z., Kolarić, D., & Nikolić, M., 2013. Tablet learning environment in iSchool Vežica. *International Convention on Information & Communication Technology Electronics & Microelectronics*, (pp. 526-528). Available from: IEEE.
28. Nouri J. & Cerratto Pargman, T. (2016). When Teaching Practices Meet Tablets' Affordances. Insights on the Materiality of Learning. In: K. Verbert, M. Sharples & T. Klobučar (Eds.) Adaptive and Adaptable Learning. EC-TEL 2016. Lecture Notes in Computer Science, vol. 9891, 179-192. Cham: Springer.
29. Preciado-Babb, A. P., 2012. Incorporating the iPad in the mathematics classroom. *Global Engineering Education Conference*, (pp. 1-5). Available from: IEEE.
30. Ramkalawon, L., & Bholoa, A., 2016. Using tablet PC in the teaching and learning of secondary mathematics: A case of a girl's class in Mauritius. *SAI Computing Conference*, (pp. 850-857). Available from: IEEE.
31. Reychav, I., & Wu, D., 2015. Mobile collaborative learning: The role of individual learning in groups through text and video content delivery in tablets. *Computers in Human Behavior*, 50. pp. 520-534.
32. Sankar, M. V., & Abdallah, S, 2015. The combined effect of class size and training on the effectiveness of iPad-based learning. *International Conference on Information and Communication Technology Research*, (pp. 194-197). Available from: IEEE.
33. Sun, J. C. Y., Chang, C., Chen, M. J., & Lin, Y. Y., 2016. Effects of enhanced element-managed instruction integrated with tablet PC-based collaborative polling on fifth graders' sight-word reading performance. *International Journal of Mobile Learning and Organisation*, 10(1-2). pp. 102-116.
34. Švecová, L., Mechlová, E., Sztwioroková, L., & Koníček, L., 2015. Tablets in classroom. *International Conference on Emerging eLearning Technologies and Applications,* (pp. 1-6). Available from: IEEE.
35. Uchiyama, K., & Funahashi, K.,,2013. Tablet VR-Learning System: Chemical Laboratory Experience System. *International Conference on Signal-Image Technology & Internet-Based Systems*, (pp. 416-423). Available from: IEEE.
36. Walubita, G., Lea, N., Robert, S., Emma, O., Heikki, L., Mapenzi, C., Maggie, K., Jacqueline, J.F., Christopher, Y. & Mwanza, N.M., 2015. Ensuring sufficient literacy practice with tablet technology in Zambian schools. *IST-Africa Conference,* (pp. 1-10). Available from: IEEE.
37. Wang, C. P., & Wang, C. H., 2013. Learning Local Culture with E-Sketch Note. *International Conference on Advanced Learning Technologies,* (pp. 485-486). Available from: IEEE.
38. Wu, Y., Lu, X., Zhou, D., & Cai, Y., 2013. Virtual Calligraphic Learning and Writing Evaluation. *International Symposium on Computational Intelligence and Design*, (pp. 108-111). Available from: IEEE.
39. Wyeth, P., McEwan, M., Roe, P., & MacColl, I., 2011. Expressive interactions: Tablet usability for young mobile learners. *Proceedings of Australian Computer-Human Interaction Conference*, (pp. 311-314). Available from: ACM.

INDIVIDUALIZATION OF INSTRUCTION USING 'SOCRATIVE' APP

Tatiana Prextova, Libor Klubal, Kateřina Kostolányová, Zuzana Homanova and Vojtěch Gybas
University of Ostrava, Pedagogical Faculty
Frani Sramka 3, Ostrava, Czech Republic

ABSTRACT

Individualization of instruction in a regular classroom is difficult. The paper explores the possibilities of using a mobile touch device and a web tool for time individualization in mathematics instruction. The paper compares the pros and cons of using an electronic and a regular (printed) test to determine students' needs. The results show that the electronic test is more time-saving than the regular test. Moreover, the paper also describes the use of an electronic test in a classroom.

KEYWORDS

Individualized Instruction, Mobile Device, Tablet, Socrative, Web Application

1. INTRODUCTION

The often used terms Individualized instruction and Individualization are a part of educational policies in a number of countries, including the Czech Republic. Published by the Ministry of Education, School and Sports, the **Framework Education Program for Basic Education** contains the following individualization-related points (2017):

- *"Apply variable organizational patterns and individualization of the learning process respecting students' needs and potential; apply differentiation to education",*
- *"Apply the principle of the differentiation and individualization of the learning process when organizing activities and determining educational content, forms and methods".*

In real instruction, however, the teacher faces the problem of how to individualize instruction in an environment where instead of 6 or 10 students, they have to deal with 25 or 30 students. What methods and technologies can the teacher use to help all of their students fully develop their potential? Is mobile technology essential in implementing individualization into instruction?

The ISTE (International Society for Technology in Education) Standards for teachers and students lead us to the conclusion that the implementation and effective use of technology in the learning process helps students fulfill their potential:

ISTE Standards for Teachers (2017):

- *"Use technology to create, adapt and personalize learning experiences that foster independent learning and accommodate learner differences and needs".*
- *"Design authentic learning activities that align with content area standards and use digital tools and resources to maximize active, deep learning".*
- *"Explore and apply instructional design principles to create innovative digital learning environments that engage and support learning".*

ISTE Standards for Students (2017):

- *"Students articulate and set personal learning goals, develop strategies leveraging technology to achieve them and reflect on the learning process itself to improve learning outcomes".*
- *"Students build networks and customize their learning environments in ways that support the learning process".*

Once every student has a mobile device, individualization of instruction becomes much more feasible.

2. INDIVIDUALIZATION

First of all, the term individualization needs to be defined as it is often confused with individual instruction, which is a face-to-face, one teacher-one student type of instruction.

The Pedagogical Dictionary (Průcha, Walterová, Mareš, 2013) defines individualization as *"a way to differentiate instruction where a heterogeneous classroom remains a basic social unit and the inner, content and methodical differentiation takes students' individual characteristics into account"*. Kargerová and Maňourová (2013) define individualized instruction similarly, arguing that it is an instruction that *"supports collective education of children with different skill levels. We take these differences into account when planning, realizing and evaluating instruction"*.

The teacher should adapt both the content and methodical part of instruction to reflect individual characteristics of their students. The teacher's role is to help the student maintain their uniqueness and develop their individual skills. Since each student has the same rights, the teacher needs to find methods that will best suit a particular student. Moreover, the teacher should be able to recognize their students' strengths and assign them such tasks that would allow them to be successful and meet their goals. In quality instruction the teacher should approach their students individually.

2.1 Individualization Principles

Individualization in the education process is based on two principles (Kasíková, Dittrich, Valenta, 2007):

Mastered Curriculum Principle

There are various ways for students to master the curriculum. Even the slower students can master the curriculum as they have more time to solve the problem. However, the teacher also needs to have additional tasks and activities (adapted to their skills and abilities) prepared for the faster students.

Continuous Learning Progress Principle

Working at their own pace, students should be able to achieve the learning objective in a given time and under the given conditions. In real instruction, the faster students often need to wait for their slower peers and therefore become bored and/or engage in extra-curricular activities. Therefore, the teacher is expected to have additional tasks prepared for the faster students. This way, working at their own pace, each student can work toward the learning objective.

2.2 Individualization Types

The following are the types of individualization of instruction, which are based on the principle of individualization of the learning content, teaching methods and strategies and learning pace (Vališová, Kasíková, 2011):

Selection of curriculum parts

Students can choose anything from the curriculum and focus on e.g. natural sciences, humanities, etc. Moreover, they can also choose a particular subject or a particular part of the subject's curriculum.

Additional instruction

It is an instruction where the basic curriculum is taught to all students, with the additional information being provided to those students who are either interested in the topic and would like to know more (additional, in-depth information) or to those who do not understand the basic curriculum and need to explore different learning strategies which would help them understand it.

Student in learning units

The curriculum is divided into parts, with students being told how to proceed. They proceed individually, choosing the sequence of tasks, their own pace, etc.

Individualization "matching"

It is matching the teacher's teaching style with the student's learning style. For instance, the teacher adapts their teaching strategies to the needs of a particular student.

2.3 Individualization Systems

Individualization systems represent different views on and approaches to individualization. The following are the best-known systems (Vališová, Kasíková, 2011):

2.3.1 Mastery Learning

This type of learning is based on the assumption that learning and its results are directly related to the amount of time we have for learning. It means that every student can reach a certain level of learning if presented with appropriate conditions, the most of important of which being time and feedback. As a result, the student becomes more motivated to study. The system works as follows: after collective instruction, students are given feedback on if they were able to meet their learning objectives (a formative test is used to acquire the feedback). The students, who have not met the learning objectives and requirements, need to work further.

2.3.2 Keller Plan

Even though the system was mainly used in university instruction, its principles could also be used at other levels of education:

- Dividing the study material into smaller learning units.
- The learning pace is individual; it is quality that is important, not time.
- Written study materials (i.e. instruction manuals) are used to guide the student in their learning process.
- For the purposes of discussion within smaller groups of students, a selected student becomes the teacher's helper.
- Instruction is motivational.
- Students are evaluated when they have successfully completed a learning unit.

2.3.3 FENI Model

It is a four-level model that is mainly used in the German education system. It consists of the following four levels:

Forderungskurs

A course that helps the student develop their skills and abilities. It consists of students who are able to deepen their knowledge of the subject matter by using critical and abstract thinking.

Erweiterungskurs

A course that provides additional information to those students who have no difficulty understanding the basic curriculum.

Normalkurs

A basic course consisting of students who have difficulty understanding the new curriculum.

Intensivkurs

A course designed to help the weaker students. It consists of those students who need intensive help from the teacher to master the curriculum.

2.3.4 Dalton Plan

This principle is based on self-studying. The student is able to master the curriculum on their own, using their own learning strategies. In this case, the teacher is only a consultant who guides the student. The main objective of this principle is to teach the student to be responsible for their own learning.

3. INDIVIDUALIZATION USING MOBILE TECHNOLOGY

3.1 Pedagogical Features of Mobile Technology

In 2012, academic scholars from the University of Hull (UK) and the University of Technology (Australia) designed the so-called iPAC Framework which identifies the specific pedagogical features of mobile devices that are used in instruction. The features consist of three main constructs – Personalization, Authenticity and

Collaboration, which are further divided into seven sub-constructs – Customization, Agency, Task, Tool, Setting, Conversation and Data Sharing (see Figure 1):

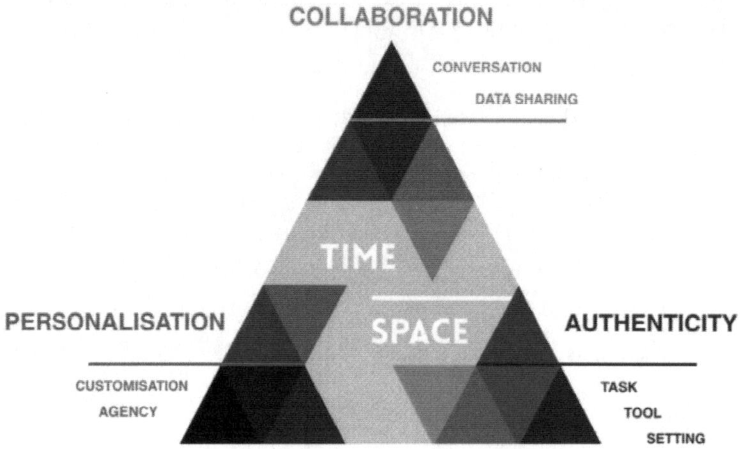

Figure 1. iPAC Constructs (Mobile Learning Toolkit, ???)

Customization

Mobile learning activities can also be customized or tailored to the needs of individual students, helping to make them more personalized. This often involves designing individual tasks for students and thus enabling them to use the features of their mobile devices, such as apps, to make their learning individual. Mobile devices are becoming context aware, thus making it possible for the device to capture information about the learner such as their location, time and the people/objects that are near them. As a result, students can be presented with additional information, resources and activities on an individual or tailored basis.

Agency

In well-designed mobile learning activities, students have a high degree of control over the places, pace and time of learning. It also includes the degree to which students have autonomy over what they learn or the learning objectives.

Task and Tool

Mobile devices enable students to undertake more authentic tasks, using more realistic tools. Students are presented with the kind of activities they might encounter outside of formal learning settings. Moreover, mobile devices also enable students to use a variety of tools and applications that are as realistic as those used by real-world professionals.

Setting

Setting is closely related to the tasks and tools with which students deal. It refers to the place or space where the mobile learning task is situated. This includes physical settings such as a field trip where students have their mobile device with them to collect and analyze data, or virtual settings such as a video conference with a scientific institution, which allows students to participate in a highly authentic exchange of ideas and information.

Conversation

Social interaction, conversation or dialogue through mobile technology can be beneficial not only to the student, but also to the teacher. It allows the teacher to provide feedback to their students and students to exchange opinions, ideas and other information.

Data Sharing

Data sharing is an important part of communication. Using mobile technology, students can create shared, socially interactive environments where they can conveniently communicate—often multi-modally—and exchange information and resources with their peers, teachers and other experts.

3.2 Individualization in Mathematics?

The actual instruction process is usually divided into the following stages: motivation – the teacher tries to make the students interested in the curriculum; exposition – the teacher transfers their knowledge to students, creating the foundation for skills and habits; fixation – which consists of repetition and leads to knowledge retention. The fixation methods are divided depending on whether we fixate knowledge or skills. (Klubal et al, 2017)

One of the fixation methods, practice is mainly used in foreign language and mathematics instruction. The repetition of facts leads to knowledge retention (fixation). In mathematics, it is multiplication of single-digit numbers, where discovering that multiplication may be done by addition can turn a skill into knowledge. Knowledge is built through practice, which is sometimes referred to as drill. This enables the student to solve more complex problems and acquire more complex skills. In foreign language instruction, this is represented by building a vocabulary. In foreign language instruction drill is often the main tool for knowledge fixation. (Klubal, Kostolanyova, 2015)

Obtaining feedback is an integral part of repetition/practice. When using non-ICT tools in repetition, feedback usually comes too late, after having been corrected by another person and/or having found the correct answer in the study material. Using ICT-based tools allows for immediate correction of errors and feedback acquisition at the time when the student is still fully focused on the task. The research results prove that electronic repetition is much more effective, especially for those students who have not yet acquired enough knowledge.

3.3 Experiment Description

Individualization during the fixation stage is facilitated through adaptation of content to students' current knowledge. As has already been mentioned, individualization of instruction in a regular classroom is difficult. The following paragraphs describe the use of the Socrative app and a mobile touch device to create such classroom conditions which would allow for a sufficient degree of individualization in terms of time management.

25 students (11 and 12 years old) participated in the experiment. The topic was decimal numbers (notation, rounding, addition, subtraction, multiplication and division). The problems used in the electronic test were chosen from a textbook which all students had at their disposal. The objective of the experiment was to determine the impact of the mobile touch device and the web tool on the time management aspect of individualization in a regular classroom, i.e. the time every student needed to understand the curriculum.

First of all, the Socrative system was used to design an electronic test which included three problems from each part of the curriculum. The purpose of the test was to determine areas in which the student needed to improve. Aside from the electronic version of the test, the teacher also had its printed version in which source tasks from the textbook were highlighted, thus allowing them to determine how the tested curriculum is represented in both the textbook and the Socrative app.

Using an iPad, each student logged into the classroom via a QR code. Students had 15 minutes to complete the test (however, they were allowed to complete it before the time limit). The test was preceded by a 3-minute preparation stage, during which the tablets were distributed to students who then logged into the Socrative app. During the pretest, feedback is displayed only to the teacher, students cannot see it.

During testing, the Socrative app displays real-time information, allowing the teacher to monitor each student's progress. Based on their results, the teacher assigned examples from the textbook to the students. All students completed the test before the 15-minute time limit. After the pretest, the teacher launched the same test in the Socrative app. This time, however, the student immediately sees whether their answer is correct or not. Afterward, the students went over the entire test one more time, which allowed them to compare their knowledge at the beginning and end of class.

*****	93%	38,225	1,00026	2,5	0,21	C	1,58	28,845	C	2,22	26,
*****	79%	38,225	1,00026	2,5	0,00206	C	1,58	28,855	C	2,22	26,
*****	43%	38,020	1,0026	2,5	0,2	C	1,58	1,451	C	2,22	26
*****	21%	38,2265	1,0026	2,600	00,26	C	1,58	26,45	A	2,22	26
*****	93%	38,225	1,00026	2,5	0,21	C	1,58	28,845	C	2,22	26,
*****	43%	38,225	1,261	2,5	0,21	C			C	2,22	26,
*****	93%	38,225	1,00026	2,5	0,21	C	1,58	28,845	C	2,22	26,
*****	50%	30,225	1,0026	2,5	0,200	C	1,58	28,251	C	2,22	1,4
*****	50%	38,225	1,00026	2,6	0,2	C	1,58	2,845	C	2,22	26
*****	36%	38,025	1,0026	2,540		C			C	2,22	26,
*****	43%	38,225	1,26 000	2,540	0,300	C	1,58	28,845	C	2,22	26
*****	50%	30,24	1,00026	2,530	1,26	C	1,58	28,845	C	2,22	26,
*****	50%		1,00026	2,6	0,21	C	1,58			2,22	26
*****	86%	38,225	1,00026	2,5	0,21	C	1,58	28,845	C	2,22	26,
*****	57%	38,225	1,26000	2,500	0,210	B	1,58	28,845	C	2,22	26,
*****	50%	38,0225	1,00026	2,540	0,2	C	158	28,845	C	2,22	26,
*****	86%	38,225	1,00026	2,5	0,21	C	1,58	8,845	C	2,22	16
*****	86%	38,225	1,00026	2,5	0,21	C	1,58	27,845	C	2,22	26,
*****	93%	38,225	1,00026	2,5	0,21	C	1,58	28,845	C	2,22	26,
*****	71%	38,225	1,00026	25,39	2,06	C	1,58	28,845	C	2,22	26
*****	57%	38,225			0,21		1,58	28,845	C	2,22	26

Figure 2. Students' Results in Socrative app

The Socrative electronic system enables the teacher to be actively involved in the student's problem-solving process, allowing them to immediately react to any problems. If it is evident that the student has not mastered the basic skills (e.g. the student in Line 10), the teacher can stop the test and make the student practice the curriculum. Moreover, the teacher can also become involved when a student is too slow and requires individual help. If the printed version of the test was used, none of the above would be possible.

Figure 3 shows the results of students in the experimental group.

Student 2	2:12
Student 23	2:49
Student 6	3:48
Student 14	3:52
Student 1	4:33
Student 13	4:37
Student 15	5:20
Student 19	5:35
Student 3	5:37
Student 4	6:12
Student 21	6:12
Student 7	6:27
Student 20	6:45
Student 25	6:53
Student 18	7:12
Student 17	7:28
Student 10	8:20
Student 11	8:48
Student 12	9:12
Student 16	9:13
Student 5	9:22
Student 9	10:52
Student 8	11:27
Student 24	11:43
Student 22	12:30

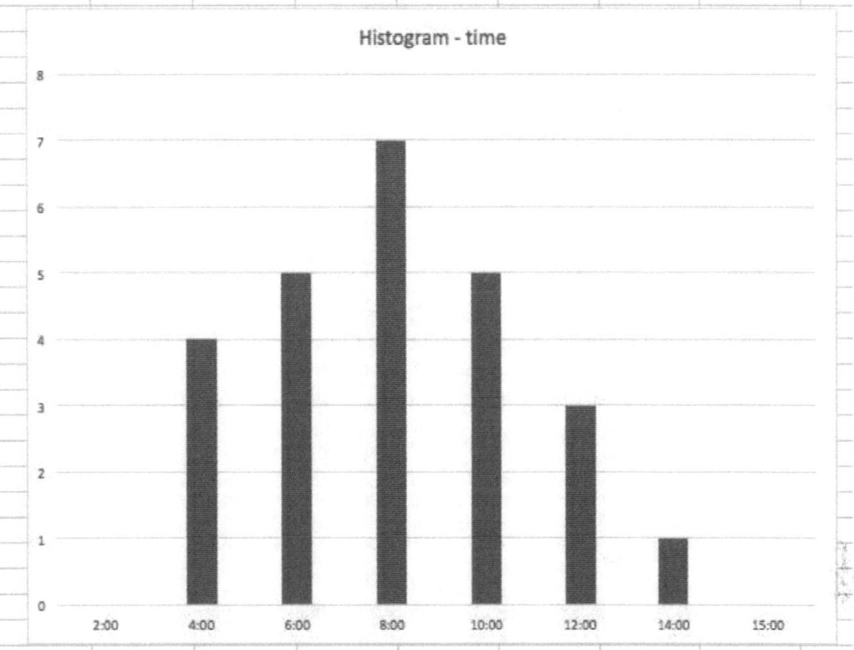

Figure 3. Results of Experimental Group

In the control group, the content of instruction was the same, but the printed version of the test (generated by the Socrative app) was used. The control group was a parallel group with the same number of students. Therefore, both groups were solving the same problems. Test distribution and instruction took as long as in the experimental group. During testing, however, the teacher could not follow the students' progress; they provided the solution key only when a student asked for it or when the teacher found out that the student had completed the test. It took the students 2 to 4 minutes, on average, to go over the test.

Student 1	6:30
Student 20	6:53
Student 23	7:12
Student 5	8:27
Student 17	8:33
Student 21	8:43
Student 7	9:15
Student 16	9:32
Student 15	9:40
Student 19	10:25
Student 1	10:26
Student 4	10:42
Student 12	11:45
Student 14	11:55
Student 3	12:05
Student 11	12:20
Student 6	12:32
Student 9	13:35
Student 8	13:56
Student 24	14:20
Student 18	14:35
Student 22	14:40
Student 13	15:00
Student 25	15:00
Student 10	15:00

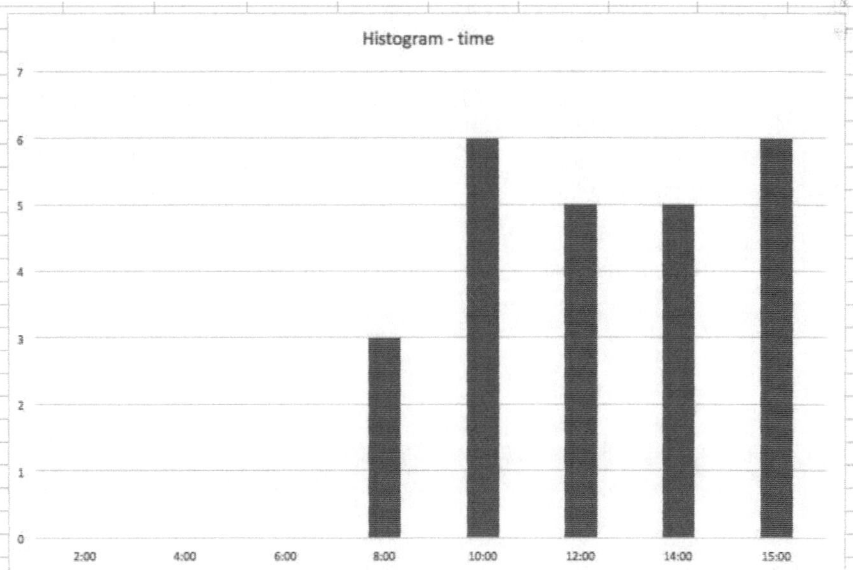

Figure 4. Results of Control Group

Since the teacher needs to grade the test manually and is unable to immediately see the errors, it takes them much longer to determine the current level of students' skills and knowledge.

4. CONCLUSION

Using the Socrative app and a mobile touch device makes individualization in a regular classroom with a high number of students much less time-consuming. Being able to follow the student's problem-solving process enables the teacher to address the problems immediately (and not only after the test has been completed). Students are given feedback on the level of their skills and knowledge and thus can spend time on the part of the curriculum that they have not yet mastered. However, the teacher remains the authority figure who can help students decide how to proceed.

Creating the electronic version of the test takes the teacher as long as creating the printed version. Unlike the printed version, the electronic version can be used repeatedly, and in different forms. The electronic test was used repeatedly during class, allowing the teacher to see the student's skills and knowledge improve in real time. This, however, will be the subject of further research.

REFERENCES

ISTE, 2017. ISTE Standards for Educators. ISTE Standards for Students. Qtd. 19. 11. 2017, available at: https://www.iste.org/standards.

Kargerová, J., Maňourová, Z., 2013. *Individualization in instruction.* Step by Step ČR, Prague.

Kasíková, H., Dittrich, P., Valenta, J., 2007. *Individualization and Differentiation in School.* In Vališová A., Kasíková, H., et al. Pedagogy for Teachers. Grada Publishing, Prague.

Klubal, L., Kostolányová, K. a Gybas, V. Using Tablet and Itunesu as Individualized Instruction Tools. In: Mobile Learning 2017: Proceedings of the 13th international conference mobile learning 2017 2017 Budapest, Hungary. Budapest, Hungary: IADIS Press, 2017. s. 139-142. ISBN 978-989-8533-61-6.

Klubal, L. & Kostolanyova, K. 2015, "Practicing in mathematics using a tablet", *Proceedings of the European Conference on e-Learning, ECEL*, pp. 712.

Mobile Learning Toolit, 2012. iPAC Framework. Qtd. 28. 11. 2017, available at: http://www.mobilelearningtoolkit.com/ipac-framework.html

MŠMT, 2017. Framework Education Program for Basic Education. Qtd. 19. 11. 2017, available at: http://www.msmt.cz/file/43792/.

Prextová, T., 2016. *Adaptation of Testing: Yes or no?.* In European Conference on e-Learning: Proceedings of the 15th European Conference on e-Learning ECEL. ACPI, Prague.

Prextová, T., 2017. *Adapt or not adapt the testing process.* In Media4u Magazine. ISSN 1214-9187.

Vališová, A., Kasíková, H., 2011. *Pedagogy for Teachers – 2nd Edition, Extended and Updated.* Grada Publishing, Prague.

Průcha, J., Walterová, E., Mareš, J., 2013. *Pedagogical Dictionary. 7th Edition, Extended and Updated.* Portál, Prague ISBN 978-80-262-0403-9.

ASSESSING MOBILE INSTANT MESSAGING IN A FOREIGN LANGUAGE CLASSROOM

Alberto Andújar
University of Almería
Crta. De Sacramento s/n, Edificio C, La cañada, Almería, 04120, Spain

ABSTRACT

The present research represents a longitudinal investigation into Mobile Instant Messaging to develop second language skills. WhatsApp application was selected as the chat-based communication tool to carry out this study, which focuses on writing and speaking skills' development. Quantitative and qualitative analyses were used to tackle students writing ability in terms of grammatical, lexical and mechanical accuracy as well as syntactic complexity together with lexical diversity. Similarly, this mobile chat-based application was also used for the creation of a speaking group where the language-related episodes were analyzed as well as students overall performance in terms of pronunciation, grammar, vocabulary, fluency and comprehension. In order to observe the differences among the participants, a control and experimental group were set at the start of the study in each of the groups. Pre-post tests were given to the students and participation was tracked throughout the interaction. Screenshots in the application were also taken at different times in order to observe students' use of the language. Positive results were found in terms of accuracy in the experimental group whereas syntactic complexity yielded no significant differences. Regarding the speaking ability, students in the experimental group outperformed those in the control in each of the aspects analyzed, becoming a constant source of language-related episodes. Overall, the application was found to be a rich environment for language acquisition and learning thanks to the social interaction taking place in the application.

KEYWORDS

Mobile Instant Messaging, Mobile Learning, Language Learning, CALL, Virtual Learning, Learning Technologies

1. INTRODUCTION

The tremendous potential that mobile devices offer has been a matter of discussion within the scientific community during the last years. In this respect, retrospective works such as Burston (2014) emphasize the lack of curricular integration even in the case of those studies that have been proved to have a positive impact on students' development through different approaches and perspectives. While mobile phone companies compete to release the latest technological devices, educational institutions continue to provide syllabuses and curriculums that do not incorporate and, in some cases, ban the use of mobile devices in a classroom environment. Due to this fact, most of the studies in this field tackle the possibilities these devices offer out of the classroom, exploiting its ubiquitous characteristics (Koole, 2009; Kukulska-Hulme, 2012).

New ways of communication have changed the landscape of e-learning and chat-based communication tools are no exception. In this vein, the number of users in this kind of applications has increased swiftly reaching almost 1500 million by the end of 2017, and that is just exclusively the case of WhatsApp application (Statista). Nevertheless, there is a growing number of chat applications providing the same functionalities as this last one such as "Line", "Telegram", "Wechat", "Tango" which exploit the possibilities that data plans offer to provide free messaging services available to everyone.

As some experts in the field point out, education is shifting towards a model where autonomous learners who cooperate actively are responsible for the creation of content, participating in a student-oriented atmosphere that little have to do with traditional classroom environments (Otto, 2017).

From the teacher's perspective, and more specifically, in terms of second language teaching, the possibilities for interaction second language learners have in class are very scarce due to the constraints of traditional classroom environment such as number of students, limited time, or amount of contents to cover during a course. Therefore, teachers struggle to develop certain students' abilities as it could be writing or speaking due to the constraints previously mentioned. Hence, in this manuscript we present Mobile Instant Messaging (MIM) as tool that allows the teacher to expand students' time, providing learners with a constant thread of conversation that fosters L2 interaction and learning. By increasing the interaction through the use of mobile chat-based conversation within a group, students have the opportunity to put into practice their second language as well as reflect on their language productions and possible errors throughout the process.

Overall, a longitudinal investigation of Mobile Instant Messaging use for second language development is presented, where social interaction, autonomous and collaborative learning, and language use create an environment that promotes second language development and learning in two different skills: writing and speaking.

2. BODY OF PAPER

2.1 Literature Review and Theoretical Background

Research in MIM has focused on the use of this kind of application and the analysis of the possibilities this platforms offer (e.g. Diaz, 2014; Morato-Paya, 2014; Padron, 2013; Tang and Foon Hew, 2017; Singh et al., 2018) as well as its technological, pedagogical and social affordances. In the field of language learning, it is worth mentioning Gutierrez Colón-Plana et al., (2016) study about improving reading comprehension through MIM as well as those regarding writing and speaking skills (Andújar, 2016; Andújar & Cruz-Martínez, 2017; Fattah, 2015) which are partly commented in this manuscript. Furthermore, WhatsApp has also been found to be a powerful tool to foster second language vocabulary as shown in different investigations where this skill was tackled (see, Hamad, 2017; Jafari & Chalak, 2016; Andujar, 2016). Its use was also explored in order to carry out peer and self-assessment of oral language proficiency (Samaie et al., 2018), nevertheless students presented a negative attitude towards the use of this kind of evaluation. Hence, further investigation of the potential and benefits this application offers for language development is needed so that teachers are able to exploit its characteristics in a second language environment.

Two main language theories underlie this investigation, firstly Vigotsky's (1978) theory about mediation and zone of proximal development. This sociocultural approach to language learning emphasizes the importance of the social context to develop cognition. In this sense, language is understood as process where interaction and collaboration facilitate acquisition (Donato, 2000; Gee, 2003). MIM becomes a fertile ground for authentic language interaction where students have the possibility to practice "on the go" (Kukulska-hulme, 2009). Secondly, Long's (1983) and Swain's (1985) contributions to interaction analysis play a fundamental role within the activity as students construct knowledge in active manner, focusing on meaning and not on isolated facts. Furthermore, because of its real-time nature, MIM contains repair moves and negotiations for meaning that have been found to promote second language development (Sotillo, 2000; Warschauer, 1996). Students modify their discourse in order to achieve understanding, collaborating and putting into practice their target language skills.

2.2 Study

The case study conducted for each of the skills differ from one another, being writing and speaking skills assessed in 2015 and 2016 respectively. Through the creation of a WhatsApp group and a series of premises given to students in advance we were able to evaluate these different skills. This premises dealt with limiting the writing WhatsApp group to the use of text messages in order to have enough data to measure writing skills and restricting the speaking WhatsApp group to voice messages so that we could measure students' speaking development. Furthermore, one student had to ask a question to their peers every day in order to maintain the conversation in the application. Image and video-sharing were allowed and no time restrictions were imposed throughout the activity. Each of the case studies had a control group in order to analyze the differences between the groups in terms of language development. Groups were composed by 30 participants each with a total of 120 students who joined a B1 course at the University of Almería.

To carry out this longitudinal investigation, different analyses were carried out depending on the skill under consideration. A mixed methods analysis was carried out where quantitative and qualitative data were investigated (Onwegbuzie, 2003). In all the cases apart from tracking students' messages in the application, pre-post test measures were taken in order to observe students' level in the different skills. An external rater was used during this process and the tests provided met the parameters set by the Common European Framework for Reference (CEFR).

In this vein, to assess students' writing skill in the foreign language, we carried out an analysis of the language gains in terms of grammatical, lexical and mechanical accuracy as well as syntactic complexity together with lexical diversity. As presented in Table 1 and Table 2, statistically significant results were found in terms of accuracy.

Table 1. Pre-post test measures of Accuracy for Texts Written in Control and Experimental Group

	Control group			**Experimental group**			**Control group**[a]			**Experimental group**[a]		
	Total	Mean	SD	Total	Mean	SD	Total	Mean	SD	Total	Mean	SD
Error-free clauses	194	4.85	2.68	206	5.15	3.5	278	6.95	2.29	341	8.53	2.65
Error-free clauses per clause		0.28	0.19		0.31	0.22		0.43	0.15		0.61[b]	0.2
Error-free T-units	140	3.5	2.3	159	3.97	3.03	201	5.03	1.9	283	7.08	2.2
Error-free T-units per T-unit		0.32	0.2		0.33	0.25		0.49	0.19		0.68[b]	0.16
Errors	646	16.15	3.7	608	15.2	2.83	449	11.23	3.1	236	5.9	2.02
Errors per word		0.16	0.37		0.15	0.28		0.11	0.31		0.06[b]	0.2

[a]Post-test results in experimental and control group.
[b]Statistically significant difference between experimental and control group ($p < .05$).

Table 2. Pre-Post Test Measures of Grammatical, Lexical, and Mechanical Accuracy for Texts Written In Control and Experimental Group

	Control group			**Experimental group**			**Control group**[a]			**Experimental group**[a]		
	Total	Mean	SD	Total	Mean	SD	Total	Mean	SD	Total	Mean	SD
Grammar errors	231	5.77	1.86	212	5.3	1.65	161	4.02	1.31	76	1.9	0.81
Grammar errors per word		0.06	0.02		0.05	0.02		0.04	0.01		0.02[b]	0.01
Lexical errors	232	5.8	1.72	223	5.58	1.79	169	4.23	1.67	40	1.1	0.64
Lexical errors per Word		0.06	0.02		0.06	0.02		0.04	0.02		0.01[b]	0.01
Mechanical errors	185	4.62	1.56	176	4.4	1.05	118	2.95	1.1	79	1.98	0.92
Mechanical errors per word		0.05	0.02		0.04	0.01		0.03	0.1		0.02[b]	0.01

[a]Post-test results in experimental and control group.
[b]Statistically significant difference between experimental and control group ($p < .05$).

No significant difference were found in terms of syntactic complexity together with lexical diversity as the mean segmental type token ratio (MSTTR) calculated yielded no significant difference between control and experimental group (See Table 3).

Table 3. Pre-post Test Measures of Complexity for Text Written In Control and Experimental Group

	Control group			Experimental group			Control group[a]			Experimental group[a]		
	Total	Mean	SD	Total	Mean	SD	Total	Mean	SD	Total	Mean	SD
Clauses	682	17.05	3.08	672	16.8	3.96	646	16.15	2.68	562	14.05[b]	2.71
T-units	438	10.95	2.85	476	11.9	3.44	413	10.33	2.7	416	10.4	2.96
Words per clause		5.86	0.67		5.95	0.58		6.19	0.6		7.11	0.54
Words per T-unit		9.13	1.97		8.4	1.89		9.68	1.87		9.61	1.8
Clauses per T-unit		1.55	0.31		1.41	0.27		1.56	0.28		1.36	0.22
MSTTR		0.68	0.07		0.68	0.05		0.75	0.05		0.82[a]	0.04

[a]Post-test results in experimental and control group.
[b]Statistically significant difference between experimental and control group ($p < .05$).

The language-related episodes (LRE) (Swain & Watanabe, 2012) resulting from the interaction within the application were also investigated in the case of the speaking group. These LREs were operationalized as situations where students collaborated to achieve understanding and were tracked throughout the exchange that lasted for four months. Similarly, students' speaking development was investigated through an extensive tracking of the language used within the voice messages sent by students during the interaction. Pre-post measures were taken and LREs were observed and divided in two categories: negotiations for meaning and negative feedback (Bueno-Alastuey, 2013). In the case of negative feedback, it was operationalized as a move from the interlocutor towards a more target-like feature. This LRE was later subdivided into recasts and elicitations (Long, 1996). It is worth mentioning the great number of negotiations that took place during the process as presented in Table 4.

Table 4. Average Number and Types of Lres Signals in the Experimental Group per Month

Month	Negotiation	Negative Feedback	
		Recasts	Elicitation
1	362 (60%)	154 (25,5%)	87 (14%)
2	331 (62,2%)	130 (24,7%)	69 (13%)
3	278 (58,5%)	145 (30,5%)	52 (10,9%)
4	260 (57,5%)	115 (25,4%)	77 (17%)
5	273 (67,2%)	96 (23,6%)	37 (9,1%)
6	224 (67,4%)	78(23,4%)	30 (9%)

As we can observe in Figure 1, the number of language-related episodes decreased throughout the interaction, suggesting a lower number of situations where possible misunderstandings occurred.

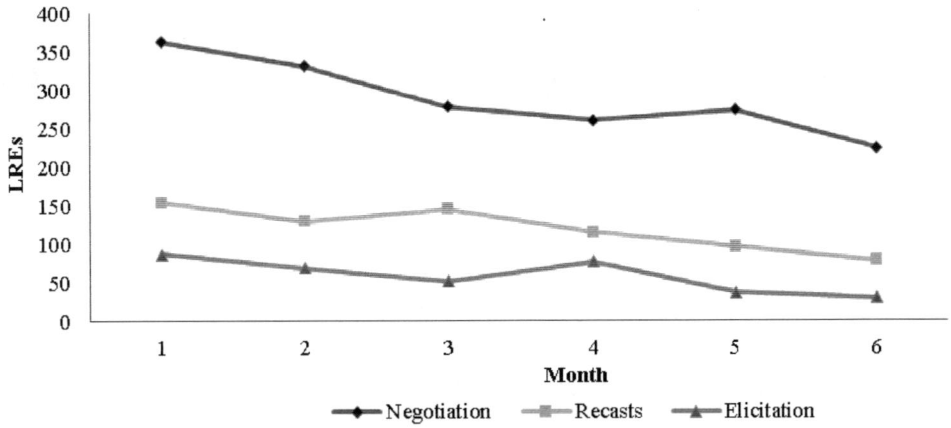

Figure 1. Trend of LREs per Month

Students performance was also analyzed with a pre-post test in the Speaking group as presented in Table 5 and 6. Results show statistically significant differences in each of the speaking skills measured, indicating a positive effect of the interaction.

Table 5. Pre-test Speaking Measures in the Control and Experimental Groups

	Pronunciation			Grammar			Vocabulary			Fluency			Comprehension		
	Total	Mean	SD	Total	Mean	SD	Total	Mean	SD	Total	Mean	SD	Total	Mean	SD
Control	40	1.23	.86	40	14.25	5.02	40	7.70	3.05	40	4.70	1.53	40	10.65	2.77
Experimental	40	1.10	1.77	40	21	4.5	40	9.85*	3.66	40	4.88	1.58	40	13.90	2.24

* Statistically significant difference between experimental and control group

Table 6. Post-test Speaking Measures in the Control and Experimental Group

	Pronunciation			Grammar			Vocabulary			Fluency			Comprehension		
	Total	Mean	SD	Total	Mean	SD	Total	Mean	SD	Total	Mean	SD	Total	Mean	SD
Control	40	1.80	.51	40	15	4.7	40	12.40	2.9	40	5.45	1.35	40	10.40	2.69
Experimental	40	2.25*	.43	40	23.40*	4.25	40	16.8*	2.74	40	8.65*	1.31	40	16.47*	2.5

* Statistically significant difference between experimental and control group ($p < .05$)

Qualitative information was also obtained through the screenshots taken from the application. These samples allowed us to observe if students kept repeating the same kind of mistakes later in the conversation. Students mistakes at the beginning were tracked and analyzed throughout the activity. It is worth mentioning cases of low-proficient students that were helped by peers when they did not achieve communication. As an example we could use the word "Great":

Student A: 'I went to Carlos' party and it was /grit/'
Student B: 'Grit'?, I don´t understand
Student A: mm.. yes /grit/
Student B: Oh! You mean great!
Student A: Yes, sorry my pronunciation is really bad…

Figures 2 and 3 show an example of the interaction carried out in the group.

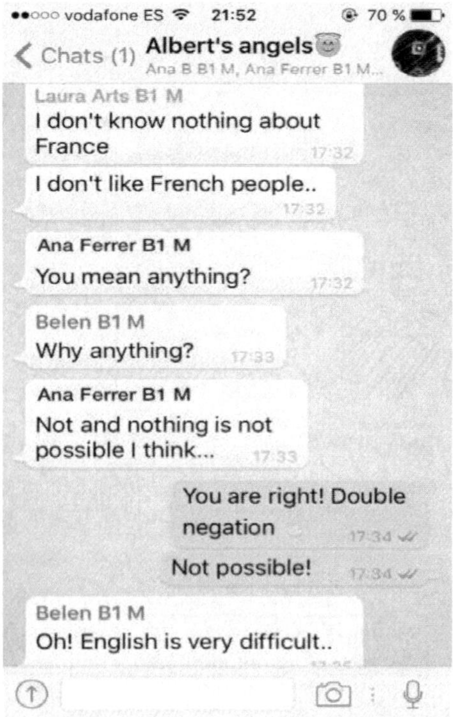

Figure 2. Sample of the conversation

Figure 3. Sample of the conversation

The characteristics this virtual environment offers for second language development are varied. Nevertheless, one of the main qualities that MIM offers with respect to other chat applications has to do with its synchronous and asynchronous character. This feature confers this virtual tool with a wide range of possibilities for language exchange, many times with interaction taking place within seconds which lead to a different kind of exchange from the one we normally find in asynchronous communication. Some of the features of face-to-face communication are present in the conversation, which adds an extra value to the language exchange.

3. CONCLUSION

Mobile instant messaging allowed students to interact outside the class on a daily basis. This possibility led to a constant thread of conversation within the application that benefitted students as they were able to increase their practice time using the target language. The application was found to be beneficial, particularly in terms of accuracy in the case of the writing WhatsApp group where students experienced a significant decrease in the number of mistakes they made, whether lexical, grammatical or mechanical. This may be due to the fact that non-native speakers when speaking a second language (L2) do not use abbreviations as, firstly, they do not have the knowledge of the abbreviations in the L2 and secondly, they aim for accuracy in order to make themselves understood. In terms of speaking development, the overall performance of the experimental group students was higher than those in the control in each of the skills tackled, emphasizing the potential of the application for second language development. Interestingly, students listen to their recordings twice, reproducing their language samples and in many cases, realizing if they have committed an error with a particular pronunciation, word or phrase. Teacher's help in these cases was not needed as students were able to perceive and repair their own errors. Thus, this chat-based environment became an enriching tool that help students overcome the tendency of mechanical repetition and traditional instruction by integrating communicative drills. Autonomy and social interaction led to negotiation for meaning, creating a learning environment that breaks temporal spatial lines.

Possible limitations during the investigation were tackled in advanced and students participation was tracked in order to guarantee that improvements did not just take place because of in-class tuition. Qualitative information was also obtained from screenshots taken in the application. Practical considerations such as owning a mobile phone or internet connectivity were also regarded.

Participation during the activity was remarkable, quickly earning students' acceptance and reducing teacher-student distance. Learners felt comfortable to tinker with the target language, creating a friendly environment for the participants and therefore facilitating learning. This environment as well as the kind of interaction taking place in the activity resembled face-to-face communication due to its often synchronous nature. The teacher role was, in this case, emphasized as he was able to provide rich input and authentic interaction, factors that may lead to second language development.

Overall, teachers cannot just limit themselves to in class teaching as the opportunities to develop a language within a classroom environment are very scarce and it is mandatory to exploit the resources technology continuously offers to expand in-class time as well as to walk in unison with the latest changes in today's society.

ACKNOWLEDGEMENT

We would like to thank professors Marisol Cruz and Tim Spratt for the assistance provided to this investigation.

REFERENCES

Andújar-Vaca, A., and Cruz-Martínez, M. S. 2017. Mobile Instant Messaging: Whatsapp and its Potential to Develop Oral Skills. *Comunicar*, 25(50), 43-52. https://doi.org/10.3916/C50-2017-04

Andujar, A. 2016. Benefits of Mobile Instant Messaging to Develop ESL Writing. *System*, 62, 63-76. https://doi.org/10.1016/j.system.2016.07.004

Bueno-Alastuey, M.C. 2013. Interactional Feedback in Synchronous Voice-based Computer Mediated Communication: Effect of Dyad. *System,* 41(3), 543-559. https://doi.org/10.1016/j.system.2013.05.005

Burston, J. 2014. The reality of MALL: Still on the fringes. *CALICO Journal,* 31(1), 103.

Diaz, J. 2014. *El WhatsApp como herramienta de intervención didáctica para fomentar el aprendizaje cooperativo* [WhatsApp as a tool of educational intervention to foster cooperative learning]. Unpublished Paper presented at *X Jornadas De Material Didáctico y Experiencias Innovadoras En Educación Superior*. Buenos Aires, Argentina. Retrieved from http://eprints.rclis.org/23597/.

Donato, R. 2000. 'Sociocultural contributions to understanding the foreign and second language Classroom', in J. Lantolf (ed*.), Sociocultural theory and second language learning,* pp. 27–50, Oxford University Press, Oxford.

Fattah, S. F. E. S. A. 2015. The effectiveness of using WhatsApp messenger as one of mobile learning techniques to develop students' writing skills. *Journal of Education and Practice,* 6(32), 115-127.

Gee, J. P. 2003. *What Video Games Have to Teach Us About Learning and Literacy*, Palgrave Macmillan, New York.

Hamad, M. M. 2017. Using WhatsApp to enhance students' learning of English language "Experience to share". *Higher Education Studies*, 7(4), 74-87.

Jafari, S. & Chalak, A. 2016. The role of Whatsapp in teaching vocabulary to Iranian EFL learners at junior high school. *English Language Teaching,* 9(8), 85-92.

Koole, M. 2009. 'A model for framing mobile learning', in M. Ally (ed.), *Mobile learning: Transforming the delivery of education and training*, pp. 25-47, AU Press, Edmonton.

Kukulska-Hulme, A. 2009. Will Mobile Learning Change Language Learning? *Recall,* 21(2), 157-165. https://doi.org/10.1017/S0958344009000202

Kukulska-Hulme, A. 2012. How Should the Higher Education Workforce Adapt to Advancements in Technology for Teaching and Learning? *The Internet and Higher Education,* 15(4), 247-254. https://doi.org/10.1016/j.iheduc.2011.12.002

Long, M. H. 1983. *Classroom-oriented research on second language acquisition*. Newbury House, Rowley.

Long, M.H. 1996. 'The role of the linguistic environment in second language acquisition', pp. 413-469, in W. Ritchie, & T. Bathia (eds.), *Handbook of research on second language acquisition*, Academic Press, New York.

Morato Paya, A. 2014. El WhatsApp como complemento del aprendizaje en la clase E/LE [WhatsApp as a learning complement in the classroom of E/LE]. *Revista Foro De Profesores De E/LE,* 10(1), 165-173.

Nakahama, Y., Tyler, A., & Van-Lier, L. 2001. Negotiation of Meaning in Conversational and Information Gap Activities: A Comparative Discourse Analysis. *TESOL Quarterly,* 35, 377-404. https://doi.org/10.2307/3588028

Onwuegbuzie, A.J., & Teddlie, C. 2003. 'A framework for Analyzing Data in Mixed Methods Research', pp. 351-383, in A. Tashakkori & C. Teddlie (eds.), *Handbook of Mixed Methods in Social and Behavioral Research*, Sage, Thousand Oaks, CA.

Otto, S. E. (2017). 'From Past to Present: A Hundred Years of Technology for L2 Learning'. In C.A. Chapelle & S. Sauro (eds.), *The Handbook of Technology and Second Language Teaching and Learning*, pp. 10-25, John Wiley & Sons, New Jersey, USA.

Padron, C. J. 2013. Teaching strategies based on WhatsApp instant messaging application only for phones (mobile learning) and its use to promote collaborative learning. *Revista De Tecnología De Información y Comunicación En Educación,* 7(2), 123-134.

Plana, M. G. C., Escofet, M. I. G., Figueras, I. T., Gimeno, A., Appel, C., & Hopkins, J. 2013. Improving learners' reading skills through instant short messages: A sample study using WhatsApp. In *Proceeding of WorldCall 2013-Call: Sustainability and Computer-Assisted Language Learning*. Glasgow, UK, pp. 80-84.

Samaie, M., Mansouri Nejad, A. & Qaracholloo, M. (2018). An inquiry into the efficiency of WhatsApp for self- and peer-assessments of oral language proficiency. *British Journal of Educational Technology*, 49(1), 111-126.

Singh, H. K. D., Lim, T. M., Woo, T. K. & Fadzil, M. 2018. 'Mobile learning support to distance learners: using WhatsApp Messenger', pp. 109-119, in Li, K. C., Yuen, K. S & Wong, B. T. M. (eds.), *Innovations in open an flexible education*, Springer, Singapore.

Sotillo, S. 2000. Discourse functions and syntactic complexity in synchronous and asynchronous communication. *Language Learning & Technology*, 4, 82-119.

Statista. Retrieved from https://www.statista.com/statistics/260819/number-of-monthly-active-whatsapp-users/. Accessed 1/03/2018.

Swain, M., & Watanabe, Y. 2012. Languaging: Collaborative dialogue as a source of second language learning. In C. Chapelle (ed.), *The encyclopedia of applied linguistics*, Wiley-Blackwell, Oxford.

Tang, Y., & Hew, K. F. (2017). Is mobile instant messaging (MIM) useful in education? Examining its technological, pedagogical, and social affordances. *Educational Research Review,* 21, 85–104.

Vygotsky, L. 1978. *Mind in society: The development of higher psychological processes.* Harvard University Press, Cambridge, MA.

Warschauer, M. 1996. Comparing face-to-face and electronic discussion in the second language classroom. *CALICO Journal*, 13, 7-26.

MOBILE LEARNING AND DIGITAL LITERACY IN THE CONTEXT OF UNIVERSITY YOUNG ADULTS

Georgi Apostolov and Valentina Milenkova
South-West University
66 Iv.Mihailov str., Blagoevgrad, Bulgaria

ABSTRACT

The present article is aimed at focusing on theoretical and practical efforts in promoting various aspects of digital literacy and mobile learning, as well as to explore its dimensions and projections in the university level.
The analysis is based on empirical information for the education process revealed specific aspects of the relationship between young people and ICT in digital society.
The basic conclusion is that the adapting of young adults to the challenges of the digitization and new training practices requires the determining of more effective ways to attract, encourage and motivate students towards the utilization of quality theoretical and applied knowledge and skills in ICT.

KEYWORDS

Mobile Learning, Digital Media Literacy, Media Competencies, Education 3.0

1. INTRODUCTION

Digital communication technologies at the start of the 21st century and their implications for a new type of involvement and advancement of people appeared the need for a mobile learning. The mobile learning goes beyond previously existing practices of education 2.0, in which new information and communication technologies are tools supporting or complementary educational content. Today we talk about education 3.0.(Frau-Meigs, 2016), where new communication technology innovations are crucial for the inclusion and participation in the mobile learning process, characterized by permanency, variation and opportunities for social creativity. Namely the decisive nature of digital technology for inclusion and participation of people in contemporary social processes give rise to the expansion of the framework of media literacy and articulation and a new type digital literacy.

The contemporary nature of the subject, as well as the importance of this new type of literacy in the modern knowledge society (European Commission. 1996; European Council.2000) is both fundamental and unprecedented in nature, because not only does it connect the success of the knowledge society with this new type of media literacy, but it also transforms the process of obtaining knowledge from a relatively passive to a more active and interactive, as well as being a phenomenon which determines the current and future social developments. Digital literacy and its permanent development is becoming a prerequisite for further digital improvements and development for people as well as of the knowledge society in a digital environment. Mobile learning as related to digital literacy is a key to successfully tackling of the challenges that the digital revolution poses to the knowledge society and its projections in the social spheres. The mobile learning, in which media and communication innovations are increasingly becoming essential tools of education and socio-cultural processes, are challenges with fundamental consequences for the prosperity of societies. In today's ubiquitous digital realia, knowledge society is faced with a new type of opportunities for participation of people with a flexible type of cooperation between them and opportunities to influence social innovations which are new in both nature and form.

The present article is focused on the following objectives related to mobile learning and digital literacy:

- To reveal significant theoretical efforts in promoting various aspects of the subject;
- To explore its dimensions and projections in society;
- To highlight its role in the transformation of society from a "collaborative" to a "knowing society";

The article develops the thesis that digital literacy development is a synthetic expression of the main knowledge resources of the social environment at both individual, group and institutional levels.

2. DIGITAL LITERACY

Digital literacy itself is examined as a concept which stands at the heart of mobile learning and its development is the result of a complex interplay between the effects of the broader social environment and the new specifics of education and training (Ferrari, 2012).

The analysis focuses on the enhanced role of people and their digital literacy in the changing complexity of the various professional landscapes. Individuals as social actors in the age of digitization interact with various social media on a daily basis (Genner & Suss, 2017). This interaction is achieved under the form of bilateral communication: on one hand the media socialize - inform, bring up, educate, advise; while on the other hand, individuals make their mark on social media via messages and images which they create, post and discuss. People increasingly acquire knowledge and information from the new mass media – the Internet, social media, e-formations of different nature (e-press, e-magazines, e-learning), etc., along with the traditional educational and media channels (Peicheva, Milenkova, 2017). This diversity of sources of knowledge brings new information, opportunities and potential for innovation, but requires a high level critical approach to both thinking and verification of understanding how to manage space and personal data, as well as awareness as to how to make informed choices, how to rationalize algorithms on digital platforms that adapt the world to our tastes and so on (Lemish, 2015).

The role of mobile learning is increasingly becoming a function of the efforts of many social actors facing different communities. Mobile learning as an approach and system of activities - is becoming more and more important in today's contexts, with the understanding that individuals need to develop their skills, to improve their knowledge and qualifications, to compete with the changing world and be able to participate actively in the labor market.

An important milestone in the studying and implementation of mobile learning is research projects. This is the project "YOUNG_ADULLLT – 'Policies Supporting Young Adulllts in their Life Course. A Comparative Perspective of Lifelong Learning and Inclusion in Education and Work in Europe', team coordinator Prof. Ph.D. Marcelo Parreira do Amaral from University of Munster, funded under the Horizon 2020 Program http://www.young-adulllt.eu/; conducts in 2016-2019. The project includes 15 partners from 9 European countries: Austria, Bulgaria, Germany, Spain, Italy, Portugal, Scotland, Finland, Croatia.

The focus of the project is European, national and regional LLL policy orientated towards young adults[1] who are active participants in mobile learning to form qualities suitable for the labor market. The project aims at gaining knowledge about the impact of LLL policies on life course, plans, strategies of young people and the ways in which these policies become more effective. Mobile learning and digital literacy have crucial role for educational process which is a subject of daily and systematic implementation and development in any particular training situation. Mobile learning is related to LLL, it acts as an incentive to develop different forms that are valued in formal and non-formal environment and its systematic impact depends on various conditions. Mobile learning has a key role for increasing personal chances in LLL process; it is necessary and important factor for taking advanced professional position, as a form of investment in better qualification and level of knowledge.

Digital media literacy, which as a concept has begun to increasingly play a major role nowadays, synthesizes in itself new resources resulting of the transition from analog to digital communication technologies and their penetration in the communications space (Verdegem, 2011). Digital literacy is actually new media literacy, as far as digitization is associated primarily with the media, with the change from analog to digital. Regardless of its digital character, however, and the subsequent on this basis interactivity, media have a strong tendency to endure not only did they not decrease, but rather expand and intensified their effects on power of all age groups and institutional formations. In both cases, digital literacy includes competencies that people should have for their social coping with communication technologies - not so much the technical aspects, but rather with their social applied aspects in the new digital environment.

---

[1] The project is accepted understanding that these are young people aged 18-29 years

European strategy for lifelong learning has listed key competences in modern conditions. The following eight key competences (Key competences are analyzed in the “Young Adulllts” Glossary, http://www.young-adulllt.eu/glossary/listview.php?we_objectID=200) are relevant to mobile learning:

1) Communication in the mother tongue;
2) Communication in foreign languages;
3) Mathematical competence and basic competences in science and technology;
4) Digital competence;
5) Learning to learn;
6) Social and civic competences;
7) Sense of initiative and entrepreneurship;
8) Cultural awareness and expression.

Digital competence is part of the wider discussion regarding media literacy, but is not limited to knowledge of digital technologies In both cases the content aspect of literacy plays an important role, its social relevance, which makes use of the new resources that digitalization has to offer. In the most important document related to digital dimensions of media literacy called "European approach to media literacy in the digital environment" (http://eur-lex.europa.eu/legal-content/BG/TXT/?uri=CELEX:52007DC0833) both traditional and new elements and concepts regarding media literacy in digital conditions were listed:

- Knowledge of all existing media - from newspapers to virtual communities; actively using media, including the use of interactive TV on Internet search engines or participation in virtual communities, more effectively exploit the potential of media for entertainment, access to culture, dialogue between different cultures, training and applications from everyday life, such as libraries digital audiovisual formats distributed over the Internet (podcasts);
- Critical attitude towards media in both terms of quality and of the accuracy of the content (e.g., ability to assess information, dealing with advertising on various media, using search engines intelligently);
- Using media creatively, as the evolution of media technologies and the increasing presence of the Internet as a distribution channel allow an ever larger number of Europeans to create and disseminate images, information and content;
- Understanding the economy of media and the difference between pluralism and media ownership;
- Knowledge of copyright issues, which is the essential "culture of legality", especially for the younger generation in its double capacity of consumers and producers of content.

All these dimensions help understanding media literacy in the digital environment, as the concept synthesizes in itself the aspects of mobile learning. Digital media literacy is therefore an opportunity for both young and old to develop their knowledge and wide range of skills and competencies for critical thinking, communication and information management, to become reasonable citizens and consumers, artists in the modern digital reality. Therefore it is important and necessary, because it aims to educate thoughtful, engaged and informed citizen.

Digital media literacy requires more than obtaining factual knowledge of media, the goal is the acquiring of skills relating to mediated communications – both in print and digital, and the ability to both code and decode their meaning encoding. (Livingstone 2004; Livingstone, 2009; Snyder, 1998). As stated by Sonja Livingston (2004) each element supports the others as part of a non-linear, dynamic process of learning: learning to create content helps people analyze what is professionally created by others; skills in analyzing and evaluating open the door to new uses for the Internet, expanding access, etc. In this sense, mobile learning assumes digital competencies and knowledge of all media and when we talk about Internet literacy, computer literacy, information literacy, we imply access and abilities for the analysis of the contents, evaluation and creation of new content in different types of media.

Digital literacy is therefore positioned as a more relevant concept of mobile learning, since it includes the skills and competencies required for effective use of new interactive media (Henriksen, 2011). It is therefore the understanding of digital literacy as increasingly focusing on the need to shift from basic skills to the use of digital tools and information resources in order to build strategies for critical and effective use of these funds.

Digital literacy has is increasingly provided significant foundation required for the adequate functioning of modern society, which, thanks to digitization, developed in compressed space and time in highly mobile environment thanks to the interchangeability of many tools and resources, as well as due to the supersaturation of informational sources and ability to influence. The mobile learning is increasingly permeated by these processes and it becomes a condition for problem-solving and prosperity in the new realms of knowledge. Very often media and mainly Internet are the basic source of information for preparing the classes and for the carrying out research tasks that are undertaken during different subjects at university; so the study processes which take place in the institutions of both formal and non-formal education are closely linked with the media. The process itself of cooperation between media and mobile learning and the strengthening role of media literacy as complementary educational processes is a subject of daily and systematic implementation and development in any particular educational situation.

Mobile learning is one of the factors for fundamental social transformations and effects in education 3.0 (Frau-Meigs, 2016), in which the foreground stand out:

- "Creativity and innovation";
- "Pedagogy for participation" and "co-design" joint problem solving;
- Interlinking of decision-makers and actors, including people from different age groups.
- Attracting potential of the creative economy in teaching and learning;
- Engagement of all ages to participate in online realities;
- Shared development of indicators and accountability mechanisms aimed at policies for the next generations;
- Data Management, including "big data" including contexts, combining opinion and facts, interpretation mechanisms and so on.

Mobile learning is crucial to deal with the modern aspects, types and forms of education typical of Education 3.0. It is defined as an evolutionary moment in the knowledge society with fundamental reflections on all aspects of life. Its absence or limited availability led to exclusion or exposure to future economic and social risk. Directing and managing mobile learning involves reviewing all existing aspects of education - from kindergarten to university, from student learning to teacher training, from some learning skills to other methods and training techniques, from formally organized to informal and open education and so on throughout people's life. Therefore mobile learning, which is implanted in modern education, builds the foundations of study content. Rapidly evolving information environment poses new challenges to teaching methods and practices to improve and adapt to it, to become the mobile learning the main focus of educational activities across all levels. Educational institutions are traditionally called up to introduce young people to the world of knowledge and experience. Today education faces a variety of digital media, but it also faces the challenge of an increasingly rapid aging of information, as well as with its different personal and social value and significance.

Some of the skills which encompass modern media literacy skills include the proficiency in the usage of digital technologies that enable students to work with computers, software applications and databases, these skills are the foundation of obtaining information and its understanding. An important aspect of education 3.0 is that students need to have the ability to search, collect and process, an ability to be able for critical and systematic use of the found information and use of Internet-based services. ICT in their full use underlie the development of creativity and innovation as important part of modern education as well as the development of basic computer skills such as spreadsheets, databases, storage and information management, understanding of the opportunities and potential risks of the Internet and computer-mediated communication to work, cooperation network. All this raises some important questions: To what extent students have access to computers? How ICTs are part of the learning process? Does this process continue to evolve over time?

2.1 Empirical Framework

This article is based in empirical plan on three surveys, used quantitative and qualitative methods, and covers the period 2003 - 2015 year.

- The survey "Integration of social- psychological sciences in a globalized world" conducted in 2013 in South-West University (SWU) with team leader prof.Valentina Milenkova. There are used two methods: structured interviews and focus groups. The sample was unrepresentative included 290 students from various faculties of the university; following "experimental design scheme". The questionnaire included questions about the learning process, digitization of education and digital culture of students. The other method used was a focus group. There were three focus groups carried out with students from Sociology and Political Science specialties of SWU. In the focus groups the discussion revealed on media literacy, forms of communication with teachers, based on digital processes.

- A survey „Cultural universals in academic environment" was carried out in 2015 at SWU with students from Social study specialties: Sociology, Political Sciences, Psychology; team leader prof. Valentina Milenkova. Topic discussed in focus groups connected with: the values that students share, communication, media literacy, digitization, significance of media environment as element of university system.

- A case study under the project "Young Adulllts", where the "Student Practices" program conducted at SWU was studied as part of the introduction to practical training and acquiring labour market skills, one of them is digital literacy. The Bulgarian team leader of the survey carried out in 2017 is prof. Georgi Apostolov. "Student practices" program is based on the understanding that during the course of their studies at the university as well as during their participation in the program, young adults actively use different digital technologies, which are a compulsory element of the academic university environment. There are carried out four in-depth interviews with young adults participated in this program.

2.1.1 Access to Computers and Internet – Condition for Mobile Learning

The implementation of digital technologies is condition for mobile learning, that's why computer literacy is one of the basic skills for competency. The students are the most appropriate age group being mobile and able to respond to environmental changes, a part of which are computers. Digital literacy has become an important part of qualification requirements and is connected with successful professional realization. It is necessity to note that the University curricula offers education for the most informational' specialties and computer technologies. At the same time the access to Internet is a basic condition required to improve the quality of education and to sustain active communication – between students and professors (through e-mails, chats, blogs, face book etc.). One of the main reasons for fast growth of the importance of computers in educational communication is the fact that this is the cheapest and the most effective way to contact with students, colleagues, friends, and peers.

The access to Internet is for all students and it's due to the increase of computers as a part of the university policy to acquire and enhance computers' meaning in university space and guarantee full access to them. The university library, with the readings' halls, computers halls, and laboratories becomes a part of the university interior and there is a constant access to computers and Internet for students. In addition, the most of students have personal laptops. The access to computers and Internet for several years has become a compulsory prerequisite for quality study process and in this direction university guarantees to students appropriate environment and conditions. The computers and access to Internet have real significance only if they support the study process as an improvement in conditions. The basic concept in this aspect is: giving and discussing homework and essays, requiring additional students' deliverances, and supporting lecturer-student networks. An important part of the whole process of new forms of modern communication is for students familiarize themselves with Internet publications and materials.

The interest of young people towards education is increasing because the sources of information are enhanced, and the real education process is being modernized. That's why it is important to expand requirements for teaching qualification through including new methods in education. The education policy reforms are oriented towards guaranteeing flexible and new technology environment. In this direction it is important to note that the syllabuses of all taught courses are uploaded on the Internet. The lectures are taught through multimedia and new technology facilities. An important part of university communication is the electronic networks, lecturers' blogs, Internet forums and active contacts supported by the university in order to facilitate dialogue between the educational actors and to improve mobile learning. The students can express their opinions for the study process and particular details of their experience as well as to discuss aspects of student preparation for seminars and exams. In the process of education the development of students' writing skills is key because it is the base for quality papers, essays, and all written assignments during the study process.

The access to any sort of required materials which may prove necessary for tasks assigned during particular courses can be viewed as a proof of conditions available for lectures and the studying process during the last few years in the university space. At the same time it is necessary to note that the advantages of Internet are not used efficiently enough in the educational and training process and there is more potential that can be utilized in the university communication and networks in order to perfect teaching and learning methods, benefiting both sides of higher education society (students and lecturers).

The students note that they have access to Internet and computers, that the education is influenced by all elements of new informational technologies. Creating conditions appropriate to interactive education, an important part of which are technologies and all traits of effective pedagogy milieu are connected with basic reforms and advanced aspects of European higher education space.

The access to computers and Internet reveals various aspects of digital literacy as the following:

- Computer literacy related to: the use of computer programs for word processing, for generating spreadsheets, presentations, photos, images, graphics; use of databases;
- Internet literacy connected to: internet access, which search engines are used, what information is extracted, using your email, social networks, blogs and websites related to the preparation during individual disciplines;
- Information literacy associated with: knowledge and use of separate library information resources on the Web;
- Independent thinking regarding: how to analyze, interpret and critically evaluate information; create of new knowledge; understanding of the ethical aspects of networking and the Internet;

It can be said that, in terms of computer literacy, students from are highly knowledgeable. In all subjects studied, the preparation of presentations using the resources of the various computer programs for the generation of tables, pictures and images is widely included; the students know and use computer tools for word processing and are able to create and format documents.

- Internet literacy is also high. Students daily access the Internet; use e-mail, participate in social networks, mainly Facebook, have profiles; read websites and blogs, in many cases, however, these activities are not related to training and academic preparation but are connected to personal pursuits and personal contacts, communicating with friends, entertainment, download movies and more.
- Information literacy of students is underdeveloped; mainly this refers to the knowing of the capabilities for the use of electronic publications - books, encyclopedias, magazines; but they are not always used. Students do not know the library information resources in the network, and do not know the electronic library of the University.
- Independent and critical thinking - this is the least developed part of literacy of students. A very minor part of respondents critically analyze what they read; they are nearly lacking in the ability to compare different sources; they find it difficult to summarize and digest what they have read; they do not think about the ethical aspect of things and copyright infringement on the Internet.

From all this we can conclude that computer and Internet literacy of students from the studied university is very high, but at the same time, it does not find a serious enough space in the formation of independent thinking and both critical and analytical skills. Often students take for granted the information Internet sources without making additional inquiries; also, we can note as part of their behavior on the Internet, is that the way they conduct themselves stands out as one devoid of an ethical approach, which is rather disappointing, given their character and values. Moreover, it is not enough to have a high-level ICT environment, access to the Internet, it is important to reflect on how digital media literacy can be actively used in school work and how students can become more team oriented.

There is a shortage of educational programs which prepare students for competences required by the contemporary labor market. In the recent decade there is a mismatch between supply and demand of working force with certain qualifications into the labor market, e.g. the Chamber of commerce revealed that 64% of employers demand engineering specialists against 27% supply of certificated engineers from the higher education institutions. According to employers, there is a discrepancy between the declared degree of knowledge and the real skills manifested during working practice. "Otherwise, there are many students, but they are not the ones the labor market needs". According to an international survey more and more employers have a problem in recruiting new employees in national conditions. Over 45% of candidates do not have the necessary qualifications and skills. Survey among employers demonstrated their belief that in the next five years the need for specialists in Biotechnology, Food and Chemical technologies will increase, as well as the need for experts in Psychology, Communication and Computer equipment and Medicine. Less demand will be for specialists in Education, History and Sports. Overall, the structure and profile of higher education does not match the needs of the market. There are deformations related to the dominant development of individual learning disciplines, such as training in, for example, economics and law. According to information from the National Industrial Association, the most wanted are the skilled workers, the engineers, the drivers, and the people working in the field of nutrition, the doctors and the managers.

One of the serious problems of skills retention is the fact that only 23% of employers have targeted policies and programs and systematically invest in training and development of human resources. This leads to the problem that people who are well qualified are gradually losing it.

Challenges to education in view of providing mobile learning students are connected with:

- Curricula and study programmes, which have to stimulate more creativity and individual approach, and to correspond to person-centred pedagogy.
- Curricula have to show higher mobility and to include more elective disciplines.
- The opening of universities towards older generations, which might turn the universities into real "life-long learning institutions". It is necessary in connection with that distance training forms to be developed further on.
- The activation of project work at universities level as well as an accent on assigning of different creative tasks to students in the process of training.

In that sense the formation appropriate students' skills is an important element under the conditions of globalisation. It depends on the specific structure, organisation and purposefulness, based on running models of training and education, the participation of students in research activities is a prerequisite for their leadership ability and individual prosperity and at the same time it is an indicator of the development of university education and its perspectives.

3. CONCLUSION

The adapting of young adults to the challenges of the digital society and new training practices necessitates the determining of more effective ways to attract, encourage and motivate towards the utilization of quality theoretical and applied knowledge and skills in ICT. Access to computers and Internet, the opportunity to work with some basic computer programs and tools in no ways guarantees the acquisition of digital media competence amongst students. Especially when taking into account that many of the young people who study at the university, do not possess the necessary skills to use digital technology due to the fragmented and superficial use of information. The need to contemplate the introduction and study of such subjects as "Digital media literacy", "Computer Literacy and Information Technology", "Ethical aspects of digital media literacy" amongst others. The ability to access online tutorials, e-books and other forms of enhancing the digital competency of trainees through which the development of a wide range of skills for search, identification, critical assessment and use of information for a more self creative and ethical behavior in the digital environment is evident. Quality of education and mobile learning, including university environment and lecturers' professionalism is connected with the modernization of higher education. In this context emerge the basic elements in the Strategy of the European Commission for supporting European higher education, connected with: improving information quality, enhancing attractiveness and competitiveness of universities, sustaining partnerships, enforcing the dialog and improving mechanisms for mobility. So, the opportunities for individuals are influenced by the specific institutional and structural settings, which have determined student's perception as supporting or discouraging a person's desire for learning.

Conceptualization of digital literacy and mobile learning, which are analyzed in the university training processes are among the most important factors for social inclusion and realization of people's formation outlining the foundations of modern knowledge society in his statics and dynamics. Awareness of the digital media skills as a factor in the full development of the knowledge society has not yet found adequacy among the cognitions of the authorized formal and non-formal social actors as well as their immediate educational practices. Digital literacy includes mobilization of resources on a personal level, which coincide with institutional values and requires a combination of successful institutional strategies and behavioral role models relating to persons of different social status.

In our country there are serious research, applied and regulatory deficits which justify the need for digital media literacy, which corresponds to modern education 3.0, as well as the challenges to opportunities for different types of interpretations, forms of participation and creativity that put constantly innovate digital communication products in all spheres of society. There are deficits in the description of existing resources in our country, in the ongoing and necessary policies, existing and future practices necessary in both the national and international comparative framework.

ACKNOWLEDGMENTS

The article has been developed in the framework of the research project "YOUNG_ADULLLT – 'Policies Supporting Young Adulllts in their Life Course.', Horizon 2020, Project No. 693176, 2016-2019. http://www.young-adulllt.eu/.

REFERENCES

Cartelli, A. 2013 *Fostering 21st Century Digital Literacy and Technical Competency.* Information Science Publishing *Digital Agenda for Europe (n.d.).* ICT & Education, Retrieved from http://ec.europa.eu/ digital-agenda/en/ict-education.

European Commission. 2010. Europe 2020 <http://eur-lex.europa.eu/legal-content/BG/NOT/?uri=CELEX:52010D

European Council. 2000. *Presidency Conclusions Lisbon European Council* 23 and 24 march.<http://www.consilium.europa.eu/uedocs/cms_data/docs/pressdata/en/ec/00100-r1.en0.htm >

European Commission. 1996. *Green paper – living and working in the information society: people* first

Frau-Meigs, Divina and Lee Hibbard 2016. *Education 3.0 and Internet Governance: A New Global Alliance for Children and Young People's Sustainable Digital Development*. Published by the Centre for International Governance Innovation and Chatham House.

Ferrari, Anusca (2012). Developing a framework for digital competence, *Information Society Policy Research,* European Commission - JRC-IPTS, Seville, Issue 6: January 2012. Retrieved from http://is.jrc.ec.europa.eu/ pages/documents/ ISNewsletter6.pdf

Genner, S. and D. Suss (2017) Socialization as Media Effect In: *The International Encyclopedia of Media Effects*. Patric Rossler (Editor –in-Chief), C.A.Hoffner and L.Zoonen.

Greenfield, P., & Yan, Z. (2006). Children, adolescents, and the Internet: A new field of inquiry in developmental psychology. *Developmental Psychology* , 42 (3), 391-394.

Henriksen, C. (2011). *Media and ICT in a Learning Perspective,* Accessed 24 November 2011, Retrieved from http://www.dpu.dk/en/research/ researchprogrammes mediaandict/

Lemish, D. (2015) *Children and Media. A Global Perspective*. Oxford, UK: Wiley Blackwell.

Livingstone, S. (2009) On the mediation of everything: ICA Presidential Address 2008. *Journal of Communication*, 59 (1), pp.1-18.

Livingstone, L. 2004 "Media literacy and the challenge of new information and communication technologies" *Communication Review*, 2004, 1(7), pp.3-14.

Peicheva, D., V.Milenkova 2017„ Knowledge Society and Digital Media Literacy: Foundations for Social Inclusion and Realization in Bulgarian Context." *Calitatea Vieţii*, XXVIII (1), pp.50-74.

Snyder, I. 1998. Beyond the hype: Reassessing hypertext. In I. Snyder (Ed.), Page to screen: Taking literacy into the electronic era (pp. 125–143). London: Routledge.

Verdegem, P. 2011 "Social Media for Digital and Social Inclusion: Challenges for Information Society 2.0 Research & Policies". *Triple C* 9(1), pp. 28-38.

Online sources

https://europass.cedefop.europa.eu/bg/resources/digital-competences

https://europass.cedefop.europa.eu/sites/default/files/dc_-_bg.pdf

https://www.eifonline.org/DigitalWorld2030# https://www.eifonline.org/DigitalWorld2030

www.translit.fr

https://money.bg/economics/za-kakvo-shte-govoryat-svetovnite-lideri-na-konferentsiyata-v-davos-tazi-godina.html

http://newtrend.bg/digitalkidz/zashho-digitalni-umeniya-tryabva-da-sa-osnoven-predmet-v-uchilishhe

http://ebox.nbu.bg/prob12/view_lesson.php?id=244

http://ukh.uni-sofia.bg/page.php?c=26&d=88

http://ec.europa.eu/education/policy/school/competences_en.htm

http://www.young-adulllt.eu/

SELFIE AS A MOTIVATIONAL TOOL FOR CITY EXPLORATION

Mark Bugeja, Alexiei Dingli and Dylan Seychell
Department of Intelligent Systems, Faculty of ICT, University of Malta
University Campus, Tal-Qroqq, Msida, MSD 2080 Malta
+356 2340 2340

ABSTRACT

This study exploits the selfie phenomenon in order to develop an application that motivates city exploration and tourism to encourage greater mobility. The application uses a reward based system that rewards the user at specific target locations by allowing the user to take pictures and selfies at these landmarks only. This in turn encourages the user the visit more sites and unlock further content. Initially the research looks at evaluating whether taking a 'selfie' is sufficiently motivating for a user to be regarded as a reward. The survey results obtained show a strong correlation between photography, 'selfie' and travel. A number of users were then given a prototype of the application to use in Valletta the capital city of Malta. The users were then interviewed, the interviews established that users find such an approach for city exploration to be meaningful. Ultimately this means that through the application tourists are encouraged to explore more of the captivating sites found in the area.

KEYWORDS

Mobile Tourism, Travel Selfie, Tourism, Gamification, Mobile Learning

1. INTRODUCTION

Mobile tourism is not a new concept. With the rapid development of smartphones from industry giants such as Apple and Samsung most users nowadays have at their fingertips small powerful computers. These machines have already started to replace traditional day to day information goods such as newspapers and magazine. This paper aims to explore how the present use of smartphones combined with selfie culture can be channeled into a mobile tourist application.

Tourism can be defined as an activity in which a person/s travel from one place to another in order to consume leisurely or business activities that are available at the destination. Traditionally the word tourism and travel are intrinsically linked. In fact, most research based on tourism assumes that time and space are linked. Thus, for a tourist to consume any of the activities available in another place they would need to travel to that location first. With the advent advancement in technology the notion that tourism is always linked to some space is slowly being revaluated. With technologies such as smart phone, Virtual Reality and Augmented Reality time and space become relative to the 'tourist' using these products. In (Letellier, n.d.) the authors proposed using Virtual Reality applications that allow users to experience in high definition detail the location of Luang Prabang a world heritage site located in Lao People's Democratic Republic. The main motivation behind this study was to allow for conservation in areas where the sheer number of tourists travelling to that location over time could potentially deteriorate the quality of the physical structures and environment of the surrounding area. Moreover, with the use of this technology more access can be given to tourists that are physically impaired and cannot travel to such sites.

The first section of the paper establishes how selfies have replaced traditional tourist photography as well as introducing the concept of selfie tourism and how it all started through smartphones (Cody Morris Paris, 2015). This leads to the exploration of what we define as tourism how users traditionally approach travelling and how this is changing. Some current tourist applications are than discussed in order to establish trends. Finally, this section is tied down with the concept of goal based systems in order to motivate users by rewarding them through actions that they currently already do in their everyday life. Such systems increase the success of a tourist mobile application as ultimately if a city is not explored than the application will not achieve its ultimate goal.

The second section introduces the profile of the users that the application is aimed for as well as discussing how this profile was obtained. It then goes into the methodology of the application and how it works by providing visual artefacts. From there we move on to the results obtained from interviewing users of this application what it means and what this will lead future research to.

2. BACKGROUND

2.1 Selfie Tourism

How is photography and the act of taking one's photo connected to tourism? In (Anja Dinhopl, 2016) the authors discuss the concept of touristic gaze or rather tourist looking. The act of looking at something is in itself is consumption. Tourists consume with their eyes what they see in front of them. "Consuming something becomes owning something" (Anja Dinhopl, 2016). This is apparent in the way tourists select places to capture and frame in order to produce digital albums of their trips. In the past years thanks to the introduction of front-facing cameras on smartphones and tablets a crucial design factor that attributed to the rise of the selfie culture. This allowed users to see themselves as they are capturing a photo (Anja Dinhopl, 2016) (Cody Morris Paris, 2015). Thanks to faster and wider coverage of wireless networks users can upload the selfie as soon as they take the photo (Cody Morris Paris, 2015), the increased use of graphics centred social networking sites to share selfies with your friends and the increase of instant messaging such as Whatsapp, selfies are becoming more and more popular. In fact, the word 'selfie' has become so popular in our everyday life, that in 2013, the word 'selfie' in itself was selected as the 'word of the year' and added to Oxford English Dictionary (Cody Morris Paris, 2015).

Selfie taking is a new way of touristic looking. The camera is not the vehicle used to frame or target a captivating destination. It has become an extension of oneself to redirect the importance of the object on the self. Portraits and self-photography is conceptually not new, but, new technology has enabled the ease of capturing photos in larger quantities. "Rather it acts as a mirror at which tourists look to take their pictures prior to, as well as when they are taking photos. Tourists are thus not looking through the screen at the destination, but at the screen to see themselves." (Anja Dinhopl, 2016)

Tourists are now looking at how to capture themselves in relation to where they are. This is emphasized by the fact that they are looking to share what they have just experienced with all the people they know. Thus, it has now become more about "Look, I am here!" rather than "This place is beautiful"

The selfie is now elevated as a touristic product and the tourist destination has become the background to set the scene for the consumption of said product. Given this new way of thinking possibilities lie in using this to produce products based on satisfying this act of consumption.

2.2 Digital Tourism

The evolution of mobile phones into fully functional computers opened a wide range of possibilities. In the previous section, we established that the innovative introduction of front face cameras adopted by smartphones introduced the selfie culture. One other emerging popular uses for these devices is in the tourism sector. Most studies in this area focus on how Smartphone's impact the touristic experience or how highly mobile travel has become. Travelling in itself is the act of planning, travelling and documenting (Craig-Smith, 1994) ICT tools play an integral part in all the stages involved in travelling. Smartphone enable interactions between the physical and the virtual world regardless of location. This is essential for most travelers as they can pre-plan the trip through virtual means and then use Smartphone's to physically interact with their environment during the travelling stage and finally document their whole experience on social media.

Smartphone use in travel is strongly associated with the everyday use of smartphones. Repeated use of something that users are familiar with influenced their use of smartphones for travel because this was consistent with their daily routines, habits, and a sense of attachment to friends or workplace (Dan Wang, 2014).

The need to access instant information is also a contributing factor to the rise of Smartphone use in travel. Users can now get information on the go and as such do not even need to pre-plan their trips as they can access that information once they are at the destination (Dylan Seychelle, 2012) (Tzu-how Chu, 2011).

An effective implementation of mobile tourism is to combine the need for instant information by using GIS technology to guide a tourist through a city or touristic landmark. These applications provide tourists with real-time information once they are at specific areas within their guided tours. This type of application is highly effective when used in heritage sites, cultural landscapes and natural areas. (Dylan Seychell, 2011) (Dan Wang, 2014)

Innovative use of mobile tourist application also introduces the concept of adding emerging technology such as virtual reality or augmented reality. Virtual Reality does not require users to be physically present at the tourist site this makes it ideal for use in marketing. Augmented reality on the other hand superimposes graphics on the camera view displayed on your smartphone. This technology can be cleverly used to provide information to users as they are moving through a city (Dylan Seychell, 2011).

2.3 Mobile Learning and Gamification

Traditionally learning is the process adopted by a person to comprehend and understand a subject or to gain the skill to perform a task. The process is mostly associated with a physical location to gain the knowledge, the use of a book or a teacher that would spread the knowledge to that person. Through mobile learning irrespective of the location and the person's ability, a person, is able to learn and obtain knowledge through the use of mobile technology that is wireless and ubiquitous (Chen, 2013). Mobile learning has shown how effective it is in various research work (Thakre, 2015) (Hussein Meihami, 2013) (Liu, 2016) where the design of the mobile learning application centers the user at the center of the learning environment. The increase of mobile usage as well as the increase of users with access to mobile data or Wi-Fi technology exemplifies the features of mobile learning that include accessibility, immediacy and interactivity. Gamification is successfully used as a means of mobile learning as one of its main principles is to wrap a set of tasks that were seemingly deemed as boring into a more enjoyable context (Gafni, 2017).

Gamification is the process that applies game concept such as game design and game mechanics. This in turn exploits the user's base need in order to increase a user's engagement and motivation to accomplish a goal (Sebastian Deterding, 2011) It is also sometimes referred to "as the selective incorporation of game elements into an interactive system without a fully-fledged game as the end product" (Seaborn, 2015). This concept of combining game elements into an interactive system is not new in tourism it was initially used by airlines in frequent flyer programs as well as other companies that made use of loyalty cards. The idea is to reward a user or in this case a 'player' for making use of your service. So, an airline user will be rewarded with discounted flights on accumulation of a number of flying miles (points) obtained with the same airline. These points can then be used to obtain free flights to a number of locations depending on the number of points accumulated. These elements in turn encourage users to fly with the same airline in order to benefit from these rewards. We can further define the process of Gamification by defining its practical application as a rule based system (Sebastian Deterding, 2011) (Feifei Xu, 2014). Users are the centre point of a game as their actions define the outcome in this rule based system. Feedback systems are then used to provide players with information in the form of scores or penalties. An example of the success of gamification in learning is presented by the authors in (Gafni, 2017) that have successfully used gamification in a vocabulary word game to increase second language acquisition.

3. METHODOLOGY

rule based system. Feedback systems are then used to provide players with information in the form of scores or penalties (Feifei Xu, 2014). This paper aims to design and develop a selfie centred mobile tourist application. A user profile was established in order to better comprehend if selfie and selfie tourism can be used as a motivational goal to encourage city exploration. This was done through a preliminary questionnaire. The survey carried out asked the users ten questions in order to establish age bracket, travel frequency, selfie frequency and the importance of taking photos when travelling. From the results obtained in the survey, it was established that most of the users that tend to take selfies are between the age of 16 and 30 with most of the participant's stating that they only take selfies on particular occasions [Figure 1].

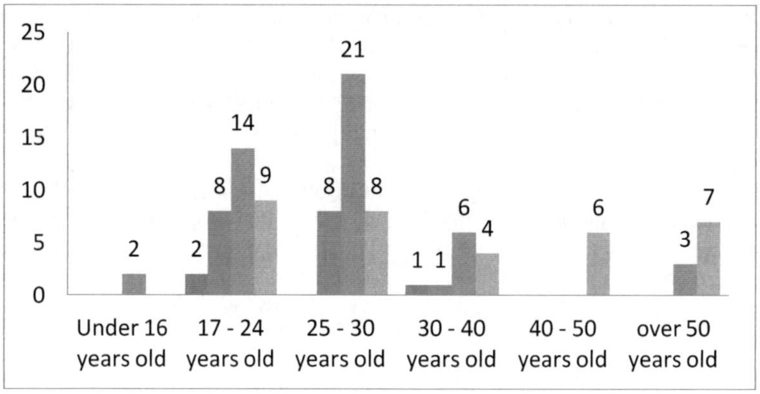

Figure 1. Percentage of Users per Age Group that Take Selfies

Surprisingly the frequency increases with the 50+ age group.

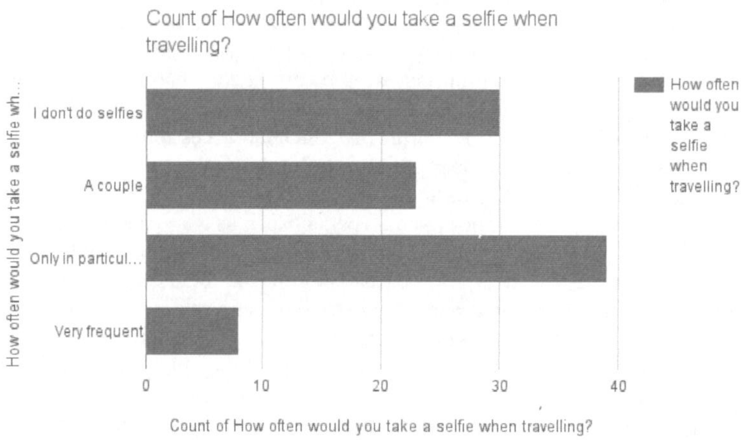

Figure 2. Chart displaying figures on selfie frequency

Almost 70% of the participants take selfie's when traveling. With an encouraging 72.2% feel that photography is very important part of traveling and tourism [Table 1].

Table 1. Photography importance in Tourism

No of Participants (%)	Rating
36.6	**5**
35.6	**4**
16.8	**3**
7.9	**2**
3	**1**

From the survey, it was also established that 80% of participants prefer visiting a lot of different landmarks in a small period of time. Which correlates with the responses gained from the activity question where 61.4% of the participants prefer to explore a city exactly when they reach it [Figure 3].

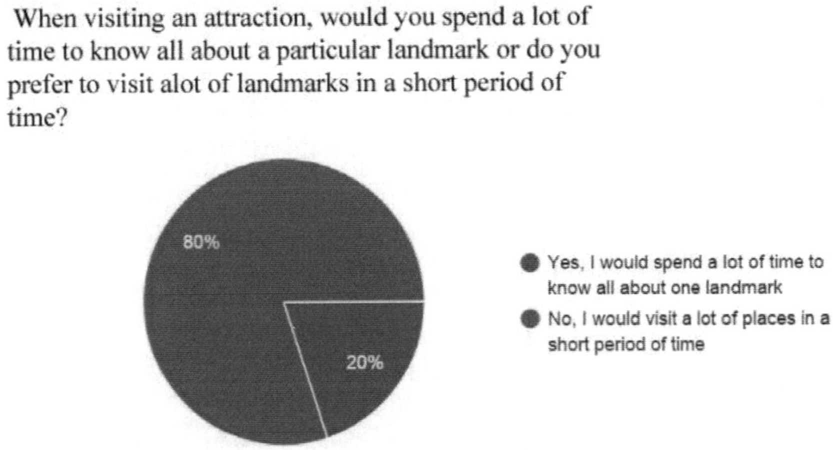

Figure 3. Chart Displaying Figures for Exploration Trends

From this survey, we established that the majority of users take selfies in particular occasions. They like to explore a city and take photos of all the attractions and landmarks that they find. They don't want to spend a lot of time learning about a particular place but they prefer taking in a lot of sights at once. The final question of the survey asked the participants if they would download an app that takes them through a tour of the most captivating landmarks in a city. An encouraging 57% of participants said yes of which the majority where from age 17 - 30. The remaining 43% where divided between 40% maybe and only 3% answered no.

As discussed in the literature the application is designed by using a gamified approach thus, the app uses is a goal based system. The survey results strongly indicate that photography and selfies are strongly related to travel. The premise used for the design approach for this application is that given this goal the application should reward the user with the chance to take a 'selfie' or 'picture' at a pre-established landmark given that the user has managed to get to that location.

The city that the application was built for is Valletta City in Malta. This choice was mainly motivated by the fact that Valletta is rich in cultural heritage, it has the same ecosystem as any large city in Europe and is a perfect test base for the application. The captivating landmarks where chosen on their Visual impact, historical and sociological importance [Table 2].

Table 2. Landmarks

Landmark
Parliament Building
Auberge de Castille
Saint John's Co-Cathedral
Palace Armory
War bell memorial

The user navigates through the city by accessing his current location through smartphone GPS accessed from the application. All the chosen landmarks are represented with an icon [Figure 4].

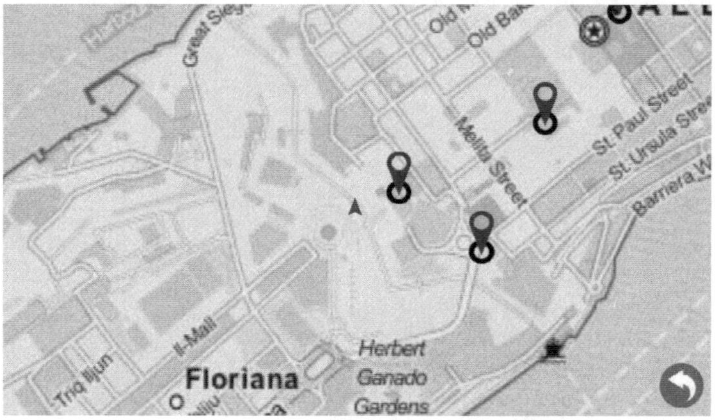

Figure 4. Screenshot GPS Map

If the user clicks on the icon he will be presented with a bit of information on the target landmark as well as an added incentive to visit the site. This incentive was in the form of unlockable camera filters [Figure 5].

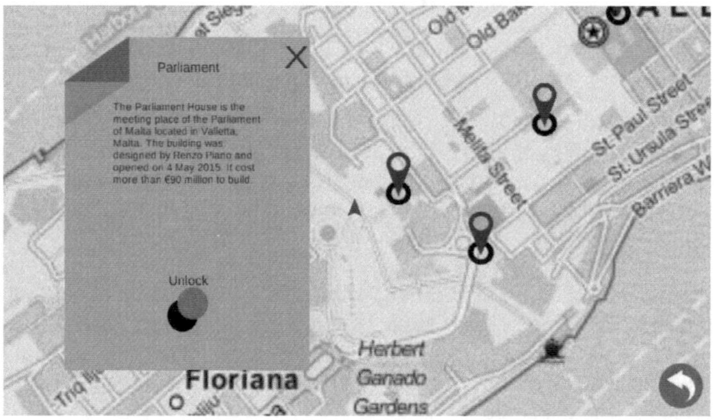

Figure 5. Screenshot Information display

The user is able to take photos only if he is within range of a target location. Once the user is within location, a camera icon will start flashing in the lower right corner. Once pressed the user has the option to take a 'selfie' as well as apply any photo filters that they have unlocked [Figure 6].

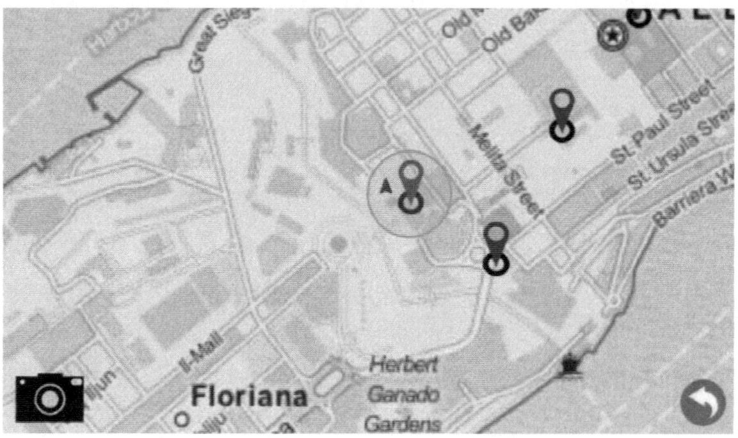

Figure 6. Screenshot of Selfie Range

Once the photos are taken they are automatically added to an auto generated album which is a visual journey of the path taken by the user to explore the city.

4. EVALUATION

The prototype application developed for this paper was evaluated by a group of participants with age group ranging from 25 – 30. The participants where given the application and briefly explained how it works. They were then left to explore the city through the app. An interview was then carried out on each individual participant. The questions asked during the interview investigated whether the participants felt motivated to explore the city through the application, how easy it was to navigate through the city by using the application and if they would download similar applications next time they visit a city.

All participants felt that the application was easy to use. One of the participants elaborated on the fact that the application was fun and educational. "It was fun and interactive, definitely something I'd use again and the info provided turned it into a learning experience. Also, knowing when to take a photo makes it easier to enjoy ones surrounding without having to worry that a photo was not taken in time".

It is encouraging to note that they felt sufficiently motivated to visit all the landmarks and would definitely, given the chance, download a similar app on their smartphones.

5. CONCLUSION

This paper intended to establish if 'selfie' and 'selfie tourism' is a sufficient motivational factor in a goal based mobile touristic application. Initial research was done to establish typical users for such an application as well as the evaluation of a selfie centred mobile application. The results from the implementation are encouraging especially as the results confirms the premise that the paper tried to establish.

More work needs to be done in order to test the application on a wider set of age groups and establish viability with certain groups which might traditionally might be averse to such technology. This will yield clearer results for future research in this area. An interesting point that came up in the survey is that the oldest age bracket where the ones more interested in covering as many landmarks as they can, in a short amount of time. Reasons cited for this was that they felt that they probably are not going to return to the area so they would prefer to make as many memories as they can. On the other hand, they were not prone to download such an application. This might be due to the problems in the digital divide and the feeling that such applications are not catered for senior citizens.

Given that this study is a proof of concept at the stage of submission further work in evaluating the application in terms of knowledge acquisition need to be conducted. This evaluation would focus on the knowledge gained by users in terms of the points of interests used in the applications as this is one of the key aspects found in both gamification as well as mobile learning.

REFERENCES

Anja Dinhopl, U. G. (2016). Selfie-taking as touristic looking. *Annals of Tourism Research, 57*, 126-139.

Chen, X.-B. (2013). Tablets for informal language learning: Student usage and attitudes. *Language Learning & Technology*, 20-37.

Cody Morris Paris, J. P. (2015). 'But first, let me take a selfie': Personality traits as predictors of travel selfie taking and sharing behaviors. *Tourism Travel and Research Association:*.

Craig-Smith, S. J. (1994). Learning to Live with Tourism. In S. J. Craig-Smith, *Learning to Live with Tourism* (pp. 401-403). Melbourne: Pittsburg Publishing.

Dan Wang, Z. X. (2014). Adapting to the mobile world: A model of smartphone use. *Annals of Tourism Research*, 11-26.

Dylan Seychell, A. D. (2011). Blending Augmented Reality with Real World Scenarios using Mobile Devices. *Technologies and Protocol for Internet Design: Reinventing the Web* (pp. 258-273). IGI Global.

Dylan Seychelle, A. D. (2012). Motivating Learning though Mobile Interaction. *IADIS Mobile Learning.* Berlin: IADIS.

Feifei Xu, J. W. (2014). Gamification in Tourism. *Information and Communication Technologies in Tourism 2014: Proceedings of the International Conference in Dublin*, (pp. 525-537). Dublin.

Gafni, R. (2017). Learning Foreign Languages Using Mobile Applications. *Journal of Information Technology Education: Research*, 301-317.

Hussein Meihami, B. M. (2013). CALL in the Form of Simulation Games: Teaching English Vocabulary and Pronunciation through Sims. *International Letters of Social and Humanistic Sciences*, 57-65.

Letellier, R. (2015). *Virtual Reality A new Tool for Sustainable Tourism and Cultural Heritage Site Management*. Retrieved from www.heritage3D.ca

Liu, G. z. (2016). Identifying learning features and models for context-aware ubiquitous learning with phenomenological research method . *International Journal of Mobile Learning and Organisation*, 238.

Seaborn, K. (2015). Gamification in theory and action: A survey. *International Journal of Human-Computer Studies*, 14-31.

Sebastian Deterding, D. D. (2011). From game design elements to gamefulness: defining "gamification". *Proceedings of the 15th International Academic MindTrek Conference: Envisioning Future Media Environments* (pp. 9-15). Tampere: ACM.

Thakre, S. (2015). Perception of medical students for utility of mobile technology use in medical education. *International Journal of Medicine and Public Health*, 305.

Tzu-how Chu, M.-L. L.-h.-w. (2011). Developing a Tour Guiding Information System for Tourism Service using Mobile GIS and GPS Techniques. *INTERNATIONAL JOURNAL ON Advances in Information Sciences and Service Sciences*, 49-58.

HOW MOBILE ARE TOP-RATED MOBILE LANGUAGE LEARNING APPS?

Heather Lotherington
Associate Dean, Research
Professor, Multilingual Education - Faculty of Education, York University, Toronto, ON, Canada

ABSTRACT

A recent survey of top-rated mobile(-assisted) language learning (MALL) apps revealed four front-runners on the digital marketplace: three proprietary language course apps: duolingo, Babbel, busuu, and one flashcard/spaced repetition system (SRS): Memrise (Lotherington, 2017). The survey was followed by empirical studies of the embedded epistemological and pedagogical approaches to language in these MALL apps. Case study findings indicated that all four apps taught language through drills, and relied heavily on dated pedagogies and structural conceptions of both language and learning. This paper overviews the potential of mobility in MALL pedagogy, and examines whether and how these four top-rated MALL apps capitalized on the affordances of *mobility* in their pedagogical approaches and content presentation, concluding that mobility was used primarily for marketing and distribution rather than for innovative instructional design.

KEYWORDS

MALL, Mobility, Everywhereness, Dynamism, Augmented Reality, Production Pedagogy

1. INTRODUCTION

Digital mediation has irrevocably changed how we communicate and learn, and in the process, challenged conceptions of what it means to know a language. Over the past three decades as literate communication has shifted from page to screen, literacy has morphed and hybridized, breaking away from limited alphabetic understandings of *reading* and *writing,* and expanding dimensionally into dynamic, interactive, multimodal, and hybridized forms and practices enfolding and merging *speaking* and *listening* in new ways. The release of the iPhone in 2007 introduced wireless Internet connection untethered to place, enabling the user to communicate interactively and multimodally on-the-go, and facilitating new linguistic communication practices. Mobile smart devices have since proliferated on the digital marketplace, with the shift from desktop computing to multi-platform devices rapidly ensuing. By 2017, mobile devices were being used for 61% of digital communication in the United Kingdom; 62%, in Canada; and 71%, in the United States (comScore, 2017. p. 4).

A digital market for *apps*—third party software programs designed for mobile devices, and available at minimal to no upfront financial cost to the user—evolved alongside digital devices. Apps have been designed for an immense array of functions; among them, language teaching and learning. A decade down the road, apps selling language learning include a variety of approaches: traditional language courses (e.g., duolinguo); digital flashcard and spaced repetition systems (e.g., Memrise); educational games (e.g., MindSnacks); social media chat-based conversation (e.g., HelloTalk), and reference programs (e.g., Google Translate) (Krzemińska, n.d.; Lotherington, in press).

Language teaching has a lengthy history going back 25 centuries (Kelly, 1969). Similarly, theoretical studies of language and language learning, including linguistics, sociolinguistics, applied linguistics and second language learning as well as developmental psychology and philology have sophisticated and multifaceted academic histories. These research disciplines, though, are based largely on language and language learning in 20th (or prior) century contexts as manifested in the mediating technologies of the era, dominated by the printed page. Conventions developed for reading and writing on the static page, and speaking and listening with identifiable interlocutors are relevant to established communication contexts and media, but they require updating for mobile contexts that enable dynamic, interactive multimodal communication, and crowd-sourced, cloud-based knowledge construction.

The capacity of apps to wirelessly network interactive multimodal communication enables just-in-time, socially-connected, customized language learning. But is that what is happening in content-oriented mobile (-assisted) language learning (MALL) apps? This paper questions whether and how top-rated MALL apps capitalize on mobile access in their approaches to language and language learning.

2. CURRENT TOP-RATED MALL APPS

An online survey of top-rated MALL apps in 2016-2017 was conducted in May 2017, using repetitive searches and varied keywords (Lotherington, 2017). The top five MALL apps from a variety of sources were tabled and weighted for frequency of rank, revealing four apps as clear market front-runners. Three of these apps offered proprietary language courses: Babbel, busuu, duolingo; one offered a flashcard/spaced repetition system (SRS): Memrise (Lotherington, 2017).

2.1 Babbel

The first of currently top-rated language teaching apps to appear in the digital marketplace was *Babbel*, founded in 2007 by Marcus Witte. Babbel claims to be the top financially grossing language app[1]. In an interview, founder Witte explains:

> Actually, our first idea wasn't about language learning at all. Prior to Babbel, all of the co-founders worked in the music technology space – we initially wanted to do something in that direction.
>
> It just so happened that one of us was trying to learn Spanish at the time. Naturally, he turned to the internet, but was surprised to find that there just weren't any viable ways to learn a language online. So we created one.
>
> Babbel has a unique approach to getting people conversational as soon as possible. And right from the very first lesson, we encourage them to communicate in their new language. (Slagel, 2016, online version).

Babbel claims, egregiously:

> Learning a language is about speaking a language, and with the help of Babbel, our novice challenge participants were able to start having conversations in just three weeks time, proving that Babbel is, indeed, the shortest path to a real-life conversation. (Stoyanoff, 2017, online version).

2.2 Busuu

Busuu was founded in 2008 by Bernhard Niesner and Adrian Hilti (busuu, 2017). The app makes the claim that "busuu is the world's largest social network for language learning, providing courses in 12 different languages on web and mobile to more than 70 million learners worldwide" (busuu, 2017, online version). busuu allies its program design with Council of Europe standards, which "provide a transparent, coherent and comprehensive basis for the elaboration of language syllabuses and curriculum guidelines, the design of teaching and learning materials, and the assessment of foreign language proficiency"[2].

> Each language course on busuu is developed using the Common European Framework of Reference (CEFR), an internationally recognised standard for creating language lessons. The CEFR is broken down into six stages, ranging from complete beginner to completely fluent. busuu courses cover the first four stages of the CEFR, from A1 to B2 level.

Our lessons are designed by experts in linguistics and pedagogy to help you achieve fluency in a structured and engaging way. Each lesson is designed around a useful topic, and contains vocabulary, grammar, and practice exercises which gradually build conversational and writing skills. We teach you all the

---

[1] https://press.babbel.com/en/releases/

[2] https://www.coe.int/en/web/common-european-framework-reference-languages/?

language we need before asking you to form sentences, have a conversation or do a writing exercise. Each lesson repeats language you've learned in previous lessons, reinforcing your memory and building your confidence. We've chosen topics that are relevant to your language level and to the types of conversation you're most likely to be having at each stage of your language-learning journey. (busuu, 2017, online version).

2.3 Duolingo

The most commonly downloaded language app in the Education category on both iTunes and Google Play is duolingo, which was founded by Luis von Ahn and Severin Hacker in 2011, and launched in 2012 (O'Conor, 2014). duolingo boasts 170 million users (Woods, 2017), though statistics on users are nebulous, given that those who download the app may not be active users.

> "What I wanted to do was create a way to learn languages for free," says von Ahn. "If you look at language learning in the world, there are 1.2 billion people learning a foreign language and two thirds of those people are learning English so they can get a better job and earn more. The problem is that they don't have equity and most language courses cost a lot of money." (vonAhn quoted in O'Conor, 2014, online version).

A deeper dive finds the principal app developer's motivation to be not quite so altruistic. According to Siegler (2011), von Ahn, who is also co-developer of CAPTCHA and reCAPTCHA, tools for distinguishing humans from nonhumans online, wanted to enable people to translate the web for him for free in order to decode fuzzy environmental print in different languages for book digitization (Jašková, 2014). duolingo was invented as a free language teaching app that could capitalize on language learners' multilingual responses to disambiguate unclear text.

2.4 Memrise

Memrise was founded in 2010 by Oxford University graduate and Grand Master of Memory, Ed Cooke and Greg Detre, a Princeton University computational neuroscientist, specializing in the science of memory and forgetting (Nicklas, 2017). Memrise describes their spaced repetition system approach as combining science, fun and community[3] in vocabulary memorization, which it must be noted does not equate to language learning. Cambridge University Press affirms the Memrise app is allied with Cambridge Dictionaries Online and the Common European Framework (Cambridge University Press, 2012), which bolsters the app's lexicographical and linguistic grounding, though this information does not feature on the app's "about us" material. Google Play awarded Memrise: "Google Play I/O Award Winner for Best App of 2017"[4]. Cambridge University Press promotional materials advertise:

> A unique approach that promises the easiest route ever to learning English words has been launched by Cambridge University Press and online language platform Memrise.
>
> The project is the brainchild of Cambridge lexicographers from Cambridge Dictionaries Online (CDO) working with experts in neuroscience and one of the world's 122 Grand Masters of Memory. Together they have created a Memrise course with 1,000 words and phrases for English learners at upper intermediate level, based on the Common European Framework levels for English vocabulary. (Cambridge University Press, 2012, online version).

2.5 Experiencing MALL

The survey and historical situation of top-rated MALL apps led me to road-test the four top apps to ascertain the pedagogical and philosophical approaches each took to language, and language learning. As an experienced language learner and research professor in the field of multilingual education, I conducted an auto-ethnographic study of my acquisition of Italian using the top four MALL apps. The results were tallied with those of a concurrent case study of experienced and inexperienced language learners similarly road-testing one or more of these apps. A question emerged from the findings as to how mobile these mobile

---

[3] https://www.memrise.com/about/

[4] https://play.google.com/store/apps/details?id=com.memrise.android.memrisecompanion&hl=en

(m-)learning apps were, given the dated pedagogical approaches evident in the highly structural presentation of language in all apps (Lotherington, in press). This paper probes the mobility of these four top-rated MALL apps.

3. WHAT IS MOBILE ABOUT MOBILE LEARNING?

How does *mobility* change the experience of language learning?

Bo-Kristensen and Meyer (2008) historicize mobile language learning technologically as a descendant of the language laboratory, which was developed in the 1950s. The language lab was a behemoth: students were established in individual booths, connected to computer terminals, equipped with headsets and microphones, and drilled in second language (L2) exercises using audio-taped material—a far cry from mobile, flexible, or contextually relevant learning. The habitual repetition pedagogy of behaviourism used in 1950s language labs fit poorly with the complex project of second language learning:

> Following Skinner's model, one is led to believe that virtually any subject matter can be taught effectively and successfully by a carefully designed program of step-by-step reinforcement. Programmed instruction had its impact on foreign language teaching, though language is such complex behavior, penetrating so deeply into both cognitive and affective domains, that programmed instruction in languages was limited to very specialized subsets of language. (Brown, 2007, p. 36).

Concurrent with language teaching pedagogy moving away from the rigidity of what Kramsch (2006) describes as 1960s drill-and-kill exercises and towards communicative, interactive and integrative pedagogies (Bo-Kristensen & Meyer, 2008), technologies shrank from large immobile computers to mobile devices that are multifunctional and wirelessly networked. Smart mobile devices merge what were once standalone technologies, such as cameras and audio-video recorders, with pedagogical software, such as online dictionaries, to offer an expanded platform for language learning that is multimodal and portable. As such, both the device and the learner are physically mobile.

Reinders and Pegrum (2015) distinguish a mobile device from a portable technology, such as a laptop, in terms of contextual use: a mobile device is on and connected for on-the-go, as-needed use, whereas a portable device is more likely to be transported from one location to another for static use. *Mobile* thus captures perpetual, context-free connection.

Scott (2015) probes how the dimension of time is understood differently in mobile communication, where interactions cross time zones and global distance in a nanosecond. He terms the ensuing expanded sense of personal reality, "everywhereness" (p. 8). Bo-Kristensen and Meyer (2008) describe a similarly conceptualized expanded sense of personal reality in terms of "immediacy" (p. 33) engendered through enhanced flexibility in time and place.

Sharples, Arnedillo-Sánchez, Milrad and Vavoula (2009) understand learning, itself, to be mobile across devices (via cloud computing), social contexts, and conceptual space. Guo (2014) describes m-learning as part of a mobile lifestyle. The mobile lifestyle includes aspects of communication that are digitally-mediated, whether mobile or not, such as multimodal affordances, immediacy in connection across global space and time zones, distributed cognition and sociality, and software tracking of the user's behaviour. *Mobile learning* is thus characterized by perpetual connection (enabling a sense of *everywhereness*), dynamic processing (of consequently dynamically changing language), and cognitive distribution across devices as well as physical and social spaces.

4. HOW MOBILE ARE TOP-RATED MALL APPS?

Given that m-learning can be locally grounded and globally shared, perpetual through instant connection across digital platforms via cloud computing, and distributed across social and conceptual space, the mobile learner can, theoretically, learn anywhere and everywhere, and connect on-the-spot learning to dynamically changing landscapes. Trail-blazing examples of language professionals working in coordination with software developers to develop innovative m-learning designs include augmented reality (AR) language trails, such as Holden and Sykes' (2011) *Mentira* AR trail for Spanish language learners in the southwestern United States, which leverages "place-based, augmented reality mobile games for language learning" (p. 1).

Similarly, Pegrum (2017), working with a Singapore-based software developer, created an urban AR trail for Asian English language learners (ELLs). On Pegrum's AR trail, ELLs make and share short videos of themselves in designated locations along the AR walk, using video-making, which is an example of a production pedagogy (Thumlert, de Castell, & Jenson, 2015). Production pedagogies require the learner to make and do, using contemporary digital tools and practices. Given these innovative professionally-designed models of experiential m-learning, using mobility in imaginative ways, I turn to top-rated MALL apps, to investigate how they exploit perpetual connection, dynamic processing, and cognitive distribution.

4.1 Perpetual Connection and Everywhereness

Everywhereness is a state generated by the potential for instant connection across space and time. All four apps could be accessed with wifi availability, technically enabling perpetual connection to course materials. But to what or whom, apart from MALL app drills, could I, as a learner, be connected?

Social media sites, such as Facebook and Instagram, facilitate and build on everywhereness in friend accumulation. busuu offered limited interactional opportunities with globally-located speakers of the target language via a social media feature, but connection was neither instantaneous nor practical, as it was geared to grammatical correction. Grammar correction is not a particularly motivating reason to connect informally with a speaker of the target language; furthermore, a random user may not be linguistically reliable. The *native speaker* cannot be tasked with canonical grammatical analysis; this requires an educated specialist. Moreover, is native language to be assumed from a user's place of residence in the same shrinking world that is characterized by social population flows and remix? Shouldn't a language course that charges for lessons beyond the basic be able to teach and correct grammatical forms without resorting to crowd-sourcing?

Language was approached as an abstract structure rather than as a medium of human social communication on all four apps, though semiotic context was included in formulaic ways that had potential for connecting the learner to a social landscape where the target language was used. Tiny video flashcards in Memrise offered single words or short phrases spoken by real people. However, the opportunity to put language in grammatical and social context was sacrificed to an authentic-looking streetscape and speaker, and the grammatical distractors were of very poor quality (see Figure 1).

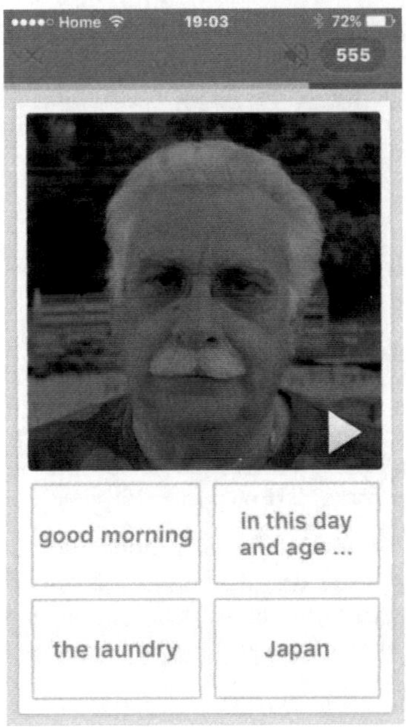

Figure 1. A video flashcard on Memrise

4.2 Dynamic Processing and Dynamically Changing Concepts of Language

Language is a complex concept. Where the edges of language lie in communication is difficult to ascertain. In contemporary society, language is visibly part of a larger suite of multimodal communication not only in physical space (with gestures and facial expressions) but importantly, in literate environments, where language is folded into suites of semiotic resources, including photos, videos, music, and voice-overs. Should language be extracted and studied in isolation from the communicatively illustrative aspects of a social media post, for example? What about the evolving grammar of tweets? Should Twitter grammar be ignored for static page grammar?

In all four top MALL apps, language was conceptualized as a static abstract structure to be learned as a *standard*. Indeed the incorporation of artificial intelligence (AI) in speech models and responses to exercises, assures a lack of the variation typical of human speech. Lessons were structured for transmission learning—content to be memorized and regurgitated—despite the fact that the material was delivered using digital multimodal forms. Structural approaches to language traditionally parse language as *reading-writing-speaking-listenin*g, despite the fact that communication has continued to morph and hybridize in digital environments, breaking out of the traditional four skills mold theorized for 20th century print and audio-video recording. Teaching the grammar of static writing for the page is limited and backward-looking in a digital era where communication is dynamic, interactive, multimodal, hybridized and multidirectional.

Where multimodality kicked in was most noteworthy in the speech record and playback feature on duolingo, where new words could be pronounced through the inbuilt microphone and checked against a programmed AI speech model. Apart from the apparent embarrassment of repeating decontextualized words in another language in public places (a strike against perpetual connection enabling constant use), the mike picked up environmental sounds without a headset and microphone, thus remixing my verbal responses with background noise, and, in the process, invalidating my tries. I could not practice spoken vocabulary in my own back yard, where duolingo captured birdsong, children's voices, and traffic rumble in my vocabulary repetitions, eliciting the programmed rejection: "Hmmm… that doesn't sound right. Give it another try."

The pedagogies tapped in all four apps relied heavily on drills and vocabulary memorization (which does not equate to language learning). These exercises, though likely easier to program, are driven by outdated theories of language learning, including behaviourism—the methodology of the ancestral language laboratory—and audiolingualism. Grammar translation, which is the oldest methodology in L2 learning and teaching, was prominent in all, but conspicuously missing the required grammatical explanations to translations in both duolingo and Memrise. The top MALL apps, thus, repackaged outdated, discredited pedagogies in shiny new digital containers. What was mobile was access to the material. Dynamic processing was not required.

4.3 Cognitive Distribution

Teamwork uses the principle of cognitive distribution. Contemporary digital devices activate cognitive distribution in a variety of ways: by facilitating crowd-sourcing knowledge, incorporating digital memory in human processing, and hosting digital role-playing games that require individuals to seek and share information.

4.3.1 Cognitive Distribution across Devices

The learner first has to locate the MALL app in a digital store, such as iTunes or Google Play, and then download it. All four MALL apps are cost-free initial downloads, though each, including duolingo, which advertises itself as gratis, requires financial or data sharing payment down the line. All four apps have desktop versions, enabling continual mobile and situated learning across mobile and desk-top devices.

4.3.2 Cognitive Distribution across Social and Conceptual Space

The four top MALL apps provided static textbooks in a convenient mobile package. Mobility was tapped for distribution and consumption of materials, not for linguistic processing, interactive communication, role game-playing, or even practice communication with voice-enabled AI conversational agents (beyond words and phrases in electronic flashcards). In fact, using an AI chatbot could be more effectively implemented were the learner to reprogram their phone in the target language, such that the digital assistant, e.g., Siri on iPhone, responded to real questions in the target language. Cognitive distribution in all four top-rated MALL apps was evident only in the learner's potential to use device memory.

5. DISCUSSION AND CONCLUSION

This paper probed whether and how top-rated MALL apps utilized *mobility* in their pedagogical designs, specifically looking at perpetual connection, dynamic processing, and cognitive distribution. Given the pedagogical engagement of virtual tours and massively multiplayer online role-playing games (MMORPG) with opponents or teammates using different languages, and opportunities to connect to geographically distant interlocutors in communicative exchanges, the opportunities to exploit the mobile character of m-learning as part of a mobile lifestyle are emancipatory in the face of centuries of desk-based language teaching.

In this study, the mobility of the device, the learner and the program, though, did not translate into mobile pedagogies for this century. MALL apps used mobility for cheap individual course delivery, changing the model from educating the learner to using the learner for profit, whether for marketable data, product advertising, or financial subscription. In return, the learner is supplied with a MALL app that provides easily accessible though boring, inflexible language drills that rely on outdated pedagogies. Perhaps drills are simply easier to program than a theoretically sound, professionally-orchestrated, communicatively interactive language resource? There is huge scope for imagination in creating production pedagogies appropriate to a mobile lifestyle, using a multifunction mobile device that captures data in multiple media, mixes modes of telling in social media genres, and shares texts instantaneously. There was unfortunately, no evidence of contemporary production pedagogies in any of these top-rated MALL apps.

With a retail orientation to learning and direct access to a product, learners are prey to advertising, online app popularity, and so forth in their choice of MALL apps, and, for novices, particularly, their understanding of how language learning works. Indeed, a skeptical view is that accessible language learning is rapidly moving online and into the hands of app developers, whose know-how and motivation privilege mobile app development and making a profit over progressive, professional language teaching and learning.

This paper discusses whether and how top-rated MALL apps utilize mobility in their pedagogical design and content presentation, finding that language is treated as static structure, grammar as print-based, pedagogy as mid-20th century drills, and mobility as a marketing ploy. Moreover, though MALL apps are marketed to the individual, they are not pedagogically flexible or customizable: they provide one-size-fits-all programming, making the methodology trademark rather than user-friendly.

The conclusion of this paper is directed to learners, teachers and software developers. Firstly, *caveat emptor* to potential language learners, who may find what little they learn of a target language was paid for in data-sharing (on duolingo), and interest in the language (on all four top MALL apps). Language teachers and professionals must become active in designing viable 21st century mobile pedagogies, such as Holden and Sykes' (2011) and Pegrum's (2017) augmented reality trails and their attendant requirements for contemporary production pedagogies. Lastly, designers cannot simply claim to be using professional standards and then come out with discredited, outdated pedagogies. Software designers and language professionals need to work together more closely and more respectfully towards pedagogical innovation that utilizes the affordances of mobility for learning, not simply for course sales and distribution.

REFERENCES

Bo-Kristensen, M. & Meyer, B. 2008. Transformations of the language laboratory. In T. Hansson (ed.), *Digital Information Technologies: Innovations, methods, and ethical issues* (pp. 27-36). Hershey, PA: Information Science Reference.

Brown, H.D. 2007. *Principles of language learning and teaching* (5th edition). White Plains, NY: Pearson Education.

busuu. 2017. *Welcome to busuu.* Retrieved from: https://www.busuu.com/en/about

Cambridge University Press. (2012, December). Cambridge and Memrise launch a world first in English language learning. *Information For The Media.* Retrieved from: http://www.cambridge.org/about-us/media/press-releases/cambridge-and-memrise-launch-world-first

comScore 2017, January. *Mobile's hierarchy of needs: How mobile evolved as the primary tool for the digital omnivore.* Retrieved from: comScore-Report-Mobile-Hierarchy.pdf .

Guo, H. 2014. *Analysing and evaluating current mobile applications for learning English speaking.* MA thesis, Birkbeck College, University of London.

Holden, C. L., & Sykes, J. M. 2011. Leveraging mobile games for place-based language learning. *International Journal of Game-Based Learning, 1*(2), 1-18.

Jašková, V. (2014). *duolingo as a new language-learning website and its contribution to e-learning education.* Unpublished Masters thesis, Brno: Masaryk University. Retrieved from: https://is.muni.cz/th/342420/pedf_m/duolingo.pdf .

Kelly, L. G. 1969. *25 centuries of language teaching: An inquiry into the science, art, and development of language teaching methodology, 500 BC-1969.* Rowley, MA: Newbury House.

Kramsch, C. 2006. From communicative competence to symbolic competence. *The Modern Language Journal, 90*(2), 249-252.

Krzemińska, M. n.d. 10 best language learning apps. *Lingualift.* https://www.lingualift.com/blog/best-language-learning-apps/.

Lotherington, H. in press. Mobile language learning: The medium is ^not the message. *L2 Journal.*

Lotherington, H. 2017, October. *English to go: A critical analysis of apps for language learning.* ICDE World Conference on Online Learning. Toronto, Ontario. Retrieved from: https://www.academia.edu/35243527/ENGLISH_TO_GO_A_CRITICAL_ANALYSIS_OF_APPS_FOR_LANGUAGE_LEARNING

Nicklas, R. 2017. Memrise. *The Electronic Journal for English as a Second Language, 21*(1). 1-12.

O'Conor, L. 2014, August. Duolingo creator: 'I wanted to create a way to learn languages for free.' Education. The Guardian. Retrieved from: https://www.theguardian.com/education/2014/aug/27/luis-von-ahn-ceo-duolingo-interview

Pegrum, M. 2017, July. Designing for situated language and literacy: Learning through mobile augmented reality games and trails. Paper in panel: *Researching digital games in language learning and teaching*, AILA World Congress, Rio de Janeiro, Brazil.

Reinders, H., & Pegrum, M. 2015. Supporting language learning on the move: An evaluative framework for mobile language learning resources. In Tomlinson, B. (Ed.), *Second language acquisition research and materials development for language learning* (pp.116-141). London: Taylor & Francis. Retrieved from: http://hdl.handle.net/10652/2991.

Scott, L. 2015. *The four-dimensional human: Ways of being in the digital world.* London, UK: Heinemann.

Siegler, M.G. (2011, April). Meet duolingo, Google's next acquisition target; Learn a language, help the web. *TechCrunch*. Retrieved from: https://techcrunch.com/2011/04/12/duolingo/ .

Slagel, J. 2016, March. Interview with Babbel founder and CEO Markus Witte. *The Young Businessmen*. Retrieved from: https://theyoungbusinessmen.com/2016/03/07/interview-with-babbel-founder-and-ceo-markus-witte/

Sharples, M., Arnedillo-Sánchez, I., Milrad, M. & Vavoula, G. 2009. Mobile learning: Small devices; big issues. In Balacheff, N., Ludvigson, S., de Jong, T., Lazonder, A., & Barnes, S. (Eds.), *Technology-enhanced learning: Principles and products* (pp. 233-250.). Dordrecht: Springer.

Stoyanoff, A. 2017. *The shortest path to real-life conversations.* Retrieved from: https://www.babbel.com/en/magazine/how-our-app-teaches-you-spanish-in-3-weeks

Thumlert, K., de Castell, S., & Jenson, J. 2015. Short Cuts and Extended Techniques: Rethinking relations between technology and educational theory. *Educational Philosophy and Theory*, *47*(8), 786-803.

Woods, J. 2017, June. How duolingo got 170 million users worldwide to learn a second language. *Techvibes*. Retrieved from: https://techvibes.com/2017/06/16/how-duolingo-got-170-million-users-worldwide-to-learn-a-second-language

TOWARDS A MOBILE AUGMENTED REALITY PROTOTYPE FOR CORPORATE TRAINING: A NEW PERSPECTIVE

Agostino Marengo[1], Alessandro Pagano[1] and Lucia Ladisa[2]
[1]*University Aldo Moro of Bari, Italy*
[2]*Osel S.r.l., Italy*

ABSTRACT

The potentials of the use of AR are showing up in a variety of ways can be used to create unique learning experiences. Recently, the advancement and popularity of handheld devices has enabled researchers to implement more effective learning methods. in educational as well as in corporate settings, from primary through to adult education. The industrial interest for such a technology is high, and in recent years, many attempts to use AR as a support for maintenance and repair processes.

In this paper, we present an ongoing research, concerning the application of Augmented Reality technology to e-learning system for corporate training purposes. More specifically, our research goal is to figure out if corporate training would get a valuable help from the implementation of AR in training programs, seeking to explore the advantages of the use of this emerging technology in maintenance contexts' needs. In particular, the research team starts from the evaluation of a previous research "Towards a mobile AR prototype for corporate training" (Marengo, Pagano, & Ladisa, 2017) and aims to go over some hurdles and criticism we highlighted during the research. The original purpose consisted in developing an Augmented Reality Web App for maintenance and repair training purposes. Going further, we noticed some critical aspects of the study, which could affect negatively the final goal of the research. The new aim is to introduce a complete new approach starting from a methodological and finishing to a technical point of view.

In this paper, we present those reinvented approaches highlighting the design and the development phases applied to achieve our goal. The last phase of our research work presented is the development of a prototype ready for further application and testing. This represent just the beginning step of our ongoing research project.

KEYWORDS

Augmented Reality, e-Learning, Mobile Learning, Corporate Training

1. INTRODUCTION

In the last few years, companies spending on corporate training grew year after year. Specifically, companies spend more money in e-learning training, always looking for more engaging and motivating experience for the employees. In fact, workers' productivity has been revolutionized by the increasing use of mobile devices on the job. This revolution leads companies in exploring how to use new technologies to increase "immersive" learning experiences for workers.

In this context, Augmented Reality (AR) represents nowadays one of the most impactful technologies on learning and training. As it is becoming more and more accessible and popular in the e-learning world, companies are attracted from the potentialities of Augmented Reality on training processes. Big companies are investing in this direction, too (Masoni, et al., 2017). Previous researches and case studies demonstrated how the use of Augmented Reality as a training system might enhance practical skills and learning processes, improving education/training outcomes (Chu, Hwang, Tsai, & Tseng, 2010; Yang, 2006; Tang, Owen, Biocca, & Mou, 2003; Hung, Hwang, Lin, Wu, & Su, 2013; Chiang, Yang, & Hwang, 2014).

In view of the above, a few months ago we started a research project concerning the development of a mobile AR prototype for corporate training (Marengo, Pagano, & Ladisa, 2017). It consisted in developing an Augmented Reality Web App for maintenance and repair training purposes, which would be useful to aid workers in the execution of some procedural tasks. While the research was going on, we found some criticism that in practical could affect negatively the results expected. Therefore, we decided to review and change the original project.

In this paper we describe our research on AR for corporate training, its origins and the change of direction in the middle of its development. We will also discuss the new perspective we have adopted to overcome the weaknesses of our previous work.

2. THE PREVIOUS RESEARCH: AN OVERVIEW

Augmented Reality is a technology that allows virtual information to be overlaid onto a live direct or indirect real-world environment in real time (Azouma R. , 1997). Our previous research is based on Augmented Reality technology, which is considered a very promising application of an emerging technology in many settings, including corporate training. We focus on the advantages of AR as directly linked to physical objects/devices of the training context, where some additional information is overlaid onto a real-world context, with the specific aim to apply it on training contexts.

The main aim of the research is to figure out if corporate training would get a valuable help from the implementation of AR in training programs, seeking to explore the advantages of the use of this new technology as a support for training on the job in maintenance contexts' needs. For this purpose, a few months ago we started the development of an Augmented Reality Web App for maintenance and repair training purposes through Wikitude, a tool providing SDKs for AR development.

In order to achieve our goal, we engaged a worldwide elevators company: Sematic-Wittur, which volunteer participated to some phases of the research. After the development of the Web App, hands-on and evaluating test sessions would have involved a focus group of the company. Future work consisted into analyzing the efficacy of AR in corporate training in comparison with the evaluation of other training methods in the same field.

Since AR has been recognized as being an interesting support in the industry for maintenance applications, assembly, and repair tasks (Azouma R. , 2016; Masoni, et al., 2017; Webel, et al., 2011; Shanmugam & Paul Robert , 2015), we expected that maintenance and repair tasks could benefit from the implementation of AR in training programs and users could take great advantage by using this new technology while performing job tasks. More details about the methodology of the project are explained in the following paragraph.

2.1 Methodology

Due to the complexity of the project, the original research consisted of three different phases:

- Phase 1: development of an Augmented Reality Web App;
- Phase 2: testing phase. Hands-on sessions and evaluation survey;
- Phase 3: analysis of the results.

The first phase concerned the development of an Augmented Reality Web App for maintenance and repair purposes. The Web App should have been mobile-based in order to be suitable for mobile devices (tablets or smartphones).

In the light of this, we had previously analyzed and compared a range of different SDKs, in order to choose the one which would have fitted better for the purposes of our project. Our choice has fallen upon the SDK Wikitude, which is an all-in-one augmented reality SDK, combining 3D Tracking technology (SLAM), Image Recognition and Tracking, as well as Geo-location AR for apps (The world's leading AR SDK). It offers markerless AR experiences, high qualitative features and an integration with Titanium (a mobile application development framework); moreover, Wikitude is community supported. The Testing phase (Phase 2) and the Analysis of the results (Phase 3) would have represented a valuable combination to assess the validity of the research and the evaluation of our research project in terms of efficacy and consistency.

3. IMPLEMENTATION OF THE FIRST PROTOTYPE AND GOING THROUGH NEW PERSPECTIVE

Recently, the advancement and popularity of handheld devices and sensing technologies has enabled researchers to implement more effective learning methods (Ogata, Li, Hou, Uosaki, El-Bishouty, & Yano, 2011). More specifically, Augmented Reality (AR) technology for maintenance aims to improve human performances and to speed up processes by providing relevant information in a highly contextual way. The kind of information to be displayed in AR permits an efficient maintenance task that accelerates the technicians' acquisition of new skill on maintenance procedures (Radkowski, Herrema, & Oliver, 2015; Cárdenas & Dutra, 2016; Elia, Gnoni, & Lanzillotto, 2016; Re, Oliver, & Bordegoni).

As explained in the previous paragraph, the first step of our original research consisted in the development of a web app for maintenance and repair tasks through the AR tool Wikitude. Before we get started the development process of the App, we made a last assessment of the potentialities of the project, making a deeper study of the target (i.e. workers) and its features. This study assessed that such a Tool could not be useful for elevator installers and repairer for several reasons:

- Mobile devices should be held with at least one hand;
- While installing/repairing elevators, workers need both hands to work;
- If they were using our web app, at least two workers would be engaged while repairing/installing onsite.

As can be seen from the points explained above, we faced some difficulties about the implementation of the App into the job process, just before starting the development. The only way to fix this hurdles were:

- Maintaining the purposes of the research and adopting hands-free technologies (i.e. Augmented Reality (AR) headset);
- Changing the purposes of the research, basing the new study entirely on mobile technology.

Firstly, we decided to change the perspective of our research, focusing the purpose of our project on training of new workers for onboarding processes. This change of direction allowed us to consider Virtual Reality Technology as one possible option, since it supports simulations of corporate settings in a virtual environment.

In regard of this, Gavish et al (2015) evaluated the efficiency and effectiveness of four training groups for industrial maintenance procedural skills. Results demonstrated no significant differences in the final performance between the VR and AR. Although this study did not directly compare the AR and the VR platform because the two platforms were different in several functions, they valued studies that compare the effects of VR and AR platforms that were in similar design (Liou, Yang, Chen, & Tarng, 2017).

However, even if VR can be considered as a more mature technology in learning contexts (Wu, Lee, Chang, & Liang, 2013), Augmented Reality provides the best scenario suited for our training goals, which is not possible with other media. Since we meant to develop an innovative prototype for corporate training, AR technology was considered the best solution for several reasons:

- Costs of development;
- Duration of development;
- The prototypal nature of our project.

From a technical point of view, we decided to evaluate the best AR software development kit (SDK) regarding the aim of our project and the company's needs. For this reason, we choose Blippar, an Augmented Reality development tool. More details are explained in the following paragraphs.

4. THE NEW RESEARCH PROJECT

Although AR has already shown promise in some corporate contexts, this immersive technology should be considered thoughtfully to ensure it adds value to the existing workflows. In regard of this, the development of an AR system involves the attentive choice of a hardware, a development software and a visualisation method (Palmarini, Erkoyuncu, & Roy, 2016). Moreover, staff should be well equipped, some hardware components have been improved (i.e. batteries), but there are still many open issues and challenges related the hardware of the technology, the content of the application and the education of the industrial market.

In the light of this, for company-specific reasons we choose to change the purpose of our AR App, shifting the focus away from repairer onto newly hired repairer. Moreover, technical aspects have been reviewed and redefined. The following paragraph will explain the details of the App development.

4.1 The Development of the App

With the changing of the purposes of the research (Paragraph 3) we have looked for a different framework or SDK to develop our project. We have chosen Blippar for several reasons, such as:

- faster development: Blippar has an app on the main app stores (also used by companies to AR marketing campaigns) that already has a powerful images and object recognition engine, so we can focus on the augmented reality experience (e.g. the image or 3D models animated on the screen, the user interface, the contents of the course), and delegate the image recognition process to Blippar;
- faster code maintenance: as explained above, the app is already on the Main app repository. By doing this, we don't need to constantly release, concerning the recognition and tracking engine. Consequently, we can focus on the course design and the user experience;
- faster prototyping: with the Blippbuilder (a drag and drop development tool) we can quickly develop a prototype in order to test the user interaction in relation to the contents of the course.

We adopted the AR technology to lead the user of a given e-learning course from the frame of the mechanical object to the learning object on the LMS Platform in an engaging and easy way through mobile devices (i.e. smartphone, tablet). By doing this, our App will:

- Frame the mechanical object;
- Detect the image with the device camera and recognize the marker;
- Display multimedia contents on the device screen (like text or video/audio contents);
- Display a button that will lead the user to the pertinent learning object

The purposed system is a mobile Augmented Reality system and a marker-based one. The choice of the marker image is a crucial part in the development process. A marker should have the following features:

- A jpeg image with RGB color space and without extra channels or paths. High resolution image are not required for the image tracking and recognition, and a too heavy image will only slow down data exchange with Blippar server;
- high contrast image with as many sharp crisp edges and corners as possible;
- a size measured in n*100 pixels.

In view of the above, we conducted some tests to choose the image better responding to the identification of the system. After evaluating several images, we choose to test the app using the logos of Osel Srl (Figure 1 and Figure 2). The test was conducted using an Android device. It revealed that the logo in the Figure 1 was identified faster than the logo in Figure 2 from different orientation and positions of the camera. This may depend on the complexity and the definition of the image. In fact, Figure 2 consists of the logo and some text, which could negatively affect the performance of image-recognition.

Figure 1. Logo Osel S.r.l.

Figure 2. Logo Osel S.r.l.

The next step to be taken is to develop the mobile AR App, basing on the above observations. Before getting started with the App, we designed the "Blipp", basing on the structure represented in Figure 3. As shown, the "Scene" is the root node containing various other types of nodes. The Model node is the root of visible entities within a blipp, that in our case consists of Sprite which is used for 2D images. The other nodes within the scene, such as Light, Material, Space and Texture have functional purpose but won't be defined because useful to 3D images. Anim could be subsequently defined.

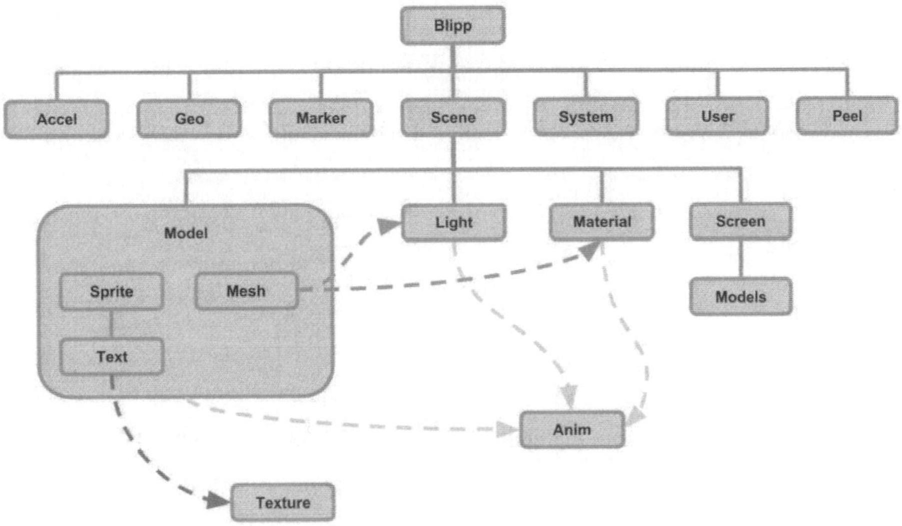

Figure 3. Diagram Showing the Relationship between the Nodes of a Single Blip

We've set the values of the Marker properties on the dimension the uploaded files and the values of the Sprite, which will cover the marker on the display:

VAR MarkerWidth ⟵ GET WidthOfMarker
VAR MarkerHeight ⟵ GET HeightOfMarker
VAR SceneSprite ⟵ SpritePath, SpriteName, SpriteTranslation, SpriteScale

The purpose of the function GET is to fetch the marker width and height from the marker file previously uploaded on the Blippar server and assign it to "MarkerWidth" and "MarkerHeight". The variable SceneSprite stores all the data of flat plane (e.g an image) that will overlap the marker during the tracking; the Blippar image recognition engine will continuously track the marker with the camera and keep the flat plane stuck on it.

IF onTouch = TRUE

THEN
OpenCourse

The User might tap the object/image displayed on the device and be led directly to course on the LMS Platform. We can add a floating frame with a brief definition or a video depending on the content of the learning object. As explained in the previous paragraph, the User might Interact with the object/image displayed on the device and be led directly to course on the LMS Platform.

5. CONCLUSION

The three characteristics of AR, combining real and virtual objects incorporated into reality, providing collaboration between real and virtual objects, and real-time interaction between real and virtual objects (Chiang, Yang, & Hwang, 2014) can empower experience-based learning and learning outcomes. More specifically, Augmented Reality as a support for maintenance AR can help to reduce time and errors of maintenance tasks (Fiorentino, Uva, Gattullo, Debernardis & Monno, 2014).

In this paper, we analyzed our previous research about the development of an AR App for corporate training in maintenance and repair, and tried to overcome the hurdles we found in the course of the research development. Basing on what highlighted in the evaluating phase described above, in our ongoing research we are developing an Augmented Reality App for training newly hired repairer and we are planning the evaluation steps.

As in the original research project, future work includes developing phase, hands-on and evaluating test sessions, aiming to evaluate the impact of our project on the training program of Sematic-Wittur on both a quantitative and qualitative point of view. Furthermore, once the results will be collected, our research will go one step further by analyzing the efficacy of AR in corporate training in comparison with the effectiveness of other training methods (such as traditional training and e-learning) in the same field.

Whereas the purposed paper presents an ongoing research, the achievement of our expected results will depend on the further steps of the study. Therefore, when the project will be finished, data will be analyzed and compared with our expectations.

ACKNOWLEDGEMENT

We wish to thank Sematic-Wittur for collaborating to our project. We would also like to thank Osel S.r.l., which is supporting the development of our ongoing project.

REFERENCES

Azouma, R. (1997). A survey of aumented reality. *Presence: Teleoperators and Virtual Environments,* 6(4), pp. 355-385.

Azouma, R. (2016). The Most Important Challenge Facing Augmented Reality. *PRESENCE: Teleoperators and Virtual Environments,* 25(3), pp. 234-238.

Cárdenas, E., & Dutra, M. (2016). An Augmented Reality Application to Assist Teleoperation of UnderwaterManipulators. *IEEE Latin America Transactions*, 14 (2), pp. 863-869.

Chiang, T., Yang, S., & Hwang, G. (2014). An Augmented Reality-based Mobile Learning System to Improve Students'Learning Achievements and Motivations in Natural Science Inquiry Activities. *Educational Technology & Society,* 17(4), pp. 352–365.

Chu, H., Hwang, G., Tsai, C., & Tseng, J. (2010). A two-tier test approach to developing location-aware mobile learning systems for natural science courses. *Computer & Education*, 55(4), pp. 1618-1627.

Elia, V., Gnoni, M., & Lanzillotto, A. (2016). Evaluating the application of augmented reality devicdes in manifacturing from a process point of view. An AHP based model. *Expert systems with applications,* 63, 187-197.

Fiorentino, M., Uva, A. E., Gattullo, M., Debernardis, S., Monno, G., Augmented reality on large screen for interactive maintenance instructions. *Computers in Industry*, 65(2), pp. 270-278 (2014)

Gavish, N., Gutiérrez, T., Webel, S., Rodríguez, J., Peveri, M., Bockholt, U., & Tecchia, F. (2015). Evaluating virtual reality and augmented reality training for industrial maintenance and assembly tasks. *Interactive Learning Environments,* 23(6), pp. 778-798.

Hung, P., Hwang, G., Lin, Y., Wu, T., & Su, I. (2013). Seamless connection between learning and assessment-Seamless connection between learning and assessmentapplying. *Educational Technology & Society,* 16(1), pp. 194-205.

Liou, H.-H., Yang, S., Chen, S., & Tarng, W. (2017). The Influences of the 2D Image-Based Augmented Reality and Virtual Reality on Student Learning. *Educational Technology & Society,* 20(3), pp. 110–121.

Marengo, A., Pagano, A., & Ladisa, L. (2017). Towards a Mobile Augmented Reality Prototype for Corporate Training. *European Conference On E-Learning (ECEL)*, (pp. 362-366).

Masoni, R., Ferrise, F., Bordegoni, M., Gattullo, M., Uva, A., Fiorentino, M., Di Donato, M. (2017). Supporting remote maintenance in industry 4.0 through augmented reality. *27th International Conference on Flexible Automation and Intelligent Manufacturing (FAIM2017)*, Modena, Italy, pp. 1296 – 1302.

Palmarini, R., Erkoyuncu, J., & Roy, R. (2016). An innovative process to select Augmented Reality. *The 5th International Conference on Through-life Engineering Services (TESConf 2016)*, Cranfield, UK, pp. 23 – 28.

Radkowski, R., Herrema, J., & Oliver, J. (2015). Augmented reality-based manual assembly support with visual features for different degrees of difficulty. *International Journal of Human-Computer Interaction, 31*(5), pp. 337–349.

Re, G., Oliver, J., & Bordegoni, M. Impact of monitor-based augmented reality for on-site industrial manual operations. *Cogn Tech Work,* 18, 379-392.

Shanmugam , A., & Paul Robert , T. (2015). Human Factors in Training for aircraft maintenance Technicians. *19th Triennial Congress of the IEA*, Melbourne, Australia, pp. 1-7.

Tang, A., Owen, C., Biocca, F., & Mou, W. (2003). Comparative effectiveness of augmented reality in object assembly. *Proceedings of the SIGCHI Conference on Human Factors in Computing Systems*, Lauderdale, USA, pp. 73-80.

Webel, S., Bockholt, U., Engelke, T., Peveri, M., Olbrich, M., & Preusche, C. (2011). Augmented Reality Training for Assembly and Maintenance Skills. *The International Conference SKILLS,* Montpellier, France, pp. 1-4.

Wu, H., Lee, S., Chang, H., & Liang, J. (2013). Current status, opportunities and challenges of augmented reality in education. *Computers & Education,* 62, pp. 41-49.

Yang, S. (2006). Context aware ubiquitous learning environments for peer-to-peer collaborative learning. *Educational Technology & Society,* 9(1), pp. 188-201.

Short Papers

PERSONALIZED ADAPTIVE CONTENT SYSTEM FOR CONTEXT-AWARE MOBILE

Ouissem Benmesbah, Lamia Mahnane and Mohamed Hafidi
LRS laboratory, University of Badji Mokhtar, P.O. Box, 12, 23000, Annaba, Algeria

ABSTRACT

The rapid development of emerging technologies for mobile devices has enabled them to contribute strongly to the creation of new paths for learning. Mobile learning helps the user to learn at anytime and anywhere and also provides him a unique experience in terms of its flexibility. The problem in mobile learning is not the availability or quality of information, but is rather its relevance to a specific context of use. The quality of a mobile learning system therefore depends on its ability to provide learners with both pedagogical content adapted to their context and processes that truly guide them in their process of learning. This paper presents a new adaptive mobile learning architecture that supports the features of mobility and context in order to enhance the learning experience.

KEYWORDS

Context Aware, Adaptive Content, Mobile Learning, Personal Characteristics, Educational Needs

1. MOTIVATION

The growth of mobile computing has drawn the attention of researchers which are interested in studying how mobile devices can be exploited for educational purposes (Baccari et al., 2015). As a result, this has led to a research trend which is commonly referred to as mobile learning (m-learning) in which researchers and educational stakeholders have been concentrating their efforts so as to consider the affordances of wireless and handheld technologies in education (Chee et al., 2017). Briefly going through m-learning history (Dennouni et al., 2017), in its early days (mid 1990s) research and educational initiatives focused on taking the most of "mobile and wireless technologies within the classroom". In this phase there was an interest on how devices, in particular PDA, laptops and mobile/cell phones, can be used for in an educational context for instruction and training. Then, in early 2000s, a second phase of m-learning focused on "learning outside the classroom". Researchers' interest was directed into highlighting the meaningful benefits that mobile technologies can bring to people outside institutionally framed educational contexts. This second phase includes field trips, museum visits, and personal learning organizers, among others. Finally, by mid 2000s, research initiatives began focusing on the "mobility of the learner" involving the design or the appropriation of learning spaces and on informal learning and lifelong learning. In this third phase, affordances of emerging technology, surrounding resources and availability of information to the learner's situation and context can be distinguished. Through these three phases, we have moved from period when human activity must be adapt to the computer location (one computer, many people), to a period when the computer is the alter ego of the man (one person, one computer), and eventually to a period of human-centered activities in which the computers are serving the learning purposes (one person, many computers) (Elhamdaoui et al., 2011). Since the beginnings of third phase of m-learning, a new research trend has been emerging; this research leads us to assess how we can provide the user with the appropriate content to its context in a radical changing environment. This focal point relies on delivering personalized and adapted mobile learning experiences to learners with regards to: i) the mobile device with which they interact (i.e. Aspects of 1st phase of m-learning); ii) their individual needs and preferences in learning situations which are different from a traditional classroom (aspects of 2nd phase of m-learning); and iii) the surrounding resources (people, ambient technologies, physical objects, etc.). That may affect the interaction between learners with anytime-anywhere available information (aspects of 3rd phase of m-learning) (Gómez. S. E, 2013). The issue that can be raised regarding mobile learning is the issue of relevance to the learner's specific context of use.

Personalization and adaptation of content is one of the fundamental aspects for developing m-learning activities (Soualah-alila et al., 2014). According to (Madhubala et al., 2017), it is important for students to have the information and educational resources in an adaptive way based on their context and needs.

2. RESEARCH QUESTIONS

During the past years, a challenging research has emerged with regards to involving ubiquitous use of mobile devices within learning strategies. Educational research initiatives has been focused on this ubiquitous characteristic combined with educational systems development, so as to offer important benefits to learning design and delivery processes, which could be summarized as follows) (Gómez. S. E, 2013):

√ Supporting pedagogical models that are based on authentic learning by exploiting real-life context.

√ Providing flexible, adaptive and personalized learning experiences by exploiting learners' contextual information.

Consequently, different educational activities have been proposed by teachers to enhance teaching and learning experiences and to introduce learners with a ubiquitous m-learning initiative including: using multimedia to stay engaged in a learning environment, for example videos, podcasts, audio as well as access to bite-sized learning, or micro learning on the go, engaging learners towards the establishment of online learning communities so as to produce collaborative projects, uploading videos with explanations about how to use tools in real situations to ensure learners can recall instruction on different process when and where they need it, making field trips to engage learners in active experience, and providing learners with supportive mobile systems that guides them through visits, among other activities. Therefore, on the plethora of teaching/learning strategies and use cases that users can be typically engaged in, Our approach is particularly focused on considering educational scenarios which may benefit from the use of mobile and wireless technologies and learners' contextual information, so as to re-think and implement them in a formal learning design that can be suitably delivered to the learners. From this stems the first research and development question of this work is:

Q1: How can adaptive and personalized learning design process, which is based on the learner's contextual information, be designed and delivered?

With the growing impact of distance learning and open educational resources, constructivist pedagogical approaches are increasingly being studied by different researchers in order to define and apply suited pedagogical theories for contextual and m-learning experiences. Accordingly, this leads to a research challenge within this research work, that is, defining optimal ways on how educational scenarios and resources can be suitable delivered to different learners according to diverse contextual information such as the characteristics of the learning place and its physical conditions, the spare time used to learn, the contributions of the surrounding people and the individual learning interests, preferences and needs in a particular moment, including the capabilities of the learners' mobile device at hand (Gómez. S. E, 2013).

In m-learning environments, providing personalized educational sequenced activities and educational digital materials (resources, tools, services, etc.) while taking into account limitations of the mobile devices such as limited screen sizes, limited memory available for page rendering and limited types of content supported may cause the loss of information for learning and the failure to achieve the learning objectives if adaptation processes are not well designed and implemented. This leads to our second research and development question:

Q2: How can educational resources, integrated in a procedural learning design, be adapted considering learner's contextual information?

Within this research work, it was important to consider the study of adaptation mechanisms based on learners' context characteristics that can be integrated into the learning process and that enable suitable delivery of educational digital materials appropriately adapted to learners' mobile devices.

3. OBJECTIVES

In a broad sense, context is (Dey, A.K., 2001) "any information which can be used to characterize the situation of an entity, an entity is a person, a place or an object which is relevant for the interaction between a user and an application including the user and the appropriate applications".

In this paper we consider some characteristics that are necessary when modelling context: Learner's profile (personal characteristics such as knowledge, skills, attitudes and individual features such as mood, preferences, needs, interests, etc), other people that influence the learning process with their role, relationships, contributions, digital devices (mobile technologies, ambient intelligence technologies, etc.) and non-digital resources (books, documents, etc) and characteristics of the status of a learning situation such as time, physical conditions of the place (such as illumination level, noise level), cultural and social milieu, among other characteristics.

Research in recent years has made considerable progress in understanding the phenomenon of context and in exploring the potentials of context-awareness. However, there are still several issues to be solved before context-aware functionality can be rolled out on a large scale. This work aims to address those issues by the following objectives:

O1: Defining Taxonomy of contextual elements for designing context-aware educational scenarios (Learning designs) and for being processed by a mobile delivery system so as to provide learners with adapted learning activities and resources.

O2: Implementing context-aware and adaptation mechanisms for both design and delivery phases of the learning design.

O3: Designing and creating a number of predefined context-aware and adaptive mobile educational scenario so as to explain and present how possible adaptations, that are realized based on learner's contextual information, can be incorporated.

O4: Developing a mobile delivery system aiming to address delivering pedagogical-enhanced and structured adaptive and context-aware educational scenarios on mobile devices.

4. SYSTEM ARCHITECTURE

In order to achieve these objectives, a client-server based architecture is developed.

- The server side:

In this part, a taxonomy of contextual elements and a set of pre defined values for those elements are defined, these elements are proposed for designing context-aware educational scenarios (Learning design) and for being processed by a mobile delivery system (Client side) so as to provide learners with adapted learning activities and resources. Moreover, it integrates an adaptation engine level 1, which produces multiple formats of the same domain model (educational scenario) according to the predefined instances of certain contextual information (mobile device capabilities, learner's profile) and pedagogical activities model used to create different forms of learning flow (canevas) based on personal characteristics (knowledge, skills and needs). These scenarios are stored on the server, and then are dynamically selected to match the contextual information captured in real time by the client side (the delivery system).

- The client side:

It is represented by the delivery system, which let deploying context-aware adaptive educational scenarios on it and executing learning activities and context-aware adaptation rules without internet connection. This is important because mobile devices are not constantly connected to the internet. The delivery system allows the contextual information acquisition (time, place, physical conditions, devices capabilities…) in real time, these information will be the entry of the adaptation engine level2, which occurs on an existing learning design created in the design phase (server side) or on a new learning design created by calling the adaptation engine level 1.

Figure 1 shows each objective in the proposed system

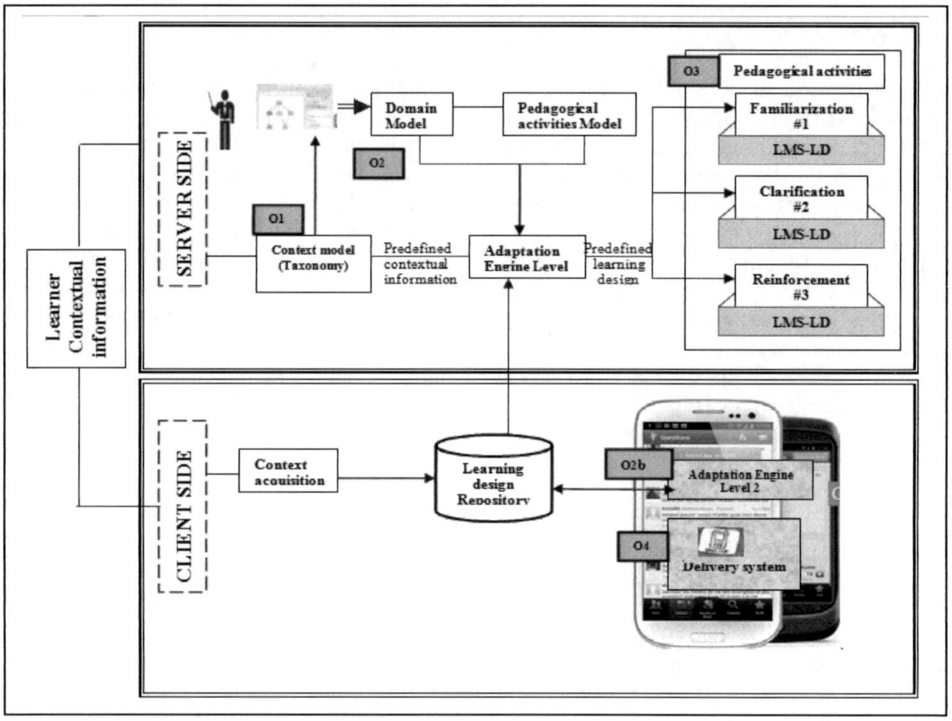

Figure 1. Proposed system architecture

5. CONCLUSION

This work provides an overview on the main facets of the research. First, we describe the research problem and express the motivation to work on it. Then, general questions for the research are introduced and discussed in brief. After that, the defined objectives and research proposal is described and the system architecture is explained. The detail implementation of the system will be published in upcoming paper.

REFERENCES

Baccari, S., Mendes, F., Nicolle, C., Soualah-Alila, F. and Mahmoud, N., 2015. *Comparative Study of the Mobile Learning Architectures. e-LEOT 2nd EAI International Conference on e-Learning e-Education and Online Training.* Novedrate, Italy. 2015.

Chee K. et al, 2017. Review of Mobile Learning Trends 2010-2015: A Meta-Analysis. *In Educational Technology & Society,* Vol. *20, No.* 2, pp 113-126.

Dennouni N. et al, 2017. Recommendation techniques in mobile learning context: A Review. *International Journal Modern Education and Computer Science,* Vol. 10, pp 37-46.

Dey, A.K., 2001. Understanding and using context. Personal and Ubiquitous Computing 5 (1), 4–7.

Elhamdaoui A. et al, 2011. Contextual adaptability platform for mobile and ubiquitous learning: a step towards a pervasive learning environment. *International journal of digital information and Wireless Communications*, Vol. 2, pp 563-571

Gómez. S. E. 2013. Learning design Implementation in Context-aware and adaptive Mobile Learning, Doctoral thesis, University of Girona.

Madhubala R. et al, 2017. Context Aware and Adaptive Mobile Learning: A Survey. *In Advances in Computational Sciences and Technology*, Vol 10, No. 5, pp 1355-1370

Soualah-Alila, F., Nicolle, C. and Mendes, F., 2014. Context-Aware Adaptive System For MLearning Personalization. IE14 *13 th International Conference on Informatics in Economy EducationBucharest*, Romania.

MOBILE LEARNING BASED GAMIFICATION IN A HISTORY LEARNING CONTEXT

Ymran Fatih, Elhard James Kumalija and Yi Sun
Student, Student, Assistant Professor
Kobe Institute of Computing, Chuo Ward, Kanocho, 2-2-7 Kobe, Hyogo prefecture, Japan

ABSTRACT

Engagement and motivation are ones of the main factors that impact the student performance during a learning process. The reason why, introducing Gamification in learning aims to improve the learning process, by making use of the motivating effects of digital game elements and techniques. However, summarizing Gamification into a set of technical concepts (points, badges and leaderboards) is a very common misunderstanding of Gamification hence greatly reducing the purposed effect on the target (students). In this paper, after exploring the key elements that can lead to a good Gamification in "History" as a learning context, driven by target (students) motivation, we will try to propose a solution based on mobile technologies, mainly Augmented Reality (AR), and design a way of evaluation and verification.

KEYWORDS

Gamification, History Learning, Digital Games, Mobile Games, Augmented Reality

1. INTRODUCTION

To keep the learner committed to what is he doing, the most important things that the e-learning system designer should care about is the student motivation and engagement. Many studies tried to tackle this topic using different approaches, one of these approach is leveraging digital games potential to keep the player engaged and motivated, - by borrowing some technics as the virtual world, points, level ..., - in order to enhance the learner capacity and commitment. In a learning based Gamification design, building a balanced system between educational content and entertainment, where providing a knowledge easy to consume in a very attractive way is the main driver, is not an easy task [1]. In history learning context, providing just a set of information about a certain historical period or era cannot be considered as an attractive teaching method. History is more complex than just to be considered as a set of information, it's an interrelation of different elements (events, people, economy, politics ...) interconnected with many events happened in a 4D environment (space(3D) and time). For the learner, 2 types of knowledge are needed to complete his learning process in such kind of environment:

- **Explicit knowledge**: developed using external factors as a set of information that can be delivered or presented in documents, teacher's explanations and point of views.
- **Tacit knowledge**: developed by the learner, it is the owned experience that can a learner get from the studied period, a self-constructed knowledge through an implicit learning process and cannot be developed by the external factors (Reber, 1989).

In our case Gamification supported by mobile technologies will be the tool used to transform the complexity of history into motivating factors for the student to a better performance during the learning process.

2. EDUCATION AND HISTORY

The current educational system considers history subject as a simple combination of three elements (time, place and people) (Chris Husbands, 2003), taught in a very simple way. Having the intention to make it simple, they omit the most interesting element, which is the story and spoiling the learning experience for the student, who cannot now relate the taught events to a consistent story. In the other hand, keeping the history as it is under the same condition of teaching will require more time for the student to understand and build a complete image of the complex story of the taught period. In order to build a learning experience that will allow to the student to assimilate the history, enjoy its story and develop an explicit as well as a tacit knowledge, we aim in this research to bride history learning with Gamification and measure the efficiency of this approach.

3. GAMIFICATION DESIGN

In the last few years, many works related to Gamification tried to come up with frameworks to support the Gamification design, using different approaches to deal with the topic, many of them identified game's technics or mechanics as drivers of the design process, but others consider them just a tool (Juho Hamari, 2014).

MDA (Mechanics Dynamics Aesthetics) one of the frameworks based on Mechanics (Gabe Zichermannand, 2011), according to the definition of this framework, Mechanics make up the functioning component of the game, they enable to the designer an ultimate control of the game and enable him to guide the player actions. Dynamics, are the player's interaction with those mechanics during the game, while Aesthetics reflect the feeling of the player during the experience of playing the game. In this Mechanics centered approach, game effects are moderated and controlled by the game technics to shape the dynamics of the game and impact the user feeling.

Yu-Kai Cho proposed also the Octalysis framework [figure 1], which in contrast with MDA, considers the player feeling or the aesthetics the driver for the Gamification design, in this framework he introduced 8 elements as a metric of player feeling or game effects: **Epic Meaning and Calling, Accomplishment, Empowerment, Ownership, Social influence, Scarcity and impatience, Unpredictability, Avoidance** (Chou, 2015), the first 4 elements deal with intrinsic motivation and the remaining 4 elements deal with extrinsic motivation elements.

In E-learning, considering the target as the main driver for the learning design is very important, for that reason a Gamification in this kind of context should consider the player (target) as the driver of the Gamification design.

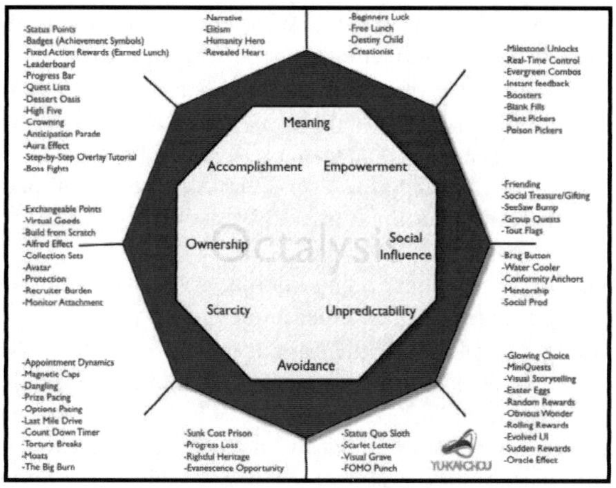

Figure 1

However, centering the design around the player is very challenging, due to the versatile nature of humans and the scarcity of the common point between them, therefore, a study conducted by Richard Bartle (Bartle, 2004) tried to classify player into categories to understand the need of each type [figure 2]:

- **Killers**: Achievement comes from another person's loss
- **Achievers**: Fun comes from point and leveling up
- **Socializers**: Fun comes from interaction with others
- **Explorers**: Fun comes from discovery

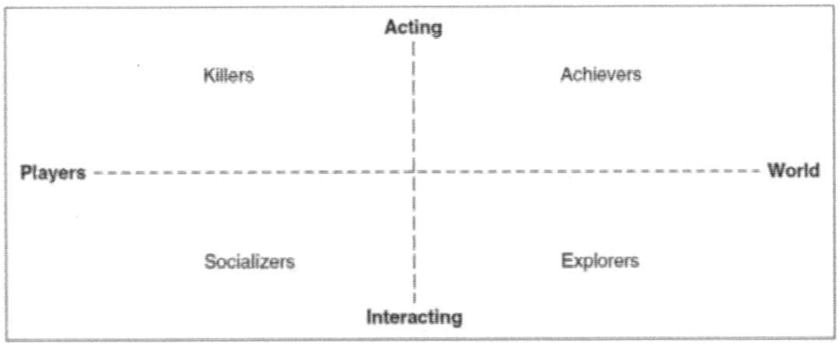

Figure 2

Furthermore, Nicole Lazzaro (Lazzaro, 2004) tried to find why people play and identified 4 reasons:

- **Hard fun**: the player plays to win
- **Easy fun**: the player plays to explore the system
- **Serious fun**: purposeful plays changes how the player thinks, feels, behaves or makes a difference in the real world
- **Social fun**: the player plays to interact with other Considering these facts, we tried to develop our own framework [figure 3] based on Octalysis and MDA framework, adapted to history e-Learning context for a Learning-based Gamification design driven by the motivation core drives.

In E-learning, considering the target as the main driver for the learning design is very important, for that reason a Gamification in this kind of context should consider the player (target) as the driver of the Gamification design.

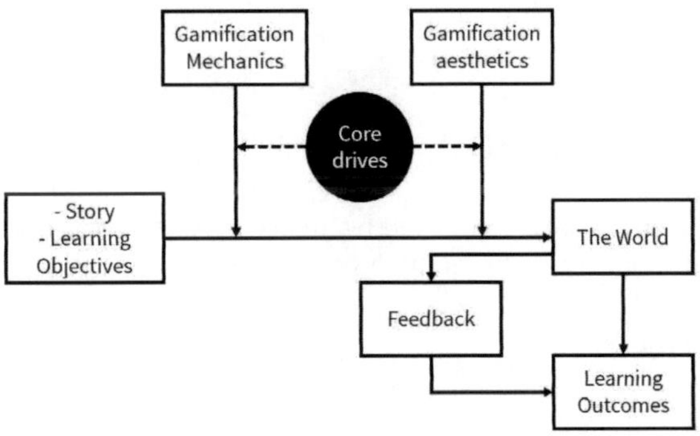

Figure 3

The process starts by extracting the learning objectives from the story of the taught period and that will be the input to build an environment that enables the learner to interact with its elements in order to achieve the learning objectives, the environment called in this framework the world [figure 3] will be built through a transformation of the input into a virtual world based on Gamification mechanics and aesthetics that are moderated and controlled by the motivation core drives, mainly based on the core drives of the Octalysis framework. The learning performance will be measured by the game elements introduced in this virtual world as well as the feedback that can be provided implicitly while progressing in the learning experience.

4. PROPOSED SOLUTION

The case study we choose for our research was the Bakumatsu era from the Japanese history, we started by a breakdown of this period events and focus on five main events. According to what happened in that era, the student will be leaping through the time between two parallel virtual worlds using AR, a virtual world where the player is the hero, and another virtual world based on Bakumatsu era, where he must clear missions to be rewarded in the other virtual world [figure 4].

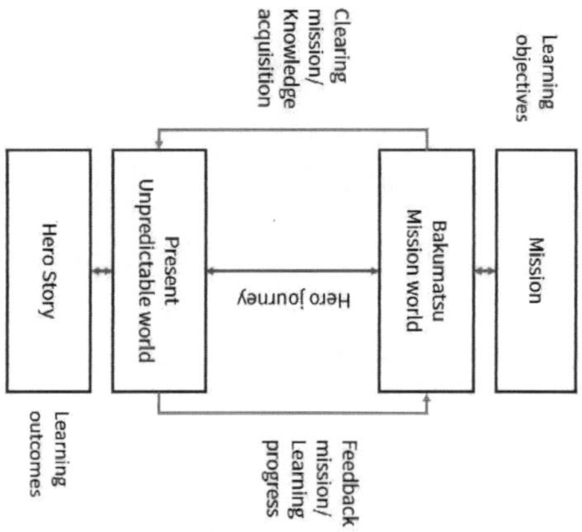

Figure 4

The story plot is divided into five chapters: *Perry, Japan opening and the Samurai era, Joui order and the enemy's reaction, The fatal encounter, The birth of dragon, Battle, enemies, alliance, The dawn of a new era.*

Each chapter retraces a part of Bakumatsu era and has its own learning objectives and feedback concerning one or many previous chapter.

The development of the solution is following an agile process based scene, and Unreal Engine as a tool for development.

5. EVALUATION METHOD

The evaluation of the result will be mainly motivation centered to explain how can game technics and effect affect the student's performance in the learning process.

5.1 Learning Outcome

At first we would like to have an idea about the learning performance of the students in this kind of environment. Learning outcome will be tested as follows:

- **Explicit knowledge**: test their knowledge about dates, events, places
- **Advanced Knowledge**: test their understanding of cause and effect of each event happened in that period
- **Tacit knowledge**: test their sense of developing and building their own picture regarding the taught era.

5.2 Motivation while using our System

Measuring the motivation of the students during the different parts of the experiment will allow us to identify the impact of game effects on the motivation, and find the most important factors that impact the motivation.

The main expected data from the participants is the time spent on the system and a questionnaire regarding the solution. The questionnaire will mainly help us to collect information about the most interesting part in the story for each participant as well as the less interesting one, in order to identify the core drive that impacts the motivation of each participant.

5.3 Experiment Design

All the participants in the experiments are high school students. The evaluation experiment is designed as following (Jonathan Lazar, 2017).

- **Individual experiment:** To have an idea about the impact of social factors during the learning process, we want to collect the needed data and perform the learning outcome test individually, the participant in that test should not interact and exchange information about what they are learning.
- **Group experiment:** The group experiment will have different participants than the individual experiment. The participants will be divided into two groups, group control and group experiment, the group control will experience a normal learning process, in contrast of the group experiment, that will use our system in its learning process.

6. CONCLUSION

Learning in an immersive world help the learner to have the better experience and quick feedback (DeFreitas, 2006). The proposed framework and the proposed solution aim to manipulate in a better way the motivation factors in a history learning context, which can make the gameplay as well as the educational content delivery spontaneous and fun as much as possible.

In a further step, a verification of these assumptions will be performed to measure the efficiency of this approach according to the evaluation design part.

REFERENCES

Bartle, R. (2004). *Designing virtual worlds.* New Riders.

Chaklam Silpasuwanchai, X. M. (2016). Developing a comprehensive engagement framework of gamification for reflective learning. *In Proceedings of the 2016 ACM Conference on Designing Interactive Systems,*, pages 45.

Chou, Y.-k. (2015). *Actionable gamification. Beyond Points, Badges, and Leaderboards.*

Chris Husbands, A. K. (2003). *Understanding history teaching: Teaching and learning about the past in secondary schools. McGraw-Hill Education (UK).*

DeFreitas, S. (2006). Learning in immersive worlds. *London: Joint Information Systems Committee.*

Gabe Zichermannand, C. C. (2011). *Gamification by design: Implementing game mechanics in web and mobile apps.* O'Reilly Media, Inc.

Jonathan Lazar, J. H. (2017). *Research methods in human-computer interaction.* Morgan Kaufmann.

Juho Hamari, J. K. (2014). In System Sciences (HICSS), 47th Hawaii International Conference. *Does gamification work?–a literature review of empirical studies on gamification* (pp. 3025– 3034). Hawaii : IEEE.

Lazzaro, N. (2004). *Why we play games: Four keys to more emotion without story.*

Reber, A. S. (1989). Implicit learning and tacit knowledge. *Journal of experimental psychology: General*, 219.

A SWOT ANALYSIS OF BRING YOUR OWN DEVICES IN MOBILE LEARNING

Santiago Criollo-C[1] and Sergio Luján-Mora[2]
[1]*Facultad de Ingeniería y Ciencias Agropecuarias, Universidad de las Américas*
Av. de los Granados E12-41y Colimes esq.
[2]*Department of Software and Computing Systems, University of Alicante*
Carretera San Vicente del Raspeig s/n 03690

ABSTRACT

In current education there is a trend called bring your own devices (BYOD), this refers to the policy of use of resources that allows students to bring their own mobile device to use in the classroom. BYOD allows students and educators to take advantage of technological tools to improve learning and instruction. Mobile devices in a BYOD environment provide educational experiences beyond the boundaries of a classroom. This trend was born in companies, where their employees are allowed to take to their workplaces personal property devices such as: laptops, tablets and smartphones. This generated several disadvantages and problems related to the security of the information. In education, many teachers and parents consider that mobile devices are a tool only for communication and entertainment and would become a distraction in the classroom. As noted, although technology and especially mobile devices have enormous potential to be used in education, there are also several factors that could limit their adoption. This article makes use of the literature review to perform a SWOT analysis of the use of BYOD in m-learning.

KEYWORDS

BYOD, Learning, m-Learning, Mobile Devices, SWOT

1. INTRODUCTION

Nowadays, the use of mobile devices is relevant in all aspects of life, especially in the educational field. This mobile technology creates new opportunities and improved learning experiences for all students, regardless of the level of education (Sanusi and Oyelere, 2017). Learning with the help of mobile devices is becoming an integral component of the modern education system. Two of the most important characteristics of m-learning are ubiquity and portability which, allow mobile users to access learning resources from anywhere and at any time (Khan et al., 2016).

Mobile technologies achieved amazing improvements for both devices and wireless networks, so today, smartphones and tablets are considered the main representatives of this category (Zappatore et al., 2015). Mobile devices in bring your own devices (BYOD) environment are gaining popularity in education due to the following reasons: most students are familiar with a mobile device they are more economical and portable compared to a laptop; portability and ubiquity make them suitable for use in the classroom. In addition, students are eager to use technology today, especially mobile devices and interactive tools (Giannakas, et al., 2015).

These new mobile technologies can play an important role in current education, informs (Mahalingam and Rajan, 2013). However, many of the teachers do not possess the necessary skills to implement a pedagogical approach supported by technology. For this reason students do not develop skills or meet the anticipated learning challenges as they gain limited support from their teachers.

This article is structured in four sections. The first section provides a brief description of the BYOD trend and defines several studies in which it is evident that BYOD is being used as a support in learning. In addition, the hypothesis and the problem are established which, deals with the investigation. The second section indicates the method used to perform the SWOT analysis and summarizes the strengths, opportunities, weaknesses and threats of BYOD in m-learning. The third section discusses of the results obtained. Finally, the fourth section presents the conclusions and provides a direction for future research. The results obtained are useful for academics who seek to include mobile devices in the teaching-learning process. The study can also be useful for educational institutions that are looking to explore innovative approaches that include emerging paradigms such as BYOD and mobile technology as support in the learning process.

2. BYOD IN EDUCATION

BYOD is a technological trend that proposes student-centered learning. Mobile devices in a BYOD environment provide teachers the ability to quickly assess students by generating almost instantaneous feedback. BYOD allows students and teachers to use the technological tools that make learning and teaching more efficient and productive (Stork et al., 2014). In traditional education, the only source of knowledge within a classroom was the teacher, without his presence the classroom is simply an empty room without any resource to learn. With BYOD, each student has access to information from around the world such as: events, places, organizations, people and other students directly and instantly (Wong, 2014). Learning in a BYOD environment tends to be easy and efficient since users are familiar with their personal devices, rather than having to learn how to operate a new device. This feature can contribute to greater learning in less time. With the help of BYOD, educators and students are learning together, thus developing communication, collaboration, critical thinking and creativity (Stork, Rose and Wang, 2014).

Although the BYOD trend gained momentum in organizations and their employees, due to many advantages such as: increased user productivity, reduced costs in purchases of hardware and software, increased mobility, flexibility, employee satisfaction, etc. (Zahadat et al., 2015). Currently, there are many initiatives that involve the BYOD trend to provide new and better ways of teaching and learning. Some studies claim that BYOD can be used to improve student engagement and collaboration (Song and Wen, 2017). Students appreciate the interaction that BYOD offers between teachers and students, they see it as a positive addition to their learning (Dobbins and Denton, 2017).

In addition, BYOD offers digital opportunities for independent learning, in and out of class and encourages innovation in teaching and learning (Stork, Rose and Wang, 2014). In Mahalingam and Rajan (2013) argue that although new technologies can play an important role in education, teachers still lack the necessary skills to implement a constructivist approach supported by technology and this leads students to get support limited to develop critical skills.

Although, the benefits are obvious there are several institutions of higher education impose a total ban on the use of mobile devices by students within the classrooms. They indicate that these devices cause distraction and are a problem for the management of the class (Olasoji et al, 2014). In addition (Olasoji et al, 2014) indicates that several professors confess that they have no idea of the benefits that technology offers in learning or how they can use mobile devices in their teaching practice. Despite all the advantages indicated in the research presented, there are also limitations and barriers that prevent the adoption of BYOD in teaching and learning environments based on m-learning. It is for this reason that a SWOT analysis involving BYOD in m-learning is presented below.

3. METHOD

The method used to carry out this investigation was a review of the literature. A search was carried out with keywords related to higher education, mobile devices, m-learning and the BYOD trend. Information was downloaded from scientific databases in which a greater number of articles related to technology, mobile devices and BYOD trend were observed. In order to avoid a theoretical expiration, the items searched belong to the last six years. The search strategy and the article exclusion criteria are detailed below.

3.1 Data sources and Search Strategy

The scientific databases were IEEE Xplore Digital Library, Scopus and Springer, two sets of keywords were searched: (1) keywords related to mobile learning; and (2) keywords related to the BYOD trend in education. The query string used to perform the searches were:

IEEE Xplore: Metadata (learning; BYOD) AND document title (mobile) AND Abstract (learning).
Scopus: Title (mobile and learning) OR (m-learning) AND Abs (BYOD) AND Key (learning).
Springer: The exact phrase (mobile) AND (learning) AND (BYOD).

For all the selected databases, the search was filtered by the type of content, only publications in journals and conferences were selected. To have the most up-to-date and relevant information on the subject, the selected articles were only from the last six years. The topics related to the search were: IT, Learning, Learning and Instruction, Education, Engineering, Psychology and Social Sciences. Owing that quantitative analysis generated too many records, more than 500 articles for each scientific library. It was decided to choose documents that were only found in conference and magazine publications related to education, learning and only written in English.

3.2 Search Results and Exclusion Criteria

In the search made we found 57 articles, of these we only chose those that were published in scientific journals and conferences. The analysis of the abstract and the introduction of each article defined the relevant articles to the topic of this research. These articles (46) were selected because in their content they included the terms searched as BYOD and m-learning, in addition the focus of these was in the educational context. For the analysis proposed by this research, a matrix of concepts was drawn up that involved all the articles and classified them according to their content of strengths, opportunities, weaknesses and threats regarding the use of BYOD and m-learning in the educational field. Of the selected articles, 15 provided information on strengths, 13 on opportunities, 13 spoke on weaknesses and 5 articles on threats, these summarized data can be seen in Table 1.

Table 1. Search Results

BDD \ SWOT	Strengths	Opportunities	Weaknesses	Threats	Total articles
IEEEXPLORE	8	6	7	3	24
SPRINGER	5	6	5	1	17
SCOPUS	2	1	1	1	5
Total thematic	15	13	13	5	**46**

4. DISCUSSES OF RESULTS

Once all the articles, summarized in Table 1, were analyzed in an exhaustive manner, the strengths and opportunities for the use of BYOD and m-learning in the educational field generate indisputable advantages. A great advantage for the adoption of this technology in the classroom is the generation of current students. Millennials have a different way of receiving and processing information, because they grew up in the era of the Internet, mobile devices and social networks. Despite all the advantages and initiatives found in the research, there are also weaknesses and threats that can represent barriers that prevent the adoption of m-leaning technology with BYOD in higher education. Some of these limitations are being addressed by several researchers to counteract them, there are currently several initiatives that indicate how to use mobile devices in education (Dobbins and Denton, 2017). Below is a summary of all the strengths, opportunities, weaknesses and threats in Table 2

Table 2. Results of SWOT analysis of BYOD in M-learning

Strengths	Opportunities	Weaknesses	Threats
1. Mobility 2. Ubiquity 3. Accessibility 4. Collaboration 5. Utility 6. Privacy 7. Adaptability 8. Portability 9. Multiplatform 10. Flexibility	1. High mobile penetration 2. Reduced costs of access to mobile internet 3. Great amount of educational app based on games 4. Learning independence, improved focus in the classroom and the link with the teacher 5. Interaction and instant feedback 6. Improvement of commitment and academic participation 7. Satisfaction of the mobile device user	1. Lack of training 2. Excessive number of applications 3. technological obsolescence of institutional mobile infrastructure 4. Low educational support, testing and applications 5. Low acceptance of the interested parties 6. Economic, technological and institutional policy factors 7. Applications not compatible with multiple mobile devices 8. Usability (screen, battery)	1. Security of personal and institutional information 2. Wide variety of devices and platforms 3. Android OS security threat 4. Costly, complex and incompatible applications on some mobile devices 5. Culture change of traditional teaching

The SWOT analysis presents several strengths and opportunities that derive from the use of mobile devices in educational environments. The most important characteristics are: mobility, ubiquity and portability, these allow mobile, independent and collaborative learning. Despite the advantages and benefits that BYOD offers in education, there are several challenges that must be overcome in order to properly implement BYOD in the teaching-learning model. The challenges that arise from the weaknesses and threats must be addressed, the solutions proposed must ensure, among other things, that there is a stable and reliable wireless network infrastructure. All educational institutions before committing to provide the services offered by the use of mobile devices focused on teaching and learning must strategically generate policies that support them. Frameworks or guidelines should be the basis of policies, guidelines should address issues such as the provision of adequate technological infrastructure, motivation to faculty and students, technological awareness, content design guidelines, technical assistance and professional and staff development.

5. CONCLUSION AND FUTURE WORK

A review of the literature is an instant photograph of the field investigated at a given time. Although the literature search was a rigorous process, many relevant articles may have been overlooked. Despite this, the research generated indicators that show the importance of measuring the impact of BYOD on teachers and addressing the impact of pedagogical approaches necessary, due to the variety of devices, functionality, operating systems and access to digital tools. The use of mobile devices and the new technologies of information and communication, both by students and teachers, generates significant changes and new ways of generating knowledge. The use of BYOD is advantageous for many reasons, above all, improving access to Internet resources and digital tools in support of teaching and learning. Despite the number of solutions and mobile learning applications currently available, there are still some limitations in terms of usability, associated costs, technological infrastructure, complexity, etc. For example, there are many educational applications available that only work on specific portable devices. This can increase the barriers in the adoption of BYOD in educational institutions. What has been said above opens new emerging paradigms that should be taken into account for future research. Students should be involved in educational experiences that make use of mobile devices, for example a combination of technologies (BYOD) and Mobile Crowd-Sensing (MCS).

REFERENCES

Dobbins, C. and Denton, P. 2017. MyWallMate: An Investigation into the use of Mobile Technology in Enhancing Student Engagement, *In TechTrends*, Vol. 61, No. 6, pp. 541–549.

Giannakas, F. et al. 2015. CyberAware: A mobile game-based app for cybersecurity education and awareness, *Proceedings of International Conference on Interactive Mobile Communication Technologies and Learning*, Thessaloniki, Greece, pp. 54–58.

han, A. I. et al. 2016. Crowd sourced testing through end users for Mobile Learning application in the context of Bring Your Own Device, *Proceedings of* 7th *IEEE Annual Information Technology, Electronics and Mobile Communication Conference*, Vancouver, BC, Canada, pp. 1–6.

Mahalingam, T. and Rajan, A. V. 2013. Cloud and mobile computing: Affordances of the 21st century teaching and learning, *Proceedings of International Conference on Current Trends in Information Technology*, Dubai, United Arab Emirates, pp. 125–128.

Olasoji, R. et al 2014. Requirement engineering for effective mobile learning: Modelling mobile device technologies integration for alignment with strategic policies in learning establishments, Federated Conference on Computer Science and Information Systems, 2, pp. 851–860.

Sanusi, I. T. and Oyelere, S. S. 2017 Exploring Students and Teachers Activities , Experiences and Impact of Opón Ìmò Mobile Learning Device on Teaching and Learning, *In IEEE africon 2017 proceedings,* pp. 809–814.

Song, Y. and Wen, Y. 2017. Integrating Various Apps on BYOD (Bring Your Own Device) into Seamless Inquiry-Based Learning to Enhance Primary Students' Science Learning, In Journal of Science Education and Technology. Vol. 39, No. 17, pp. 1–12.

Stork, M., et al. 2014. Global Perspectives on BYOD: A Reflection on the EdMedia 2015 Conference, *In TechTrends*, VOL. 59, No. 6, pp. 13–14.

Wong, G. K. W. 2014. Engaging students using their own mobile devices for learning mathematics in classroom discourse: a case study in Hong Kong, In International Journal of Mobile Learning and Organisation, VOL. 8, No 2, p. 143.

Zahadat, N. et al. 2015. BYOD security engineering: A framework and its analysis, *In Computers & Security*, VOL. 55, pp. 81–99.

Zappatore, M. et al. 2015. Mobile Crowd Sensing-based noise monitoring as a way to improve learning quality on acoustics, *Proceedings of International Conference on Interactive Mobile Communication Technologies and Learning,* pp. 96–100

THE CATEGORISATION OF THE PUPILS' WORK WITH IPAD IN A SPECIAL ELEMENTARY SCHOOL

Mgr. Vojtěch Gybas, Doc. Ing. Kateřina Kostolányová, Ph.D. and Mgr. Libor Klubal
University Of Ostrava, Pedagogical Faculty, Department Of Information and Communication Technologies
Fráni Šrámka 3, Ostrava, Mariánské Hory, 70900, Czech Republic

ABSTRACT

The contribution introduces the detailed categorization of pupils with iPads at special primary schools in the Czech Republic. The first half of the contribution deals with a part of the survey. It refers to the methodology and selection of the informants who were used to create the final categorization. Based on this categorization, special teachers in the Czech Republic should be able to classify their pupils in order to find out what expected outputs they can expect from their pupils when working with iPads. Then a comprehensive verification across specialized primary schools will be in the second part of the survey. The aim is to verify whether the proposed categorization is applicable to a comprehensive sample, and whether any pupil with special educational needs can really be included in the category.

KEYWORDS

Categorisation, iPad, Special Elementary School, Individualization

1. INTRODUCTION

Nowadays, the use of ICT is an indispensable part of the work of a teacher and it can be considered as one of the pedagogical key skills. Using iPad mobile touch devices does not require the development of cognitive abilities as much as using other digital technologies. (Chmiliar 2015), therefore using these devices, which we rank among ICTs, may seem justified. Using iPads in a special elementary school for pupils with special educational needs, can bring many benefits but also a lot of negatives. Rahman (2012) said that iPad tablets are motivating especially for their interactivity. Two years later, Flewit, Kucirkova and Messer in their case study (2014) state, that writing on the iPad requires less effort and control of precise graphics and facilitates visual and sensory learning. We can say about Vygotsky's notion of gesture being 'writing in the air'. That is all right if we consider iPad as a new learning tool that offers a different kind of working on graphomotorics. MacDonald, Hill (2014) report that these devices can be sort, based on the primary use of pupils, such as in augmentative and alternative communication. Wianwright (online, 2016) adds that starting slowly with just one or two applications is natural, and it is very important to establish a clear and consistent policy for mobile devices for teachers, employees and students. Everyone needs to know what is expected, so it is important to set the rules in advance before we start using the iPad in the classroom. Epps (online, 2016), in his study "Special Education Teachers' Experience in the Implementation of the iPad as an Instructional Tool for Students with Intellectual Disabilities, says that using iPad tablets, when teaching pupils with moderate mental disabilities, greatly increases attention at work.

Tablets are attractive for the pupils. Working with tablets, compared to common teaching materials, is motivating for pupils. Allen (2016) in the study states, that digital touch technology provides a unique advantage and opportunity to adapt to the individual deficiencies of each pupil, that common paper material can not provide. Among the negatives, that are often mentioned, are the claims, that the iPad seems to be too expensive for potential users or that the App Store offers most of the apps for a fee. This is confirmed by Chmiliar (2017). As part of our dissertation on "Individualization of teaching in a special primary school using iPads", the research goal has appeared:

- to categorize pupils with special educational needs in the context of direct work with iPads in the educational process;
- to categorize the recommendation of using iPads in the classroom.

There is no such categorization in the educational process of pupils at special elementary schools in the Czech Republic, and special educators, when trying to implement iPads into teaching process, learn mostly from the experiment - what to do, when a pupil is not interested in iPad; a very common hypothesis - when this pupil cannot do the work, then the one, with worse diagnosis, will not be able to do it, etc. Chmilliar (2017) at the conclusion of his study confirms, that iPads can make a positive contribution to the education even of small children with disabilities. As a part of our dissertation, several partial studies have been carried out to confirm the positive effect of using iPads in education in the Czech Republic. These results were published in The ICDLSE 2017: 19th International Conference on Distance Learning and Special Education and at the 13th International Conference on Mobile Learning 2017 in Portugal, Algarve (04/2016). Partial researches have also shown that the absence of missing categorization, which clearly determines the content of the expected outcomes and the inclusion of a pupil, is very important for all teachers surveyed in the Czech Republic. However, the facts, how a teacher can categorize his pupils by working with iPads and fulfilling expected outcomes in the context of working with iPads, do not exist. In the framework of the 18th Annual International Conference on Information and Communication Technologies in Education, another sub-study was conducted, in which 115 special educators pronounced "for" the formation of categorization that would allow sorting of pupils in the context of working with iPads. This categorization will be an entry point for educators to know which pupils can individualize iPad lessons.

2. METHODOLOGY OF RESEARCH

In accordance with established research questions and qualitative research techniques, as reported by Hendl (2008), Švaříček, Šeďová et al. (2007), the most appropriate method of collecting data was participative (participatory) observation, in the natural educational situations, induced especially by the teachers, because of mental retardation of the pupils. We can characterize this method as open observation, because the author of this survey actively participates in the "iPad in Teaching process" class project, and pupils are used to it for a long time. For this reason, the investigation has simplified the phase of contact with the research team and the search for a key informant. An advantage was also the knowledge of the school environment, school management inclined to test new teaching practices, and knowledge of the pupil's usual school work prior to iPad's intervention in the classroom. Another positive criterion for choosing this data collection technique was that the author had unlimited time for this work.

2.1 Research File

The entry research team was 21 special elementary school pupils, ranging from the 1st year to the 10th year of the special elementary school. Those were watching while working with iPads during classes.

Table 1. A detailed overview of student diagnoses, their associated partial deficits, the number of pupils in a given group and their age

Diagnosis of the pupil	associated defects	number of pupils	y.o.
moderate mental retardation IQ 35-49	0	8	7-16
moderate mental retardation IQ 35-49	Glaucoma, a great potion in a fine motorcycle	1	15
moderate mental retardation IQ 35-49	Down syndrome, impaired communication ability	1	13
moderate mental retardation IQ 35-49	autism, impaired communication ability	3	7-16
moderate mental retardation IQ 35-49	deaf - hearing loss	2	9
moderate mental retardation IQ 35-49 - lower boundary band	autism, impaired communication ability	3	11-15
severe mental retardation IQ 21-34	autism, impaired communication ability	3	7-10

2.2 Evaluation Criteria and Rating Scale

Because of the specifics of each pupil, the interaction pupils - iPad, the school work with this mobile device is not united. Due to the partial deficits of each individual pupil who is involved in this project, the iPad tablet's instruction must be individualized, so that each student is able to achieve his / her maximum school output in the course of his / her learning in his / her medium-term mental retardation and any associated disabilities. The results of the "iPad in Teaching process" sub-research study pointed to the need to introduce a certain categorization of pupils. It subsequently simplified the selection of teaching methods in relation to the work on the iPad, made it easier for a pupil to understand the working in groups on pupils' outputs and it was a prerequisite for individualizing school work on the iPad Based on the results of this pre-survey, the following three criteria were set for the relevant rating scales.

Table 2. Evaluation Criteria

difficulty	Evaluation criteria
↓	1. capability (from a technical point of view) to serve the iPad,
	2. level of pupil's ability to work in content-based applications,
	3. the degree of the pupil's ability to work with creative applications or so-called app smashing.

Table 3. Rating Scale

	Rating scales for criterias				
Difficulty ↓	Criterion nr. 1	manages self-services	work with the teacher's support	working with iPad only with the help of a teacher	does not have a job
	Criterion nr. 2	Individual work	After compensating for associated defects, he manages to work with mild aid	Only with the help of a teacher and assisted access	the pupil appears to have only a small visual / hearing interest or rejects the iPad
	Criterion nr. 3	work with the teacher's support	with teachers help	does not have a job	does not work and the iPad rejects it

Independence →

3. CATEGORISATION OF THE PUPILS' WORK WITH IPAD

The students of the research team were always familiar with the iPad technical device; they were repeatedly provided with explanation of intuitive control and basic service, including charging and maintenance of cleanliness, and they were gradually acquainted with individual applications during one school year. During this training, the principles of proportionality, repetition, progress from simpler to more complex were followed. The pupils were part of the attendance of the teachers, who made the notes of individual pupils during this training and together they evaluated the work according to the set criteria. The set conditions and criteria described above, the study group has disrupted into 4 categories. It also follows, from the results of this five-year research study, that all pupils in a given research group, may be included in one of the categories after a certain period of time, with no possibility, that the pupil will "move" to another category, after another long- practical work with these pupils. Each pupil of a given category is an individual and finding two identical pupils, due to the manifestations of a given disability, is impossible. Therefore, it is also necessary to state, that within the category, pupils, when working with iPad, may have some differences, different specifics, or fluctuations, according to the actual health and mental state. The resulting categorization was complemented by expected outcomes, that do not agree with the currently valid Framework Education Program for the Specialized Primary School, because this educational program in the Czech Republic does not count on the use of modern ICT in teaching process. This Framework Education Program was established in 2008 and has not been revised so far. This study also aims to show that iPads (and tablets in general) can be of great benefit and that the Framework Education Program should be reviewed.

Table 4. Categorisation of the puppils' work with iPads

Expected Output	1. category	2. category	3. category	4. category
Operation on the iPad off / on; brightness adjustment, volume adjustment; desktop orientation; Launching and running the application keyboard orientation; typing text on the keyboard; put the iPad on the charger; working with web browser, App Store App; working with email; storing the camera; using gestures; lock the iPad	Manages self-service	work with the teacher's support	working with iPad only with the help of a teacher	does not have a job
Working with content-specific applications the ability to manage application instructions; keep your attention on the application desktop; Understand the importance of application and its use; ability to control individual application features	Individual work	After compensating for associated defects, he manages to work with mild aid	Only with the help of a teacher and assisted access	the pupil appears to have only a small visual / hearing interest or rejects the iPad
work based on own content creation - Appsmashing ability to switch between apps; to understand the individual application usage for each task - here I will do this, here, export the final output	work with the teacher's support	with teachers help	does not have a job	does not work and the iPad rejects it

difficulity ↓ independence →

4. CONCLUSION

Two-year day attendance, video recording, photographs and data interpretation clearly showed, that the pupil's diagnosis and the extent of his mental as well as associated deficits are not the primary factor for his place in the category. In practice, this means, that the pupil, who has a severe diagnosis, can be a level higher in the final categorization. The assumption, that a pupil would shift to a higher category, after a certain time, is disproved by two-year observation. None of the 21 pupils involved could do this. The two-year survey has also confirmed the fact, that iPad reduces the burden on the pupil's graphics, does not require the development of cognitive features as much as other ICTs or common teaching material require.

The purpose of further research is to verify this proposed categorization of work for pupils across the Czech Republic (only special elementary schools). The data obtained will be compared to those inputs. If the area verification brings new data, then the categorization of pupils will be adjusted, according to a higher number of informants, up to the final form. Our goal is to create a final categorization of pupils' work with iPads, where the teacher will be able to classify his pupils and know exactly how much work his pupils will handle with the pupil's own efforts and with the teacher´s help.

However, we can already say, that the diagnosis of a pupil, the degree of his / her disability, is not the primary determinant for the pupil's categorization. If a pupil accepts the touchscreen devices, then he is capable of successful interacting: the mobile touch device x student. Teacher´s assistance at a certain level is already secondary factor. If the pupil does not accept the mobile touch device then the interaction of the learner x the pupil x the mobile touch device is irrelevant. We can also say, that the successful implementation of mobile touchscreen devices, clearly eliminates and reduces the pupil's graphical load, co-ordination eye x hand. It is clear, that the iPad mobile touchscreen device can compensate for writing equipment, where the pupil is unable to use it efficiently. Since the touchscreen device has a so-called visual keyboard, this device can eliminate the difficulties in fine motoring, which are a very common symptomatic disorder of a pupil within a range of mental disabilities. Then the pupil is capable of realizing a lesson, that he would normally not be able to realize with a computer keyboard.

REFERENCES

Chmiliar, L., Anton, C. Journal on Technology and Persons with Disabilities Santiago, J. (Eds): Annual International Technology and Persons with Disabilities Conference, 2015 California State University, Northridge.

Rahman, S. Getting started: iPad special needs. Houston: Rahman publishing. 2012.

Flewitt R., Kucirkovat N., Messer D. - Touching the virtual, touching the real: iPads and enabling literacy for students experiencing disability. Australian Journal of Language and Literacy, Vol. 37, No. 2, 2014.

Flewitt R., Kucirkova N., Messer D. New directions for early literacy in a digital age: The iPad. Journal of Early Childhood Literacy published online 20 May 2014 DOI: 10.1177/1468798414533560.

Macdonald, P., Hill B., Brown G. S. Is Apple transforming special education? Assessing the effcacy of the iPad as an assistive technology for students with special education needs. In Special education perspectives.

Wainwright A. 8 Things to Remember When Preparing for iPads in the Classroom.

EPPS, S.T. Special education teachers' lived experiences in the implementation of the iPad as an instructional tool for students with intellectual disabilities.

Allen M.L., Hartley C., Cain K. (2016) iPads and the Use of "Apps" by Children with Autism Spectrum Disorder: Do They Promote Learning? Front. Psychol. 7:1305. doi: 10.3389/fpsyg.2016.01305.

Chmiliar L (2017) Improving Learning Outcomes: The iPad and Preschool Children with Disabilities. Front. Psychol. 8:660. doi: 10.3389/fpsyg.2017.00660.

Gybas V., Klubal L., Kostolányová K.. Mobile touch screen devices as compensation for the teaching materials at a special primary school in 12th International conference on Mobilelearning 2016. Algarve, Portugal. s. 157-161, 5 s.

Gybas V., Klubal L., Kostolányová K.Mobile technologies in the hands of special pedagogues. In ICTE 2016. Information and Communication Technology in Education. Ostrava: Ostravská univerzita, 2016. s. 40-48.

Gybas V., Klubal L., Kostolányová K.. Assisted Approach as a Tool for Increasing Attention When Using the iPad in a Special Elementary School: Action Research. IN ICDLSE 2017: 19th International Conference on Distance Learning and Special Education, Venice, 16. - 17. 2. 2017.

Švaříček, R.. a Šeďová,, K.,Qualitative research in pedagogical sciences. 1st ed.. Prague:: Portál,, 2007, 384 s.

WHATSAPP AS A SITE FOR MEANINGFUL DIALOGUE

Conor Keogh and Heydy Robles
Universidad del Norte, Colombia

ABSTRACT

Smart-phone technology is pervasive across Colombia, even among those of lower economic means. This has greatly changed the face of society and the world of education is no different. Instant messaging services like WhatsApp allow for an extension of the traditional classroom. This study is concerned with how such technology allows learners of a second language a space where true dialogue and meaningful interaction may occur.
This report presents progress of an ongoing investigation into how a shared WhatsApp group may be used as a site for dialogue for students of International Relations. The study consists of analysis of the interaction which occurs in the group as well as learner reflection on the benefits of the space.
The data generated thus far have demonstrated examples of interaction between participants in their second language on complex themes related to their country and the international community. Participant responses have been positive on the benefits of the space.
The study adds further credence to a growing body of work on the benefits of such a space for encouraging discussion, participation and enhancement of learner identity.

KEYWORDS

Mobile Learning, Dialogue, Virtual Spaces, Community of Learners, WhatsApp, Blended Learning

1. INTRODUCTION

Nowadays, teachers' pedagogical practices try to establish dialogical communications in an effort to avoid imposition of monological positions or discourses. However, there is still a resistance towards changing teaching methods in order to privilege students, and allowing them to make decisions. The role of the traditional teacher tends to result in pedagogical discourses that suppress student voices (Drewery, 2005). If educators consider themselves to be the ones who always know best, instead of fostering critical awareness, they assume rigid and imposing positions which may leave their students with uncritical opinions that may lead them to oppressive social practices (Giroux & McLaren, 1998).

The revolutionary concept of dialogism was introduced for the first time by Bakhtin (1986), who emphasized that all the power of language is generated in the relationship with others, that is, in dialogue. In the process of interaction with the other, it is when a subject is really formed; "...the *I* only exists in so far as it is related to a *you*" (Bakhtin, 1982, p.102). It takes a speaker and an active interlocutor to generate dialogues.

Furthermore, Bakhtin (1986) explains why language should point to a dialogical process. In other words, the listener's opinions are recognized and accepted, therefore favouring an active understanding. It is necessary for teachers to be aware of students' ′voices in order to identify their beliefs, ideologies, social and cultural contexts in order to build meaningful knowledge and break with traditional paradigms that are dedicated to eliminating or ignoring voices. Regarding this, Wegerif (2013) argues that education must be dialogic in order to empower voices. This implies "the ability to participate in dialogues constructively without the need to oppress or be oppressed" (p.35).

The variety in emergent technologies in schooling has grown enormously in recent years. Currently, teachers of different disciplines in higher education are integrating technology to support students' learning processes. In particular, the implementation of mobile technology in the classroom has become a unique way to innovate teachers' pedagogical practice (Fraga & Flores, 2011; Herrington et al, 2011; Park, 2011). Mobile learning refers to the use of such devices for academic purposes. Some examples of equipment used for this purpose include cell phones, smart phones, laptops, tablets, and audio players, among others

(Kukulska-Hulme & Traxler, 2005). The use of mobile instant messaging apps such as WhatsApp in classes has allowed students to construct meaningful knowledge and to have peer support through synchronous discussions (Hou & Wu, 2011; Ngambi & Brown, 2009; Scornavacca et al., 2016)

The increased focus on the importance of classroom interaction and the potential benefits of a dialogic approach within education has coincided with the establishment of additional educational spaces made possible by the development of such technology. The ubiquitous presence of smartphones is simply a modern fact of life and one which is having dynamic effects on nearly all walks of life in the 21st century. The effects of this technology, be they interpreted negatively or positively, are keenly debated by many within education, with many questioning if the devices should be prohibited within schools. What can be under no dispute is the fact that smartphones have changed the manner in which communication occurs. Social networks, web forum and various apps such as WhatsApp have created virtual spheres where communication can take place. Despite questions over the benefits or otherwise of smartphone technology, the premise of this study is that such a space as created by a WhatsApp group, offers learners an additional field where communication can take place in a meaningful manner outside of traditional class times. Furthermore, this technology provides an opportunity to surpass the traditional barrier between classroom and leisure time, meaning that learners in the 21st century are increasingly blurring the line between work and play (Coffin, 2009). Research into the area has indicated that learners of a second language have benefitted from the use of WhatsApp in terms of exposure to the language (Almekhlafy & Alzubi, 2016) and that the use of WhatsApp groups have had a positive impact on interaction and rapport among learners (Bouhnik & Deshen, 2014, Keogh, 2017).This current study is seeking to build on this emerging body of work in order to explore how such a virtual chat offers learners an ongoing, portable and dynamic space where they may enter into enriching dialogue which is "...reciprocal, supportive, cumulative and purposeful" (Alexander, 2008, p 13).

2. PARTICIPANTS

The participants in the study are students of International Relations English from a private university in the north of Colombia. They form part of an 8 level English for International Relations program and they range in age from 17-21. Thus far in the study there has been 25 participants (8 at level 2 in the first cycle of the study from the second semester of 2016, 17 at level 6 from the second cycle in the second semester of 2017). The students take four hours of English per week across a sixteen week university term as part of their undergraduate degree. The level 2 students should boast a pre-intermediate (A2) level of English according to the Common European Framework, while the level 6 students are at an intermediate level (B1). The third cycle of the study has begun recently with a further 20 students from level 7 (B1-B2 level). These learners share the WhatsApp group space throughout the whole semester along with their teacher (one of the co-authors of this paper). The responsibility of the teacher in this instance has been to encourage the students to offer opinions and discuss topics by posting discussion prompts. The learners have been encouraged to participate and engage in discussion but their participation has not been obligatory.

3. METHODS

In order to explore how instant messaging apps like WhatsApp could offer additional spaces for dialogue, participants in the study have been encouraged to extend discussion of topics covered during class time to the space offered by a shared WhatsApp group. At times this has been assigned as homework tasks with students given a prompt to discuss in the group. Furthermore, participants have been encouraged to initiate their own discussions on topics of interest to them. The topics discussed have related mainly to political issues and societal debates related to Colombia and beyond. It was hoped that this additional space would provide a safe space where all of the participants could feel confident to voice their opinion, something which does not always occur within the classroom due to factors ranging from confidence in linguistic competence to learner identity and issues of anxiety.

In one sense, the WhatsApp group space is an ideal format to assess learner participation and interaction as the space opens a continuous dialogue between group members with all of the interactions saved and accessible for analysis at a later date. The principal instrument in this study is therefore the group space itself and the interactions which have occurred there. All of the interactions throughout each cycle of the study have been recorded using screenshots. These interactions are then reviewed by the co-authors and relevant examples where meaningful examples of discussion and dialogue are identified are then selected for analysis. These conversations have been analysed with a particular focus on turn taking and learner participation as well as reflections on the content of these interactions. While the nature of the dialogue itself is obviously of huge importance, the perception of this dialogue within this additional space on behalf of the participants is also sought to gain a perspective of what value, if any, participants attribute to the additional space. In order to achieve this, participants have provided feedback related to the space and its uses.

4. PRELIMINARY RESULTS

Some of early data to emerge from the study was interesting as it was in relation to a discussion in the level 2 group. The topic discussed was a keenly debated decision by the then Minister of Education to include educational content relating to gender and sexual diversity in the national school curriculum. The issue prompted controversy among conservative elements of society and also polarised opinion on a national level. It provided a topic that learners at that level of language proficiency and academic experience (the participants were first and second semester students) might be reluctant to voice opinions on. However, the WhatsApp group space (Figure 1) afforded a more comfortable setting for discussion.

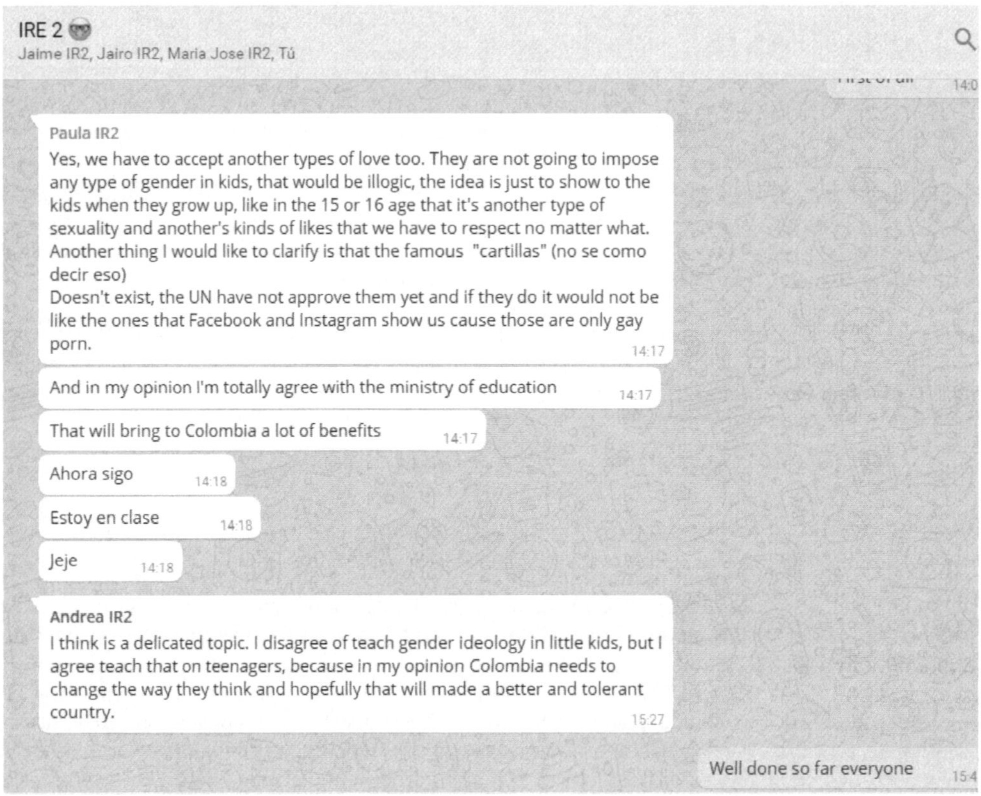

Figure 1. Excerpt of Interaction from Level 2 Group (2016)

Furthermore, the level 6 participants demonstrated how the group space can offer students an extended space beyond class time where concepts covered in class (the language of othering in this instance) could be discussed in relation to examples from the world they see around them (Figure 2).

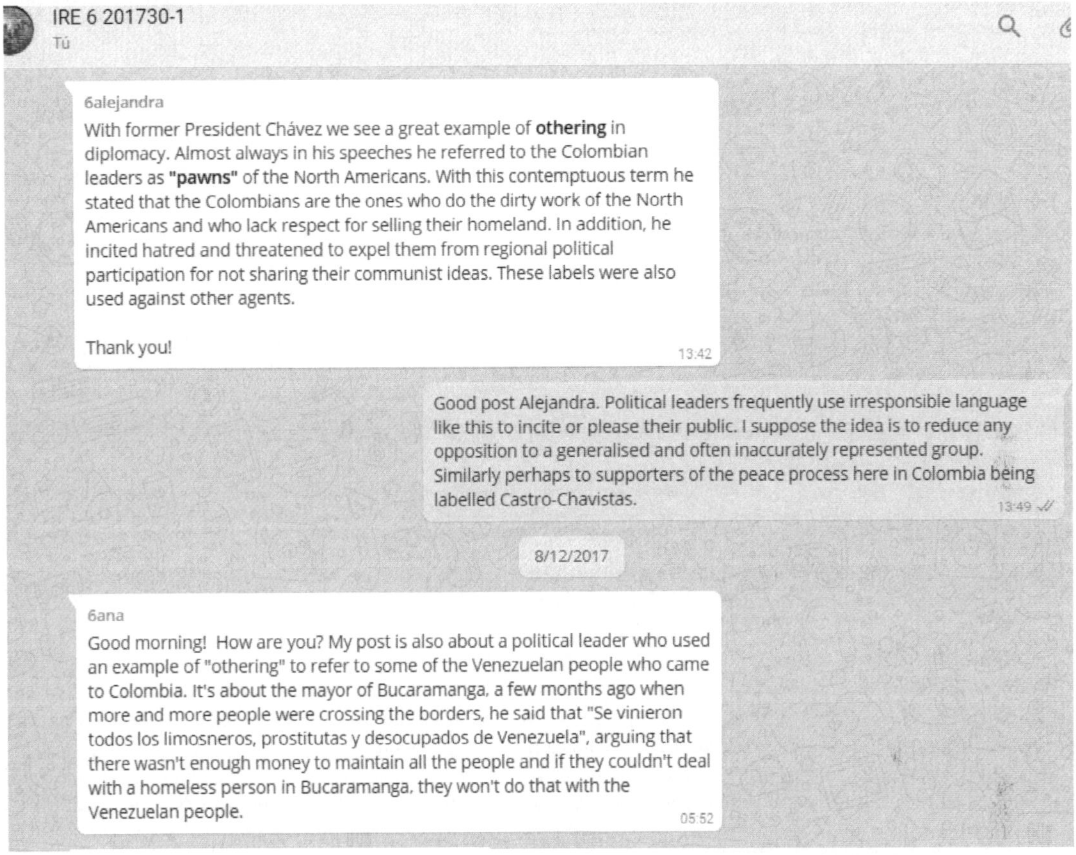

Figure 2. Excerpt of interaction from Level 6 group (2017)

5. PRELIMINARY CONCLUSIONS

The interactions between teachers and students have always been one of the most recurrent and studied subjects in scientific research due to the control of the teacher's speech in the classroom and of the students' voices without being heard (monological and traditional approaches). The use of WhatsApp in this study has been meaningful for students in that it has created an additional space beyond the traditional classroom where topics developed in class can be further elaborated on and new topics, be they prompted by the teacher or the students themselves, may be discussed. Furthermore, there has been indications that learners view such a group as a "safe space" where voices which are often silent within the four walls of the classroom offer their opinion, something which has been indicated through previous work on behalf of the author (Keogh, 2017). As the study moves into its third cycle, the benefits of the WhatsApp group as a site for meaningful and fulfilling interaction will continue to be explored as will how the space is perceived by its participants.

REFERENCES

Alexander, R. (2008). Towards Dialogic Teaching. York: Diálogos.

Almekhlafy, S. & Alzuby, A. (2016). Mobile Mediated Communication: A Tool for Language Exposure in EFL Informal Learning Settings. Arab World English Journal, 7, 388-407.

Bakhtin, M. (1986). Problemas de la poética de Dovstoievski. México: Fondo de Cultura Económica.

Bakhtin, M. (1982). *Estética de la creación verbal.* Buenos Aires: Siglo XXI Editores.

Bouhnik, D. & Deshen, M. (2014). WhatsApp Goes to School: Mobile Instant Messaging between Teachers and Students. Journal of Information Technology Education: Research, 13, 217-231.

Cazden, C. (Ed.). (1972).The functions of language in the classroom. New York: Teachers' College Press, Columbia University.

Coffin, C. (2009) Contemporary Educational Argumentation: A Multi-Modal Perspective. Argumentation, 23, 513. https://doi.org/10.1007/s10503- 009-9161-z

Drewery, W. (2005). Why we should watch what we say: Position calls, everyday speech and the production of relational subjectivity. Theory & Psychology, *15*(3), 305–324.

Fraga, L. M., & Flores, B. B. (2011). Mobile learning in higher education.PhD, The university of Texas, San Antonio.

Giroux, H. & McLaren, P. (1998). Escrito desde los márgenes: geografías de identidad, pedagogía y poder". In P. McLaren. Multiculturalismo Revolucionario. Mexico: Siglo XXI.

Herrington, J., Herrington, A., Mantei, J., Olney, I. W., & Ferry, B. (2009). New technologies, new pedagogies: Mobile learning in higher education.

Hou, H. T., & Wu, S. Y. (2011). Analyzing the social knowledge construction behavioral patterns of an online synchronous collaborative discussion instructional activity using an instant messaging tool: A case study. *Computers & Education*, *57*(2), 1459-1468.

Keogh, C. (2017). Using WhatsApp to Create a Space of Language and Content for Students of International Relations. *Latin American Journal of Content & Language Integrated Learning*, *10*(1).

Kukulska-Hulme, A., & Traxler, J. (Eds.). (2005). *Mobile learning: A handbook for educators and trainers*. Psychology Press.

Mercer, N., & Littleton, K. (2007). Dialogue and the development of children's thinking. London: Routledge.

Ng'ambi, D & Brown, I. (2009). Intended and unintended consequences of student use an online questioning environment.British Journal of Educational Technology, *40* (2) 316-328.

Park, Y. (2011). A pedagogical framework for mobile learning: Categorizing educational applications of mobile technologies into four types. *The International Review of Research in Open and Distributed Learning*, *12*(2), 78-102.

Scornavacca et al. (2016). Mobile instant messaging support for teaching and learning in higher education. *The Internet and Higher Education*, *31*, 32-42.

Wegerif, R. (2013) Dialogic: Education for the Internet Age. London: Routledge (ISBN-10: 0415536782 ISBN-13: 978-0415536783).

SOFTWARE PLATFORM FOR GAMIFICATION IN THE UNIFIED STATE EXAMINATION PREPARATION ACTIVITIES

Airat Khasianov and Irina Shakhova
Higher School of Information Technologies and Information Systems, Kazan Federal University
Kremlyovskaya St., Kazan, Russia

ABSTRACT

In the paper we present a software platform for applying gamification to the Unified State Examination (USE) preparation activities in the Russian Federation.
The USE is a final examination at school as well as a university entrance examination. Students' preparing for the examination takes a long time and is accompanied by solving a large number of similar tasks. Over time students' interest in these activities is reducing, which leads to unsatisfactory results.
We developed a mobile learning tool for the USE preparation which uses game mechanics to increase the involvement of students in the process of preparing for the USE. These mechanics are based on our model of implementing the gamification in the educational process and include the particular properties of the Unified State Examination. We've implemented the model in a platform consisting of mobile applications (iOS, Android) for students and a web-application for a teacher. The platform provides a support for the USE preparation activities at school and outside it. It lets students execute different types of the USE tasks as a training and simulate the examination with a complete set of tasks and a time limit. The processes are accompanied by visualization of user's progress, competition in a form of other students' success rating, receiving badges for special sets of actions, etc. Detail description of the game mechanics and capabilities of the platform are presented in the paper. This is a follow up paper to the preliminary report (Khasianov and Shakhova, 2017).

KEYWORDS

Mobile Learning, Education, Software Engineering, Unified State Examination

1. INTRODUCTION

Gamification application in preparing for the Unified State Examination is considered in this research. Universal State Examination (USE) preparation takes about two years and includes a lot of routine and stressful for students activities. The preparation at large consists of solving a large number of similar tasks that leads to decrease of students' motivation. The students don't have any relevant feedback neither about their progress nor on growth of their competences of solving of the USE tasks. Students have opportunities to pass training examination a few times, but it isn't enough. The training becomes a stressful event and often doesn't allow to adequately measure competences because of it, but organization of extra trainings requires a significant share of teacher's time for assessment of the students' submissions.

The general idea of this research is to transfer routine work to a digital tool implemented as a software platform which was developed with some game mechanics as was stated in the earlier work where the general model was described (Khasianov and Shakhova, 2017).

Aparicio at. al 2012 describe a general method how gamification can be involved as a tool to improve participation and motivation. Essentially we follow the same steps: *Identification of the main objective* (USE preparation); *Identification of the transversal objective* (to perform better in solving tasks, to get a higher USE grade); *Selection of game mechanics support* (described separately), *Effectiveness analysis* (comparison of performance of the experimental and control groups). A very recent and a thorough review of advantages and disadvantages of using gamification in education is done by Sobocinski, 2018, where the author also mentions that education is already naturally gamified. It is indeed so, but it is important to underline importance of mobile learning in the context of gamification for education. Namely, there are certain properties of mobile platform that make it a must for education gamification best practices: *continuous data collection*; *constant timely feedback*; *IoT infrastructure integration*. There's also a recent review on most preferred mobile apps for gamification in the higher education context done by Bicen and Kocakoyun, 2017. It generally supports the fact that majority of students access digital tools on their mobile devices, and that proper utiliseion of these tools improve participation and motivation, although this was not stated by the authors explicitly. There's no so far a study if the effect of using mobile learning in USE preparation.

The solution provides the opportunities to: a) transfer the USE activities from the classroom activities to the mobile application; b) track students' progress and get some awards which allows to support student's interest; c) model training examination with over 400 different random the USE questions any time; d) automate assessment of the major part of the assignments submitted by students.

Despite of the transfer of the USE preparation activities to the online platform we should keep the opportunity for the students to receive adequate and timely feedback by the teacher. That is our solution has to support at list minimal communication. We should also note that teachers' a feedback and asynchronous nature of training is necessary for the platform to work for most of the students.

The paper includes the information about game mechanics which are used in the software platform and the description of the system capabilities.

2. GAME MECHANICS

The game mechanics of the platform are based on approaches of implementing the gamification in the educational process described in *Gamification in higher education: Kazan Federal University prime*r (Khasianov et al., 2016) and model presented in *New model of mobile learning for the high school students preparing for the Unified State Exam* (Khasianov and Shakhova, 2017). In the software platform we use the same mechanics that were confirmed to be effective for the educational process: *goals*, *challenges*, *feedback* and *social interaction*.

According to *Practical proposals for motivating students* (Forsyth and McMillan, 1991) it is important to identify valuable goals as it increases motivation. The goal should be positive, realistic, behaviorally specific and personally important (Danish et al., 1983). In our case the student's goal is achievement of the maximum score on the examination. The score consists of points for the solved tasks in each examination discipline. The student must pass only two exams - the Russian language and mathematics. Other subjects can be selected by the student if it's necessary to provide these results for admission to the university. Obviously, the maximum score is an individual index depending on a student's personal wishes and abilities. For maintaining an individual approach to achieving the goal our system lets students solve tasks of different levels in any order.

The Unified State Examination consists of two types of tasks: tasks with a short answer and tasks with a detailed answer. The tasks are challenges that are necessary for tracking student's progress in the process of achieving the goal (Brothy, 2010). The scores that are obtained as a result of these tasks form a final score of the discipline. The tasks with a short answer support automatic checking and scoring. The tasks with a detailed answer that require a teacher's mark are sent for peer review.

Preparing for the Unified State Examination takes a long time and the absence of a continuous feedback may have a negative effect on students' motivation. It means that students can be uncertain about their position in achieving goals or need help. It is crucial to get the fast feedback throughout the whole process (James, 1998). It allows participants to control the process of proceeding towards their goals and correct their behaviour depending on the current progress indices. Although most of the tasks are checked by the system automatically what provides instant updates of the user's progress, a teacher is an important object of the model.

The opportunity to compete with other students or groups of students has a positive effect on extrinsic motivation and stimulates learning activity (Deci et al., 1991). The individual student's rating is the main component of the Unified State Examination and it forms the status of a student depending on his progress.

3. THE PLATFORM

Described game mechanics were implemented in the software platform consisting of mobile applications (iOS, Android) for students and a web-application for a teacher.

The goal is to obtain a maximum number of points for each topic of a discipline. The goal is measured in the number of earned points. The topic can consist of two types of tasks: tasks with a short answer and tasks with a detailed answer.

The challenge (or task) is measured in points that can be obtained by solving the task. Simple tasks with a solution in a fixed form the points are given if the answer is correct. This type of tasks is checked by the system automatically, students can see their performance virtually in real-time manner. Tasks with an elaborate answer required score the maximum points that can be reached. A solution to this type of a task can be submitted in a form of a digital scan or photo of the solution. The solutions are sent to a teacher and become available in the teacher's user account. The school and the teacher should be selected by the student via the student's interface of the platform. The teacher assigns a score in the system after checking the task and the score is displayed in the student's mobile application.

The software platform also includes one more game feature called a *badge*. A *badge* is an award which can be received through a student's activities in the mobile application. The *goal achievement* is completed with a *badge*, in addition, *badges* can be obtained by performing certain challenges or combinations of certain actions with the mobile application. This opportunity was added for a surprise effect that supports the students intrinsic motivation (Deci E.L., 1971), and helps avoid decrease of it. All of the obtained *badges* are available in the user's profile of the mobile application.

The total number of points creates an individual rating of the student. This allows addition of competitive effect and visualize the student's progress.

The mobile application features ability to:

- choose topics for training, solve the tasks of the topics in any desired order, get a fast feedback about correctness of the answers and accumulate points;
- pass training examination with a complete set of tasks and a time limit;
- track progress of a specific student, get the students' rating compared against other students' performance;
- receive and collect badges;
- get information about other students and their successes.

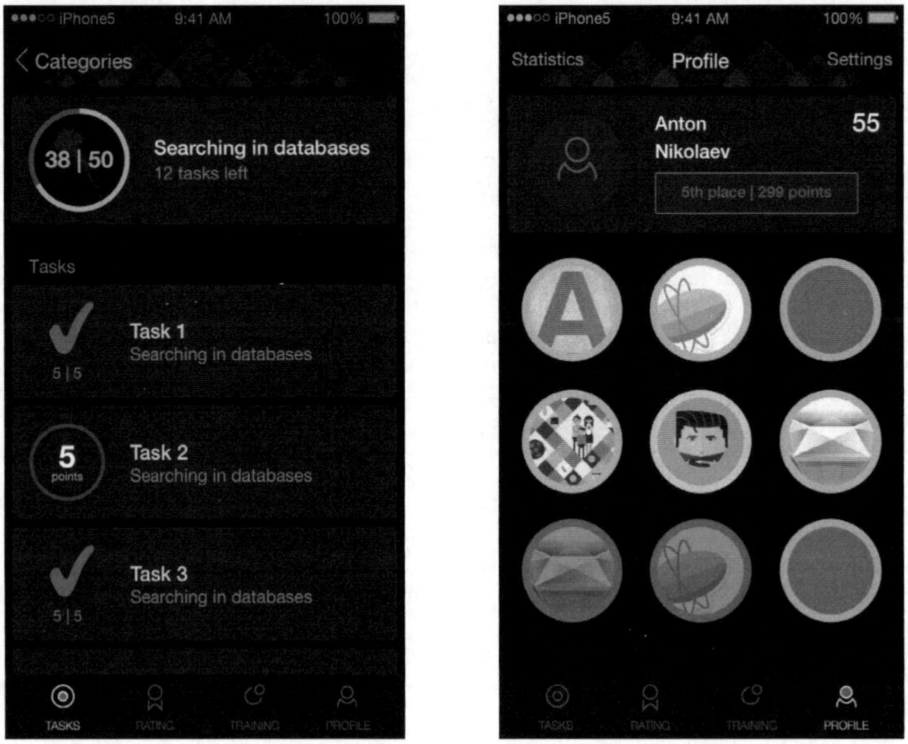

Figure 1. The User Interface of Mobile Application for Students

In order to illustrate the interface two screens of the application are presented on Figure 1: The screen with a list of tasks (solved tasks are checked) and the screen of a user's profile. The first screen has information about possible/achieved points of the topic, tasks remaining to solve, solved tasks, points for the specific tasks. The second screen provides the data of a user's profile: name, number of points in the system and position in the rating, received badges and the Unified State Examination point of the last training attempt.

The web-application lets teachers:

- view their students' solved tasks, check the answers and assign a score for the tasks with a detailed answer;
- get information about their students' successes and the common rating of the students.

4. CONCLUSIONS

The application has been developed with .Net technology on the server side and the teacher's web-interface and Objective C for iOS mobile application, and Java for Android mobile application.

The first version of the described platform will be introduced as an experiment in the Unified State Examination preparation activities of one of Russians schools. The students of the 10th grade get an opportunity to prepare for the USE of Informatics. We carried out a poll shown that one hundred percent of students (22 persons) are owners of mobile devices with one of two operating systems (iOS, Android). The statistics of mobile operation systems showed that 15 mobile devices running Android 5.0 and higher, 3 devices - Android 4.4, 3 devices - iOS 10 and higher, 1 device running Android 4.2.

Full audience coverage enables to track all students' indices and get correct results in analysis. The students' indices of the Unified State Examination in training attempts will be collected during this stage of the experiment and analysed after its completion.

After the experiment we'll get information about new game mechanics which could be added to the software platform and the next direction of the research.

REFERENCES

Aparicio, A. F., Vela, F. L. G., Sánchez, J. L. G., & Montes, J. L. I., 2012. Analysis and application of gamification. *Proceedings of the 13th International Conference on Interacción Persona-Ordenador*. ACM, p. 17.

Brothy, J., 2010. *Motivating Students to Learn, 3rd edition*. Routledge, New York, USA.

Bicen, H. & Kocakoyun, S., 2017. Determination of university students' most preferred mobile application for gamification. *World Journal on Educational Technology: Current Issues*, 9(1), pp. 18-23.

Danish, S.J., Galambos, N.L., Laquatra, I., 1983. Life development intervention: skill training for personal competence. *In Preventive Psychology: Theory, Research, and Practice*. Pergamon Press, New York, USA, pp. 49-61.

Deci, E.L., 1971. Effects of externally mediated rewards on intrinsic motivation. *In Journal of Personality and Social Psychology*, No.18, pp. 105-115.

Deci, E. L. et al., 1991. Motivation and Education: The Self-Determination Perspective. *In Educational Psychologist*, No. 26 (3 & 4), pp. 325-346.

James, W., 1998. Capturing and Directing the Motivation to Learn. *Speaking of Teaching, Stanford University Newsletter on Teaching*, Vol. 10, No. 1.

Forsyth, D. R. and McMillan, J. H., 1991. Practical proposals for motivating students. *New Directions for teaching and learning*, No. 45, pp. 53-65.

Khasianov, A., Shakhova I. and Ganiev B., 2016. Gamification in higher education: Kazan Federal University primer. *Proceedings of the 12th International Scientific Conference eLearning and Software for Education*. Bucharest, pp. 519-522.

Khasianov A. and Shakhova I., 2017. New model of mobile learning for the high school students preparing for the Unified State Exam. *Proceedings of the 13th International Conference Mobile Learning 2017*. Budapest, Hungary, pp. 127-130.

Sobocinski, M., 2018. Necessary Definitions for Understanding Gamification in Education A Short Guide for Teachers and Educators. Working paper. https://www.researchgate.net/publication/319646230

THE INTRODUCTION OF A PEER-EVALUATION APP FOR IN-CLASS PRESENTATIONS

Peter Gobel and Makimi Kano
Kyoto Sangyo University, Kamigamo, Motoyama, Kita-ku, Kyoto, Japan 603-8555

ABSTRACT

PeerEval is a mobile app created for evaluating student presentations. This paper covers the rationale for creating such an app, the features of the app, and the benefits for both teachers and students. The details and initial findings of ongoing research into the efficacy of PeerEval will be briefly discussed.

KEYWORDS

Peer Evaluation, Assessment, Grading Rubric, iOS

1. INTRODUCTION

This short paper deals with in-class presentations and a new mobile app that can be used for peer evaluation. Japanese students have been called "mobile natives" (Gobel & Kano, 2014) who are more at home using mobile devices than desktops and laptops. Previous research (Kano & Gobel, 2013; Lockley, 2011) has shown that given the choice many Japanese students will choose completing assignments using smartphones rather than computers. Some Japanese universities have tried to accommodate this propensity by offering software such as PowerPoint and Word as applications that can be downloaded to their smartphones.

1.1 Introduction to PeerEval

PeerEval is a mobile application that allows students to listen to presentations and evaluate them in real time. The results are compiled in a database and are then available to the teacher and the students.

The application was developed in response to the increasing popularity of simultaneous in-class presentations. This kind of presentation, since they are given to a small group of people, reduces the stress involved in addressing a group, while the peer evaluation promotes greater involvement of the students in the presentations to which they are listening (Cote, 2013).

1.2 Benefits of Small in-class Presentations

Getting students to practice speaking in class is challenging since they do not possess the skills or confidence to speak spontaneously. Short talks allow students to prepare in advance, but whole class presentations can be stressful. Small in-class presentations allow students to speak in small groups, thus reducing stress.

One significant problem with this approach, however, is the fact that it is impossible for the instructor to evaluate all presentations when multiple presentations are going on simultaneously. Thus the students' presentations must be evaluated by their peers. With proper planning, this can have an advantageous effect on both L2 acquisition and general presentation skills (Hansen & Liu, 2005). Evaluation on paper, however, creates considerable paperwork for the instructor, who has to compile the results into a spreadsheet. In addition, students are often reluctant to fairly evaluate their peers or give critical comments on paper-based rubrics. Using the forum function of a CMS, such as Moodle, poses different problems, since the students can see each other's grades and comments, they are reluctant to grade or comment critically. In addition, grading and commenting on Moodle may be asynchronous, thus affecting the reliability of the ratings and comments. The PeerEval system was designed to overcome these problems.

1.3 Concerning the Reliability of Peer Assessment

In the field of language teaching, peer assessment has mainly been used as a means of giving students feedback on their writing. Some work, however, has been done on peer assessment of speaking. Patri (2002) found in a controlled experiment with multiple classes that "peer-assessment was in high agreement with the teacher-assessment. This suggests that, in the presence of peer feedback, the students were able to make judgments of their peers' oral presentations comparable to those made by the teacher." In our situation, however, the primary purpose of the assessment is not so much to evaluate the students' ability so much as to encourage them to prepare well and to provide them with multiple chances to speak. Additionally, the assessment procedure gives their peers a clear purpose to listen and to compare the speaker's production skills to their own.

2. PEEREVAL IMPLEMENTATION

The system consists of two components, a browser-based system for the instructor to create the evaluation criteria, to upload the student name list, and to download the results, and the app that the students use for their assessments.

2.1 The Browser-based System: http://peereval.mobi

Any teacher can use PeerEval with their students. The teacher needs to go to http://peereval.mobi, where are two login choices. Teachers may use the system without registration, but they must configure their session, conduct their class and download their results within a set time period. Teachers with login-access, however, can create multiple rubrics, sessions and classes which remain in the system until the teacher elects to delete them. Figure 1 shows part of the teachers' page that allows them create or reuse rubrics, set up multiple sessions (a "session" is a combination of a class list with a rubric set that can be used for one activity in the class), view or download the results. Teachers can choose one of the default rubrics or create their own. A set of up to six rubrics can be set up for one session, with a choice of four-point or five-point Likert scales.

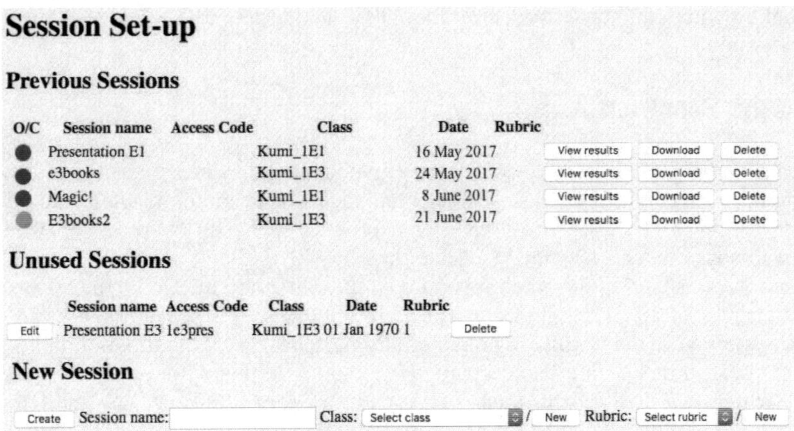

Figure 1. Teacher's Control Panel

Red and green clickable icons allow a session to be closed so that students cannot continue to submit evaluations after the activity is complete. In cases where the activity takes two or more classes to complete, the session may be opened and closed as needed.

2.1.1 Output of the Results

The teacher can show the results instantly on the class screen if s/he is not concerned about student privacy, or print them out and supply the students with their own scores which also shows the class averages (Figures 2 & 3).

Total Scores

Name	Ending?	English only?	Good job?	Interesting?	Well-Prepared?	Average
Ay	3.8	3.9	3.3	3.5	3.4	3.6
Ch	4.3	4.4	4.2	4.0	3.6	4.1
Ch	4.2	4.7	4.2	4.1	4.1	4.2
Ch	3.8	3.1	3.2	3.8	2.8	3.3
Da	3.5	3.3	2.8	3.8	2.3	3.1
Hi	3.8	4.4	4.0	4.0	4.1	4.1
Ka	3.9	3.9	3.6	3.5	3.2	3.6
Ko	3.7	3.0	3.3	3.8	2.9	3.3
Mi	4.0	3.8	3.1	3.3	2.6	3.4
Mi	4.2	3.9	3.6	4.3	3.2	3.8
Mi	4.2	4.6	3.9	4.3	3.6	4.1
Mi	4.1	3.3	3.6	3.9	3.4	3.7
Na	3.6	3.7	3.3	3.6	2.9	3.4
Ri	3.7	3.8	3.7	3.9	3.3	3.7
Ry	3.8	4.1	3.8	3.9	3.2	3.8
Sa	3.9	4.5	3.6	3.5	2.8	3.7
Ta	3.8	4.3	4.0	3.8	4.1	4.0
Yu	3.8	3.9	3.3	3.9	3.1	3.6
Yu	3.6	3.6	2.8	3.4	2.3	3.1
Yu	3.7	4.2	3.2	3.3	2.8	3.4
Average	3.9	3.9	3.5	3.8	3.2	3.7

Figure 2. Complete Session Report

Student Scores

Name	Ending?	English only?	Good job?	Interesting?	Well-Prepared?	Average
	3.8	3.9	3.3	3.5	3.4	3.6
Average	3.9	3.9	3.5	3.8	3.2	3.7
	interesting Very clear speech. I like love romance too!! love is interesting I like love story. love story is good I want to read this book I want to try to read.					

Figure 3. Individual Score Report

The scores can also be output as a standard CSV file which allows the instructor to manipulated the results as needed and create grades for the students. A future improvement will allow the instructor to stipulate a weighting for each rubric. For example, in a low-level English class, an important aspect of the presentations is the students' preparation so that they speak from memory rather than read their talk from notes or from sentences that appear on the slides. Thus that aspect can be given more weight in the final grade determination.

2.2 Using the PeerEval App

The iOS app is downloadable from the App Store (free of charge). When students activate the app, they log in with an access code provided by their instructor and their first name (or handle). Android users and people who want to use their PCs to evaluate can use a browser to log in by accessing the PeerEval website (http://peereval.mobi) and choosing the "Students" link.

A screen such as that in Figure 4 then appears with the rubric constructed by the teacher and, when slid to the right, the names of all of the students. Touching the name of a student then sets the main screen to evaluate that particular student, with the presenter's name appearing at the top of the screen. All evaluations are on a Likert scale. Students are also encouraged to enter a comment in the box provided at the bottom of the screen. Each student then submits their evaluation to the server. It is possible, however, for a student to return to a previous evaluation during the same session, revise the scores and re-submit. Once a student has finished presenting and the peers have input their scores and comments, students can view their scores for each rubric, the total score for the presentation, and the class average.

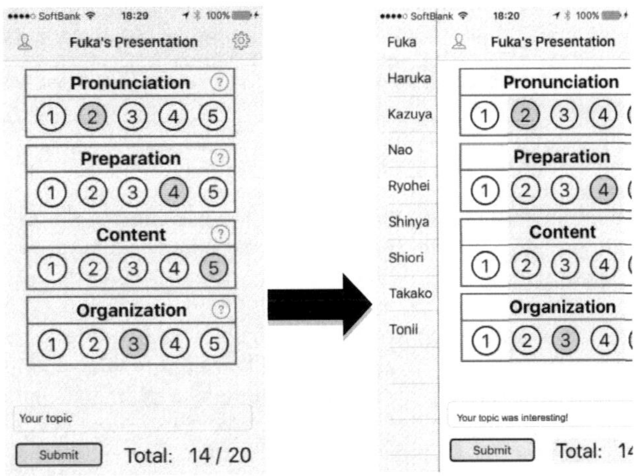

Figure 4. Main Screen with Name List of Students When Slid to the Right

2.3 Student Attitudes towards the PeerEval App

To informally measure students attitudes towards PeerEval, a twelve item questionnaire was created and administered to students who had experience with both paper-based and PeerEval peer evaluation procedures. The rubrics for both procedures were similar. The questionnaire was divided into five questions about the PeerEval app itself, three questions comparing paper-based and app-based evaluation from the presenter's point of view, and four questions comparing paper and app-based evaluation from the point of view of the audience.

In general, students felt that the app was easy to install and use. They felt that the evaluation system was clear and that the comments and feedback would help them prepare more for subsequent presentations. From the presenters' standpoint, the feedback speed was a major plus, and the ability to quickly read peer comments was viewed as helpful. One negative point was that presenters felt that students might be paying more attention to the app (or their phones) that the presenter. From the point of view of the audience, everyone preferred the privacy and feedback speed of the app, and felt that the app gave them the feeling that the presentations were more interactive. Students also felt that the app allowed them to evaluate more accurately than using paper-based methods.

3. CONCLUSION

The PeerEval app has a number of advantages over paper-based or CMS (Moodle) based evaluation. Firstly, the interface is simple and easy to use for mobile natives, allowing for faster evaluation and display of results. In addition, privacy of the evaluations is greater than Moodle forum or paper-based systems, hopefully resulting in more accurate grading and more salient comments. From the teacher's side, there is far less work inputting the data and summarizing the results.

Table 1 shows a sample of comments from students. Since the comments are anonymous, they tended to be quite direct and on point.

Table 1. Selected Student Comments

Session	Comment
44	it is generally good presentation but I couldn't understand a little about the content so if you prepared little more, that would be great.
	hard to follow. too many characters on the slides.
	Good job. Overall good, but some explanation was not totally accurate.
	Slide and organization was good but if you speak more slowly and clearly, that would be better.
68	The present ion was slightly long. Maybe you should tell us why you choose this topic more.
	Thesis is little bit unclear and not really enough. I am curious how do you broaden your idea.
	References are not enough. You should look for reference of books.

The preliminary results of comparing PeerEval with paper-based forms of peer evaluation allowed us to take student preferences into account. Students generally had a favorable impression of the system, but presenters felt audience members were paying less attention to presentations and more attention to their phones. This preliminary result suggests that rules and/or procedures should be put into place regarding when students are allowed to input their evaluations.

Finally, since the initial review of the app, the developers have added a student peer evaluation section to the PeerEval website, allowing students to evaluate from browsers as well as the iOS app. Browser-based peer evaluation functions in exactly the same way as the PeerEval app. This addition helps alleviate the problem of having a peer evaluation system on one single platform.

ACKNOWLEDGEMENT

PeerEval was created by Thomas N. Robb and Tetsuya Nagare.

REFERENCES

Cote, R. (2013). The Role of Student Attitude Towards Peer Review in Anonymous Electronic Peer Review in an EFL Writing Classroom. Unpublished Ph.D. Dissertation available: http://arizona.openrepository.com/arizona/bitstream/10150/307005/3/azu_etd_13017_sip1_m.pdf

Gobel, P., & Kano, M. (2014). Mobile natives: Japanese university students' use of digital technology. *APACALL Book III*. Cambridge Scholars Publishing. 21-46.

Gobel, P., & Kano, M. (2017). The complexities of digital storytelling: Factors affecting performance, production, and project completion. In T. Issa, P. Kommers, T. Issa, P. Isaias, and T. Issa (eds.) *Smart Technology Applications in Business Environments*. IGI Global. 343-360.

Hansen, J.G. & Liu, J. (2005). Guiding principles for effective peer response. *ELT Journal, 59(1)*, 31-39.

Kano, M., & Gobel, P. (2013). Mobile Natives: KSU Students' Use of Digital Technology. *Sogo Educational Research Bulletin, Volume 8*, pp. 1-19.

Lockely, T. (2011). Japanese students' experience of ICT and other technology prior to university: A survey. *Jaltcall journal, 7(1)*, 93–102.

Patri, M. (2002). The Influence of Peer Feedback on Self and Peer-Assessment of Oral Skills. Language Testing. 19, 109-131.

DYNAMIC PROGRAM VISUALIZATION ON ANDROID SMARTPHONES FOR NOVICE JAVA PROGRAMMERS

Elhard Kumalija, Sun Yi and Ymran Fatih
Kobe Institute of Computing
〒650-0001, Chuo Ward, Kanocho, 2−2−7, Kobe, Japan

ABSTRACT

Dynamic program visualization tools helps to reduce the cognitive load of students in learning programming. However, to authors' understanding there is no dynamic program visualization tool that can be used in a widely available smartphones. In this study, we design a Dynamic visualization engine for java programs that is integrated to java code interpreter that runs on android smartphones. This tool will be valuable to students who don't have access to computers. It can also increase productivity in smartphone usage among lower secondary schools students.

KEYWORDS

M-learning, E-learning, Program Visualization, Java Programming

1. INTRODUCTION

We are surrounded by digital technology everywhere we are than ever before. Computer science literacy is now the needed basic skill as mathematics. Computer science is now being integrated in primary and secondary schools curriculum to equip students with the basic skills needed in this digital society. The computer science curriculum now puts emphasis in computation skills than previous. Visual approach to teaching computational skills through program visualization has seen as an effective way to motivate students to learn programming and reduce the cognitive load of understanding programming. Despite higher ownership of smartphones compared to personal computers there is no program visualization tool for learning programming using smartphones known to authors. Time spend by individual in using smartphones is higher than time spent in using PCs. Students are always accompanied with smartphones when commuting to school and on the way back home. More than 70% of their time is spend in social, entertainment and gaming activities while only 4% is spent on productivity (Jesse G.R., 2015). This paper presents a design of Dynamic program visualization on android smartphones for novice java programmers. The tool is expected to be a great aid to lower secondary schools students in schools where there is no computer laboratories but also to help students in schools with computer laboratories to use their smartphones in a productive way.

2. BACKGROUND

Nowadays computer science literacy is important skill for every career. Many countries are introducing compulsory computer science subjects in all levels of education. In 1997, the Ministry of Education of China emphasized importance of computing in college education regardless of discipline (Pan T.Y., 2017). In 1996 the Government of Tanzania launched computer science curriculum for secondary schools. These early initiatives were focused on skills to use computer tools. However needed computer literacy skill is shifting from learning computer tools towards equipping students with computation skills.

Every country is thriving to empower its youth in computer science and computational thinking skills. In 2016, the then President of United States America started a new initiative to empower a generation of American students with the computer science skills they need to thrive in a digital economy. The focus of computer science for all is students from kindergarten through high school to learn computer science and be equipped with the computational thinking skills they need to be creators in the digital economy, not just consumers, and to be active citizens in our technology-driven world (Megan 2016). Basic computer skills for college students (CS0) reform happening in China that shifts the focus of the course from computer tools and skills to computational thinking (Pan T.Y., 2017). There are also different campaigns like coder dojo and hour of code that are motivating students all over the world to learn computer science skills.

2.1 Computational Literacy and Digital Divide

Despite all efforts to teach computational skills to students in primary and secondary schools the goals are still far from being attained. Moreover there is a big difference between developed and developing countries. According to United Nations statistics division, data shows that the proportion of youth and adults with information and communications technology (ICT) skills to write a computer program using any language in all countries is less than 10% but in developing countries the results are worse, with less than 1% in some countries. Moreover, the proportional of primary and secondary schools with access to computers for pedagogical purposes varies from 90% to less than 7% in other countries (Sustainable Development Goals (SDG) Indicators | United Nations Statistics Division, 2017). The low computer literacy can be attributed not only to lack of computer laboratories in primary and secondary schools in developing countries but also the low usage of computers among youth.

The low computation literacy is due to difficult in comprehension of computation and digital gap. Programming is a difficult cognitive skill to learn. Mastering the basis of a programming language is a huge problem for many students. In order to write a simple program they need to have a basic knowledge of variables, input/output of data, control structures and other areas. There are much more complex concepts such as pointers, abstraction or exception handling. Moreover, Students in resource challenged environments lack opportunity to learn computation skills due to lack of computer labs.

In SDGs goal 4 is to ensure inclusive and quality education for all and promote lifelong learning. The one of the aim is by 2030 to ensure that all girls and boys complete free, equitable and quality primary and secondary education. Recognizing that computer science is a new basic skill necessary for economic opportunity and social mobility to ensure that students get equitable and quality education the digital divide needs to be addressed.

2.2 Program Visualization on Android Smartphone

Different tools have been developed to help, motivate and make learning computation skills and programming an interesting endeavor. These tools employs visual approach to programming and can be categorized into visual programming environments like Scratch and AppInvetor and Program visualization tools for example Jeliot and Python tutor.

Program Visualization tools are promising programming teaching tools in early stages of the learning path of a programmer, teaching the students the basics of programming and algorithms. Software Visualization tries to represent software systems in ways that help the user, developer, or student to understand them (Bhattacharya, P. Et al, 2011). A study of 600 students in a programming course with focus on visual approach showed increase in pass rate from 12% to 23% (Cisar S.M. Et al. 2011). According to Bhattacharya et al (2011) visualization would help novice programmer understand many abstract concepts and how to implement the concepts easier and better.

Furthermore, there is a widespread use of smartphones and nowadays smartphones are so powerful that there is no different between a laptop and smartphone apart from screen size. Youth are accompanied with their smartphones when commuting from home to school and back, the mobility of smartphones make their usage simple and everywhere.

To address the digital divide gap, **dynamic program visualization on android smartphones for novice java programmers** is proposed. The proposed solution capitalizes on youth preference to use smartphones and advantages of visual approach to learning programming. Students in resource challenged environments will be able to write java code, compile and visualize code execution on android smartphones. The target is primary and lower secondary school students.

3. RELEVANT WORK

This work involves two aspects the first is programming using smartphones and the second is providing dynamic program visualization.

3.1 Program Visualization Tools

Program visualization is graphical presentation of code execution. Jeliot3 is a program visualization application. It visualizes how a Java program is interpreted. Method calls, variables, operation are displayed on a screen as the animation goes on, allowing the student to follow the execution of a program step by step. Programs can be created from scratch or they can be modified from previously stored code examples; all the visualization is automatically generated (Moreno, A. Et al. 2005).

mJeliot supports interactive visualization of program behavior where learners become actively involved in testing their knowledge in an environment where they receive direct feedback about their own hypotheses (Pears, et al. 2011). What is missing is program visualization tool on smartphones as all tools (known to authors) can be used with personal computers.

3.2 Smartphones in Learning Programming

The growth of mobile technologies was evolutionary in the progress of technology; it opened a revolution in computing in a quicker time frame. The easy availability and extreme mobility with rich set of applications made smartphones an inevitable tool for students.

Different approaches has been adopted to utilize the potential of mobile phone to students studying programming, example delivering education content, introduction to programming where students learn directly by developing smartphone applications and using smartphone to write programs that will be run on smartphones (John M.S. & Ran, M. 2015). There are mobile platforms for learning programming on smartphones like mobProg a mobile-based application that provides students with a smart phone based platform for learning Java programming (Hashim, A. 2007) and Microsoft TouhDevelop a programming environment intended to enable anyone to use a phone to program the phone using scripts for their windows based smartphones (Athreya, B. Et al. 2012).

Holz et al (2011) researched on integrating smartphones as interesting everyday objects into computer science courses to raise motivation and the results show that using smartphones can have a highly motivational effect on students of both sexes and the usage of the latest media and technologies is generally far more motivating than the usage of the old and long-known ones. Eighth grade students were taught programming using TouchDevelop the results are, 7% of the students stated that they thought the development of a mobile application with TouchDevelop was easy, 48% thought it was somewhat difficult, and 45% said it was difficult. However, 86% of the students wanted to create more applications using TouchDevelop. 92% of the girls wanted to continue writing applications whereas only 38% of them had an idea of what applications they could create prior to the class (Tillmann N. et al. 2012). This shows the potential of using smartphones as a tool for teaching programming. However, Alsaggaf (2012) points out that while most students today own and use mobile devices, these devices are not obviously utilized as practical learning aids in lectures. Furthermore, these tools also lack visualization which is very important in learning programming.

4. DYNAMIC PROGRAM VISUALIZATION ON ANDROID PHONES

Dynamic program visualization engine on android smartphones is designed to support basic common programming concepts written in Java programming language syntax. Dynamic visualization is provided for sequential instruction execution, variable declaration and assignment, Expression Evaluation, data input, message output, selection, loop and function calls.

4.1 System Architecture

The system contains the user interface, Tokenizer, Parser, Interpreter and visualization Engine as shown in figure 1. User interface includes Editor and Visualization Pane. User writes code using editor and source code is tokenized and parsed before interpretation.

Interpreter sends command to visualization engine which animates code execution on visualization pane (4,5), during code execution visualization user can enter input to the program (6) and line of code in execution is highlighted in the Editor (7).

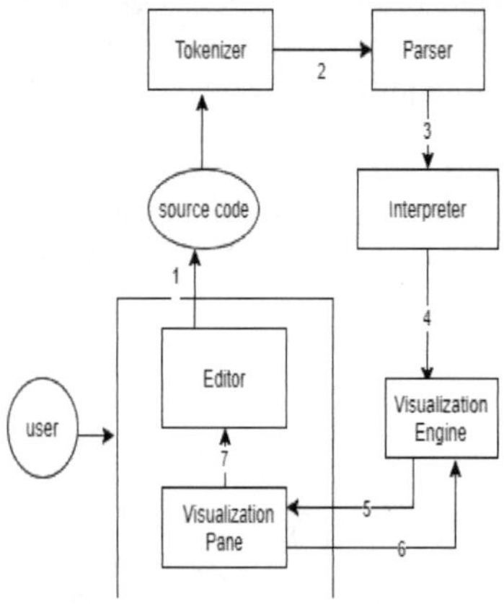

Figure 1. System Architecture

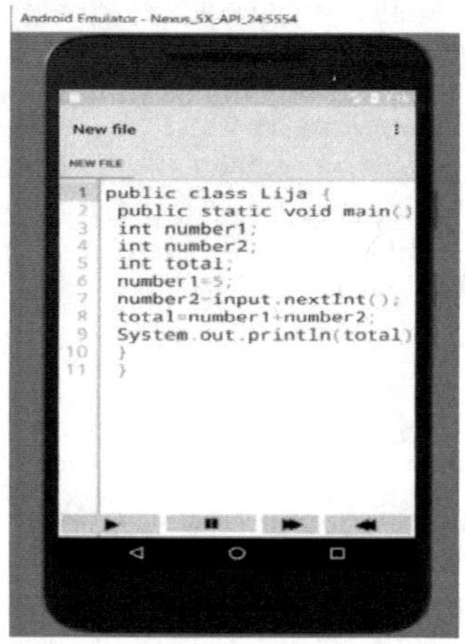

Figure 2. Source Code Editor

4.2 Program Visualization and Animation Control

The first stage in dynamic program visualization is to write source code in the source code Editor The editor contains buttons for compiling and controlling program visualization as shown in figure 2. Play button is used for compiling and starting program animations. It changes to stop button during program visualization so user can stop program visualization and go back to edit code. Forward and backward buttons are used for step wise animation. Forward and backward buttons are activated by pressing pause button.

During program execution, user is provided with graphical representation of program execution. Program in figure 2, includes sequential instructions, variable declaration and assignment, data input, message output and Expression Evaluation is used to demonstrate the dynamic program visualization. Sequence of instruction execution is animated by highlighting with pale dark blue color the instruction number of the current instruction (see instruction number 4 in figure 3).

Variable declaration is shown by adding a row in a table with first column presenting variable name and second column shows data stored in that variable. When data assignment instruction is executed, the corresponding data field in a variable table changes from null to the assigned data value. Instruction number 7 of the source code, the program asks input. In executing this instruction a EditText view pops up to the right side of variable declaration, where user can type in the value. The typed in value is assigned to the corresponding variable as is entered. Figure 4 above shows the presentation.

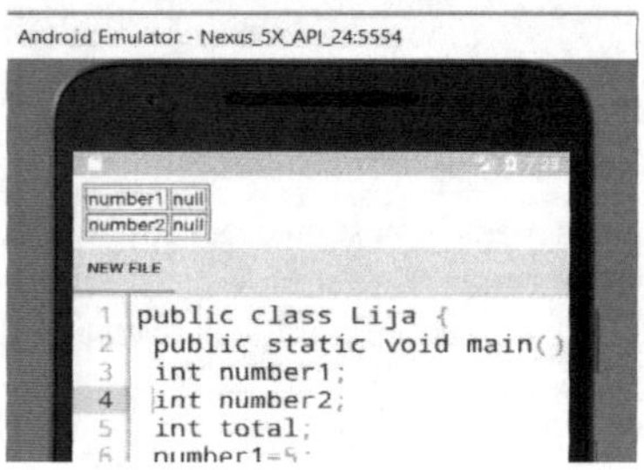

Figure 3. Variable Declaration

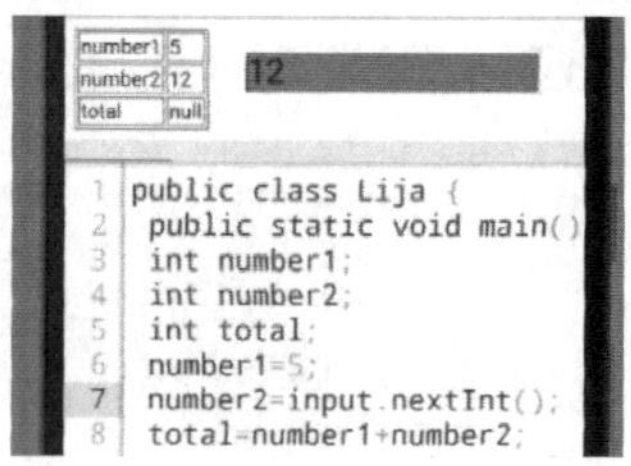

Figure 4. Data Input

Note that visualization designed does not support Object oriented programming concept. Hence input.nextInt() is not related to a method nextInt() in Scanner class of the java.util package but it is defined as the instruction to get input from the user so that user can input data during visualization. Same case applies to System.out.println().

Expression Evaluation is visualized by a pop up TextView which appears to the right of variables declaration. This region is used also for data input and output message. Instruction number 8 is expression evaluation, a TextView pops up to the right of the variable declaration visualization and shows the values of variables instead of variables names of the expression, the expression result is stored to the variable. Expression evaluation is shown in blue color to distinguish it from data input which is shown in red color and message output which is show in yellow.

Finally message output instruction number 9, message output is acting like a console in standard compilers and IDE. The message is shown with yellow background TextView to the right of the variable declaration.

5. CONCLUSION

Currently, program visualization for Selection, Loop and Functions are under development. Due to small screen size it is challenging to visualize classes and objects therefore the visualization of these programing concepts will not be provided. However it is expected that the tool will be useful for novice programming learners in learning basic programming concepts. It is also expected that the tools can enable a large number of students in resource challenged environments to learn computation skills as it can be accessed on widely available smartphones. The process of evaluating this tool in learning environment is under way.

REFERENCES

Alsaggaf, W., 2012. Enhancement of learning programming experience by novices using mobile learning: mobile learning in introductory programming lectures. *Proceedings of the ninth annual international conference on International computing education research*, ACM , pp. 151-152.

Athreya, B. et al, (2012). End-user programmers on the loose: A study of programming on the phone for the phone. *In Visual Languages and Human-Centric Computing (VL/HCC), 2012 IEEE Symposium,* pp. 75-82.

Bhattacharya, P. et al, 2011. A Collaborative Interactive Cyber-learning Platform for Anywhere Anytime Java Programming Learning. *In Advanced Learning Technologies (ICALT), 11th EEE International Conference,* pp. 14-16.

Čisar, S. et al, 2011. Effectiveness of program visualization in learning java: a case study with jeliot 3. *International Journal of Computers Communications & Control*, pp. 668-680.

Hashim, A., 2007. Mobile Technology for Learning Java Programming-Design and Implementation of a Programming Tool for VISCOS Mobile. *Unpublished Master's thesis*, University of Joensuu, Finland.

Holz, J. et al, 2011. Using smartphones to motivate secondary school students for informatics. *In Proceedings of the 11th Koli Calling International Conference on Computing Education Research* , ACM, pp. 89-94.

Jesse, G. R., 2015. Smartphone and App Usage Among College Students: Using Smartphones Effectively for Social and Educational Needs. *In Proceedings of the EDSIG Conference,* pp. 3424.

John, M. S. and Rani, M. S., 2015. Teaching Java Programming on Smartphone-pedagogy and Innovation; Proposal of its Ontology Oriented Implementation. *Procedia-Social and Behavioral Sciences*, *176*, 787-794.

Moreno, A. et al, 2005. Jeliot 3, an extensible tool for program visualization. *In 5th Annual Finnish/Baltic Sea Conference on Computer Science Education.*

Pan TY., 2017. Reenergizing CS0 in China. *In: Rich P., Hodges C. (eds) Emerging Research, Practice, and Policy on Computational Thinking. Educational Communications and Technology: Issues and Innovations*. Springer, Cham

Pears, A. and Rogalli, M., 2011. mJeliot: ICT support for interactive teaching of programming. *In Frontiers in Education Conference (FIE)*, IEEE, pp. T1J-1.

Smith M., 2016. Computer Science For All, https://obamawhitehouse.archives.gov/blog/2016/01/30/computer-science-all, accessed Nov 2017.

Tillmann, N. et al, (2012). The future of teaching programming is on mobile devices. *Proceedings of the 17th ACM annual conference on Innovation and technology in computer science education,* ACM, pp. 156-161.

United Nations Data., 2017. http://data.un.org , accessed December 2017

IMPROVING MUSIC PRACTICE WITH A MOBILE LEARNING SMARTPHONE APPLICATION

Yuanzhu Chen, Alan Klaus, Yeni Liang and Chen Zhang
Memorial University of Newfoundland, St. John's, Newfoundland, Canada

ABSTRACT

Learning musical instruments requires a significant amount of independent, unsupervised effort by students in the current post-secondary pedagogical context. A vital role of the teacher is therefore to help a student improve at the art of independent practice. The theory of contextual interference in skills learning has demonstrated better retention, but its essence of interleaved practices demands even more discipline in its execution. To respond to such a challenge, we developed an iPhone application for music students of our university to assist them with the planning, execution, and tracking of interleaved practice. The app allows users to create templates, log/record practices, and review practice outcome, and has a potential for social interaction and big-data analysis; it can also be used in many other areas of skill learning.

KEYWORDS

m-Learning, Music, Contextual Interference, Interleaved Practice

1. BACKGROUND

Learning musical instruments requires a significant amount of independent efforts in the current post-secondary pedagogical context. A vital role of the teacher is therefore to help a student improve at the art of independent practice. The theory of contextual interference in skills learning has demonstrated better retention, but its essence of interleaved practices demands even more discipline in its execution. To respond to such a challenge, we developed an iPhone application for music students of our university to assist them with the planning, execution, and tracking of interleaved practice. The app allows users to create templates, log/record practices, and review practice outcome, and has a potential for social interaction and big-data analysis; it can also be used in many other areas of skill learning.

2. CONTEXTUAL INTERFERENCE

"The contextual interference effect is a learning phenomenon where interference during practice is beneficial to skill learning. That is, higher levels of contextual interference lead to poorer practice performance than lower levels while yielding superior retention and transfer performance" (Magill and Hall, 1990).

An effective way to benefit from the contextual interference effect is to frequently alternate the material being practiced, which is know as interleaved practice, as opposed to the traditional routine of completing each task in a single block before moving on. Carter and Grahn (2016) showed the increased retention through interleaved practice by advanced clarinetists. Explaining its counter-intuitive impact, they wrote that interleaved practice "involves more effortful processing, resulting in increased long-term learning." There has been a considerable amount of research demonstrating improved retention of skills in various disciplines including basketball (Landin et al., 1993), badminton (Goode and Magil, 1986), mathematics (Rohrer et al., 2015), electrocardiogram diagnoses (Hatala et al., 2003), and other areas.

While the effortful processing improves retention, it can also be difficult for students to find the discipline to undertake interleaved practice. Due to the poorer in-practice performance noted by Magill and Hall, it can feel like more progress is made during traditional blocked practice, even if retention is frustratingly lacking the following day. Another drawback is that planning and tracking a balanced and complete interleaved practice routine can be an onerous task, especially in a complex field such as music. It is simpler to complete a block of ten minutes for a skill, working on finger speed for instance, than it is to return to the skill multiple times for short bursts, all in varied and balanced rotation with other skills that also need to be tracked. Our application is designed to alleviate this challenge.

3. RATIONALE FOR THE PRACTICE APP

Figueiredo et al. (2016) highlighted that today's students are of "the generation of digital games and social networks. We cannot ignore that they are no longer the same for which the education system was designed a few decades ago. See, for example, the prospect of Heide and Stilborne (2000), for whom 'the technological revolution has produced a generation of students who grew up with multidimensional and interactive media sources. A generation whose expectations and world views are different from those that preceded it' (p. 27). In this context it is wise to consider the integration of digital media and mobile devices (tablets, phablets, smartphones), allowing students to set personal goals, to manage educational content and to communicate with others in the right context."

Many musicians are already in the habit of using mobile applications during daily practice, but not commonly for the planning, tracking, or improvement of practice. Applications have replaced and significantly upgraded the functionality of what used to be common stand-alone devices such as a tuner (for pitch) and metronome (for pulse and rhythm). Other applications provide further functionality such as recording, playback (some can adjust the speed and/or pitch of existing tracks on playback), decibel readers for volume, and specialized pedagogical games or drills. In a broader scope, there is a known market for mobile applications that help users with many aspects of self-improvement such as fitness, nutrition, sleep, and daily planning. This highlights the potential desire for and benefits of an application that could help musicians improve their practice effectiveness.

We created a prototype iPhone application with the five main targets:

1. Make it easier to plan practice, track progress towards practice targets, and adjust practice plans. The app must be able to effectively manage interleaved practice but also work well for traditional blocked practice. Flexibility is imperative to the design of the app in order to support individual users in open experimentation around the effectiveness of freely altering their practice routines.
2. Create a user-friendly interface that guides students efficiently through their practice plan. This will avoid the waste of mental energy on logistics, instead prioritizing the increased processing demands of intense practice itself.
3. Enhance the feedback loop between teacher and student, including opportunities to connect outside of lessons, through the capability to share progress recordings, practice assignments, practice plan templates, and practice logs.
4. Provide a framework for students to access the power of "social and participative web technologies" and the "creation of mobile communities of practice" (Figueiredo et al., 2016) through a mobile learning network where users can share ideas, upload and download practice templates, and send recordings to each other.
5. An essential feature of the application is that it is not instrument-specific and can work for all musicians. It is also flexible enough to branch out into other broad areas such as athletics and academics.

4. DESIGN OF THE APP

We developed a prototype practice application for the iPhone (iOS 9 or later) using Apple's classic programming language Objective C in Xcode, Apple's integrated development environment. The app has three modules: a calendar for practice scheduling, a timer to log execution of practice plans, and a recorder to track how students improve their skills. These modules plus a Settings module are organized in a typical "tab"-based touch user interface.

- The Home View is where much of the user interaction happens. It provides a venue to view, edit, and execute practice items. The individual practice items can be accessed under the headings "skills" (Figure 1(a)) or "repertoire" (Figure 1(b)), depending on the user perspective at the moment. For example, when teaching trumpet, some of the skills may be tonguing, long tones, articulation, finger speed, etc. Repertoire refers to the pieces of music being studied. The users can edit any item by adding, removing, and modifying descriptions and goal practice times (Figure 1(c)). The practice items can be organized as a "stored set" (Figure 1(d)) to facilitate interleaved practice. The practice program will cycle through the stored set as the user practices (Figure 2(e)), with an option for randomization of the item order. With each practice item, a timer is automatically started to track the time spent, with an option of record- ing the practice with the phone's built-in microphone. The time for a practiced item is accumulated for the corresponding skill and repertoire item, and can be viewed as a progress graph on the Home View (Figures 1(a) and (b)).

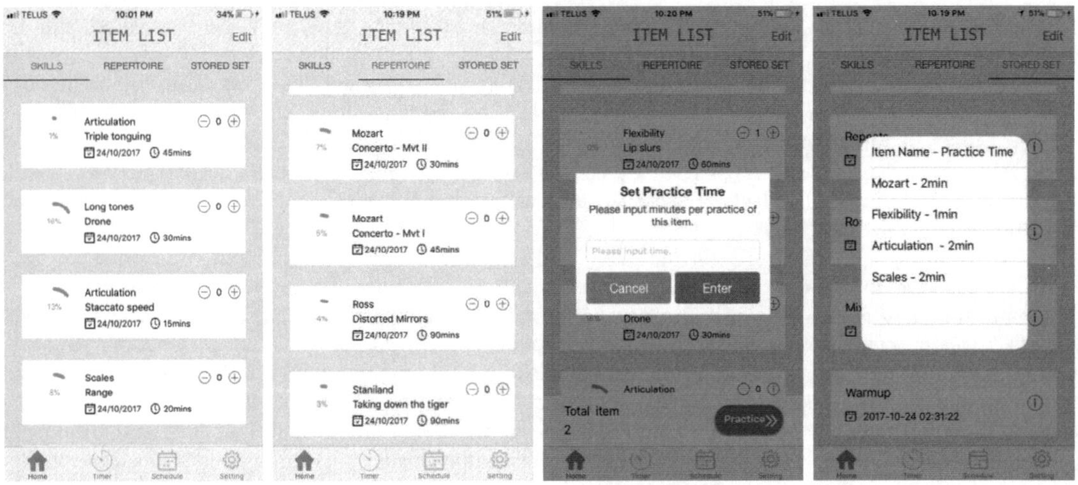

(a) (b) (c) (d)

Figure 1. Application Workflow 1/2

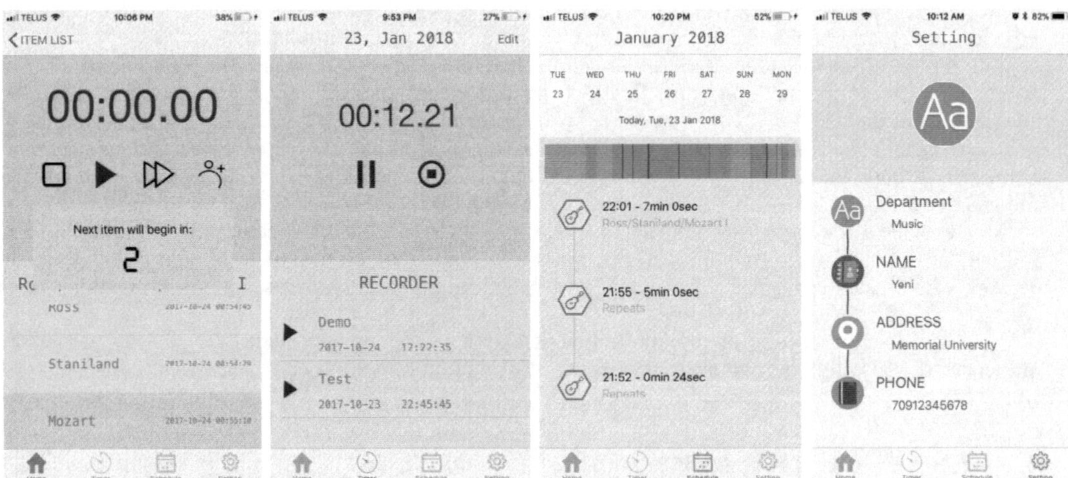

(e) (f) (g) (h)

Figure 2. Application Workflow 2/2

The Timer View (Figure 2(f)) allows the user to freely practice any skill or piece without being associated with any stored set item. The time spent can still be tracked as general practice. The Timer View gives users direct access to the timer, recorder, and also stored recordings.

- The Schedule View (Figure 2(g)) summarizes the planning and execution of the user's practice plan using a calendar-style user interface. It provides a weekly navigation tool at the top of the screen, and displays detailed information about the selected day of that week underneath. Such information is colour-coded for the different skills and pieces in a general progress bar, and then listed with time and text annotation.
- The Settings View module (Figure 2(h)) allows users to edit profile information, control app behaviours, and set permissions to access certain hardware components, such as the microphone and location sensor.

Under the hood of the app, the recording module is built on top of Apple's AVFoundation and AVAudio frameworks. All recorded audio clips are stored after encoding with ADPCM (Adaptive Differential Pulse Code Modulation) to achieve a compression ratio of about 1:4. The recordings, practice templates, and practice logs are managed through SQLite, a lightweight embedded relational database system used commonly in small computer systems, with an FMDB wrapper.

For initial testing, we deployed the app to a number of faculty members and students at School of Music in Fall 2017. We ran an open workshop on the app and obtained valuable feedback from users about improving functionality for the next phase of the app. Incorporating what we already have on our agenda with such feedback, the app can be extended in a few interesting ways with anticipated completion of April 2018.

- We will develop a utility for the creation of practice templates separately with the option for users to load them to the app from the cloud. This utility may be a Web application to allow the creator to work in more space without being limited to the small screens of smart phones. Teachers could help adjust practice routines for students, even between lessons, and users could share ideas with each other. Once a template is loaded to the phone, a user would still be able to customize some of its parameters.
- The users can currently save and playback audio clips as a way to observe their own progression in learning. Next, we will allow users to submit these clips to teachers for evaluation and to enhance possibilities for feedback loop between lessons. The submitted clips will be managed and accessed through a Web utility, which can be integrated with the previous template-creation tool.
- The app will facilitate social interaction amongst students to synergize their learning efforts. With this future module, users can share well-crafted practice templates, plan to practice together, and provide feedback on shared recordings. This can be implemented with a cloud service, or among students them- selves via direct peer-to-peer radio links.
- Once a high volume of practice data is voluntarily loaded to a central server, we can apply artificial intelligence techniques to compare a user's practice performance over time and to compare different users. Such a big-data approach could provide significant information for pedagogical analysis.
- In consultation with various faculty members, we will put an initial library of practice templates available for user download from the cloud. This is to allow users to quickly and easily get started and experiment with the application. As with all templates, these will be adjustable by the user if desired.
- We are creating a more robust user interface, including an option to automatically distribute the allotted weekly practice time across all items based on priority values assigned by the teacher or student.

5. CONCLUSION

The current common pedagogy of applied music instruction is to practice in blocks, similar to other disciplines. However, the theory of contextual interference suggests that frequent alternation of the materials being practiced would yield a better learning outcome, entailing a different way that music could be taught for increased effectiveness. With a smart phone application built as reported in this article, adhering to a prescribed practice template can be easy and rewarding, which otherwise could be mentally stressful and seem extraneous to the subject without the technology. Following the completion upgrades and the creation of the Web functionality in April, we will release the application once again to the university community. There will be a testing and feedback period for the remainder of 2018. The purpose is to obtain proof of concept and guide final upgrades before a targeted open release date in 2019.

ACKNOWLEDGEMENTS

Chen's research is supported by a Memorial University Teaching and Learning Framework fund, and an NSERC Discovery Grant. Klaus' development of this project has been supported by the Memorial University Scholarship in the Arts Fund, and by Dr. Ian Sutherland, Dean of the School of Music. Klaus would like to acknowledge Christine Carter for her inspiring research on interleaved practice in music.

REFERENCES

Carter, C. E. and Grahn, J. A., 2016. Optimizing music learning: Exploring how blocked and interleaved practice schedules affect advanced performance. *Frontiers in Psychology*, 7:1251.

Figueiredo, M. et al, 2016. The development of an interactive mathematics app for mobile learning. *Proceedings of 12th International Association for Development of the Information Society (IADIS) International Conference on Mobile Learning*. Algarve, Portugal.

Goode, S. and Magil, R. A., 1986. Contextual interference effects in learning three badminton serves. *Research Quarterly for Exercise and Sport*, Vol. 57, No. 3, pp 308–314.

Hatala, R. M. et al, 2003. Practice makes perfect: The critical role of mixed practice in the acquisition of ECG interpretation skills. *Advances in Health Sciences Education*, Vol. 8, No. 1, pp 17–26.

Landin, D. K. et al, 1993. The effects of variable practice on the performance of a basketball skill. *Research Quarterly for Exercise and Sport*, Vol. 64, No. 2, pp 232–237.

Magill, R. A. and Hall, K. G., 1990. A review of the contextual interference effect in motor skill acquisition. *Human Movement Science*, Vol. 9, No. 3-5, pp 241–289.

Rohrer, D. et al, 2015. Interleaved practice improves mathematics learning. *Journal of Educational Psychology*, Vol. 107, No. 3, pp 900–908.

DEVELOPMENT OF A COLORIMETRIC MEASUREMENT MOBILE APP FOR ACTIVE LEARNING IN ANALYTICAL CHEMISTRY

Eric H. C. Chow[1], Prof. Christopher Keyes[1], Dr. Koon-Sing Ho[2], Prof. Albert W. M. Lee[2], Wai-Yee Lee[2] and Nga-Wing Fong[2]
[1]*Apps Resource Centre, Hong Kong Baptist University, Hong Kong*
[2]*Department of Chemistry, Hong Kong Baptist University, Hong Kong*

ABSTRACT

This paper describes the development of a mobile application to engage students in active learning in analytical chemistry. Colorimetry is a topic in analytical chemistry that can effectively be learned through the use of mobile devices to perform colorimetric measurement in the real-life environment. Previous attempts in the development of colorimetry mobile apps have been described in the literatures, however, shortcomings exist in their ease of use for teaching and learning and dissemination. We herein propose a colorimetry mobile app design that allows anyone to download, and easily perform colorimetric measurements and engage in active learning anytime, anywhere. Pedagogical underpinnings of the mobile learning activity and app design will also be discussed.

KEYWORDS

Active Learning, Informal Learning, Experiential Learning, Chemical Education, STEM

1. INTRODUCTION

Today's learners are always on the move, and a great deal of learning happens outside the classroom (Sharples et al., 2005). With mobile devices, students can acquire knowledge anytime, anywhere, achieving ubiquitous learning outside the classroom walls. Mobile learning can thus be perceived as a "natural" way of learning, as suggested by Low and O'Connell (2006): "learning has always been mobile: we all learn as we go about our lives, with inherent dynamism and personal mobility." In science education, Zydney (2016) also notes that "much of science takes place outside of the classroom and is arguably better studied in its natural environment", and she postulates that "science learning are well aligned with the mobility of newer devices as well as their ability to display interactive, three-dimensional graphics and simulations." On the other hand, active learning in science-related subjects and respective benefits are extensively researched and described in the literatures (de Caprariis, 2012; Freeman, 2014; Kontra, 2015). Therefore, rather than passively learning in the confines of a classroom, students can acquire scientific concepts more effectively through the use of mobile devices through active learning in the real-life environment.

The current study focuses on active learning in analytical chemistry, which is the study of instruments and methods applied to separate, identify and quantify matters. Colorimetry is a technique in analytical chemistry for the quantitative determination of colored compounds in a solution. For example, colorimetry can be used to measure the concentration of heavy metals, sugars, proteins, food preservatives, environmental pollutants and other molecules in sample solutions. Colorimetric measurement is typically performed by the UV-visible spectrophotometer, which could cost up to USD50,000; this may not be worthy for some school laboratories. Yet, colorimetric measurement is a common topic in chemical education, and its practical applications can be valuable for anyone to learn and apply in daily life. Therefore, a colorimetric measurement mobile app that is fully functional on common mobile devices is an ideal tool for chemistry students to perform active learning in the real-life environment.

2. MOBILE APP DEVELOPMENT

As the affordability of mobile devices and the quality of their built-in cameras continually increase, the use of mobile devices for colorimetric measurement has been explored in various studies (Kehoe, 2013; Campos, 2015; Koesdjojo, 2015; Knutson, 2015). The general workflow described in these studies are as follows: use the mobile phone's native camera app to take color images of the sample solution, and use a general-purpose color-picker app or desktop software to extract the RGB (Red-Green-Blue) values in the images. Then, use a spreadsheet app or desktop software (e.g. Excel, Google Sheets) to tabulate the RGB values, and compute the absorbance, calibration profile and concentration of the sample solution. These studies use a combination of different apps and/or software on multiple platforms to complete the different steps in the workflow of colorimetric measurement, which may be inconvenient to the users, and may lead to erroneous results due to human errors when copying data from one software or platform to another. Lopez-Ruiz (2014) and Hussain (2016) studies attempted to create a single mobile app that integrates the different steps of the measurement workflow. However, their apps were designed specifically to function within the context of their studies and publications (i.e., pH value, nitrite content, and fluoride content), and their user-interfaces were not designed to cater for a general audience with no prior knowledge in colorimetry. Furthermore, the app by Hussain (2016) require a special device to fixate the sample solutions in front of the mobile phone camera lens, limiting both portability and practicality. Moreover, at the time of this writing, both apps were only compatible with Android mobile devices, and were not made publicly available on Google Play store.

2.1 App Design & Usage

The current study will design and produce a mobile app (tentatively named "SPECTRAL") which will be compatible for both Android and Apple iOS mobile devices, and made freely available on Google Play and Apple App Store. The app will allow anyone with a mobile device to perform colorimetric measurement using the built-in camera at anytime, anywhere without any external apparatus. Our mobile app will consist of two modes of operation: calibration and measurement modes. In calibration mode, the phone's built-in camera will capture color image of standard solution placed in front of the mobile phone. This image capturing is repeated several times for the same type of standard solution of different known concentrations and the RGB values of these images are automatically extracted and stored with the respective concentration values (input by the users). These values will be used to calculate the absorbance and construct a calibration profile. The absorbance obtained is a normalized value which is dependent of the concentration of sample solution (provided that the optical path is fixed). Once the sample container is the same as that of standards used for calibration, the quantification would be accurate. In measurement mode, the user uses the app to capture a color image of sample solution of unknown concentration, and based on the calibration profile of the same type of solution previously measured in calibration mode, the app will compute and output the extrapolated concentration of this solution.

The app's user-interface design will employ on-demand tooltips, so that instructions will be revealed just-in-time as user progresses through the measurement workflow. Another important feature of the mobile app design will be its support for informal learning experience. Active learning in the real-life environment may not necessary occur within the context of a formal learning experience led by an instructor. Informal learning using mobile apps usually occurs during out-of-school time, which means users can be with highly varied age, interest, background, and prior knowledge (Land, 2015). In light of this, when designing the app, self-guided instructional material on the topic of colorimetry will be strategically embedded into the measurement workflow, so that users who have no prior knowledge can also use the mobile app to informally learn and apply colorimetric measurement in the real-life environment.

The completed app will eventually be applied in undergraduate level chemistry, integrated science and general education courses at the Hong Kong Baptist University and other sister institutions in Hong Kong. It will first be introduced to students in formal learning settings: during laboratory classes when pre-designed laboratory experiments involving colorimetric measurement takes place, and during project-based learning experience, such as field trips and undergraduate final-year projects, when students will use the app as an active learning and investigative tool to study a chemistry related problem. We are also partnering with the Hong Kong Education Bureau, which will introduce the mobile app to the Hong Kong secondary schools for promoting active learning in STEM (Science, Technology, Engineering and Mathematics) education.

It is expected that about 700 local Hong Kong secondary school students will be using this app each year for their study in chemistry.

As mentioned previously, the app will be designed to support active learning in an informal learning context as well. It is hoped that university and secondary school students will continuously use the app after their formal learning experience; they would use the app to observe their surrounding environment through a critical lens, and tackle problems creatively that few of their current generation of instructors can imagine. Furthermore, as the mobile app will be available freely on the app store, anyone from around the world can download and use the app to learn and conduct colorimetric measurement in their own personal and localized context. For instance, an environmental NGO worker from a low-income country could use the app to perform colorimetric measurement and determine the cleanliness of drinking water samples taken in a river without using an expensive spectrophotometer.

2.2 Pedagogical Underpinning

For formal learning in laboratory experiment, our mobile app design must support the associated learning outcomes, which are as follows:

1. Explain the technique, theory, and building components of colorimetric measurement.
2. Compare the technique of conventional and mobile app colorimetry.
3. Solve analytical science problems using mobile app colorimetry.
4. Develop analytical methods using mobile app colorimetry to address real-life problem.

These four learning outcomes require students to actively *construct* knowledge in colorimetry and *experience* first-hand the use of colorimetry for tackling analytical science and real-life problem. More specifically, these learning outcomes are related to two well-established theories of constructivist learning and experiential learning. Recent work by Parsons (2017) provides a rubric-based framework for guiding and evaluating mobile learning activity design with respect to different learning theories, among which are constructivist and experiential learning. For constructivist learning, Parsons describes that the mobile activity should "involves (inter)active construction of knowledge by learners", and learners should "have control of the learning process, and time and opportunity to reflect and develop personal meaning". For experiential learning, on the other hand, the mobile activity should be "designed around a cycle of experience, observation, conceptualization, and experimentation, transformed through reflection into new knowledge". These guidelines will serve as useful pedagogical underpinnings to guide the colorimetry mobile apps and laboratory experiment design.

3. CONCLUSION

The current study design and create a mobile app that supports active learning in analytical chemistry. Specifically, it makes learning and performing colorimetric measurement more accessible to chemistry students as well as the general public. For further development, a database of different common solutions calibration profiles can be stored on a cloud-base server, which could be accessed by anyone though the mobile app for measuring the concentration of those common solutions. This would help users bypass the calibration process to increase the ease of use. For instance, a housewife could use the app to download the calibration data of off-the-shelf products such as orange juice or salad dressing sauces, and easily measure their concentration using the app to determine whether the sampled product has been diluted. As a result, this app can serve both as an educational and a monitoring tool for the wider general public for causes such as consumer right and environmental protection.

ACKNOWLEDGEMENT

The authors would like to thank the University Grants Committee (UGC) of the HKSAR government for their funding of "Developing Active Learning Pedagogies and Mobile Applications in University STEM Education" (PolyU2/T&L/16-19) under the Funding Scheme for Teaching and Learning Related Proposals (2016-19 Triennium).

REFERENCES

Campos, A.R., Knutson, C.M., Knutson, T.R., Mozzetti, A.R., Haynes, C.L. and Penn, R.L., 2015. Quantifying Gold Nanoparticle Concentration in a Dietary Supplement Using Smartphone Colorimetry and Google Applications. *Journal of Chemical Education*, Vol. 93, No. 2, pp. 318-321.

de Caprariis, P., Barman, C., and Magee, P., 2012. Monitoring the benefits of active learning exercises in introductory survey courses in science: an attempt to improve the education of prospective public school teachers. *Journal of the Scholarship of Teaching and Learning*, Vol. 1, No. 2, pp. 13-23.

Freeman, S., Eddy, S.L., McDonough, M., Smith, M.K., Okoroafor, N., Jordt, H. and Wenderoth, M.P., 2014. Active learning increases student performance in science, engineering, and mathematics. *Proceedings of the National Academy of Sciences*, Vol. *111*, No. 23, pp. 8410-8415.

Hussain, I., Ahamad, K.U. and Nath, P., 2016. Low-cost, robust, and field portable smartphone platform photometric sensor for fluoride level detection in drinking water. *Analytical chemistry*, Vol. 89, No. 1, pp. 767-775.

Kehoe, E. and Penn, R.L., 2013. Introducing colorimetric analysis with camera phones and digital cameras: an activity for high school or general chemistry. *Journal of Chemical Education*, Vol. 90, No. 9, pp. 1191-1195.

Koesdjojo, M.T., Pengpumkiat, S., Wu, Y., Boonloed, A., Huynh, D., Remcho, T.P. and Remcho, V.T., 2015. Cost effective paper-based colorimetric microfluidic devices and mobile phone camera readers for the classroom. *Journal of Chemical Education*, Vol. 92, No. 4, pp. 737-741.

Kontra, C., Lyons, D.J., Fischer, S.M. and Beilock, S.L., 2015. Physical experience enhances science learning. *Psychological Science*, Vol. 26, No. 6, pp. 737-749.

Knutson, T.R., Knutson, C.M., Mozzetti, A.R., Campos, A.R., Haynes, C.L. and Penn, R.L., 2015. A Fresh Look at the Crystal Violet Lab with Handheld Camera Colorimetry. *Journal of Chemical Education*, Vol. 92, No. 10, pp. 1692-1695.

Land, S.M. and Zimmerman, H.T., 2015. Socio-technical dimensions of an outdoor mobile learning environment: a three-phase design-based research investigation. *Educational Technology Research and Development*, Vol. *63*, No. 2, pp.229-255.

Lopez-Ruiz, N., Curto, V.F., Erenas, M.M., Benito-Lopez, F., Diamond, D., Palma, A.J. and Capitan-Vallvey, L.F., 2014. Smartphone-based simultaneous pH and nitrite colorimetric determination for paper microfluidic devices. *Analytical chemistry*, Vol. 86, No. 19, pp. 9554-9562.

Low, L. and O'Connell, M., 2006, September. Learner-centric design of digital mobile learning. *In Proceedings of the OLT Conference*, pp. 71-82.

Parsons, D. and MacCallum, K., 2017. A Learning Theory Rubric for Evaluating Mobile Learning Activities. *International Journal of Online Pedagogy and Course Design (IJOPCD)*, *7*(4), pp.24-38.

Sharples, M., Taylor, J. and Vavoula, G., 2005, October. Towards a theory of mobile learning. *In Proceedings of mLearn*, Vol. 1, No. 1, pp. 1-9.

Zydney, J.M. and Warner, Z., 2016. Mobile apps for science learning: Review of research. *Computers & Education*, Vol. 94, pp.1-17.

EMERGING DOUBLE REPEATED MODEL FOR LANGUAGE LEARNING MOBILE APPS

Norjinbuu Baljinnyam
Beijing Normal University, Beijing China

ABSTRACT

Nowadays technology development is so fast. Among this development, mobile usage, especially number of smart mobile users is rapidly increasing. So more and more researchers study focus on learning users' tendency of mobile phone and mobile app usage. As a result, every year many education-related, especially language learning mobile apps are born. This study is firstly aimed to learn a Chinese language foreigners' mobile apps usage situation, second to analyze popular mobile app types in Chinese language learning, and third tried to suggest emerging language learning app model to double repeated model.

KEYWORDS

Mobile App, Language Learning, Double Repeated Model, Design, Content

1. INTRODUCTION

1.1 Language Learning Mobile Apps

Today, learning foreign languages is one of the main interests and needs of students. It is on one hand because there are plenty of self-study and online study opportunity whenever and wherever, even free of charge. Information technology development already made it possible. Therefore more and more researchers are focusing on making and creating lots of learning mobile APPs. Then plenty of them are language learning apps. For example, among the 2674 publications in the selected journals between 2008 and 2012, 214 of total are related to the usage of mobile technologies in educational field. It was found that the top four applications are for language learning (37/214) (Gwo-Jen Hwang, Po-Han Wu, 2014). Another example is a self-directed language learning program, Duolingo that is used by more than 120 million people around the world, for learning 28 different languages (www.duolingo.com, 2017). 95,5k of its users are learning Chinese. Mobile apps and broad usage in language learning led to the development of the theory of learning foreign languages using mobile technology. For example, the second language acquisition SLA, Mobile Assisted Language Learning (MALL) using mobile phones to learn theory.

1.2 Space Repeated Language Learning

While experimenting with this method since 1932, Professor Mace came to the conclusion that it is simple, but effective technique to memorize new language patterns. Now most of self-study paid apps used a space repeated model.

Spaced repetition is a learning technique that incorporates increasing intervals of time between subsequent reviews of previously learned material in order to exploit the psychological spacing effect. Alternative names include spaced rehearsal, expanding rehearsal, graduated intervals, repetition spacing, repetition scheduling, spaced retrieval and expanded retrieval (Alan D. Baddeley, 1997). If there is no duplication: After one year 33% of the learned knowledge will be forgotten. Two years later 50% will be forgotten etc…

So experts say that up to 90% of today's applications are based on repetitions submitted in this or any other situation (Cull, W. L, 2000).

1.3 Purposes of This Study

This study focused on learning foreigners' usage of mobile apps in China and those apps' design and types, their current situation and found answers to following questions:

- What types of apps are used by Chinese foreign students for learning language?
- What are the designs of those apps used by Chinese foreign students?
- What are problems that encounter self-study of Chinese foreigners?
- What types and designs of apps are needed for language learning foreigners in China?

Finally, it is aimed to give a suggestion of emerging model self-study language learning app design through this research.

2. METHOD

2.1 Participants, Design and Implementation

Study 1, this study used questionnaire survey. The survey covered 96 international students from 13 countries around the world. All the participants are students of different universities of China. 34 of them are male, 62 are female.

Study 2, this study used an exploratory-qualitative-interpretive approach. I chose 40 of Chinese language learning apps, and some of them are dictionary (learning support tool), some are self-learning Chinese, some are quiz apps, etc. 20 of them are paid apps, 20 are not paid app. 29 are Android, 16 are IOS and 5 are possible on double platform.

2.2 Platforms and Instruments

Study 1 survey has 12 sub questions and developed on www.wjx.cn, involved students used Wechat. This sub 12 questions first five is general information, next seven is about app's question.

Study 2, for now, haven't examined those mobile apps' standards and contents, design checker. So I prepared this requirements based on (Catherine R. H,..., 2016) read paper's research used examiner and student requirement and add own design requirement. Next I examined this apps' designs and types.

Table 1. Examine Requirement and Apps' Score (Total 40 Apps, Some App is not Included this table)

Requirements			Duoling	Rosetta	Memris	Penyop	Mindsna	LingoAr	Innovati	Busuu	Hello	LearnP	Hanping Chinese	Pinyin Chart	Memori ze	Phraseb ook	Learn& PlayLan	Learn Chinese	Langua geLearn	MangoL anguage	LearnJa panese/	Learn Chinese
Content	Type	Video	1	1	1	1	1	0	1	1	1	0	0	0	0	0	0	0	1	0	0	0
		Picture	1	1	1	1	1	1	1	1	1	1	1	0	1	1	1	0	1	1	1	0
		Text	1	1	1	1	1	1	1	1	1	1	1	0	1	1	1	1	1	1	1	1
		Systematic content	1	1	1	1	1	0	1	1	1	1	1	1	1	1	1	1	1	1	1	1
		Culture content	1	1	1	0	1	0	0	0	1	1	1	0	0	0	0	0	0	0	0	0
		Vocabulary	1	1	1	1	1	1	1	1	1	0	1	0	1	1	1	1	1	1	1	1
		Pronuncation	1	1	1	1	1	1	1	1	1	1	1	1	1	1	1	1	1	1	0	1
		Grammar content	1	1	1	0	1	0	1	1	1	0	0	0	1	0	0	0	0	0	0	0
		Assessment	1	1	1	1	1	0	0	1	1	0	0	0	1	0	0	0	0	0	1	0
	Output	Alert	1	1	1	0	1	0	0	0	0	0	0	0	0	0	0	0	0	0	0	0
		Listen audio	1	1	1	1	1	1	1	1	1	1	1	1	1	1	1	1	1	1	1	1
		Read content	1	1	1	1	1	1	1	1	1	1	1	0	1	1	1	1	1	1	1	1
		Feedback(output)	1	1	1	0	1	0	0	1	1	0	0	0	1	0	0	0	1	0	0	0
		Study skill results	1	1	1	0	1	0	0	1	1	0	0	0	0	0	0	0	0	0	0	0
	Input	Possible insert word	1	1	0	0	1	0	0	0	1	0	1	0	1	0	0	0	0	0	0	1
		Possible insert voice	1	1	1	0	0	0	0	0	1	0	1	0	0	0	0	0	0	0	0	0
		Possible examine user speak voice	1	1	1	0	0	0	0	0	1	0	1	0	0	0	0	0	0	0	0	0
		Possible examine student writing hand	1	1	0	0	0	0	0	0	1	0	1	0	0	0	0	0	0	0	0	0
Design		Line						1	1	1		1	1	1		1	1		1	1	1	1
		Branched																1				
		Repeated	1	1	1	1	1				1				1							
		Double repeated																				
Type		Dictionary											1									
		Flash cards																				
		Writing characters																				1
		self-study app	1	1	1	1	1	1	1	1	1	1		1	1	1	1	1	1	1	1	
		Pinyin app																				
User		Android	1	1	1	1	0	1	1	1	1	1	1	1	1	1	1	1	1	1	1	1
		IOS	1	1	1	1	1	1	1	1	1	1	0	1	0	1	1	0	1	1	1	0
		offline use	0	0	0	0	0	1	1	1	1	1	1	1	1	1	1	1	0	0	0	1
		Free	1	0	0	0	0	0	0	0	0	0	0	0	0	0	0	0	0	0	0	0
		Total	23	22	20	13	18	11	14	17	22	12	16	8	15	12	12	10	13	11	11	11

2.3 Results

Study 1 role is know, now learn Chinese foreigner used in app's situation. I take this survey after process and based on this survey result did study two. Some important outcomes of the study one are described here. For example: 85.4% of participants answered that they involved in face to face language learning, 8.3% of them learning online, and 29.1% of them are using Chinese language self-study mobile apps. Most of participants are involved in face to face language learning. For those students, they think most useful app is dictionary apps (see chart 1).

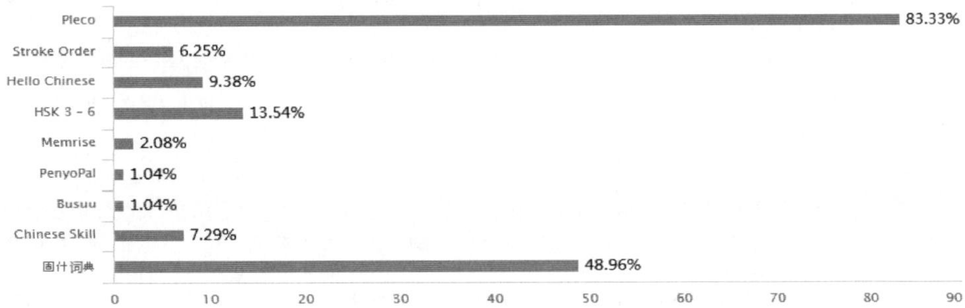

Chart 1. Participants Answer to Chinese Most Useful Language Learning Mobile Apps

Consider the chart 2, “Which of the Chinese language learning mobile apps help you most?” Answers have multiple choices, and 72.9% of the participants answer they use vocabulary learning apps. Because most of participants are involved in face to face learning, more useful apps are dictionary apps. So answers are as following result:

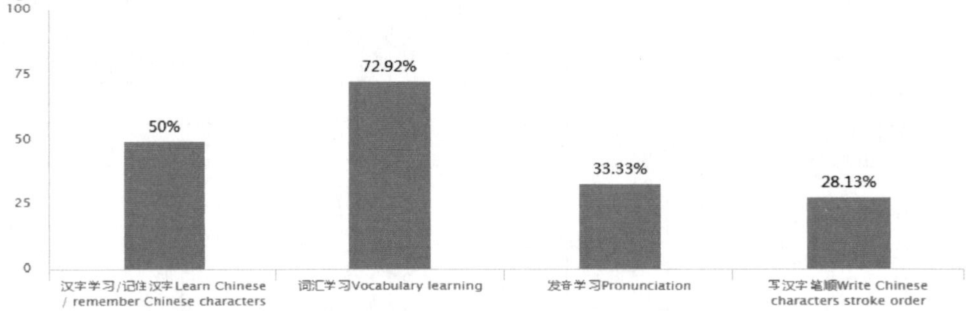

Chart 2. Language Learning Apps’ Usage

Now let’s discuss result of study 2. This study examined content, types of apps that foreigners in China use for language learning. Commonly used mobile apps can be divided into 5 types: Dictionary, Flash cards, Writing characters, Practice apps, Pinyin apps. Most of these apps are one skill based (dictionary, flash card, pinyin, writing hanzi). It means if foreigners choose self-study for learning Chinese using mobile apps, at least three or five apps are needed to be downloaded (some of them are free, some are paid). Another problem is that contents of those apps are not good and not systematic enough. Therefore, foreign students use practice type apps. Those are most comfortable apps for self-study.

The apps on both the Android and IOS platform are the dictionary, pronunciation, write Chinese characters, flash card apps etc… Among them, linear structure mobile app are too many. As well as branch structure, another is the structure repeating self-learning mobile apps.

Linear Structure Mobile apps are one of the supporting tools for face-to-face learning. So design and contents of those apps are simple. There are not many weakness in those apps.

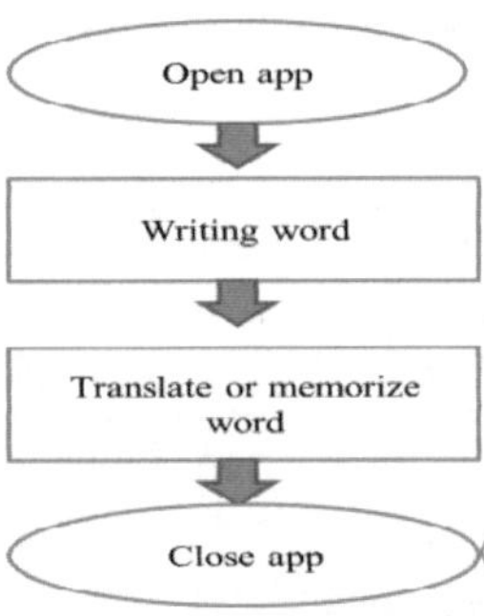

Figure 1. Line Structure

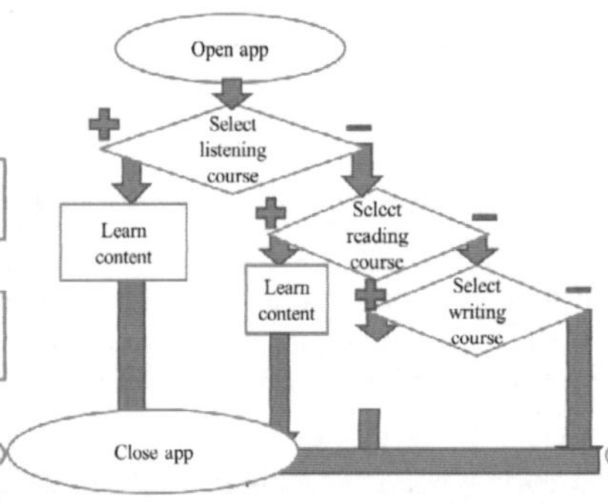

Figure 2. Branched Structure

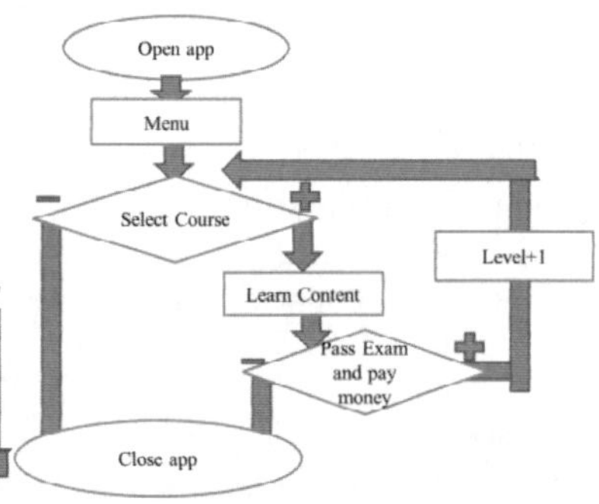

Figure 3. Repeated Structure

Branched mobile apps are rare. Those test mobile apps are created for foreigners for preparing for the HSK(Chinese Proficiency Test) exam.

Repeat structure is self-learning foreign language mobile apps. This kind of mobile apps are most popular and usually paid, as well as independent. Language learning mobile app should have a complex design and content. But current 40 mobile apps’ analysis result shows that most of them are impossible to input information (speaking, writing Chinese characters). So it means self-learners using these apps are only possible to learn to recognize Chinese characters and know what they mean. But learners can’t write Chinese characters and can’t correctly pronounce them. Another problem is that there are design related problems in those apps. Because of design problem, results are low.

The results of other researchers’ study in this field are following: Most of the paid apps focus on direct translation of words and phrases (Patrik Allan, 2017). Our review has shown that, in the commercial apps field, there is a predominant focus on teaching language as separate words rather than contextualized usage.

Most of them use drill-like mechanisms and offer very little explanatory corrective feedback, and there is little adaptation to the needs of individual learners. Despite the advances in language teaching that stress the importance of communicative competence in language learning, MALL technology is still primarily utilized for vocabulary instruction rather than fluency-building (Catherine R. H, …, 2016).

3. DISCUSSION

Now learn foreign language mobile app problems before we introduced. Most problems are content-related, especially related to the relevance between content and design. The reason I'm doing this double-repeat model is to fix the design and content of mobile apps that are now in use. There are also several language learning mobile apps that their design is advanced to a new level.

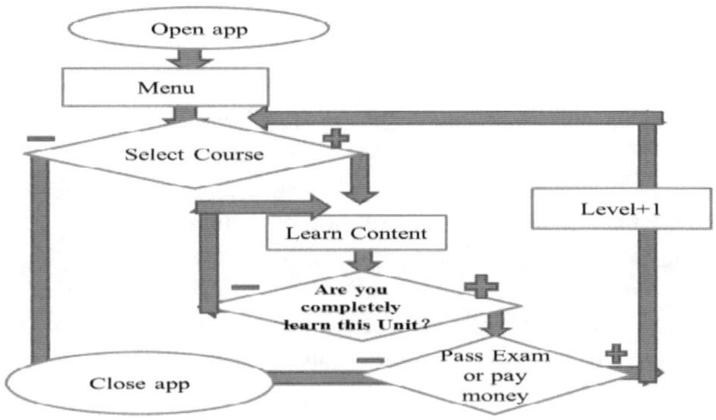

Figure 4. Double Repeated Model

This model is featured by two checkers. One is "Are you ready for the final exam?" Yes, "Take the exam". But how do you know that students are ready for the final exam? (Do you complete this unit?) We can calculate it as following. If students open their mobile app every X1 day and take lesson in listening, speaking, reading and writing, they should learn or master Y1% of contents. Then this means the learner is ready to take exam. Even if students open their mobile apps, but time interval between lessons is too long, this means that learner is impossible to take exam. If students do not participate in class, then those students can't participate in the final exam and are impossible to go up to the next level.

But for now there is no such limitation in currently used mobile apps. When we closely look into the current usage cases of language learning apps, most of the users first download mobile app and learn a few days, and then forget that mobile app. Or open a mobile app to learn one and forget for some time. And then open it and learn after very long time. At that time, they have already forgotten what they learned last time. And their knowledge and skills are less than others and learning process is slower than others.

Figure 5. Now self-learn app used repeated structure (break off)

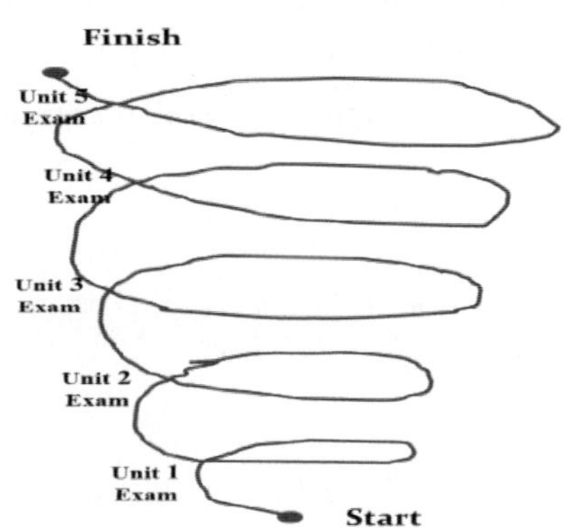

Figure 6. Double repeated model (continuously)

FIGURE 5 LINE: OPEN APP LEARN TIME OR DAYS.
FIGURE 5 SPACE: APP'S CLOSED TIME. LEARNERS' NOT USED DAYS.
FIGURE 6 IF STUDENT'S APP NOT USED DAYS IS MANY, SENT ALERT。
FIGURE 6 IF STUDENTS DON'T LEARN X_2 DAYS, IMPOSSIBLE TAKE EXAM. AFTER EVERY Y_2 DAYS OF CONTINUOUS LEARNING, THEY WILL BE POSSIBLE TO TAKE THE EXAM AND POSSIBLE TO GO UP TO THE NEXT LEVEL.
X1=UNIT.CONTENT / LEARNER.USE.MOBILE.A.DAY.POSSIBLE.LEARN.ABILITY
Y1=UNIT.CONTENT / X1
X2=NOT LEARN DAYS NUMBER
Y2=$\sqrt{X_2}$ LEARNER PRECAUTIONS DAYS

4. CONCLUSIONS

Nowadays there are too many foreign language learning self-study mobile apps. However, most of those apps are paid and used repeated model. This model has its own weakness. It can't control or examine the time interval (not only time interval but also some users' skill) of learning of users. So for that kind of control for improving quality of learning, double repeated model can be used.

As for learning foreign languages, learner the more repeat, the better the result is. All the teachers give one advice to the foreign language learners is that "learn continuously is most useful method".

If we want emerging language learning apps, first, of course, we should focus on this app's content. Content possibly include language learning four skills (speaking, reading, listening and writing), and is based on activities and knowledge (grammar, culture, vocabulary, pronunciation). Another is that they must provide students with feedback. Second important thing that must be considered is the app's design. Double repeated model should be used in designing.

REFERENCES

Alan D. Baddeley, *"Human Memory: Theory and Practice"*, 1997

Crompton, H. (2013). *"A historical overview of mobile learning: Toward learner-centered education"*. In Z. L. Berge & L. Y. Muilenburg (Eds.), Handbook of mobile learning (pp. 3–14). Florence, KY: Routledge.

Trentin G. & Repetto M. (Eds) (2013). *Using Network and Mobile Technology to Bridge Formal and Informal Learning*, Woodhead/Chandos Publishing Limited, Cambridge, UK, ISBN 978-1-84334-699-9.

Catherine Regina Heil, Jason S. Wu, Joey J. Lee, Torben Schmidt (2016). "*A review of mobile language learning applications: trends, challenges and opportunities*", The EUROCALL Review, Volume 24, No. 2, September 2016.

Cull, W. L. Untangling the benefits of multiple study opportunities and repeated testing for cued recall. Applied Cognitive Psychology, 14, 215–235, 2000

Gwo-Jen Hwang, Po-Han Wu *"Applications, impacts and trends of mobile technology-enhanced learning: a review of 2008–2012 publications in selected SSCI journals"*, Mobile Learning and Organisation, Vol. 8, No. 2, 2014

Crescente, Mary Louise; Lee, Doris (March 2011). "*Critical issues of m-learning: design models, adoption processes, and future trends*". Journal of the Chinese Institute of Industrial Engineers. 28 (2): 111–123. doi:10.1080/10170669.2010.548856.

COMPARATIVE STUDY OF THE CONTEXT-AWARE ADAPTIVE M-LEARNING SYSTEMS

Mahnane Lamia, Benmesbah Ouissem and Hafidi Mohamed
LRS laboratory, University of Badji Mokhtar, P.O. Box, 12, 23000, Annaba, Algeria

ABSTRACT

In technology-enhanced learning (Tel), the use of mobile applications is increasing, which improves learning experiences, allowing learners to carry out daily activities anytime and anywhere. However learners might lose interest and motivation to learn using their mobile devices if content adaptation and learning personalization processes are not appropriately designed. This has led to an increasing interest on context-aware adaptive and personalized mobile learning systems aiming to provide learning experiences delivered via mobile devices and tailored to learner's personal characteristics and situation, increasing user satisfaction and facilitating learning achievement. This paper includes the detailed survey about context aware and adaptive m-learning, which serves as the base for new researches in this area.

KEYWORDS

Context-Aware Adaptive, Personalized Mobile Learning Systems, Educational Needs

1. INTRODUCTION

The rapid development of emerging technologies for mobile devices has enabled them to contribute strongly to the creation of new paths for learning; it has drawn the attention of researchers in Technology-enhanced Learning (TeL). They have been interested in investigating how these technologies can be exploited for educational purposes aiming to enhance learning experiences. As a result, this has lead to a research trend which is commonly referred to as Mobile Learning (ML). Context-aware learning has recently got attention of many researchers. It will be a key area for m-learning in the oncoming years because it is moving beyond content delivering in place and it is getting involved with issues surrounding how information from context can be retrieved, stored, represented so as to support tools and services be delivered in optimal ways (Madhubala.R and Akila 2017; Gómez 2013) .

Before this work, many surveys have been conducted on context aware mobile learning systems with diverse perspectives (Baccari, 2015; Hassanov 2017), however, these works reveal two major shortcomings: one is the lack of published surveys on this topic and their missing extension & comprehensiveness since many of them are outdated and do not include newer proposals. The other shortcoming is that there has not been a recent study which would thoroughly analyze contemporary learning environments from the perspective of the two main issues in the design of context-aware adaptive and personalized mobile learning systems, namely, the learner's contextual information that influence adaptations, and the type of adaptations that can be performed based on retrieved learners contextual.

2. BASIC CONCEPT

2.1 Learner's Contextual Information

In this paper, we use the definition of context as a set of entities that constitute the learner's situation:

- Learning context: Includes:
  - **Learning Design**: Learning objectives, pedagogical strategy, learning activities and Resources
  - **Learner profile:** Competence profile (Knowledge, skills, attitudes) role

- Mobile context: Includes Learner temporal information (mood, needs, interest…), People (relationship, role...), Place, Artifact (Technological and non-technological), Time and Physical conditions (noise, illumination…) (Gómez, 2012).

2.2 Type Adaptation

We can identify two main categories of adaptation in context-aware m learning systems: (a) Adaptations related to Educational Resources and (b) Adaptations related to Learning Activities (Gómez. S, 2013):

a. Adaptation of Educational Resources:

- Selection: This type deals with selecting appropriate educational resources and presenting them to the learners based on different learners' contextual elements.
- Presentation: This type considers that educational resources are adaptively structured for access via mobile devices by taking into account parameters related with the learners' type of mobile device, the learner's profile, location, physical conditions

b. Types of adaptations related to Learning Activities:

- General Adaptation: This type of adaptation deals with automatic generation of individual learning activities based on contextual information (Gómez, 2016; Soualah-Alila, 2014; Harchay, 2015).
- Feedback and Support (scaffolding): This type of adaptation includes personalized hints at the right time and suggestion of suitable learning activities depending on different criteria derived from learner's contextual elements (Gómez, 2014).
- Navigation to locations: This type of adaptation includes mostly location-awareness and planning of suitable learning activities in real-world (Hsu, 2015).
- Communication and interaction: Used for finding peers based on their location with whom they can meet virtually, build learning groups and share knowledge or experts with whom they can communicate for asking advice (Gómez. S, 2013)

3. METHOLOGY

3.1 Search Criteria

First, we defined literature search criteria as follows:

- A combination of predefined keywords (e.g., personalized mobile learning systems, context-aware systems, context aware mobile learning);
- Publication time range 2010-2017;
- Type of papers: conference and journal publications;
- Digital libraries/search tools: Google Scholar, Research gate, Freefullpdf, SNDL.

3.2 Classification Criteria

Before the presentation of the overview, we define in this section the criteria of the classification:

- Context acquisition Taxonomy: Sensor (S), Derived (D) and User input (IU).
- Context modeling Taxonomy: There are several popular context-modeling techniques: Key-value, Markup scheme, and Graphical, Object-based, Logic-based, Ontology and Database based models Context entities Taxonomy: previously listed.
- Sensors: We identified six groups of sensors that have been used as sources for context data: RFID/NFC, GPS, Camera, Microphone, IR (infrared)-based sensors, and network (e.g., bandwidth)
- Mobile devices: PDA Smartphone, Tablet
- Adaptation strategy: explained in section 2.

4. OVERVIEW

Here we present an overview of the context aware learning environments. We have focused on two main issues namely, the learner's contextual information that influence adaptations, as shown in table 1.

Table 1. Overview of Context-Aware Learning Environments

System	Description
Gomez et al. (2016)	Delivers contextualized content to the students in nursery, medicine and systems engineering
Gomez et al. (2014)	Supports semi-automatic adaptation of learning activities, particularly for learning English
Hsu et al. (2016)	Able to actively provide the required learning support to individual students when they approach the corresponding real-world learning targets (Museum).
Sevkli et al. (2017)	Leverages the pervasive nature of mobile computing and utilizes context-aware mobile application features to encourage and promote Hadith learning in daily life.
Soualah et al. (2014)	Presents a general architecture that aims to offer a new approach for designing and recommending learning contents as part of industrial training.
Marcelo (2016)	Context4Learning is a mobile application used in educational program based on cloud computing and LMS (Moodle),
Harchay et al 2015	Semantic web-based system that supports personalized self-assessment in mobile environments for computer science students

5. ANALYSIS AND DISCUSSION

We can infer from the results presented in Table 2 that is the most popular clients of the context aware mobile learning environment are PDAs. Their popularity exceeds that of Smartphone, this is probably due to their integration of RFID and NFC reader modules, which made them smart in terms of sensing capabilities.

Location as one of the context dimensions is present in the reviewed contributions that give more attention to the location awareness in the mobile learning systems. In such systems, it is essential that the learning environment can adapt its behavior to match the learner's location by the use of Sensors. The popularity of Location awareness is aligned with the popularity the Spatio-temporal context entity group.

We can also notice from the table that Input user (IU) and Sensors (S) are the most used between the context acquisition methods.

Ontology is the most popular between contexts modeling approaches. Ontology is a very promising instrument for modeling contextual information due to their high and formal expressiveness. We expect that ontology will keep their dominant place as a context modeling approach in context-aware learning environments, although novel approaches based on machine learning are likely to emerge in the future.

In the other hand, it is remarkable that the most used adaptation strategy is the general adaptation, it focuses on not only one specific adaptation aspect but on a general learning process, moreover we can also find out that there is no contribution based completely on the communication and interaction strategy, This type of adaptation helps learners to Find peers based on their location. According to our interpretation, the reason for this is that most context aware learning environments are not developed to be used in closed spaces (classrooms, laboratory...). In fact they represent informal learning environments located beyond the physical space boundaries, in contrary to the principle of communication and interaction adaptation strategy that promotes collaboration between close learners. However as said before, we can find a part of these features integrated in the general adaptation strategy (Gómez, 2016; Soualah 2014; Harchay, 2015), that includes adaptation related to communication.

Table 2. Classification of Context-Aware M learning System

Authors	Adaptation	Context entities							Context modeling	Context acquisition	Sensors	Device
		Learning context	Mobile context									
			LTI	p	Pl	Art	T	PC				
Gomez et al 2016	**Feedback & Support**	√	√		√	√	√	√	Ontology	Ui Sensors	GPS-BLE-QR-RFID	PDA, Smartphone
Gomez et al. 2014	**General Adaptation**	√	√	√	√	√	√	√	Ontology	Ui	/	PDA, Smartphone
Hsu et al. 2016	**Navigation to locations**	√			√		√		DB Rel	UI Sensors	RFID	PDA
Sevkli et al. 2017	**Selection**	√	√		√		√		Ontology	Ui Sensors	GPS	Smartphone
Soualah et al. 2014	**General Adaptation**	√	√		√	√	√	√	Ontology	UI Sensors	Wifi GPS	PDA, Smartphone, Tablette
Marcelo 2016	**Selection**	√			√	√	√	√	/	UI Sensors	Wifi GPS	PDA, Smartphone
Harchay et al 2015	**General Adaptation**	√			√	√	√		Ontology	UI	/	PDA
Bingxue et al 2016	/	√				√			Ontology based, DB (relational)	UI Sensors	/	PDA

LTI: Learner temporal information Art: Artifact T: Time PC: Physical conditions P: People PI: Place

This in-depth analysis can help us to propose our specific learning system with proper structure and functionalities. Synthesizing from the above systems and referring to the relevant work of Gomez we identify four Objectives, which need to be considered when we design a context-aware mobile learning system, including

- O1: Defining a context model for identifying and describing the information that can be used to characterize the situation of a particular entity.
- O2: Implementing context-aware and mobile adaptation processes for both design and delivery approaches of the learning design.
- O3: Designing exemplary context-aware mobile educational scenarios so as to explain and present how possible adaptations can be incorporated.
- O4: Delivering pedagogical-enhanced and structured adaptive and context-aware educational scenarios via mobile devices.

6. CONCLUSION

This paper presented the literature review of context-aware learning systems. This is an active research field that has been produced, since the last decades. We noticed that although, a large body of proposals covering the context- aware learning systems under various different perspectives and some proposals report further enhancements on learning systems, the field still suffer from the major limitation of context-aware learning systems. We believe that this survey will be useful for researchers and practitioners interested in the area of context-aware u- learning system to do research on new dimensions.

REFERENCES

Baccari. S, et al 2015.Comparative Study of the Mobile Learning Architectures. In e-LEOT 2nd EAI International Conference on e-Learning e-Education and Online Training, Novedrate.

Gómez. E et al.2012. Context-Aware Adaptive and Personalized Mobile Learning, *In Advanced Digital Systems and Services for Education and Learning (ASK).*

Gómez. S. E et al.2016. Context-aware adaptive and personalized mobile learning delivery supported by UoLmP, " *Journal of King Saud University-Computer and Information Sciences*, 26(1), 2014, pp. 47-61.

Gómez. S. E. 2013. Learning design Implementation in Context-aware and adaptive Mobile Learning, Doctoral thesis, University of Girona.

Gómez. S. E., et al. 2016. A contextualized system for supporting active learning, *IEEE Transactions on Learning Technologies*, 9(2), pp. 196-202.

Harchay.A et al.2015. A Context-aware Approach for Personalized Mobile Self-Assessment, *J. UCS*, 21(8), pp. 1061-1085.

Hassanov.A and Laine.T. 2017. A Survey of Context-awareness in Learning Environments in 2010-2016, *In Proceedings of the 9th International Conference on Computer Supported Education (CSEDU 2017)*, pp. 234-241.

Hsu. T. Y, et al. 2016. Development and evaluation of an active learning support system for context-aware ubiquitous learning, *IEEE Transactions on Learning Technologies*, 9(1), pp. 37-45.

Hwang. G. J and Tsai. C. C. Research trends in mobile and ubiquitous learning: A review of publications in selected journals from 2001 to 2010, *British Journal of Educational Technology*, 42(4), 2011, pp. 65–70.

Laine.T.H and Joy. M. 2009. Survey on Context-Aware Pervasive Learning Environments, *International Journal of Interactive Mobile Technologies*, 3(1), pp. 70–76.

Madhubala. R and Akila. A. Context Aware and Adaptive Mobile Learning: A Survey, *Advances in Computational Sciences and Technology*, 10 (5), 2017, pp. 1355-1370, 2017 .

Marcelo. C et al. 2016. Learning in mobility with Context4Learning: developing a context-aware mobile learning, " application. International *Journal of Mobile Learning and Organisation*, 10(4), pp. 203-222.

Sevkli. A. Z. et al. 2017. The design and implementation of a context-aware mobile hadith learning system, "*International Journal of Mobile Learning and Organisation*, 11(4), pp. 295-313.

Soualah-Alila. F et al.2014. Context-Aware Adaptive System for M-Learning Personalization, *In IE14 13th International Conference on Informatics in Economy Education.*

Verbert. K et al, 2012. Context-Aware Recommender Systems for Learning: A Survey and Future Challenges, *Learning Technologies, IEEE Transactions on*, 5(4), PP. 318–335.

Reflection Papers

COUNTERFACTUALS, POSSIBLE WORLDS AND SMARTPHONES

Giuseppe Cosimo De Simone
Carovigno, Italy

ABSTRACT

This paper outlines a proposal to use smartphones and counterfactual reasoning to overcome rote and passive learning. Some historians and history teachers have highlighted the usefulness of counterfactual reasoning for a deeper understanding of the past. In a classroom history simulation, it is proposed here that counterfactuals can be developed by a discussion between two groups of students via video call. Counterfactuals and smartphones can be linked by the concept of "possible worlds" conceived within the context of modal logic. Though smartphones are not the only possible technology, they make the experience technically simple and engaging. To conclude, a few critical points in implementing this activity are mentioned.

KEYWORDS

History Teaching, Counterfactuals, Video Calls, Possible Worlds, Simulation

1. THE PROBLEM OF ROTE LEARNING

When teaching and learning are reduced to the transmission and storage of information, many dimensions of knowledge are lost. Bruner, for example, says that «while a body of knowledge is given life and direction by the conjectures and dilemmas that brought it into being and sustained its growth, pupils who are being taught often do not have a corresponding sense of conjecture and dilemma. The task of the curriculum maker and teacher is to provide exercises and occasion for its nurturing» (Bruner 1966, p. 159). A classic example of this problem is history learning, which often consists in the memorization of notions, dates and characters (Jensen 2005). However, mnemonic learning impoverishes the wealth of history. A different way of teaching could be a didactic activity that combines counterfactual reasoning with the use of video calling. In the following paragraphs we will try to link the teaching of counterfactual history with smartphones through the intermediate passage of modal logic.

2. COUNTERFACTUALS AND HISTORIANS

A counterfactual hypothesis consists in imagining an alternative outcome of a historical event which we already know to have occurred in a certain way, e.g. "if Hitler had won the Second World War, he would have landed on the moon". Counterfactuals are often criticized - "History is not made with ifs". However, they are also recognized as being useful both in historical research and in the field of psychology (Wenzlhuemer 2009; Kray et al 2010; Buchsbaum et al 2012). In particular, it has been pointed out that historians often implicitly consider alternative outcomes (Bunzl 2004). Maar (2014) lists three possible advantages in counterfactual experiments: they provide helpful insights, weight different causes and show that history is essentially chaotic. He maintains however that only the second point can have a solid basis. In fact, by comparing what happened with what might have happened, it is possible to highlight the relative importance of some factors. It can also be useful to understand why things turned out in a certain way and not in another. Historical figures were always faced with situations where they had to make choices based on the possibilities given to them. Revisiting the possibilities they were given and those they eventually chose without knowing the outcome, allows us to better understand why they acted as they did, providing an "antidote to determinism" (Ferguson 2011, p. 89). These reflections were transposed by some teachers who, when looking for a way to make the teaching more critical, have also adopted counterfactuals.

3. COUNTERFACTUALS AND TEACHERS

In school education, the need for active teaching that involves collaborative activities and role-playing, as opposed to teacher-centered learning, is recognised (McCarthy and Anderson 2000). When teaching history, we must therefore encourage reflection on alternative scenarios and put the students in the condition to relive the dilemmas of a given historical period (Jensen 2005), "thinking historically" about the past, while considering different perspectives (Stradling 2003; Jackson 2005; Corbeil and Laveault 2011). In this sense counterfactuals can be employed to increase the understanding of historical events (Scott 2011).

An example of application is offered by Huijgen and Holthuis (2014). They proposed that training teachers address the construction of a counterfactual reasoning task to students in their last year of pre-university education. The task consisted of four steps:

1) choosing a historical narrative
2) choosing a point of divergence
3) developing an alternative narrative from the point of divergence
4) comparing the two stories (the real one and the counterfactual).

The authors analyse an example concerning the fall of the Berlin Wall. The point of divergence chosen is the moment in which Harald Jäger, the commander of the border crossing, orders the opening of the border to the crowd of people coming from East Berlin. The alternative scenario reconstructs what may have happened if Jäger had instead given the order of firing at the crowd. Envisaged consequences are: many are wounded, Bush revokes all the disarmament treaties achieved with the USSR, Gorbachev is dismissed and replaced by the head of the KGB Vladimir Kryuchkov who governs the Soviet empire with a firm hand. The Cold War then reaches its lowest point since the Cuban missile crisis and the Wall remains standing.

In order to create interest around the causes, the counterfactuals must be concrete through games or role-playing, and by promoting the discussion among students (Chapman 2003; Chapman and Woodcock 2006). The idea of developing counterfactuals through smartphones recalls both the experience of narratives of Huijgen and Holthuis and the simulations of Chapman. But to do this, we must first go through the modal logic.

4. HOW TO LINK COUNTERFACTUALS AND VIDEO CALLS

For this proposal, it is necessary to translate counterfactuals in "possible worlds", as it is done in modal logic: «a counterfactual (or subjunctive') conditional is an invitation to consider what goes on in a selected 'counterfactual situation'; which is to say, at one other possible world. [...] We can say that a counterfactual conditional 'If it were that A, then it would be that C' is true iff C is true at the selected A-world» (Lewis 1986, pp. 20-21). A counterfactual of the type "if Hitler had won the Second World War, he would have landed on the Moon" is to say "there is at least a possible world in which Hitler won the war and went to the moon". The possible worlds can be interpreted in a more or less metaphorical manner. Kripke. for example, disagrees with the use of the concept of "possible worlds" as "distant planets" and believes that the expression «'possible state (or history) of the world' or 'counterfactual situation'» is preferable (Kripke 1980, p. 15). In our case, however, the possible worlds must be interpreted as if they were "distant planets" from where it is possible to simulate a link.

The application of counterfactuals with smartphones starts by considering the possible worlds as "real" entities (thus not the Kripke's hypothesis). In the classroom situation, we can simulate a trip to one of the infinite alternate worlds. The class is divided into two groups, one group travels to an alternate world while the other stays behind. The link between the two groups will be by video. Let's try to better understand how this would work.

5. COUNTERFACTUALS IN CLASS USING VIDEO CALLS

The two groups of students are: the "travellers" and the "interviewers". Each group is in a different room and will be equipped with a single smartphone through which they will communicate with each other. The group of "travellers" will simulate "a journey to a counterfactual world", as in the Huijgen and Holthuis example, where a world materialises after Jäger fires at the crowd. The group of interviewers will begin with questions such as "What can you see?", "How is the situation over there?". They then move on to the whys, e.g. "Why are things as they are?".

At least four phases should be included:

1) a first phase of historical documentation on the fall of the Berlin Wall is performed by the entire class (duration of two lessons)

2) the teacher will have to choose a point of divergence from which to start the possible world (in our example, it was the decision of Jäger firing at the crowd)

3) then the two groups are created (the "travellers" and the "interviewers"). Each group will have a week to prepare a response to what happens after the point of divergence which will have been decided by the teacher. The "travellers" will construct and "prepare to defend" an alternative world starting from the point of divergence. The group of "travellers" are free to choose whichever alternate world, as well as the consequences of the decision to shoot. One possibility is the one seen in Huijen and Holthuis, but there are also other outcomes. This creates a surprise effect because the "interviewers" should study and "prepare to attack" an alternative world they do not know exists up to the moment of contact. The alternative world constructed by the "travellers" foresees some documentation and elements of creativity. First there is the knowledge of the context, the characters and their motivations (which serve to explain the possible reactions of Bush and Gorbachev in the counterfactual world). The part of creativity instead arises from the construction of a narrative (White 1978; 1987) and representation of the alternative world given by the students. Once connected through video calling, they can use costumes or symbolic objects from the alternative world, read articles in newspapers or testimonies (ones they had previously created). The video call allows them to add a visual dimension which gives the students room to be creative (e.g. by getting dressed in accordance with the fashion of the time, by displaying objects from that world or adding filters, such as clack and white, etc.).

The connection will occur with the use of two smartphones and one of the many apps that allow you to video chat (i.e. WhatsApp, Skype, Messenger, Hangouts, etc.): one in the room of the "interviewers" and one in the room of "travellers". The use of the smartphones in this proposal is not the only possible option. Obviously a computer or a tablet could be used instead, but the cameras of the smartphone (even the front ones) often provide a better quality. Though the smartphone screen is smaller, it can be linked to an Interactive Whiteboard or a projector.

Although smartphones offer many possible applications at school, their basic purpose as a communication device is sometimes underrated. The activity presented in this paper uses the smartphone as a "simple" means for video calling, facilitating a didactic experience that can be both immersive and significant.

4) Finally the video call can be recorded (for example using a screen recording app) and then loaded onto a page especially created in Facebook. The page will collect and store all the "travels in possible worlds" staged from different classes and schools. The posted travels may be commented by students themselves, highlighting the strengths and weaknesses of each video link. This creates a wider environment of discussion of historical topics, thus recovering the sense of the dilemma mentioned by Bruner.

6. SOME QUESTIONS

Many questions, both practical and theoretical, emerge. We mention three.

1) What will the discussion between the two groups be based on? Also, how should the "travellers" "defend" the alternative world that they themselves have built and the "interviewers" "attack"? Bunzl (2004) comes to our aid. He distinguishes good counterfactuals (based on the laws of nature or the considerations of rationality) from bad counterfactuals (more linked to the imagination). He affirms that every counterfactual can be translated in a causal claim and it is on this causal link that our judgement on the validity of the counterfactual hypothesis must be drawn. The "travellers" and the "interviewers" should discuss the soundness of the assumptions that support the constructed world. For example, let's say that "travellers" build a world in which after firing at the crowd, "Bush retracts agreements on disarmament". This decision can be translated as "agreements were based on fragile foundations and easily revocable". This causal link can be debated by the students on the basis of the research that were carried out previously.

2) How can the teacher evaluate an experience of this kind? One thing to keep in mind is that teachers would have the video recording at their disposal to calmly analyse various aspects such as the participation of the individual kids and the soundness of their interventions. But another solution is to set up the experience as a competition between various teams of "travellers" and "interviewers", and who would be evaluated on Facebook by the students themselves.

3) At what age is it possible to propose this experience? It is necessary to consider the psychological development of students. In the light of experiences from previously made counterfactuals, it would appear that high school students are the preferable target age group.

REFERENCES

Bruner, J., 1966. *Toward a Theory of Instruction*. The Belknap Press of Harvard University Press, Cambridge.

Buchsbaum, D. et al, 2012. The power of possibility: causal learning, counterfactual reasoning, and pretend play. *Philosophical Transactions of The Royal Society B*, Vol. 367, pp. 2202-2212.

Bunzl, M., 2004. Counterfactual History: A User's Guide, *The American Historical Review*. Vol. 109, pp. 845-858.

Chapman, A., 2003. Camels, diamonds and counterfactuals: a model for teaching causal reasoning. *Teaching History* 112, pp. 46-53.

Chapman, A. and Woodcock, J., 2006. Mussolini's missing marbles: simulating history at GCSE. *Teaching History* 124, pp. 17-27.

Corbell, P. and Laveault, D., 2011. Validity of a Simulation Game as a Method for History Teaching. *Simulation & Gaming*, Vol. 42, No. 4, pp. 462-475.

Ferguson, N. (ed.), 2011. *Virtual History*. Penguin Books, London.

Huijgen, T. and Holthuis, P., 2014. Towards bad history? A call for the use of counterfactual historical reasoning in history education. *Historical Encounters: A journal of historical consciousess, historical cultures, and history education*, Vol. 1, No. 1, pp. 103-110.

Jackson, N., 2005. Creativity in History Teaching and Learning, Subject Perspectives on Creativity in Higher Education. Working Paper. Available from: http://www.creativeacademic.uk/uploads/1/3/5/4/13542890/creativity_in_history.pdf [Accessed 9/02/2018]

Jensen, B. E., 2005. Counterfactual History and its Educational Potential. In: P. Kemp, ed., *History in Education. Proceedings from the Conference History in Education* (Held at the Danish University of Education, 24-25 March 2004), Danish University of Education Press, Copenhagen.

Kray, L. J. et al, 2010. From What Might Have Been to What Must Have Been: Counterfactual Thinking Creates Meaning. *Journal of Personality and Social Psicology*, Vol. 98, No. 1, pp. 106-118.

Kripke, S., 1980. *Naming and necessity*. Harvard University Press, Cambridge.

Lewis, D. K., 1986. *On the Plurality of Worlds*. Blackwell, Oxford.

Maar, A., 2014. Possible Uses of Counterfactual Thought Experiments in History. *Principia – An International Journal of Epistemology*, Vol. 18, No. 1, pp. 87-113.

McCarthy, J. P. and Anderson, L., 2000. Active Learning Techniques Versus Traditional Teaching Styles: Two Experiments from History and Political Science. *Innovative Higher Education*, Vol. 24, No. 4, pp. 279-294.

Roberts, S. L., 2011. Using Counterfactual History to Enhance Students' Historical Understanding. *The Social Studies*, Vol. 102, No. 3, pp. 117-123.

Stradling, R., 2003. *Multiperspectivity in History teaching: a guide for teachers*. Council of Europe. Available from: https://rm.coe.int/1680493c9e [Accessed 9/02/2018].

Wenzlhuemer, R., 2009. Counterfactual Thinking as a Scientific Method. *Historical Social Research*, Vol. 34, No. 2, pp. 27-54.

White, H., 1978. The Historical Text as Literary Artifact. In: H. White. *Tropics of Discourse: Essays in Cultural Criticism*, John Hopkins University Press, Baltimore, pp. 81-100.

White, H., 1987. The Value of Narrativity in the Representation of Reality. In: H. White. *The Content of the Form: Narrative Discourse and Historical Representation*, John Hopkins University Press, Baltimore, pp. 1-25.

OPPORTUNITIES AND CHALLENGES OF USING AMAZON ECHO IN EDUCATION

Neil Davie and Tobias Hilber
South Westphalia University of Applied Sciences
Lindenstrasse 53, 59872 Meschede, Germany

ABSTRACT

This paper offers a first look at the opportunities and challenges for educators offered by the Amazon Echo smart speaker. As with all new technologies, educators have been quick to wonder how and if it could be adopted for use in educational contexts. Although at present most Amazon Echo and compatible devices need to be connected to mains electricity and are therefore relatively immobile, the Echo is designed to be switched on and left on permanently meaning that it conforms with the ubiquity often given as a defining factor of mobile learning. A review of articles as well as personal experiments will explore the possibilities Echo offers, especially with regard to language learning, and attempt to clarify whether it does offer teachers and students an additional value in the classroom. The issue of privacy is also discussed.

KEYWORDS

Amazon, Echo, Alexa, Language Learning, Skills

1. INTRODUCTION

The original Amazon Echo device was given a limited US-only launch in 2015 and has since become available in 36 countries, including Canada, the UK, Germany and Portugal. Described as a smart speaker, the Echo reacts to voice instructions, then uses Amazon's Alexa operating system to connect to Amazon's servers to make queries and carry out commands.

2. THE AMAZON ECHO

Since the launch of the original Amazon Echo, the product has expanded to include a whole range of different devices, as shown in Table 1. Amazon has also licensed the Alexa software so that other companies like Sonos and Harman Kardon have also launched Alexa-power devices, these tend however to be high-range smart speaker systems.

Table 1. Amazon Echo & Alexa Devices

Device	Price (US $ - Feb 2018)	Features
Echo Dot	49.99	Wifi, small size
Echo (2nd generation)	99.99	Wifi, larger speaker
Echo Show	229.99	Screen & camera
Echo Look	199.99	Camera, no screen
Amazon Tap	129.99	Battery, Bluetooth
Fire TV Stick	39.99	TV required
Fire Tablet	49.99-149.99	7, 8 or 10" tablet

2.1 Requirements

The Amazon Echo is an internet-connected smart device running the Alexa software. A compatible internet connection which the device can connect to by wifi is the first operating requirement. Unfortunately, the Enterprise network in our university was not compatible with the Echo Dot we tested. Furthermore, an Amazon account is required in order to setup, configure and use the device. This configuration is done using the Amazon Echo app installed on a compatible smartphone. During the setup process the user can select the language the Echo should use (which also affects the range of functions available) as well as the "wake word" – the spoken command which causes the device to come out of sleep mode and await your command.

2.2 Standard Alexa Skills

The programs or commands which Alexa can perform (like the apps on a smartphone) are called "skills". Setting up the Echo with English as the chosen language brings a range of skills which can be used in the classroom. At its simplest, the Echo can perform classroom management tasks like setting a timer. The timer can be paused and when requested will say how much time is remaining. Alexa can also pick a number or flip a coin which could both be used to choose an activity or select student from a group. There are also built-in commands which could be of special interest to language learners. For example, Alexa can act as a dictionary by asking "Alexa, what is the definition of...?" a chosen word and the device will (attempt to) give an answer or by being asked "Alexa, how do you spell...?". It is also possible to use the Echo as a thesaurus by asking "Alexa, what is a synonym for...?" the word of your choice. Additional skills for language learning are also available. Most commonly these are Flashcard-style services typically link to established sites like Quizlet or Chegg. In addition, an Echo device can also be used to play listening comprehension audio files or calming music for relaxation or quiet study time.

3. LITERATURE REVIEW

The review of articles on the use of Amazon Echo in education found that only Echo Dot and Echo devices have reportedly been put into use. Reasons for this could be the lower costs of the devices, the fact they have been available the longest, and that due to the lack of camera they do not cause as many concerns about privacy. Due to the smaller speaker the Echo Dot has been found to be more suited to a smaller classroom or when attached to an external speaker. The Echo (2nd generation) has a larger speaker and is loud enough to be used with no additional speakers. The articles found covered pre-school, school and higher education levels. Arias (2017) explored the possibilities of using Echo to help a five-year-old daughter learn English as a foreign language. The interaction with Alexa was exciting and fun, a sentiment also expressed by Ellis (2017) with regard to classroom use. In addition, the possibility to use Echo to replace routine classroom tasks like selecting pupils or practicing vocabulary in preparation for standard tests.

An important distinguishing feature of the Amazon Echo is the voice interface which means that no special control system or commands have to be learnt. Learningabledkids (2017) emphasize this as being a benefit for children with reading difficulties, for example, people with dyslexia and non-readers. Selak (2017) emphasizes that this simplicity allows first and second-grade students to have more control over their own learning and thereby free their teachers up to deal with more complicated tasks.

The very uniqueness of this device is however also identified as a weakness in several articles. Although Metz (2017) finds that even pre-kindergarten children now have access to huge amounts of information, the voice activation interface

"...can still be difficult even for the clearest-speaking adults, and young kids often don't enunciate that well"

Selak adds that managing expectations is an important factor in introducing the Echo to the classroom – the device will not be able to understand and answer all questions and students should not expect it to. In addition, there is presently no way to limit the content the device has access to or restrict what it does.

4. CUSTOM SKILLS

Amazon themselves have also identified the educational potential of Echo and Alexa. They even describe it as being a transformational technology. One of the first tutorials published by Amazon to encourage educational use provides a six-step model to develop a quiz application. This quiz allows educators, having created the necessary Amazon developer accounts, to copy and paste the Javascript code to create a quiz skill about the topic of their choice. The example skill is a quiz about the states of the US, their capitals and the year they joined the United States. In addition to acting as a quiz, the skill can also act as a reference work and give details when asked about a particular state.

Once the appropriate accounts have been created, reusing the existing code is a simple process. Providing a set of questions and answers already exist it is possible to create a fully-functional quiz within an hour. Apart from editing the text, an icon and skill description for the appstore are required. As a test, we adapted the sample to create a quiz about Scotland to use with students ahead of an excursion. The students all found using the Echo and the skill to be entertaining and different. As previous articles have suggested, especially for non-native English speakers, there were problems with the voice recognition which caused the skill to misunderstand an answer or judge a correct answer to be false. Students however adapted to this limitation and accepted it.

5. PRIVACY

Only one of the articles examined mentioned the topic of privacy (Simpson, 2017). In order to function correctly the Echo device has to be permanently switched on, connected to the internet and listening for its wake word command. According to Amazon it will only then become active. Security experts (Wueest, 2017, Stegner, 2018) have however raised concerns about this and the potential risk of the devices being abused by hackers too. There are also reports of Echo devices randomly speaking or of adding items to shopping lists without being asked to.

6. REVISING MODELS FOR EVALUATING TEACHING TECHNOLOGY

The prevalent models of technology acceptance, Davis's TAM (1989) and Venkatesh's UTAUT model (2003), include neither cost nor privacy which are now very real concerns for educators wanted to introduce new technologies into their classrooms. It would therefore seem wise to add these factors when considering the use of a device like the Amazon Echo. Both cost and privacy are relative factors which have to be considered in relationship to the perceived educational benefits of the device, see figure 1. If the lower cost Echo Dot device is acceptable for an institution then cost will play a less important role. If a more expensive model is required then the educational benefits would need to be higher to outweigh the negative concerns.

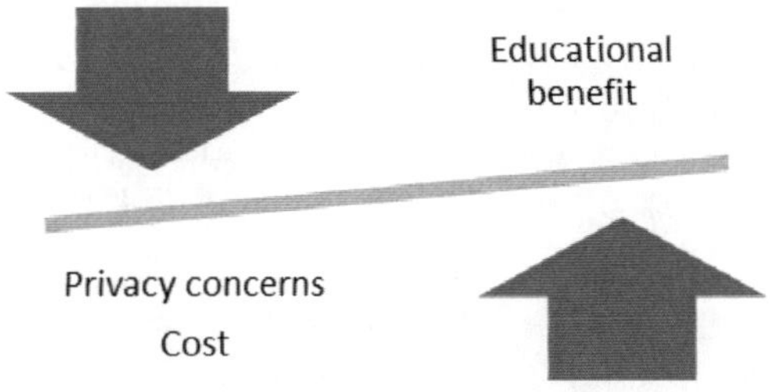

Figure 1. Teacher Considerations

7. CONCLUSION

The most fundamental requirement for using an Amazon Echo in the classroom is a functioning internet connection. The compatibility problems with Enterprise networks mean that for some schools this rules out the use of such devices. If a connection is available, the school, teacher, parents and pupils all have to be aware of the potential privacy issues regarding the use of such a device. The built-in and additional skills already available offer basic functions to both students and learners alike. The problems of speech recognition can present a challenge but they do also encourage students to think about their pronunciation and how human-computer interaction works.

Further scientific work will be required to establish the genuine and longer-term benefits of the Amazon Echo. However, the initial findings suggest it can be a useful addition to the classroom.

REFERENCES

Alhadlaq, A. et al. 2017 *Privacy in the Amazon Alexa Skills Ecosytem.* https://petsymposium.org/2017/papers/hotpets/amazon-alexa-skills-ecosystem-privacy.pdf

Amazon.com. 2018 *Alexa in education.* https://developer.amazon.com/de/alexa/education

Amazon.com. 2018 *Build an Alexa Quiz Game Skill in Six Steps.* https://developer.amazon.com/public/solutions/alexa/alexa-skills-kit/content/quiz-game-skill

Arias, C. 2017 *How I am improving my daughter's English skills using Amazon Echo.* https://medium.com/@caioarias/how-i-am-improving-my-daughters-english-skills-using-amazon-echo-f5eeca3ce245

Blankenburg, J. 2017 *Technical Tutorial: Build an Alexa Quiz Game Skill Using Our New Template.* https://developer.amazon.com/de/blogs/alexa/post/fa962f53-4d7e-47a2-933b-302b833d716c/technical-tutorial-build-an-alexa-quiz-game-skill-using-our-new-template

Davis, F.D. 1989 *Perceived Usefulness, Perceived Ease of Use, and User Acceptance of Information Technology.* MIS Quarterly, Vol. 13, No. 3 (Sep., 1989), pp. 319-340. https://www.jstor.org/stable/249008

Druga, S. et al. 2017 *"Hey Google is it ok if I eat you?" Initial explorations in child-agent interaction.* https://www.media.mit.edu/publications/hey-google-is-it-ok-if-i-eat-you-initial-explorations-in-child-agent-interaction/

Ellis, B. 2017 *Alexa: Your new teaching assistant.* https://www.tcea.org/blog/alexa-teacher-assistant/

Erin*tegration. 2016 *Using the Amazon Echo Dot and Alexa in the classroom.* https://www.erintegration.com/2016/12/26/amazon-echo-dot-and-alexa-in-the-classroom/

Kim, J. 2017 *How the Amazon Echo Show Will Revolutionize Higher Education.* https://www.insidehighered.com/blogs/technology-and-learning/how-amazon-echo-show-will-revolutionize-higher-education

Learningabledkids. 2017 *Amazon Echo enables your child's learning independence.* http://learningabledkids.info/assistive-technology/amazon-echo-for-independent-learning/

Metz, R. 2017 *Growing up with Alexa.* https://www.technologyreview.com/s/608430/growing-up-with-alexa/

Morris, K. 2017 *30 ways to use Amazon Echo Dot in the classroom.* https://kaysemorris.com/30-ways-use-alexa-classroom/

Nazerian, T. 2017 *Amazon Pushes Echo Smart Speakers on Campus.* https://www.edsurge.com/news/2017-08-28-amazon-pushes-echo-smart-speakers-on-campus

Selak, B. 2017 *Amazon Alexa in the classroom.* http://www.coolcatteacher.com/amazon-alexa-classroom/

Simpson, J. 2017 *Amazon Echo in education?* http://www.edugeek.net/blogs/simpsonj/2291-amazon-echo-education.html

Stegner, B. 2018 *7 Ways Alexa and Amazon Echo Pose a Privacy Risk.* https://www.makeuseof.com/tag/alexa-amazon-echo-privacy-risk/

Venkatesh, V. et al. 2003 *User Acceptance of Information Technology: Toward a Unified View.* MIS Quarterly, Vol. 27, No. 3 (Sep., 2003), pp. 425-478. http://aisel.aisnet.org/misq/vol27/iss3/5/

Warren, E. 2016 *30 ways the Amazon Echo can assist struggling learners.* https://learningspecialistmaterials.blogspot.de/2016/02/30-ways-amazon-echo-can-assist.html

Wueest, C. 2017 *Everything You Need to Know About the Security of Voice-Activated Smart Speakers.* https://www.symantec.com/blogs/threat-intelligence/security-voice-activated-smart-speakers

TACIT KNOWLEDGE IN VIRTUAL UNIVERSITY LEARNING ENVIRONMENTS

Cathrin Vogel[1], Birgit Großer[2], Ulrike Baumöl[1] and Theo J. Bastiaens[2]
[1]FernUniversität in Hagen , Universitätsstr. 41, Hagen, Germany
[2]FernUniversität in Hagen , Universitätsstr. 33, Hagen, Germany

ABSTRACT

Knowledge work has become a major component of value creation, especially in industrialized countries. Processing knowledge in virtual ways becomes increasingly possible with emerging technological innovations. This leads to the important question, how to transmit elusive tacit knowledge in a virtual setting. Education at universities benefits from the use of virtual environments for passing on knowledge, such as by setting up MOOCs and using learning apps. How to manage tacit knowledge in virtual learning environments as well as how to prepare students for virtual organizational knowledge processes become crucial. Although knowledge management and processes have already been widely analyzed, research on harvesting tacit knowledge in virtual educational environments is still rare, in particular regarding the use of intelligent tutor systems for knowledge management processes. Therefore, the central question addressed in this paper is, how university knowledge processes concerning tacit knowledge can be supported by intelligent systems, such as bots and tutor systems.

KEYWORDS

Virtual Teams, Tacit Knowledge, Education, Learning Environment, Intelligent Tutor Systems, Educational Bots

1. INTRODUCTION

Universities work on adapting to the needs of a new generation of students. And new technological solutions provide efficient environments for teaching a growing student body, as well as enabling mobile learning. Especially studying mobile and remotely and forming virtual teams (VTs) allows students to integrate their studies into their lives while still being able to choose from rich options of universities and fields of study (Benson & Samarawickrema, 2009). Studying in VTs induces new chances and challenges for learners and lecturers alike regarding the processing of knowledge. In this paper, we focus on virtual teams as an option for organizing knowledge work in teaching and learning processes and consider the ensuing consequences for capturing tacit knowledge (TK). We want to understand the mechanisms of processing the valuable but elusive TK in an individual knowledge environment, such as in the context of mobile academic learning processes. When focusing on virtual work, the deployed information and communication technology (ICT) plays a major role. Therefore, we aim at deriving guidance for how to manage TK in the knowledge processes of virtual teams in a university learning environment with a special focus on deploying bots and intelligent tutor systems (ITS) as technological enabler. Thus, we concentrate on how these technologies relying on artificial intelligence can support these processes. As a consequence, we aim to answer the following question:

How can bots and ITS support the processing of Tacit Knowledge in a virtual university learning environment?

In order to answer the question, knowledge processes regarding TK for virtual teams are analyzed (Chapter 2). A framework and approaches for knowledge processes regarding TK in virtual learning environments (VLE) are constructed (Chapter 3). Finally, a discussion, possible limitations, as well as suggestions for future research are presented (Chapter 4).

2. CONCEPTUALIZATION

Tacit knowledge is regarded to enable people to create ideas through their experience of the past and anticipation of the future. This ability is crucial for developing advanced and innovative ideas (Leonard & Sensiper, 1998). To show how to support knowledge management processes, in particular TK in virtual settings, the concepts of tacit knowledge, knowledge processes and virtual learning environment (VLE) are presented in the following. Then the state of the art on managing TK in knowledge processes of VTs in university settings is described.

Virtual teams are not only used by organizations as an additional way of organizing work but as driver for meeting requirements of a future workforce and so staying competitive. That also applies for universities and the way education is designed. The options reach from partly virtual forms of learning processes (e.g., blended learning, flipped classroom) to a fully VLE (e.g., online mobile learning). Researchers strive to reveal the dynamics and dependencies regarding processing of TK in VTs, e.g., Alavi and Tiwana (2002) as well as Leonard and Sensiper (1998). Being able to analyze and process knowledge in virtual teams is of major importance for modern mobile learning settings and thus requires further insights on how to support the processing of tacit knowledge in virtual teams.

Knowledge can be regarded as a construct that consists of both, tacit knowledge and explicit knowledge (EK), with varying proportions (Virtanen, 2013). A difference between tacit knowledge and EK is that explicit knowledge focuses on how knowledge is organized while TK focuses on practice, on how work is done. Examples of TK are experiences, strategic thinking, and ideas (Liu, et al., 2008; Martins & Meyer, 2014).

TK cannot always be passed on easily via written documents (Martins & Meyer, 2014) as educational media, human interaction is needed for creating, retaining and transferring TK in VLE. The ways of human interaction in VLE are different for virtual teams compared to traditional teams. In traditional teams, students meet during lectures and study groups and can learn from each other. ICT, as for instance collaboration tools (e.g., Slack), established video call applications (e.g., Adobe Connect), or intelligent tutoring systems (e.g., AutoTutor) preserve the support for gaining experience for mobile and distance communication and enable virtual teamwork (Schweitzer & Duxbury, 2010; Rossi & Fideli, 2012). Thus, knowledge related processes need to be designed differently, if the teams in focus work virtually, due to the nature of tacit knowledge and prerequisites of virtual teams and their ICT use.

Knowledge processes use knowledge as object of alteration. Many different concepts of knowledge processes are derived in literature. The distinction of knowledge processes into creation, retention, transfer and application is common (Fang, et al., 2014) and allows for allocating all knowledge related activities to these processes. EK uses structured elements, e.g., documents, to retain and transfer data (Liu, et al., 2008). These can be used directly or altered for subsequent use, following explicated rules. TK is "stored" individually in people as carriers, and does exist even if not recognized consciously (Stenmark, 2000; Diptee & Diptee, 2013). Here, the carriers are the students as well as the lecturers. Regarding the use of ICT, explicit knowledge is primarily represented by documented information, whereas TK is already involved through the ways carriers of the tacit knowledge actually approach and use the available ICT (Alter, 2010). *Creation* of tacit knowledge is the process of generating new knowledge (Hao, et al., 2016). Knowledge creation can as also be a conversion of already existing knowledge into new knowledge. These conversion processes are based on human interaction (Nonaka & Takeuchi, 1995; Liu, et al., 2008). Knowledge can be *retained* through holding on to students and lecturers (Leonard & Sensiper, 1998) and supporting the transfer of knowledge (Martins & Meyer, 2014). This applies especially to tacit knowledge, as TK cannot easily be stored detached from the carrier without prior conversion to explicit knowledge. This conversion includes, e.g., discussions and written documentation. Knowledge *transfer* refers to the transfer between applications by the same person or team and to the transmission of knowledge from one person or team to another (Argote & Ingram, 2000). Considering a VLE, knowledge is transferred between students as well as from lecturer to student. ICT, such as chat rooms and virtual classrooms support the transfer of knowledge within their VTs. Factors influencing the transfer of TK are, e.g., trust, reciprocity and organizational structure (Hao, et al., 2016). The process of knowledge *application* regarding TK in a university setting is presented by solving tasks or guiding fellow students (Kapur, 2008; Bohle Carbonell, et al., 2014). TK is crucial for being able to recognize limits of and gain new strategies for problem solving (Kapur, 2008; De Arment, et al., 2013).

These conditions are necessary for dealing with and making decisions within a fast-changing environment with unknown parameters (Venkitachalam & Busch, 2012).

The idea of using ICT for supporting tacit knowledge processes is discussed in literature (Venkitachalam & Busch, 2012; Butler, 2016). Insights conclude that ICT supports online communication with non-verbal information, like video-calls and in virtual worlds (Ketcha, et al., 2015). Another study finds ITS useful for supporting teamwork and collaborative problem solving to enhance shared mental models (Sottilare, et al., 2017). To follow up this discussion, Venkitachalam and Busch (2012) as well as Ketcha et al. (2015) state that empirical studies focusing on the connection between TK processes and ICT are required.

By enlightening the role of TK in a VLE, we aim to describe approaches for lecturers in universities who strive for transmitting TK via bots. The benefits of VLEs, e.g., independence in time and place, stand against the segregation between the learners as well as the learner and the lecturer. The more teaching happens online, the more flexible it can be, but the more not only physical but also psychic distance between the participants is inherent (Benson & Samarawickrema, 2009). Addressing this challenge, suitable educational methods for the use of bots for teaching is presented in the following.

3. EDUCATIONAL BOTS FOCUSING ON TACIT KNOWLEDGE

Regarding the main question, the role of bots in supporting tacit knowledge processes in VLEs is described in the following. The terms ITS and bots, as used here, differ in one important aspect: ITS have been used for about 25 years for supporting particular non-complex learning (Rossi & Fideli, 2012). Traditional ITS are currently being enhanced with machine learning technology, resulting in systems mostly (and here) called bots. Both belong to the cluster of Artificial Intelligence Tools (Rossi & Fideli, 2012) and are educational tools that can be used to enhance TK creation, retention, transfer, and application. To simplify reading and because all assumptions we make are valid for bots and ITS alike, we will now only use the term "bot" for both characteristics. In general, bots are computer programs that provide individualized instructions by being able to connect the user's input with given information (Rossi & Fideli, 2012). They are deployed in diverse subject areas (e.g., algebra, medicine, law, reading), helping learners acquire domain-specific, cognitive and metacognitive knowledge. Some advantages are the immediacy and response-specificity of feedback, more opportunities for practice and feedback, an increase of learner control as well as individualized task selection (Ma, et al., 2014). The role of ICT becomes crucial when managing TK in virtualized knowledge processes. Figure 1 shows the relationships between the knowledge processes with respect to managing TK and the ensuing need to document and communicate knowledge in a virtual team setting. Documentation and communication can be done via bots. Insights on using bots for notably enhancing the creation, retention and transfer of TK are provided. Therefore, some existing educational approaches are introduced that are suitable for supporting TK-learning via ICT.

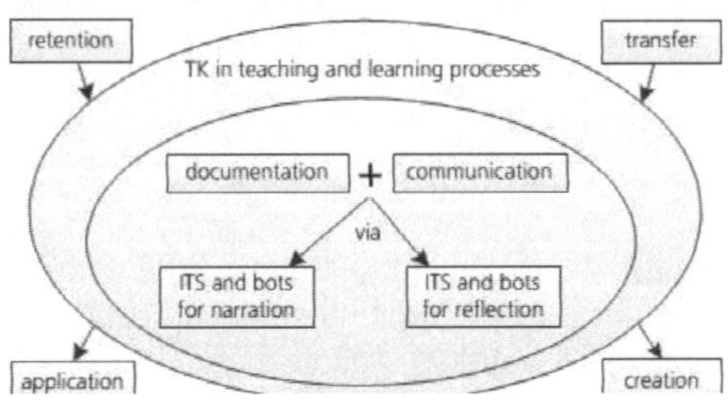

Figure 1. Documentation, Communication and the ICT Support as Enabler of Knowledge Processes

Students work together virtually and also need to share their knowledge and experiences virtually. The task of a lecturer is to prepare content and create possibilities of sharing TK in virtual teamwork to provide TK processes. In VLE, in which blended or mobile online learning defines the structures of teaching and learning, holistic contact is minimal (Falloon, 2012). Asynchronous communication as well as synchronous media-supported communication potentially lead to a lack of structure and intended meaning of information (Morgan, et al., 2014; Butler, 2016).

It is possible to enhance the existing knowledge system through information given by students, facilitators and employees with the proposed artificial intelligence tools. Narratives can be taught to the machine which is then able to build clusters from the information given. Bots have the advantage to be able to store knowledge that is encoded in spoken language, reducing the effort to express TK in written symbols (Lane & VanLehn, 2005): the need to have a continuous and consequent transparency of TK as well as the high effort for documenting TK (Rossi & Fideli, 2012, Bastiaens, et al., 2014). The systems are also able to recognize patterns in the narrations and store the respective information. This mechanism simplifies the search for information by assigning patterns found in an inquiry to patterns of stored information automatically. As a consequence, the transfer of TK from a database to a person and the awareness for and retrieval of existing knowledge can be supported (Rossi & Fideli, 2012). In addition to this, students teaching an avatar (teachable agent) supports the students' reflection of their knowledge and their skills to explicit meaningful patterns and converts TK to EK (Pipitone, et al., 2012). This also supports the students in being aware of the limitations of their own thinking and the willingness to communicate and reflect on competencies and limitations in, e.g., VTs which again supports TK processes (De Arment, et al., 2013). Though these are all valid advantages of using bots in academic teaching, the effort of developing such a setting and the necessity of working in an interdisciplinary team, should not be underestimated (Sottilare, et al., 2017).

4. CONCLUSION

TK proves to be a valuable but elusive resource in knowledge processes of virtual teams in university learning environments. All four identified knowledge processes are recognized to be a challenge for these VTs. But these challenges can be addressed by educational and technological solutions for academics as shown in this paper. Opportunities for enhancing the processing of tacit knowledge by applying educational methods on bots were presented in order to provide guidance for lecturers as well as starting points for future research on how to process knowledge in virtual teams, especially in VLEs.

Challenges occur driven by the degree of virtuality concerning knowledge creation and transfer. These can be approached by using bots for storing and sharing experiences. A limitation of this paper is the missing empirical foundation regarding the influence of ICT on tacit knowledge-processes. Further research is needed to determine the impact of an educationally sound designed bot.

In order to support learning and cooperation, students must be aware of the limitations of their own knowledge (Nonaka & Takeuchi, 1995). In this regard, the use of intelligent systems, such as bots, has a high potential for supporting students in their individual reflection. They can be designed to support transfer of TK, and also the creation of new knowledge through collaborative problem solving (Kapur, 2008). For the next steps, we see a high demand for further research that may elicit which combinations of ICT and educational methods are most effective for supporting knowledge processes for virtual teams in VLEs.

REFERENCES

Alavi, M. & Tiwana, A., 2002. Knowledge integration in virtual teams: The potential role of KMS. *Journal of the American Society for Information Science and Technology*, 53(12), pp. 1029-1037.

Alipour, F., Idris, K. & Karimi, R., 2011. Knowledge Creation and Transfer: Role of Learning Organization. *International Journal of Business Administration*, 2(3), pp. 61-67.

Alter, S., 2010. Work systems as the core of the design space for organisational design and engineering. *Int. J. Organisational Design and Engineering*, 1(1/2), pp. 5-28.

Argote, L. & Ingram, P., 2000. Knowledge Transfer: A Basis for Competitive Advantage in Firms. *Organizational behavior and human decision processes*, 82(1), pp. 150-169.

Bastiaens, T., Wood, L. C. & Reiners, T., 2014. New Landscapes and New Eyes: The Role of Virtual World Design for Supply Chain Education. *Ubiquitous Learning: An International Journal*, 6(1), pp. 37-49.

Benson, R. & Samarawickrema, G., 2009. Addressing the context of e-learning: using transactional distance theory to inform design. *Distance Education*, 30(1), pp. 5-21.

Bohle Carbonell, K. et al., 2014. How experts deal with novel situations: A review of adaptive expertise. *Educational Research Review*, Band 12, pp. 12-29.

Butler, C., 2016. Being appropriately professional: the interaction between professionalism, ICT and knowledge transfer. *New Technology, Work and Employment*, 31(2), pp. 132-145.

De Arment, S. T., Reed, E. & Wetzel, A. P., 2013. Promoting Adaptive Expertise: A Conceptual Framework for Special Educator Preparation. *Teacher Education and Special Education: The Journal of the Teacher Education Division of the Council for Exceptional Children*, 36(3), pp. 217-230.

Diptee, D. & Diptee, J., 2013. *Tacit knowledge acquisition in virtual teams.* s.l., s.n., pp. 1-8.

Falloon, G., 2012. Inside the Virtual Classroom: Student Perspectives on Affordances and Limitations. *Journal of Open, Flexible and Distance Education*, 16(1), pp. 108-126.

Fang, Y., Kwok, R. C. W. & Schroeder, A., 2014. Knowledge processes in virtual teams: Consolidating the evidence. *Behaviour & Information Technology*, 33(5), pp. 486-501.

Gouvêa, M. T. A., Santoro, F. M., Capelli , C. & Pimentel , M., 2016. *Knowledge Management in Distance Education.* New York, s.n., pp. 1-8.

Haase, T., Termath, W. & Martsch, M., 2013. *How to Save Expert Knowledge for the Organization: Methods for Collecting and Documenting Expert Knowledge Using Virtual Reality based Learning Environments.* s.l., s.n., pp. 236-246.

Hao, J., Zhao, Q., Yan, Y. & Wang, G., 2016. *A brief introduction to tacit knowledge and the current research topics.* Jeju, South Korea, s.n., pp. 917-921.

Kapur, M., 2008. Productive Failure. *Cognition and Instruction*, 26(3), pp. 379-424.

Ketcha, A., Johannesson, J. & Bocij, P., 2015. Tacit Knowledge Acquisition and Dissemination in Distance Learning. *European Journal of Open, Distance and E-learning*, 18(2).

Lane, H. C. & VanLehn, K., 2005. Teaching the Tacit Knowledge of Programming to Novices with Natural Language Tutoring. *Computer Science Education*, September, 15(3), pp. 183-201.

Leonard, D. & Sensiper, S., 1998. The role of tacit knowledge in group innovation. *California management review*, 40(3), pp. 112-132.

Liu, Y., He, J. & D. Xiong, Z. Z., 2008. *Managing Tacit Knowledge in Multinational Companies: An Integrated Model of Knowledge Creation Spiral and Knowledge Fermenting.* Tianjin, China, s.n., pp. 1-5.

Martins, E. C. & Meyer, H. W. J., 2014. Organizational and behavioral factors that influence knowledge retention. *Journal of Knowledge Management*, 16(1), pp. 77-96.

Ma, W., Adesope, O. O., Nesbit, J. C. & Liu, Q., 2014. Intelligent Tutoring Systems and Learning Outcomes : A Meta-Analysis. *Journal of Educational Psychology*, 106(4), pp. 909-918.

Morgan, L., Paucar-Cacares, A. & Wright, G., 2014. Leading Effective Global Virtual Teams: The Consequences of Methods of Communication. *Syst Pract Action Res*, 19 February, Band 27, pp. 607-624.

Nonaka, I. & Takeuchi, H., 1995. *The Knowledge-Creating Company: How Japanese Companies Create the Dynamics of Innovation.* Oxford: Oxford University Press.

Pipitone, A., Cannella, V. & Pirrone, R., 2012. Cognitive Models and their Application in Intelligent Tutoring Systems. In: G. Paviotti, P. G. Rossi & D. Zarka, Hrsg. *I-Tutor - Intelligent tutoring systems: an overview.* Lecce, Rovato: Pensa multimedia, pp. 57-84.

Rossi, P. G. & Fideli, L., 2012. Intelligent Tutoring System: a short History and New Challenges. In: G. Paviotti, P. G. Rossi & D. Zarka, Hrsg. *I-Tutor - Intelligent tutoring systems: an overview.* Lecce, Rovato: Pensa multimedia, pp. 13-57.

Schweitzer, L. & Duxbury, L., 2010. Conceptualizing and measuring the virtuality of teams. *Information Systems Journal*, 20(3), pp. 267-295.

Stenmark, D., 2000. *Turning tacit knowledge tangible.* Hawaii, s.n., pp. 3020-3029.

Sottilare, R. A., Baker, R. S., Graesser, A. C. & Lester, J. C., 2017. Special Issue on the Generalized Intelligent Framework for Tutoring (GIFT): Creating a Stable and Flexible Platform for Innovations in AIED Research. *International Journal Artificial Intelligence Education*, September, pp. 1-13.

Venkitachalam, K. & Busch, P., 2012. Tacit knowledge: review and possible research directions. *Journal of Knowledge Management*, 16(2), pp. 357-372.

Virtanen, I., 2013. In Search for a Theoretically Firmer Epistemological Foundation for the Relationship Between Tacit and Explicit Knowledge. *Electronic Journal of Knowledge Management*, May, 11(2), pp. 118-126.

BETTER TEACHING AND MORE LEARNING IN MOBILE LEARNING COURSES: TOWARDS A MODEL OF PERSONABLE LEARNING

Vanessa Ament[1] and Richard Edwards[2]
Ball State University
[1]BC 201F, Department of Telecommunications, Muncie, IN 47306, USA
[2]BC 220B, Division of Online and Strategic Learning, Muncie, IN 47306, USA

ABSTRACT

In this reflection paper, we argue, contrary to many positive assessments of the use of new technologies, data analytics and artificial intelligence (AI) in mLearning, it is worthwhile to look again at the process and agency that comes from human teachers and that live teaching acts should be prioritized in the creation of mLearning courses. The mLearning community should re-evaluate how teachers are part of the "most irreplaceable aspect of education: inspiration." (Schrager and Wang, 2017). We will review existing trends in 21st century education that marginalize the role of the teacher and propose a new model that introduces the need for personable mobile learning to place teachers back into their primary role within communities of learners. If mLearning is going to be a dominant trend in 21st century education, it must resist technological determinism and a belief that learners on their own are to be primarily in control of their educational experiences. A model of personable learning restores teaching to its rightful place—as a both powerful source of connection among learners and at the center of any learning experience.

KEYWORDS

Personalized Learning, Teacher Presence, Constructivism, Pedagogy

1. THE PROBLEM WITH PERSONALIZED LEARNING

Someday, bots could be integral to college. They could be your tutor, advisor, grader—essentially, the bulk of teachers' work. Students already are taking lectures online and consuming personalized software instead of reading textbooks. It's not a stretch to imagine the university of the future as a series of private dorm rooms, filled with students chatting with programs all day long. (That teacher bot may have even been built by a bot who was built by a bot.) (Schrager and Wang, 2017).

As evidenced by the above quote, trends in 21st century learning, coupled with advances in mobile technology, are moving towards what is being commonly called "personalized learning." Students are shifting from older forms of knowledge delivery (such as printed textbooks) and embracing newer forms such as computer bots, software programs, and artificial intelligence. As the quote further suggests, the "teacher" in mLearning will increasingly be a non-human teaching program, algorithm or "bot." In this reflection paper, we argue, that contrary to many positive assessments of the use of new technologies, analytics, and artificial intelligence (AI) in mLearning, it is worthwhile to look again at the process and agency that comes from human teachers. In our reflection, we want the mLearning community to reevaluate how teachers must remain the "most irreplaceable aspect of education: inspiration." (Schrager and Wang, 2017). We review three prevalent methods and approaches in 21st century education and demonstrate how they marginalize the role of the teacher in the educational process. Against these trends in mLearning, we propose a new model that advocates for personable learning environments that place human teachers back into a primary role among communities of learners.

The growing ubiquity of mobile technologies offers promises of new educational approaches, often coupled with the power of data analytics. Several teaching and learning methods and approaches have been advanced in educational circles that are closely linked to mLearning. Among the three most prominent are (1) personalized learning; (2) connectivism; (3) learning analytics. Each of these approaches have their adherents among researchers, teachers, and administrators, yet each potentially has limitations and problems when utilized as a core or pervasive methodology in 21st century education.

1.1 The Shift from Teacher-Centered to Student-Centered Learning

The rise of personalized learning as a method seems to be an ideal fit for mLearning. The personal, intimate, and interactive nature of handheld or wearable technologies maps to the kind of learning experience promised by proponents of personalized learning. According to a report by Hanover research:

The shift from teacher- and curriculum-centered learning to student-centered learning has long been underway in the U.S. school system, with roots in the theories of John Dewey, Lev Vygotsky, and Jean Piaget. Personalized learning, on the other hand, has only more recently developed prominence in the K-12 education community. Now, a recent (and presumably ongoing) Department of Education spotlight on personalized learning has firmly established the approach as a pillar of high-quality 21st century learning. (Hanover Research, 2012)

Personalized learning has had a long and complex history. For our purposes here, even in its many manifestations, personalized learning tends to be broadly contrasted with older, more established teacher-centered pedagogies (Wink, 2011). The promise behind personalized learning (as advanced by such organizations as the U.S. Department of Education) is that it will improve individual learning performances and outcomes through adaptive pathways, data-driven assessments, and artificial intelligence (AI), while shifting the economics of the learning paradigm from hiring and compensating teachers and towards non-human technological solutions. In almost all cases, personalized learning approaches require investments into new kinds of adaptive or flexible learning technologies and/or environments to achieve its goals. However, personalized learning necessarily advances the notion of a self-centered learner, often with no connection to other learners. In many cases, personalized learning can remove the need for a live human teacher altogether. Personalized learning raises concerns on how educational experiences will be led, organized, and conducted in mLearning, especially as key educational tasks previously handled by qualified and trained instructors—such as control over the curriculum or the lesson plan—shift primarily to the learner.

1.2 The Limitations of Connectivism

With the rise of MOOCs and online learning in the last ten years, approaches such as connectivism have gained traction in education circles. Connectivism, as defined by George Siemens, directly seeks to address new cultures of learning that are opening up due to online networked realities and social media. As Siemens states, he believes that connectivism moves beyond the limitations of behaviorism, cognitivism and constructivism: "Connectivism is the integration of principles explored by chaos, network, and complexity and self-organization theories. Learning is a process that occurs within nebulous environments of shifting core elements – not entirely under the control of the individual." (2004) As part of his view of connectivism, Siemens states view of what is limiting in most learning theories: A central tenet of most learning theories is that learning occurs inside a person. Even social constructivist views, which hold that learning is a socially enacted process, promotes the principality of the individual (and her/his physical presence – i.e. brain-based) in learning. These theories do not address learning that occurs outside of people (i.e. learning that is stored and manipulated by technology). They also fail to describe how learning happens within organizations. Learning theories are concerned with the actual process of learning, not with the value of what is being learned. In a networked world, the very manner of information that we acquire is worth exploring. (2004).

However, his critiques of earlier learning theories underplay the importance of critical thinking. Siemens never directly addresses how learners are supposed to acquire the critical thinking skills necessary to benefit from the abundance of information nodes made through interconnected networks of users. While his theory seems to privilege the power of connections, he fails to understand how collaboration and symbiosis between individuals in the network operate in terms of learning or socially constructed acts of knowledge. Through his technologically determinist viewpoint, Siemens posits that "the pipe is more important than the content within the pipe." (2004) However, neither the pipe nor the content is decisive in the act of learning; rather, the broader relationships between individuals and teachers are. Moreover, a focus on the pipe can create an effect of the "echo chamber," as learners select certain parts of "the pipe" but without a qualified guide or mentor, they will not necessarily be exposed to new ideas nor challenged to encounter new concepts. The role of teachers and peer learning in a collective sense counterbalances this tendency.

1.3 The Problem with Learning Analytics

The present moment in mobile learning also concerns itself with learning analytics. Mobile learning technologies seem ideally suited towards generating, storing, and evaluating data analytics around acts of learning. As we increase our ability to capture quantitative data during mobile learning, the accumulation of big data promises more accurate measurement of learning outcomes to create more sophisticated adaptive learning environments (Alhadad, 2015). However, while offering new ways to measure both teaching and learning, such data-driven approaches must proceed along the premise that teaching and learning can be accurately measured and quantitatively verified. As we consider such problems in mLearning, there is a role for analytics and big data. Yet these efforts should not come at the expense of what is immeasurable: the ability of a human teacher and a group of peer learners to provoke each other to pursue their critical and creative thinking. In this sense, learning analytics may have a more limited role to play in teacher-centered approaches to mLearning.

2. MAKING LEARNING PERSONABLE: THE CASE FOR A BETTER MODEL OF TEACHING AND LEARNING IN MLEARNING

Education is a process of mutual and continuous adaptation of both the teacher and student. Education is a collaborative process with participants engaged in genuine activity. (Vygotsky, quoted in Wink, 2011)

Given the prevalence today of certain pedagogical approaches in 21st century education such as discovery learning, project-based learning, socio-constructivist learning and self-directed learning (Crompton, 2013), it is likely that there are more roles in the creation of mLearning courses for instructional designers, UX experts, game designers, solutions architects, or software developers than for actual teachers. With a reliance on the new technology capabilities of mLearning, many personal learning environments remove the instructor almost entirely from direct interaction with the learner. If an instructor does have a pedagogical function, it tends to be in the construction and implementation of an adaptive lesson plan, and the curation of learning materials. Furthermore, in many mobile learning applications, the central role of the instructor is neither as a "sage on the stage" nor as a "guide on the side" (Morrison, 2014) as much as a subject matter expert who is expected to have minimal teaching presence for a community of learners. Even when mobile courses deploy a Community of Inquiry model (Swan, et. al., 2009), the active presence of a live and engaged teacher still tends to be underdeveloped in mLearning theories and thus infrequently utilized in practice. The reason seems not to be a limitation of technology or bandwidth. Rather it appears to be a systemic issue that has arisen as part of the anywhere/anytime mythos that underpins many approaches to mLearning, and in this regard, has much in common with informal mLearning practices that have de-emphasized the centrality of a live instructor (Udell, 2012)

In cases where teaching presence has diminished (or disappeared altogether) in mLearning, the prioritization of the learner has reached new heights in the age of tablets, smartphones, wearables, and big data. Many research studies, pedagogical theories, and instructional design approaches related to mLearning focus almost exclusively on the crucial role of the learner. It is quite common to read about learner-centered pedagogies in mLearning (Shrunk, 2012; Crompton, 2013; Heick, 2017) that positions a self-directed learner in a flexible learning environment as a needed correction against the teacher-centered or curriculum-centered pedagogies that emerged in the 20th century.

2.1 The Symbiotic Relationship of Teachers and Learners in mLearning

Rather than positioning mLearning and the rise of the learner as a shift away from a mass educational model of the 20th century, we propose that mLearning pedagogies reconsider how teachers and learners alike will benefit from symbiotic relationships. Through a symbiosis that shapes both teacher and learner, comprehensive knowledge can be created, nurtured, and transmitted. Rather than identifying either the learner or the teacher as a center of the learning enterprise, we propose that it is more useful to think of teachers and learners together, holistically, as part of a dynamic set of relationships. Together, they can generate interactions, spur communications, and produce artifacts that hone critical and creative thinking skills, and deeper knowledge. Whether face-to-face or in mobile environments, acts of learning should not be seen as isolated and isolating events, but rather part of both the individual and collective development of a learner in a meaningful and situated context. In this sense, the more that a teacher can have an authentic, empathetic, and engaged relationship with a student, or a community of students, in mLearning, the more likely such a learning environment will be experienced as personable.

2.2 Defining Personable Learning

We advocate for a model of *personable learning* and for more teacher/learner connections, or TLC. As an acronym, TLC also can mean "tender loving care," and this additional layer of meaning works well with the concept of personable learning that we seek to advance. An ethos, based in caring for one's students, should be present in a personable learning environment as the presence of the teacher can imbue a mobile learning environment with "purpose, structure, and leadership" (Wink, 2011; Tharp and Gaillimore 1989) that directs the cognitive and social connections with and among the students. These teacher/learner connections can take many forms and utilize a wide array of current available communication possibilities in mLearning that support synchronous and complex interactions via video, chat, or social media. These connections, under the supervision of a teacher, can also be peer-to-peer and/or communities of inquiry where many learners engage to explore creative or critical ideas.

The more TLCs that are created, the more the mobile learning environment will be *personable.* In this regard, our concept of personable learning is much more than an offshoot or a different manifestation of personalized learning. Personable learning is an inversion of the latter approach in its heightened focus on being teacher-centered rather than learner-centered. A model of personable mobile learning proposes a critical role for the agency of the teacher, who sustains an intentional process of continual connections and symbiosis, built upon and sustained by mutual and frequent engagements between a qualified teacher and an engaged student. These engagements should focus on being empowering, relational, dialogical, and equalitarian. Furthermore, personable mobile learning recognizes that learning occurs when knowledge is co-constructed interdependently among teachers and learners, and that such relationships and interdependences inject a humanistic "warmth" and human "touch" into the mobile learning environment—thus allowing mobile, digital environments to be more equal to the traditional face-to-face classroom in terms of teaching presence and social interactions.

3. CONCLUSION: PERSONABLE LEARNING AS AN AUTHENTIC PEDAGOGICAL RELATIONSHIP IN MLEARNING

Transformative pedagogy requires a classroom that allows a democratic setting where everyone feels a responsibility to contribute. (hooks, 1994).

Personable learning is more about multiple entry points into the learning experience than end points or measurable learning outcomes. Personable learning emphasizes the processes by which teachers and students interact with each other more than the presentation of content or the pursuit of pre-ordained results. At this point in the development of mLearning applications and platforms, authentic pedagogical relationships are possible through video conferencing, interactive chats, message boards, and social media (among other instructional media choices.) The authors have begun to experiment with personable learning in their design, teaching, and assessment of outcomes of innovative mLearning courses taught through Ball State University, Instructure's Canvas Network, and Turner Classic Movies (TCM); particularly the use of peer-to-peer engagements in Canvas, Twitter social media interactions, live events hosted on Shindig.com's interactive video chat platform, and TCM.com's moderated message boards.

Through communication technologies and high-speed data connections, the best parts of the teaching act can be sustained in mobile learning classrooms. A master teacher can model particular behaviors as lively as in a face-to-face classroom. As bell hooks aptly argues:" ...most professors must practice being vulnerable in the classroom, being wholly present in mind, body, and spirit." (hooks, 1994). Paolo Freire articulates: "the pursuit of full humanity, however, cannot be carried out in isolation or individualism, but only in fellowship and solidarity." (Freire, 2006) This element of "mind, body, and spirit" or "full humanity" is not something that is reducible to a quantifiable outcome or measured by learning analytics. As evidenced by learning theories such as constructivism, teaching is not something that we should delegate to algorithms and data science. If mLearning is going to be a dominant trend in 21st century education, educators, designers, and learners all must resist technological determinism and a belief that learning can be controlled or predicted. In the end, a model of personable learning seeks to restore teaching to its rightful place at the center of any learning experience.

REFERENCES

Burden, K. and Kearney, M., 2006. Conceptualizing Authentic Mobile Learning. D. Churchill et al. (eds.), *Mobile Learning Design,* Lecture Notes in Educational Technology, DOI 10.1007/978-981-10-0027-0_2

Crompton, H., 2013. A Historical Overview of M-Learning: Toward Learner-Centered Education. *The Handbook of Mobile Education*, pp 80-107.

Dewey, J., 1916. *Democracy and education: an introduction to the philosophy of education*, New York: Macmillan.

Freire, P., 2006. *Pedagogy of the Oppressed.* Trans. Myra Bergman Ramos. New York: Continuum

Hanover Research, 2012. Best Practices in Personalized Learning Environments. Retrieved from http://www.hanoverresearch.com/media/Best-Practices-in-Personalized-Learning-Environments.pdf

Heick, T., 2017. 9 Indicators of Authentic Mobile Learning Retrieved from https://www.teachthought.com/learning-models/9-characteristics-shift-learning-tablets/

hooks, b., 1994. *Teaching to Transgress: Education as the Practice of Freedom.* New York: Routledge

lhadad, S. et al., 2015. The Predictive Learning Analytics Revolution: Leveraging Learning Data for Student Success. *Educause.* Retrieved from https://library.educause.edu/resources/2015/10/the-predictive-learning-analytics-revolution-leveraging-learning-data-for-student-success

Liu, C.H. and Matthews, R., 2005. Vygotsky's philosophy: Constructivism and its criticisms examined. *International Education Journal*, 6(3), pp 386-399

Morrison, C.D., 2014. From 'Sage on the Stage' to 'Guide on the Side': A Good Start. *International Journal for the Scholarship of Teaching and Learning*: Vol. 8: No. 1, Article 4. https://doi.org/10.20429/ijsotl.2014.080104

Nicholas, H. & Walta, C., 2016. Sustaining learning with mobile devices through educational design for teaching presence. *Sustaining Mobile Learning: Theory, Research and Practice*. pp 149-172.

Parsons, D., Thomas, H., and Wishart, J., 2016. Exploring Mobile Affordances in the Digital Classroom *12th International Conference Mobile Learning 2016*, pp 43-50

Richey, R.C., et al., 2011 *The Instructional Design Knowledge Base: Theory, Research, and Practice*. New York: Routledge

Schrager, A. and Wang, A.X., 2017. Imagine how great universities could be without all those human teachers. *Quartz*

Schunk, D.H., 2012. *Learning Theories: An Educational Perspective*. Boston: Pearson

Siemens, G., 2004. Connectivism: A Learning Theory for the Digital Age. *Elearnspace*. Retrieved from http://www.elearnspace.org/Articles/connectivism.htm

Swan, K., Garrison, D, and Richardson, J., 2009. A constructivist approach to online learning: The community of inquiry framework. *Information technology and constructivism in higher education: Progressive learning frameworks*. pp 43-57. 10.4018/978-1-60566-654-9.ch004.

Tharp, R. & Gallimore, R., 1989. *Rousing Minds to Life: Teaching, Learning, and Schooling in Social Context*. American Educator.

Udell, C., 2012. *Learning Everywhere: How Mobile Content Strategies Are Transforming Training*. Alexandria, VA: Rockbench Publishing

Wang, L. and Ma, Q., 2017. Community of Practice: Building a Mobile Learning Community in a Higher Education Institution to Promote Effective Teaching and Learning. S.C. Kong et al. (eds.), *Emerging Practices in Scholarship of Learning and Teaching in a Digital Era*, DOI 10.1007/978-981-10-3344-5_2, 19-38

Wink, J., 2011. *Critical Pedagogy: Notes from the Real World*. Fourth Edition. Boston: Pearson

Poster

MAKING INNOVATION VISIBLE

Ilaria Bucciarelli and Elisabetta Mughini
INDIRE , Florence, Italy

ABSTRACT

Audiovisual and mobile technologies seem to be full of promises for teacher training and professional development. Within the INDIRE project "Making Innovation Visible" we have therefore designed an "online video showcase" drawing on the heritage of innovative educational practices and knowledge gathered by the Avanguardie Educative project (www.avanguardieeducative.indire.it). We prototyped this video showcase in order to build a flexible tool that can guide the progression towards 21st century learning environments. Working with teachers confirmed that instructional and educational video content through a tutorial format, used on mobile devices, could support them on a double direction: while they are trained and when they are working with their own classroom students. The use of video showcase through mobile devices supports the building up of teachers' competence.

KEYWORDS

Lifelong Learning, Professional Development, Coaching, Video Education, Innovation, Documentation

1. INTRODUCTION

Teachers' professional development is an issue of great interest both to the national as to the international policies, since it is considered a strategic element in the modernization of the educational systems. According to research evidences (Gaudin et al., 2012), audiovisual language appears to be a particularly effective tool in knowledge transfer, especially in relation to the quality of teaching interactions, as they are linked to direct observation of processes and practices. Starting from these premises, the first step of the INDIRE project "Rendere visibile l'innovazione" (Making innovation visible) was the implementation of the Youtube channel with the same name (www.youtube.com/c/Renderevisibilelinnovazione[1]). The channel hosts videocontents related to innovative teaching practices: good practices are selected among those existing in the community of the Avanguardie Educative project (http://avanguardieeducative.indire.it). Specific features of the channel are:

1. Video-modeling, disintermediation and peer learning, with the explanation through visualization of an activity carried out by an "expert" peer who assumes the role of *model* - In modeling (Bandura, 1977) this model is usually represented by the most important people in a given context, in this case senior teachers of the Avanguardie educative project;
2. Modular structure ("Minilesson") - Content format has a modular structure: the whole "practice" is divided into small highly focused elements, lasting from one to three minutes. The single minilesson focuses on a small part of the practice, highlighting from time to time only one phase, or making a lunge on a particular skill or on the use of a specific technology. The minilesson is also the idea of a short content, which can be enjoyed on the move, during a break or in a waiting room, to simplify and enrich the professional life of the teachers;
3. Use of standards - The choice to start the service through the YouTube platform has been suggested by the need to make the delivery of content as simple as possible. This choice guarantees high standards of interaction and dissemination - as in social or protected environments - but it is also a guarantee of interoperability and easy reuse within different platforms (and therefore in different contexts and educational ecosystems).

[1] See content in English at https://www.youtube.com/watch?v=p59mH4Y7S3g&list=PLctxbT0kZm0Fpn4_s5_LKqSpArbEhipbU

2. HOW THE VIDEOS WERE RECEIVED

From January to March 2018 videos from the Youtube channel were used in a professional development course involving fifty-four teachers from a primary and lower secondary school in Foligno - Perugia, Italy. During the first lesson one of the video was showed, asking teachers to implement the same methodology in their classroom within one month. During that month video documentations of teachers' generated practices were shared on the elearning platform Edmodo then discussed during the second lesson. Some issues emerged in the discussion related to the use of the video example that could be considered interesting insights for future researches. The main elements are as follows:

1. Teachers agree that video format have been very helpful while working with the classroom, not only to generally get a better understanding of the methodology;
2. Teachers agree that is very helpful to be able to watch the video any time they needed, in order to implement the methodology with their students, as showed in the example;
3. More than half the teachers agree that the video example was actually more useful as a tutorial for classroom work than as a general source of inspiration;
4. More than half the teachers watched the video from a desktop computer, the others from mobile devices;
5. A vast majority of teachers watched the video alone when at home, the others at school with their colleagues; in most interesting cases they used to watch the video during the implementation of the new methodology in the classroom activity either with their colleagues or with students;
6. Teachers used the video example to make their students understand what they were going to implement in the classroom activity.

3. CONCLUSION

Audiovisual and mobile technologies seem to be full of promises for teacher training and professional development. We prototyped the "Rendere visibile l'innovazione" channel in order to build a flexible tool that can guide the progression towards 21st century learning environments. Working with teachers confirmed that instructional and educational video content through a tutorial format, used on mobile devices, could support them on a double direction: while they are trained and when they are working with their own classroom students. Video content on mobile devices allow teachers to bring, share and study new educational methodologies directly into the classroom, together with their students and colleagues. Students could better understand proposals and help teacher in implementing innovation. Lifelong learning services can take great advantage from the audiovisual and mobile adventure, in order to improve and innovate the education system.

REFERENCES

Bandura, A., 1977. *Social learning theory*, Prentice-Hall, Englewood Cliffs, NJ

Gaudin C. et al., 2014. *An exploratory study of the influence of video viewing on preservice teachers' teaching activity: normative versus developmental approaches,* Form@re . Open Journal per la Formazione in rete

Micheletti S., 2014 . *La videoeducazione per la formazione degli insegnanti: sviluppi e prospettive nel web 2.0*, ECPS Journal - 10/2014

Doctoral Consortium

CELLPHONE USE AND TECHNOLOGICAL APPROPRIATION AMONG HIGH SCHOOL STUDENTS IN JALISCO, EDUCATIONAL STRATEGIES AND TIES BETWEEN FORMAL AND INFORMAL EDUCATION WITHIN A SCHOOL RANGE

Yesica Cecilia Núñez Berber
University of Guadalajara, Mexico

ABSTRACT

Cellphones are considered a convergent technology since their use goes beyond making a simple phone call, they are smart phones used as technological devices that have a series of applications as well as Internet connection. The use and appropriation of cellphones, consequently, require a series of learning and competence that is generated which goes beyond the instrumental use, since they place the user before another type of cognitive and symbolic learning that, in many Sometimes, they are not valued in other social areas (for example, the school), generating a false belief that when using and appropriating the cell phone, nothing is being learned. This research intends to know and analyze if high school students develop some type of learning with this mobile technology and if these learnings can link them with what they learn in the school environment.

KEYWORDS

Cellphone, Students, Learning, Strategies, Educational

1. INTRODUCTION

Last March 7th, a current High School Number 10 student of the University of Guadalajara published on social media a video he had previously recorded during a class where a teacher used a foul and misogynistic language to give examples on the subject he was addressing; said video had been edited by the student to only present fragments of the session, in such a way that the audio seemed a reprehensible act on the part of the teacher when using that type of language in the classroom and during a class. The video went viral in such a way on social networks that even national and international media talked about the case. The previous situation evidenced the need for a program of media literacy and ethical management of social networks for the university community, in addition to demonstrating that students have achieved appropriation of the cell phone to have the ability to plan the recording and, later edition of the video to publish it in the social networks out of context, causing the disqualification of the teacher.

As a result of this event, the University of Guadalajara headmaster declared that in view of the reality that in high schools and university centers, more than 90 percent of the students attend classes with their smart phones, the Normativity Commission of the General University Council studies the releasing of a regulation that establishes clear rules on the use of electronic devices in classrooms (Pérez, 2017). It is important to note that prior to this event, the internal regulations of the high schools already established the condition that the cell phone can be used in the classrooms only for educational purposes; but, you might think, what are those educational uses to which the regulation refers? since the fact that it was news shows that the student "knows" to use the cell phone to "create" videos and publish them, did he learn that in high school? In what class did he learn to do it? They also taught him the ethical management of social networks, but he forgot?

The reality is that even though the use of cellphones in classroom is prohibited by rules and regulations, students will use them for educational purposes or not. It is why that the present investigation pretends to know the diverse educative strategies that young high school students use in order to build bridges between informal learning that they develop with and through cellphones and formal learning that they acquire at school. How students recover or can recover skills that they have developed with the use of cellphones, and even appropriation that they have achieved from cellphones to tie them with what is learned in classes of the educational high school program.

For Katz (2003), cellphones have turned out to be machines and such machines have become us; They are gadget-technology that goes beyond being a tool or gadget, for the author could be a represented of oneself. Young High School 10 students are not exempt from the influence and the widespread use of cellphones, that is why the present investigation intends to know in first instance what are the uses that such students give to such cellphones, as well as the appropriation that they give to those, so we can later analyze what they have learned with the use and appropriation of cellphones and what ties them with their formal learning development at school environment, in other words, what are the implications of cellphone use to students in a school setting.

In this research we have chosen to select cellphone as the analysis technology, not only because of its convergent capacity -since it is a mean that contains others- but also because such technology is mostly used by young people. The National Survey of Audiovisual Content Consumption 2016, conducted by the Federal Institute of Telecommunications in Mexico, presents in its results that cellphones are the most used device to view Internet content, 70% of survey respondents, while 77% of Mexican households have a cell phone.

2. MAIN QUESTION

What are the uses and appropriations granted to cellphones by High School 10 students of the University of Guadalajara and what educational strategies do they create to link the formal and informal learning within the school environment?

2.1 Prompt Questions

- How do High School 10 students of the University of Guadalajara create educational strategies in order to tie what is learned through cellphones with formal learning what is taught in classrooms?
- How have High School 10 students of the University of Guadalajara taken appropriation of cellphones and how have they incorporated it into their school environment?
- What kind of meaning do High School 10 students of the University of Guadalajara give to cellphones and what kind of learning tools have they acquired through this gadget-technology?

3. OBJECTIVE OF THIS RESEARCH

Analyze and interpret the uses and appropriation that High School students of the University of Guadalajara have regarding to cellphones, as well as knowing and analyzing which educational strategies they create in order to tie what is learned with such mobile devices to the formal learning development in a school setting.

3.1 Specific Objectives

- Analyze the way in which High School 10 students of the University of Guadalajara create educational strategies in which they tie their technological appropriation of their cellphones to their formal learning process that is taught in the classroom.
- Point out and interpret the way in which High School 10 students of the University of Guadalajara have owned cellphones and how this has affected the incorporation of this technology in a school setting
- Describe the meaning that they give to cellphones, as well as the learning process that the High School 10 students of the University of Guadalajara develop with this technology.

4. METHODOLOGY

4.1 The Method and its Methodological Decisions

It is by using qualitative research methodology they way is sought to acquite and analyze the uses and owenership given to cellphones by the High School 10 students of the University of Guadalajara and what educational strategies they create to tie the learning process that they can develop with it. and the type of learning developed in a school setting.

4.2 The Field of Study

Understand the meaning given to cellphones by the High School 10 students of the University of Guadalajara involving understanding of the symbolic value and the meaning of this object (already cultural) within their daily and educational practices and this implies necessarily the construction of a qualitative approach, since it is about making the object of study visible through the methodology.

4.3 Analytical Categories and Methodological Tools

This research intends to analyze and interpret the uses and appropriation that students have regarding cellphones, as well as the way in which such students use educational strategies to link what they learn in the school environment with the informal learning setting that they have developed with such technological tool.

In order to get to know it, we start from the categories proposed in the theory of technological domestication; which are: appropriation, which has to do with how and in what situations cellphones can take over a place in the lives of students; incorporation, aimed directly at the location and the role played by cellphones according to the needs, knowledge and preferences of the students; objectification, which refers to the cognitive and aesthetic values that give cellphones and how they acquire a place and a specific meaning in the lives of students; and, conversion, which implies the way in which cellphones are part of the image of the students and how they project a certain position with their possession and use in front of the other students.

Discussion groups are considered the most appropriate methodological tool, since by forming the group with young students who share age, tastes and interests, it will be possible to generate greater interaction among them, so that they can expand their knowledge to discuss the uses, appropriation and learning that they give to the cellphones; which is the objective of the present investigation. It is intendeded that among them, it will generate a discussion topic with their points of view and not that it is a direct group, that is why we opt for the discussion group as it is considered that this gives the participants freedom to express themselves as they wish.

4.4 Discussion Groups and Qualitative Interviews

What is this methodological tool about? For Chavéz (2013), the discussion group as a methodological tool comprises three stages, which are: preproduction, which includes the semantic field that determines the theme of the session and which is vital, since it defines the discourse produced around the conversation and that in the case of this research allows to recover the collective discourse of a specific generation that has grown with using cellphones. The first topic for this moment of the discussion group is taken from what was raised in one of the research questions and has to do with, in what way and in what situations do students use cellphones; according to categories of analysis of the theory of technological domestication, which will be help us to know the appropriation that High School 10 students give to those mobile devices.

A second stage of the discussion group is the construction of categories of analysis on global topics; the categories of analysis that are pre-constructed statements with the intention of obtaining the lecture on the part of the students; Chávez (2013) suggests that these statements are not explicitly imposed or stated, so that they do not interfere with the course that could take the conversation in the discussion group. In the case of the current investigation, the units of analysis or observables are: a) cellphones as a communication tools;

b) cellphones used as cameras; c) cellphones to connect to the internet and consult social networks; d) cellphones to connect to the internet and search for information; e) cellphones to perform school tasks.

The aforementioned categories are aimed to providing information regarding the category of incorporation proposed in the theory of technological domestication, which has to do with the location and the role played by cellphones in the lives of students according to their needs, knowledge and preferences, as well as the development of invisible learning process in the High School 10 students of the University of Guadalajara, which according to the theoretical framework has to do with the ability to use the search engines on the internet, o the ability to interact in social networks; informal learning developed by the students with the use and appropriation of cellphones and, if they also use them to do homework, they would be making the connection with such school setting.

4.5 Detonators and Analytic Strategies for the Discussion Group

Regarding the third stage of the discussion group, for Chávez (2013), detonators are presented, which once they have triggered the discursive situation with the phrases or assumptions that are going to generate conversation, are thought-provokers of the lecture and represent the only tool that the researcher can use to intervene in the group's discussion, if he considers it necessary to motivate the participants to speak. For the case of this study, the first detonators to use are: a) what would they feel at the moment if they lost their cell phone? b) At the time of getting your cellphone, Did you consider any educational or learning criteria?; c) Do they use cellphones to carry out research and tasks assigned by teachers in their activities within the school?

With the first detonator that encourages students to discuss how they would feel if at that moment they lost the cellphones; it is intended that the answer or information that they provide on the subject, allows them to know the meaning that mobile devices have for them; since the empirical context tells us that cellphones are the most used technological tool by young people and, when questioning what would happen if they lost it, it would make obvious in their speech, the meaning cellphones have for them as an object. The above is related to the category of objectification, raised in a technological domestication, which has to do with cognitive and aesthetic values and the way in which mobile devices acquire a place and meaning in the lives of the High School 10 students of the University of Guadalajara.

4.6 Field Work

The first stage of the fieldwork was piloted by conducting three discussion groups, in which in one of them participate five students of the second, third and fourth high school grade-semesters who. The first discussion group was formed by four men and one woman, the invitation was opened and the participants decided to do it voluntarily.

The second discussion group was formed with students of fifth and sixth semester, conformed by three men and three women to whom the invitation was made to them and of voluntary they decided to participate. For the third group, the same amount of students is presented in terms of men and women, with six participants, all of them in the sixth semester. The three groups were formed with students from both the morning shift and the afternoon shift. The invitation was made to the students of these semesters since they attended the first high school semesters learning the subjects Information Technology I and II.

Being part of these organized groups with different students and different semesters to know how the interaction occurs and how much they express themselves to colleagues they do not know, but who are their peers in terms of age, educational level and in this case hobbies to use of cellphones, since all the participants have a smartphone. Of the three sessions one lasted about 50 minutes, and the other two 40 minutes.

As detailed in the methodological section, the group work dynamics of the discussion groups followed what Chávez (2013) proposed, regarding follow up and processes, while the categories of the questions or phrases were chosen so that triggered the discussion, they take up the processes proposed in the theory of technological domestication and invisible learning.

Regarding the field work carried out. It has been fascinating for myself on how the approach on high school students has been carried out and in this case being researcher and not a teacher makes a big difference, since it has allowed me to "see them in their own environment", listen to the talks outside the classroom, listen directly from their voice what it is like to actually own a cellphone, how and what they use it for, to hear their side of the story that some professors do not want to see a cell phone in their classes and, on the other hand, they shared me how they manage to take photographs from the whiteboards so that they do not have to write on their notebooks what teachers have written down; but they also talked about how they use those photographs after and they share them through WhatsApp groups with the rest of their classmates.

All students talk about having created WhatsApp groups with their classmates and through that social network-app they ask and share what the teacher leaves for homework, updates on what the teacher can send them, those groups in the social network are only of students, except for what a fourth-semester student who shared an experience about a math teacher they had in the second semester asking them to create a WhatsApp group since that teacher missed a lot of classes and used the group of the social network to send them activities or tasks for when he did not attend those classes.

To the question expressed in the discussion group on how do they know that the information they get from the internet is correct in order to do their homework, the students point out that when they want to search for information on the internet they go to google and put the word and the information that appears check several pages, if they match then it's true; Besides, when they arrive at school, they ask their classmates what they investigated and, if it coincides, then that is fine. This also speaks of the efficient use of Internet search engines, how students unknowingly create learning networks when they consult and contrast with their peers the information gathered from the Internet. In addition to selecting, discriminating and comparing the information that the search engine provides them.

By not seeing myself as an authority at all, as someone who can "affect" their grades for because of what they say or do, in some way allowing them to express themselves with greater freedom. For example, when they say they do not remember what they were taught in the Information Technology class, or that they did not learn anything; that something they saw something regarding a cloud or something like keeping information but that they do not remember, except one of them. Or, saying that the internet connection at high school 10 is very slow, that better they go to the library "that is on the other side" (Juan José Arreola Library), because there is a good internet connection.

Explanatory note: The field work carried out has been an actual approach to the proposed methodology, mistakes are acknowledged by analyzing that it was necessary to work on more detonators in order to encourage students to speak and explain their educational strategies, the centrality of what was done was in technological domestication. Therefore, it is expected to be resolved in the second stage of the fieldwork which will be carried out during the months of February and May of 2018 by using a greater creativity in the design of how to work the discussion groups with these high school students.

REFERENCES

Chávez, M. (2013). El grupo de discusión: técnica de investigación con utilidad práctica. En Chavez, M, Covarrubias, K. y Uribe, A. (Coord.) *Metodología de investigación en ciencias sociales. Aplicaciones prácticas.* Pp. 133-158. Colima, México. Universidad de Colima.

Katz, J. (ED.) (2003). *Machines that become us: The social context of interpersonal communication technologies.* Piscataway, NJ. Transaction Publishers.

Haddon, L. (2005). Empirical studies using the domestication framework. In: Berker, T. Hartmann, M., Punie, Y. y Ward, K. (eds) *Domestication of Media and Technologies.* Open University Press, Maidenhead, pp. 103-122. ISBN 9780335217687. Recuperado de: http://eprints.lse.ac.uk/64591/1/Empirical domestication pdf.pdf

Instituto Nacional de Estadística Geografía e Informática (2016*). Encuesta Nacional sobre Disponibilidad y Uso de Tecnologías de la Información en los Hogares.* Recuperado de: http://www.inegi.org.mx/saladeprensa/aproposito/2016/internet2016_0.pdf

Instituto Federal de Telecomunicaciones. *Resultados nacionales Encuesta nacional de consumo de contenidos audiovisuales 2016.* Recuperado de: http://www.ift.org.mx/sites/default/files/contenidogeneral/comunicacion-y-medios/encca2016vf-compressed_1.pdf

Pérez, I. (15 de marzo de 2017). La UdeG pretende regular el uso de teléfonos celulares dentro de las aulas de clases. *UDGTV. com.* Recuperado de: http://udgtv/.com/noticias/la-udeg-pretende-regular-uso-telefonos-celulares-dentro-las-aulas-clases/

MOBILE LEARNING ZIMBABWE- LECTURERS' PERCEPTIONS

Lydia Maketo
Curtin University
Kent Street, Bentley, Perth, Western Australia, 6102, Australia

ABSTRACT

The benefits of mobile-learning (m-learning) have been widely publicised. Research on m-learning is predominantly from developed nations, with a dearth of empirical studies on m-learning at tertiary institutions from developing nations. This study investigates the feasibility of implementing m-learning in the developing nation of Zimbabwe by investigating factors that influence m-learning implementation and adoption, assessing learners and lecturers' perceptions towards m-learning and challenges of m-learning implementation. This study will develop a new model for m-learning especially for Zimbabwean universities and other tertiary institutions in similar developing countries.

KEYWORDS

M-learning, Developing Countries, Tertiary Institutions

1. INTRODUCTION

Education is widely accepted as a leading tool in economic development (Brown and Lauder 1996, Gylfason 2001). In developed nations, mobile learning (m-learning) is used to support and enhance traditional learning and teaching approaches in tertiary institutions. Lack of access to quality education continues to be a major impediment to economic growth in developing countries. Most research on m-learning has been done in developed countries with little empirical research being conducted in developing countries Hwang and Tsai (2011). This research aims to develop comprehensive m-learning model for Zimbabwe tertiary institutions, one which takes into account learners, instructors, challenges, factors influencing adoption and pedagogy. The study will be carried out in Zimbabwe's five top ranked universities with a student population of 48000.

The major objectives and research questions of the study are given in Table 1.

Table 1. Research Objectives and Research Questions

Research Objective	Research Questions
To identify the factors that influence m-learning implementation in Zimbabwe.	What are the factors that influence the implementation of m-learning in Zimbabwe?
To assess students and lecturers perspectives and perceptions towards m-learning.	What are students and lecturer perspectives and perceptions towards m-learning?

2. RELATED WORK

There are encouraging results from ongoing m-learning projects in developing countries such as learning language in India Kam, Kumar et al. (2009), m-learning for Mathematics in South Africa Roberts and Vänskä (2011), m-learning with physician trainees in Botswana Chang, Littman-Quinn et al. (2012) however there is a paucity of empirical research on m-learning in tertiary institutions in emerging economies. A major impediment to m-learning implementation in developing countries is lack of infrastructure in the form of unreliable electricity supplies and poor Internet connectivity. While Internet connectivity is almost ubiquitous in developed countries this is not the case in most developing countries (Andersson and Grönlund 2009, Ford and Leinonen 2009). Electricity constraints in developing nations have largely prohibited the adoption of information technology (IT) related activities (Hosman and Baikie 2013, Armey and Hosman 2016).

There are cultural norms and social concerns to be considered when implementing m-learning. Cultural differences in relation to perceptions and attitudes toward technology are key factors for acceptance of m-learning and its future use particularly in developing countries. Keengwe and Bhargava (2014) stress that understanding the cultural boundaries and social environment of developing countries before implementing mobile technologies for teaching and learning can play a substantial role for their success. Another major obstacle to m-learning adoption and implementation is training. Sife, Lwoga et al. (2007) identified the need for staff development when integrating information and communication technologies (ICT) with education, not only for improving skills but to also facilitate the process of integrating ICT with education. Handal, MacNish et al. (2013) detail the diverse training required by instructors ranging from basic training, application of technologies, disciplinary training, and specific training. (Schuck, Aubusson et al. 2013) suggest the need to further explore understandings of m-learning rather than mobile usage.

3. METHODOLOGY

The mixed-methods approach will be employed for this study. Mixed methods have been lauded for producing a complete and holistic understanding to a phenomenon (Denscombe 2008, Flick 2009, Venkatesh, Brown et al. 2013) and complementarity by seeking clarification from one method using results from another method Greene, Caracelli et al. (1989). The study will follow an exploratory design because of the scant previous research on m-learning in tertiary education in Zimbabwe, starting with the in-depth interviews and then a survey. This research aims to develop a comprehensive m-learning model for Zimbabwe tertiary institutions, one which takes into account learners and instructors, challenges, factors influencing adoption, pedagogy and characteristics of m-learning.

Qualitative techniques will be employed to collect data from instructors. NVivo will be used for some of the mechanical tasks involved in qualitative analysis such as coding and storing of data as well as retrieving and aggregating previously coded data, and making connections among coding categories.

A survey will be used for the quantitative research. The researcher intends to use SPSS which supports statistical analysis of data and allows for in-depth data access and preparation, analytical reporting, graphics and modelling. SPSS will be used to conduct a number of tests including factor analysis and cluster analysis.

4. WORK DONE SO FAR

This paper discusses some findings of the instructors' perceptions on m-learning so far. It is noteworthy that this study will be one of the few studies that follows qualitative techniques to investigate instructors' adoption of m-learning, from the papers reviewed for this study a majority of them employ statistical techniques with the exception of two studies. The study by Schuck, Aubusson et al. (2013) involved seven lecturers while the study by Handal, MacNish et al. (2013) involved 177 lecturers who participated in an online survey. To assess academic staff perceptions and gain better understanding towards m-learning, the main research question was formulated as: What are the instructors' perspectives and perceptions towards mobile learning? One of the open ended specific questions was:

- What are the constraints of using mobile devices in teaching and learning?

The survey for the qualitative study involved sending emails to the potential respondents with the questions and a link for the online survey. Most respondents chose to respond to the questions via email rather than use the online survey. Twenty instructors have responded to the survey.

5. RESULTS AND THEMES

The themes on constraints to m-learning revolve around infrastructure, lack of mobile devices, and training.

5.1 Infrastructure

Most academics indicated that constraints to m-learning were inadequate infrastructure in terms of bandwidth and poor electricity supplies characterised by frequent power cuts. Closely related to poor bandwidth was poor connectivity. Most instructors remarked that electricity outages affected Internet connectivity. Other lecturers lamented the lack of continuous access to Internet for both students and instructors. While other lecturers described connectivity as slow or no Internet connections. Most instructors cited bandwidth as a major constraint to m-learning. Some instructors bemoaned the cost of Internet access as they have to foot the bill themselves. This was supported by other instructors who stated that *"data is expensive in Zimbabwe"*.

This study indicates inadequate bandwidth at universities in Zimbabwe based on the comments from the lecturers. However an earlier study by (Chitanana 2012) suggests that although bandwidth demand at Zimbabwe universities continues to increase due to increased enrolment there is inappropriate use of the bandwidth by some students. (Chitanana 2012) asserts the need for bandwidth management at Zimbabwe tertiary institutions given the high demand. (Chitanana 2012) further argues that the bandwidth is essentially for productive use at these institutions to yield quality academic work. With the limited bandwidth at tertiary institutions it may be important for the Zimbabwe institutions to come up with bandwidth management policies that do not infringe on the learners' academic rights. Bandwidth management strategies may be a priority in Zimbabwe tertiary institutions since it is a strategic resource. The control, monitoring and optimisation of the resource may enable learners and lecturers access to academic resources. It may also be important to educate the various stakeholders at universities on how to efficiently and effectively use the available bandwidth to meet the institutions' educational needs.

(Traxler 2013) proposes that the major issue of electricity can be remedied by use of solar panels. (Traxler 2013) concedes that this solution is more expensive than commercial power but more practical and can be implemented incrementally. Mobile networks are cheaper and quicker to install compared to fixed telephony systems (Motlik 2008).

Although it seems the current infrastructure in Zimbabwe universities is inadequate for m-learning at a large scale, an improved use of the available resources particularly bandwidth could slightly ease the demand of this resource. Solar chargers would be very costly for mass adoption initially in m-learning implementation however there is a possibility that solar chargers may prove to be cheaper and more sustainable in the long run. M-learning also provides an opportunity for Zimbabwe to by-pass high investment costs in fixed telephone infrastructure and invest more in installation of mobile phone networks. In so doing m-learning provides a more viable opportunity to expand education programs on a larger scale. It is imperative to improve the quality and access of Internet infrastructure for m-learning to be successful in Zimbabwe

5.2 Lack of Mobile Devices

Most academics were of the opinion that students did not have mobile devices suitable for m-learning. Some cited mobile devices not compatible with modern technology. Some instructors indicated that some students did not have mobile devices at all and could not afford mobile devices. It was noted that in some institutions instructors were expected to use their own devices for m-learning instructions which was perceived as unfair by the academics. This was further buttressed by comments like:

"No such devices (mobile) have been provided to lecturers and students"

"Availability of mobile phone may also be a challenge since students come from different backgrounds and have different resources endowments."

Literature suggests the continuous growth in the near ubiquity or ubiquity of mobile devices (Gikas and Grant 2013, Ally and Tsinakos 2014) with (Kabanda 2014) claiming that the mobile phone density in Zimbabwe is above 100%. While it would appear that there is a contradiction between the findings and literature it may be that mobile devices are ubiquitous even in Zimbabwe but that some of these mobile devices may not be suitable for m-learning, for example some learners may have basic mobile phones which are not smartphones. It may be concluded that in Zimbabwe mobile devices suitable for m-learning are not ubiquitous. This presents a challenge in m-learning implementation as m-learning adoption cannot rely on the ubiquity of mobile devices or Bring Your Own Device, since some learners may not afford to purchase suitable devices due to costs.

5.3 Lack of Training

The academics in Zimbabwe acknowledge the need for training in using mobile technologies for teaching and learning. While a majority of lecturers have no problems using mobile technologies for their personal use, they concede that they have basic skills in utilising the mobile technologies for teaching and learning. Most academics feel they are not fully equipped to utilise mobile technologies for teaching and learning as they are *"learning as they go"*. Most academics felt they had inadequate skills to use mobile technologies for teaching and learning purposes citing the need for skill acquisition, with one instructor declaring *"no requisite training have been provided to lecturers and students"*. Some instructors professed basic knowledge on how to use mobile technologies for teaching and learning, there was a suggestion that *"Both lecturers and students need to be introduced and taught on how to use whatever online platforms used by their institutions"*.

These results are consistent with the previous study by Handal, MacNish et al. (2013), that highlight the need for diverse training required by lecturers when implementing m-learning. Comments by most lecturers indicate that these instructors are comfortable with mobile-device usage however they appreciate the need to be trained in utilising the mobile devices for teaching and learning purposes, which corroborate the ideas of Schuck, Aubusson et al. (2013) who suggested that the need to further explore understandings of mobile learning, as opposed to mobile usage.

Isaacs (2007) states that Zimbabwe adopted a National Information Communication Technology (ICT) policy in 2005, which made significant references to the promotion of ICTs in education including their pedagogical use in educational institutions including provisions for staff development. The study by Musarurwa (2011) gives an example of an externally-funded project with positive results of ICT integration with Education in Zimbabwe including staff development.

The findings of this study indicate a lack of staff development regarding m-learning. Notwithstanding the fact that there is a policy to support ICT integration with education in Zimbabwe and that the lecturers are willing to adopt m-learning the lack of staff development would clearly hamper m-learning implementation. A possible explanation for the lack of staff development could be socio-economic challenges currently in Zimbabwe. Although there is a National ICT policy in place in Zimbabwe to integrate education with ICT the lack of training in m-learning for lecturers could also be attributed to: inconsistencies in applying the policy when it comes to m-learning, or the policy not addressing m-learning specifically or an outdated policy. It may be concluded that a policy alone is not enough as it needs to be embraced, understood and backed by all relevant stakeholders for it to be effective.

6. CONCLUSION

This paper is one of the few empirical studies on m-learning in developing countries, which aims to develop a comprehensive m-learning model for Zimbabwe tertiary institutions. The mixed-method approach is expected to provide an extensive understanding of m-learning implementation and adoption on a large scale from a developing country perspective. The initial findings highlight and confirm some key aspects and constraints to m-learning from a developing country perspective which are infrastructure and staff development. Although infrastructure may not be fully in place in Zimbabwe the available resources could be used wisely and more efficiently particularly in academic institutions to further academic endeavours. If the various stakeholders in these institutions were more informed on the efficient and effective use of bandwidth coupled with guided bandwidth management policies which would not infringe on the learners' rights or stifle learner creativity and exploration this could possibly somewhat ease the demand on the bandwidth. There may be a need to review the National ICT policy to see how it aligns with m-learning.

ACKNOWLEDGEMENT

Lydia Maketo extends her gratitude to Dr Tomayess Issa, Dr S Zaung Nau and Dr Theodora Issa her Academic Supervisors at Curtin University for their on-going advice and guidance as she pursues her PhD studies which inspired this paper.

REFERENCES

Ally, M. and A. Tsinakos (2014). Increasing access through mobile learning, Commonwealth of Learning (COL);.

Andersson, A. S. and Å. Grönlund (2009). "A conceptual framework for e-learning in developing countries: A critical review of research challenges." The Electronic Journal of Information Systems in Developing Countries 38.

Armey, L. E. and L. Hosman (2016). "The centrality of electricity to ICT use in low-income countries." Telecommunications Policy 40(7): 617-627.

Brown, P. and H. Lauder (1996). "Education, globalization and economic development."_Journal of education Policy 11(1): 1-25.

Chang, A. Y., R. Littman-Quinn, D. Ketshogileng, A. Chandra, T. Rijken, S. Ghose, A. Kyer, A. K. Seymour and C. L. Kovarik (2012). "Smartphone-based mobile learning with physician trainees in Botswana." International Journal of Mobile and Blended Learning (IJMBL) 4(2): 1-14.

Chitanana, L. (2012). "Bandwidth management in universities in Zimbabwe: towards a responsible user base through effective policy implementation." International Journal of Education and Development using Information and Communication Technology 8(2): 62.

Denscombe, M. (2008). "Communities of practice a research paradigm for the mixed methods approach." Journal of mixed methods research 2(3): 270-283.

Flick, U. (2009). An introduction to qualitative research, Sage.

Ford, M. and T. Leinonen (2009). "MobilED–mobile tools and services platform for formal and informal learning." Mobile learning: Transforming the delivery of education and training: 195-214.

Gikas, J. and M. M. Grant (2013). "Mobile computing devices in higher education: Student perspectives on learning with cellphones, smartphones & social media." The Internet and Higher Education 19: 18-26.

Greene, J. C., V. J. Caracelli and W. F. Graham (1989). "Toward a conceptual framework for mixed-method evaluation designs." Educational evaluation and policy analysis 11(3): 255-274.

Gylfason, T. (2001). "Natural resources, education, and economic development." European economic review 45(4): 847-859.

Handal, B., J. MacNish and P. Petocz (2013). "Adopting mobile learning in tertiary environments: Instructional, curricular and organizational matters." Education Sciences 3(4): 359-374.

Hosman, L. and B. Baikie (2013). "Solar-powered cloud computing datacenters." IT Professional 15(2): 15-21.

Hwang, G. J. and C. C. Tsai (2011). "Research trends in mobile and ubiquitous learning: A review of publications in selected journals from 2001 to 2010." British Journal of Educational Technology 42(4): E65-E70.

Isaacs, S. (2007). "ICT in education in Zimbabwe: Survey of ICT and Education in Africa." Zimbabwe Country Report.

Kabanda, G. P. (2014). "Technology Affordances and Diffusion for Mobile Connectivity and Applications in Zimbabwe."

Kam, M., A. Kumar, S. Jain, A. Mathur and J. Canny (2009). Improving literacy in rural India: Cellphone games in an after-school program. Information and Communication Technologies and Development (ICTD), 2009 International Conference on, IEEE.

Keengwe, J. and M. Bhargava (2014). "Mobile learning and integration of mobile technologies in education." Education and Information Technologies 19(4): 737-746.

Motlik, S. (2008). "Mobile learning in developing nations."_The International Review of Research in Open and Distributed Learning 9(2).

Musarurwa, C. (2011). "Teaching with and Learning through ICTs in Zimbabwe's Teacher Education Colleges." Online Submission.

Roberts, N. and R. Vänskä (2011). "Challenging assumptions: Mobile learning for mathematics project in South Africa." Distance Education 32(2): 243-259.

Schuck, S., P. Aubusson, M. Kearney and K. Burden (2013). "Mobilising teacher education: A study of a professional learning community." Teacher Development 17(1): 1-18.

Sife, A., E. Lwoga and C. Sanga (2007). "New technologies for teaching and learning: Challenges for higher learning institutions in developing countries." International Journal of Education and Development using ICT 3(2).

Traxler, J. (2013). "Mobile learning in international development." Global mobile learning implementations and trends: 45.

Venkatesh, V., S. A. Brown and H. Bala (2013). "Bridging the qualitative-quantitative divide: Guidelines for conducting mixed methods research in information systems." MIS quarterly 37(1): 21-54.

AUTHOR INDEX